The Economic Effects of Aging in the United States and Japan

A National Bureau
of Economic Research
Conference Report

The Economic Effects of Aging in the United States and Japan

Edited by   Michael D. Hurd and
Naohiro Yashiro

The University of Chicago Press

Chicago and London

MICHAEL D. HURD is professor of economics at the State University of
New York, Stony Brook, and a research associate of the National Bureau
of Economic Research. NAOHIRO YASHIRO is professor of economics at the
Institute of International Relations, Sophia University.

The University of Chicago Press, Chicago 60637
The University of Chicago Press, Ltd., London
© 1997 by the National Bureau of Economic Research
All rights reserved. Published 1997
Printed in the United States of America
06 05 04 03 02 01 00 99 98 97   1 2 3 4 5
ISBN: 0-226-36100-4 (cloth)

Library of Congress Cataloging-in-Publication Data

The economic effects of aging in the United States and Japan / edited by
Michael D. Hurd and Naohiro Yashiro.
      p.   cm.—(A National Bureau of Economic Research conference
   report)
   Includes bibliographical references and index.
   ISBN 0-226-36100-4 (cloth : alk. paper)
   1. Aged—United States—Economic conditions—Congresses.   2.
Aged—Japan—Economic conditions—Congresses.   3. Age distribution
(Demograpy)]—Economic aspects—United States—Congresses.   4.
Age distribution (Demography)—Economic aspects—Japan—Con-
gresses.
I. Hurd, Michael D.   II. Yashiro, Naohiro, 1946–   .   III. Series: Con-
ference report (National Bureau of Economic Research)
HQ1064.U5E244 1997
305.26'0973—dc20   96-23921
                                                                        CIP

⊗ The paper used in this publication meets the minimum requirements of
the American National Standard for Information Sciences—Permanence
of Paper for Printed Library Materials, ANSI Z39.48-1984.

Since this volume is a record of conference proceedings, it has been exempted from the rules governing critical review of manuscripts by the Board of Directors of the National Bureau (resolution adopted 8 June 1948, as revised 21 November 1949 and 20 April 1968).

Contents

Preface

This volume consists of papers presented at a joint Japan Center for Economic Research–National Bureau of Economic Research conference held in Hakone, Japan, in September 1993. Financial support from the Department of Health and Human Services, the National Institute on Aging (grants P01-AG05842 and R37-AG08146), and the Japan Foundation Center for Global Partnership is gratefully acknowledged.

Any opinions expressed in this volume are those of the respective authors and do not necessarily reflect the views of the National Bureau of Economic Research, the Japan Center for Economic Research, or the sponsoring organizations.

Introduction

Michael D. Hurd and Naohiro Yashiro

A common theme of the papers in this volume, by both the Japanese and the U.S. authors, is that population aging in these two countries will have both micro- and macroeffects and that in some cases these effects will be substantial. The most obvious effects will be on the social programs that specifically serve the elderly, such as the public pension systems and provisions for the medical needs of the elderly. But aging will also affect labor markets, capital markets, the housing market, and the market for health care services. It will affect firms through their participation in the demand side of the labor market and through their provisions for pensions. Aging will have macroeffects on saving rates, the rate of return on assets, the balance of payments, and, most likely, economic growth.

The fraction of the population that is elderly (aged 65 or over) is expected to increase rapidly in Europe, the United States, and Japan as the result of falling fertility rates, the aging of the baby boom cohort, and increases in life expectancy at age 65 (Hurd, chap. 2 in this volume; Yashiro and Oishi, chap. 3 in this volume). The change is likely to be particularly rapid in Japan. For example, the elderly made up about 12 percent of the Japanese population in 1990; they are forecast to be 25 percent of the population by 2020. By comparison the corresponding change in the United States will be rather modest: from 12 percent to 16 percent. The working-age population (aged 15–64) has already started to decline in Japan, whereas it will continue to grow for several decades in the United States.

The most important cause of the difference between forecasts for the Japanese and U.S. populations, particularly in the long run (more than 30 years in

Michael D. Hurd is professor of economics at the State University of New York, Stony Brook, and a research associate of the National Bureau of Economic Research. Naohiro Yashiro is professor of economics at the Institute of International Relations, Sophia University.

1

the future), is the assumption about the fertility rate. In 1990 the fertility rate in Japan was 1.6 births per woman, whereas in the United States it was about 2.1. A second reason for more rapid aging in Japan is more rapid growth in life expectancy at age 65. In Japan between 1960 and 1990 the life expectancy of both women and men increased by about 40 percent, whereas in the United States the gains were 19 and 16 percent for women and men, respectively. The increase in life expectancy will lead to a large increase in the elderly population after the large baby boom cohort reaches age 65.

Even if the increase in the elderly population were the same in the two countries, we would expect the consequences of aging to differ because of institutional and cultural differences. Indeed, an objective of the JCER-NBER conferences is to try to understand economic behavior better by observing how these differences cause behavior to be different. The main objective of this Introduction will be to make some comparisons, drawing on the results of the papers in this volume.

As measured by income the elderly in the two countries are about as well off as the nonelderly (Yashiro, chap. 4). The composition of income, however, is very different. The elderly in Japan are much more dependent on public pensions. A good benchmark is the fraction of the elderly that get 80 percent or more of their income from public pensions. In Japan about half of elderly couples who live independently and about three-fourths of nonworking elderly couples receive more than 80 percent from public pensions (Takayama, chap. 10). In the United States, only about one-fifth of elderly couples get at least 80 percent of their income from Social Security. One explanation for the difference stems from the differing structure of the public pension system: Japan has a basic pension that provides a minimum level for all to which is added a wage-related component, which can be substantial. In the United States, Social Security benefits increase at just 0.15 of average indexed monthly earnings in the top bracket with the result that the maximum benefit is low compared with

Table 1   **Comparison of Demographic Characteristics and Projections**

| | Fertility Ratio | | Life Expectancy at 65 | | | | Percentage of Population 65 or Over | |
| | | | Japan | | U.S. | | | |
Year	Japan	U.S.	Males	Females	Males	Females	Japan	U.S.
1960	2.00	3.61	11.6	14.1	12.9	15.9	5.7	15.9
1990	1.55	2.07	16.2	20.0	15.0	19.0	12.0	12.3
2020	1.80	1.90	17.8	22.6	16.5	20.2	25.5	16.4

Sources: For Japan, Ato et al. (1992); for the United States, Board of Trustees of the Federal OASDI Trust Funds (1994).

the earnings of many workers. Thus, there is a greater need for private pensions in the United States.

The Japanese elderly have more income from earnings because their labor force participation rate is considerably higher. They have considerably less asset income because they hold a much greater fraction of their wealth in the form of housing. Besides the obvious explanation of very large increases in housing and land prices in Japan, this great housing wealth is partly the result of the high rate of homeownership among the Japanese elderly. It is likely that the elderly retain their homes because of the very low property taxes in Japan, and because of the custom of bequeathing the house to a child in exchange for the child's taking care of the elderly parents.

Comparisons of income and wealth between the Japanese and U.S. elderly are tenuous, however, because of the very large difference in living arrangements (Yashiro, chap. 4). In Japan, about 33 percent of elderly women and 42 percent of elderly men either live alone or with their spouses, compared with 81 and 91 percent in the United States, respectively. The rest live in extended households in which the elderly person is not the head of the household. This fact has two consequences. First, because of returns to scale in consumption it is difficult to assess the economic status of individuals in multiperson households. Second, when an elderly person is not the head of the household, the income of the household is associated with the nonelderly head, so that figures on the average income of the elderly cover only about 40 percent of the elderly. In that the well-to-do elderly tend to live independently and the less well-to-do tend to live in extended families, the percentage included in income statistics falls with economic status. For example, only 28 percent of those in the lowest income quintile (those who are household heads) are covered in the household statistics. As a consequence, age-income or age-wealth paths will be too steep because at older ages only the wealthy of the cohort are included in the sample (Yashiro, chap. 4). There is no easy or obvious solution to this data problem: the income and assets of the elderly who live in extended families are reported with the income and assets of the family unit.

Having said this, we do not mean to imply that we cannot learn a good deal from the available data. There are several major household-level surveys, and for the most part, they form the basis of the empirical papers in this volume. The most widely used is the *Monthly Report on the Family Income and Expenditure Survey* (MRFIE), which is published by the Management and Coordination Agency (MCA). The National Survey of Family Income and Expenditure (NSFIE) is the most extensive survey on households, but it is published only every five years by the MCA. The NSFIE covers a number of types of households, including single persons and nonworking households, that are not covered by the MRFIE. The Basic Survey on People's Life by the Ministry of Welfare has extensive information on family income and savings by type of household, and it partly includes information on the single elderly. Nonetheless, the problem of constructing a sample that is representative of elderly individuals remains in all of these surveys.

In the United States there has been a considerable volume of research based on household-level data aimed at verifying the life-cycle hypothesis about consumption (LCH). In Japan there has been a good deal of research about the consequences of aging for the national saving rate: under the LCH the projected aging of the population will cause the saving rate to fall because the elderly consume more of their income than the nonelderly. However, because of data limitations it has been difficult to verify or even study the LCH at the microlevel. First, cross-sectional wealth holdings may not give a good estimate of the wealth paths of individuals because it is hard to control for cohort effects, living arrangements, and differential mortality. In the United States these problems are overcome by using panel data, but in Japan there are no panel data. Second, in synthetic cohorts there is no control for differential mortality or living arrangements. Third, because consumption is difficult to measure in household surveys, it is often underestimated, so saving rates are overestimated. Fourth, because of the high rate of homeownership among the elderly, the apparent high saving rate in old age would be reduced were the implicit high income and consumption flows from housing taken into account; this adjustment would make the lifetime pattern of consumption and saving conform more closely to a life-cycle pattern.

An alternative to studies based on household data is to estimate directly the effect on the national saving rate of changes in the age composition of the population. In the context of the LCH, however, age is not just years since birth. Age should also take into account life expectancy: holding age constant, an increase in life expectancy should increase an individual's saving rate and retirement age. Indeed, in the forecasts of Yashiro and Oishi (chap. 3), which control for increases in life expectancy, the national saving rate would be 10 percent in 2020–25 rather than −5 percent with no change in life expectancy.

In the United States, even though the household saving rate as measured in panel data varies with age, the aging of the population will probably have only small effects on household-level saving: the life-cycle pattern is not large enough to produce a substantial aggregate change because the population will age rather slowly (Hurd, chap. 2). But, as pointed out by Poterba, Venti, and Wise (chap. 9), saving for retirement purposes through employer-provided pension plans is a large fraction of total personal saving in the United States: in 1989 this kind of saving amounted to about $120 billion; personal saving as measured in the national income and product accounts amounted to $152 billion. Changes in the fraction of the population that works could cause substantial changes in this kind of saving. Indeed, Schieber and Shoven (chap. 5) estimate that real saving through private pensions, which is now almost 4 percent of payroll, will become negative in about 2024.

Another aspect of saving for retirement through private pensions is that we expect the consumption rate of annuitized wealth to be higher than the consumption rate of bequeathable wealth. The reasoning is that if there is no bequest motive, a cohort will completely consume its annuitized wealth by the time the last survivor dies whereas a cohort will accidentally bequeath (not consume) some fraction of its bequeathable wealth. If there is a bequest motive, the difference will be reduced but not eliminated. In the United States, retirement saving through 401(k) plans and, to a lesser extent, individual retirement accounts is becoming the primary mode of retirement saving. This trend should increase the fraction of wealth that is annuitized in the United States and by itself reduce the saving rate. In Japan, little retirement income comes from private pensions, and as a result, little household wealth is in the form of private pensions: in 1992 pension reserves were 4 percent of household financial assets in Japan whereas they were 28 percent in the United States (Yamauchi, chap. 6).

There are a number of similarities in the pattern and determinants of retirement in Japan and in the United States. In both countries the labor force participation rate of 60–64-year-old males fell rather sharply during the 1970s and early 1980s, a period when real public pension benefits increased rapidly. Particularly in Japan, where most retirees are heavily dependent on income from public pensions, it is hard to imagine that the decline would have happened without the increase in pensions. Workers seem to be very responsive to retirement incentives. In Japan there is substantial bunching of workers at the point on the annual budget constraint where the earnings test becomes binding (Seike, chap. 12), just as in the United States. In Japan the structure of separation pay (a lump-sum defined-benefit pension) is very similar to a typical backloaded defined-benefit pension in the United States. This structure causes annual compensation to increase substantially until separation, and in the United States it reduces worker mobility before separation (Lumsdaine, Stock, and Wise, chap. 11). In both countries, the public pension system encourages retirement at age 65 in that the increase in benefits from a year's work after age 65 is less than the actuarially fair increase. Consequently, the labor force participation rate falls sharply after age 65.

There are, however, a number of differences between the labor markets. The most striking is the rate of work among the elderly. For example, in 1992 the labor force participation rate of 65–69-year-old Japanese men was 56.5 percent.[1] In the United States just 25.9 percent of men aged 65–69 were in the labor force. Part of the explanation for the high participation rate of the elderly in Japan is the prevalence of self-employment: among male workers aged 70 or over, 64 percent were self-employed or worked for other family members. This kind of employment offers flexibility in the choice of hours, which can keep workers in the labor force. In addition, however, we imagine that the difference in the number of expected years of retirement could be an important determinant of the differences in retirement patterns. As we discussed pre-

---

1. Of these, 80.6 percent worked full time.

viously, the increase in life expectancy at age 65 has been much greater in Japan, so it is reasonable to suppose that retirement-age workers forecast even greater future increases in life expectancy. Furthermore, in Japan mandatory retirement from the career job is mostly at age 60, while in the United States, where mandatory retirement is illegal, the retirement hazard rate has large peaks at ages 62 and 65. The net result is that a 60-year-old retiree in Japan probably anticipates financing many more years of retirement than a 62- or 65-year-old worker in the United States, possibly as many as seven or eight more years.

Financial explanations probably play a role. Few retired Japanese have income from private pensions: most separation pay is a lump sum, which benefits from favorable tax treatment. In the United States many defined-benefit private pensions encourage retirement, and new jobs are difficult to find for older workers.[2] In addition, some private pensions are employment conditioned so that pension income is lost if earnings are too great. This, of course, would not be the case in Japan, where separation pay is a lump sum.

The overall financial wealth of the Japanese elderly may be less than that of the U.S. elderly, although because of the difference in living arrangements it is hard to be precise. What is clear is the important difference in the level and composition of total wealth due to the value of housing. In 1989, the average value of housing and land among those aged 70 or over was 82 million yen, or about $820,000, which represents about 84 percent of their assets.[3] If this could be monetized either through the sale of housing or through home equity conversion mortgages (reverse annuity mortgages), the income of the elderly could be increased substantially (Noguchi, chap. 8). However, because the children of the elderly cannot afford to buy housing, most elderly live with their children in their own houses, which are eventually bequeathed to the children. The conclusion is that, although total wealth among the elderly is considerably higher in Japan than in the United States, the resources available for nonhousing consumption may not be any greater, and are possibly even less. This would encourage a longer work life.

As we have indicated, the housing market apparently operates very differently in the two countries. In the United States the evidence suggests (or at least does not contradict) some downsizing with age. This implies that housing prices may fall as the population ages, although, to the extent that the housing prices can be forecast from population change, adjustments in housing choice and in the supply of housing can moderate price change (Hoynes and McFadden, chap. 7). Should prices fall as the baby boom generation moves past retirement, the ability to finance nonhousing consumption by reducing housing consumption will be reduced, and the baby boom generation may find itself with

2. In the United States the wage rate falls by 35–50 percent when a postretirement job is taken. In Japan the wage falls by about 50 percent on a new job after the career job ends (usually at age 60; Seike, chap. 12).

3. This figure is calculated over independent households excluding singles.

fewer resources in retirement than anticipated. In Japan, children move in with their elderly parents because they cannot afford to buy a house, and then the house is passed on to the children. Of course, demographic changes could cause housing prices to fall, but that would not affect the flow of real housing services of the two closely linked generations. A possible effect, however, is that separation of the generations, which has been happening fairly slowly, could accelerate: if housing becomes more affordable, the working generation could choose to buy housing rather than live with parents.

The public pension system in Japan is in debt in the sense that promised future benefit payments are greater than the fund dedicated to paying the benefits (Hatta and Oguchi, chap. 14). That is, the public pension system is not fully funded, and the amount of shortfall is about equal to the GNP. This has happened because of windfall gains to the start-up generation and because the future benefits of current workers exceed the value of their past contributions. As in the United States, this causes transfers across generations.

Because of the aging of the population, keeping the system solvent will require increases in tax rates: Ogura (chap. 1) forecasts that with no changes in benefit structure, the tax rate will have to increase from 15 percent today to about 40 percent in 2040.[4] This is much greater than the required increase in the tax rate in the United States: a more relevant comparison is with Germany or Austria, which forecast similar tax rates. The main causes of the very high rate are the replacement rate (about 60 percent in Japan compared with about 45 percent in the United States), greater life expectancy, and low fertility.

It seems unlikely such a high tax rate will be realized, which means that benefits will have to be reduced. In Japan, as in the United States, a natural response is to increase the age for full benefits because of the increase in life expectancy and better health. Increasing the age for full benefits to 65 from 60 would reduce the required tax rate to about 35 percent. Indexing benefits to prices rather than wages and taxing benefits could reduce the required tax rate to about 25 percent. All of these reforms seem reasonable from the U.S. point of view because they are already part of the Social Security system.

The part of the U.S. Social Security system that funds retirement benefits is forecast eventually to become negative, but the tax rates required to keep the fund solvent are not particularly large, especially from the Japanese point of view: in 2040 the cost rate is forecast to be greater than the income rate by 3.4 percent of taxable payroll, which means that the fund would be stabilized if the tax rate were increased by 3.4 percent to 16.6 percent of taxable payroll (Hurd, chap. 2). This is, of course, very different from the 40 percent rate that is forecast for Japan.

The major problem facing the U.S. Social Security system is health care costs. The increase in such costs is only moderately due to the aging of the

---

4. This is higher than the official government forecasts because Ogura forecasts a lower total fertility rate.

population: most of the increase comes from price inflation in medical services and increasing real consumption per capita. If medical care costs are not controlled, they will probably eventually influence the Social Security retirement trust fund though interfund borrowing.

In Japan the delivery of medical care to the elderly is also a major policy issue. While total medical costs have stabilized at 6 percent of national income for the last 10 years, the medical costs of those aged 70 or over have doubled, and their per capita consumption of medical services is about four times the average. An apparent cause is generous medical benefits, which have resulted in care being provided in hospitals rather than in less costly settings.

We conclude by noting that, despite the differences in culture and social and government structure, there are many similarities in the economic status and behavior of the elderly in the two countries. Furthermore, some of the apparent differences are due to measurement: for example, even though the elderly in Japan have much higher saving rates than the elderly in the United States, the difference would be reduced if the saving rate of the dependent elderly (who are missing from Japanese household statistics) could be included. At the macrolevel both countries face substantial difficulties associated with population aging: in Japan the public pension system has a large cash surplus on current account, but in fact it has large future liabilities, just like the U.S. Social Security system. Although population aging in Japan will be much more rapid than in the United States, the effects from an associated fall in the saving rate may be similar because Japan starts from a considerably higher saving rate. We believe that this volume shows that a comparison of similarities and differences can increase our understanding of the possible future effects of population aging in each of the two countries.

References

Ato, Makoto, et al. 1992. Nihonnoshoraijinnkousuikei (Japan's estimated future population). *Jinkoumonndaikennkyuu* (Journal of Population Research) 48, no. 3 (October).
Board of Trustees of the Federal OASDI Trust Funds. 1994. *The 1994 annual report.* Washington, D.C.: U.S. Government Printing Office. Ato et al. (1992) is used as the official Japanese government forecast.

I Demography and Macroeconomic Impact of Aging

1　Projection of Japanese Public Pension Costs in the First Half of the Twenty-First Century and the Effects of Three Possible Reforms

Seiritsu Ogura

1.1　Introduction

Only very recently has aging started to attract national attention. During the past two decades, however, Japan has been aging very rapidly. In fact, some people claim that no other country in history has aged more rapidly, although it is obviously very difficult to verify this assertion. Two factors that usually contribute to the process of aging—declining mortality and declining fertility—have indeed been present in Japan. Of these two factors, the most dominant since the mid-1960s has been the decline in mortality. Almost all newborn babies are now expected to reach age 65 (fig. 1.1), and more than half of them are expected to reach age 80. This is the best mortality record in the world, and probably in the history of humankind.

In 1960, there were only 501,000 men and women who were 65 years old. Thirty years later, in 1990, 1,193,000 Japanese were this age. The life expectancy at this particular age was 11.6 years for men and 14.1 years for women in 1960. In 1990, it was 16.2 years for men and 20.0 years for women (fig. 1.2). As the size of the population at age 65 doubled and the life expectancy increased by 50 percent, we would expect the size of the elderly population to have at least tripled over these 30 years. This is, in fact, what happened in Japan.

This alone is a very dramatic change, but it is only part of the story. Close to 2 million baby boomers born during the years immediately after World War II will reach age 65 in the second decade of the twenty-first century. At that time, the number of elderly will be at least twice that in 1990 if life expectancy remains the same.

Moreover, in the past 10 years the decline in the birthrate has started to

Seiritsu Ogura is professor of economics at Hosei University and chief economist of the Japan Center for Economic Research.

Financial support from the Abe Foundation is gratefully acknowledged.

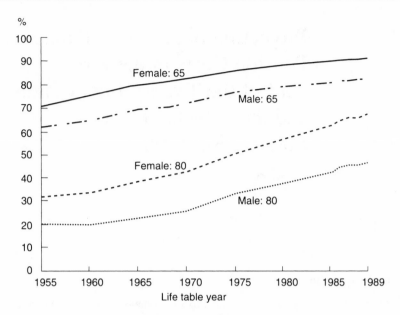

Fig. 1.1   Probability of survival to ages 65 and 80 (newborn babies)

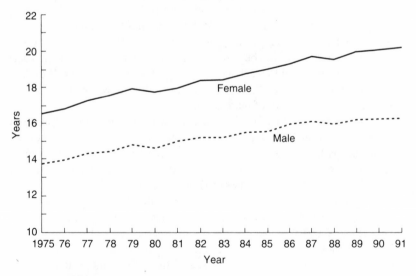

Fig. 1.2   Life expectancy at age 65

accelerate Japan's population aging process. In 1960, 1,606,000 babies were born in Japan. In 1990, 1,221,000 babies were born, a decline of almost 25 percent. The total fertility rate (TFR) of Japanese women was 2.0 in 1960 but only 1.54 in 1990. If this low fertility rate persists, and we believe that it will, in the first quarter of the next century only three-quarters of the present working population will be supporting almost twice the present elderly population. Thus, the ratio of the elderly to the working population will be about 8/3, or more than 2.5 times, the present ratio.

Judging from the current population structure, by the first quarter of the twenty-first century, the rapid population aging process will be over in Japan, but it will be followed by a slow, steady aging process as long as the low fertility rate persists. In May 1991, at JCER, we published our own population projection for the next 30 years (Ogura 1991). We followed it with a series of demographic studies (e.g., Ogura 1992; Ogura and Dekle 1992). All available evidence so far indicates that the birthrate is very unlikely to rebound in the next few years, as is expected in the government's 1992 official population forecast. Not only is the low fertility rate here to stay, but a further decline in TFR is very likely to occur in the next few years. In fact, the government recently announced that TFR dropped to 1.47 in 1993, but it has not abandoned its optimistic projection. It is almost certain that new public policies will be introduced to help raise the fertility rate, but it is not clear how effective these interventions will be in this delicate area unless we are willing to abandon the present family structure in Japan.

We must, therefore, take the expected increase in the elderly population relative to the working population up to, say, the year 2020 as a given. It is either too late or too expensive to try to change that substantially. In contrast, in spite of our projections here, changes in public policies and social institutions could have substantial effects on the population structure in the second quarter of the twenty-first century.

Although aging is expected to have far-reaching effects on all aspects of our lives, many public systems have not had time to adjust to these expected changes, particularly since the government is not yet fully convinced of the need to adjust. In terms of the effects on the national economy, the most serious effects will be those on health care costs and public pension costs. Both will almost directly reflect the expected increase in the elderly population, and we should carefully examine whether present financing mechanisms will be able to withstand the crunch.

In this paper, we estimate the costs of public pension benefits, and the insurance tax rates needed to support them, using the Social Insurance Model developed by this author and others. The results of our analyses clearly illustrate the instability of the Japanese public pension systems. The insurance tax rates of pension programs for employees will climb in an almost straight-line fashion, from less than 15 percent today to 40 percent in the second quarter of the next century. This paper investigates three alternative measures that can control the cost of future benefits: (1) delay of the start of old-age pensions, (2) disposable income slide or benefit taxation, and (3) price indexation. Measure 1 will reduce the required tax rate by only 5 percent, while measures 2 and 3 will reduce it by 10 percent each. Various combinations of these measures will have greater effects than any one measure alone, but much less effect than the simple sum of these measures.

In the next section, we outline our public pension simulation model and its key variables, providing necessary accounts of Japanese public pension systems. We then present the simulation results, showing what will happen if we maintain the present public pension structure as the baseline scenario. Finally, we discuss the effects of the three possible reforms, which could be introduced separately or in various combinations, on the total cost of public pensions.

1.2   Outline of the Simulation Model

Our simulation model consists of the Population Model and the Social Insurance Model, which in turn consists of the Public Health Insurance Sub-Model and the Public Pension Sub-Model.

1.2.1   Population Model

Assumption on mortality. The Population Model was run for every year from 1990 to 2050; the rest of the model was run for every five-year period. The initial values for population regarding age and sex were set at 1990 census values, and the numbers of deaths by age and sex were estimated using the mortality data in the 1990 life table. Contrary to the government's projection of a continued decline in mortality, we assumed that long-run mortality rates will remain as they are. In the past few years, for several major diseases such as cancer, cerebrovascular disease, and cardiovascular disease, the mortality rates of the most elderly group have either stopped declining or started to rise more sharply, suggesting the possibility of an upturn in the long run.

Assumption on fertility. Our Population Model includes an innovative method of estimating the number of new births. In the past, government estimates were based on the projection of the number of married women and their fertility rate at each age. This simple method could be easily manipulated by the fertility rate projection, as is evident in the government's notorious 1986 official projection. In this regard, Ogura (1991) presented the empirical fact that the fertility of a married woman of a given age is determined more by the number of years since her marriage than by her biological age itself, and they proposed to use this fact as the basis for fertility rate projections. For instance, two 30-year-old married women can have completely different likelihoods of giving birth in the course of a year if one has been married for 10 years and the other for 1 year. The odds of the former giving birth are slightly better than 50 to 1 (2 percent), while those of the latter are better than 2 to 1 (54 percent). Averaging these two probabilities involves a considerable risk in population projection if there is no guarantee that the "vintage" mix will remain reasonable constant over time.

The methodology we adopted was very simple. If we denote the number of women of age n who have been married z years in year t as $k(n, z; t)$ and the probability of a woman giving birth to her first child as $\pi_1(n, z)$, the number of first children born out of this group is given by

$$c_1(n, z; t) = \pi_1(n, z)k(n, z; t).$$

As an example, figure 1.3 shows the probability π_1 for women aged 18–41 who have been married one to five years. In the projection, z runs up to 9 years for first children and 12 years for other children. Probabilities were obtained as averages of the ratio $c_1(n, z; t)/k(n, z; t)$, where values of t were chosen to be 1980, 1985, and 1989. We should note that the data for $c_1(n, z; t)$ and $k(n, z; t)$ were obtained directly from *Vital Statistics* (Ministry of Health and Welfare, various years), which excludes the case of couples whose cohabitation started prior to the calendar year when they reported their marriage. This group accounts for about 10 percent of all marriages reported, but in the absence of detailed information on the childbearing behavior of these couples, we computed the $\pi_1(n, z)$ ratios without data for them. We believe that this will not affect the results of our fertility projection too much, but it is possible that the probability shown in figure 1.3 may have a small bias.

Summing $c_1(n, z; t)$ over z, we obtained the total number of first children for women of age n, or

$$c_1(n; t) = \Sigma c_1(n, z; t).$$

We then summed $c_1(n; t)$ over n and obtained the total number of first children born to women of all ages, or $C_1(t)$:

$$C_1(t) = \Sigma c_1(n; t),$$

out of which 50.37 percent were assumed to be boys and the rest girls. In our model, we repeated the same procedure two more times—once for second children and again for third or more children.

Assumption on marriage rates. The number of women getting married at age n was assumed to be a fixed proportion ($\kappa(n)$) of the female population of that age, or $f(n; t)$; hence,

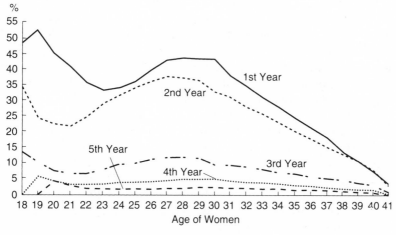

Fig. 1.3   Probability of giving birth to a first child

$$k(n, 0; t) = \kappa(n)f(n; t).$$

For $\kappa(n)$, or the rate of marriage at age n, we took the number of women married in 1989 whose cohabitation and marriage coincided in the same calendar year and divided it by the female population of age n in 1989. In year $t + 1$, all married women who survive increase by one year in both age (n) and years married (z), or

$$k(n + 1, z + 1; t +1) = s_f(n)k(n, z; t),$$

where $s_f(n)$ is one minus the mortality rate at age n. The marriage rate as computed from 1989 data includes both first marriages and second or third marriages. In view of the increasing share of second marriages, it may be worthwhile to model divorce behavior in future population projections. One valid criticism of this procedure is that the marriage rate should be replaced by the marriage probability conditional on being single. More specifically, according to this view the number of women getting married in their thirties (numerator) is small simply because the number of single women in their thirties (denominator) is small, but as the size of this latter group increases, the size of the former should increase as well. Thus, by directly linking marriage to population, our projection may have a downward bias, particularly for women in their thirties.

Results of population projection. At the start of industrialization, in 1872, the Japanese population was estimated to be around 34.8 million, and it has continued to increase during each of the past 120 years, with 1944 being the only exception. According to the projection of our model, however, this phase will be over in 10 years.

Births will increase in the next 10 years, reflecting childbirths to the second baby boomers, but this third baby boom will be a very modest one, peaking at less than 1.4 million, compared with 2 million births for their parents' generation. Following the third baby boom, the number of births will continue to decline for the first quarter of the twenty-first century, which will be interrupted only briefly by the fourth baby boom around the year 2030. The fourth baby boom will be very feeble, producing slightly over 900,000 babies, and the number of births will start to fall quickly; by the middle of the twenty-first century it will be about half of the current number.

In contrast, the number of deaths will continue to increase monotonically until it reaches 1.8 million in 2025, and it is expected to remain at that level for almost a decade and a half. As a result of these two divergent trends in births and deaths, the total Japanese population will reach its peak in 2005 and will decline at an accelerating rate thereafter. The rate of decrease will stabilize in the second quarter of the twenty-first century, but in 2025 the number of deaths will be almost twice the number of births, reducing the population by almost 900,000 people a year.

Age composition of population. Table 1.1 shows the composition of the Japanese population in different age groups. In this table, people in their sixties and eighties are grouped in five-year age groups, while the rest are shown in ten-year groups. From this table, we can see that in 1990 about 11.5 percent of the population was 65 years of age or older, but according to our projection the proportion will more than double by 2020. By 2040, the proportion will be close to 30 percent.

1.2.2   Social Insurance Model

Our Social Insurance Model inherited its basic structure from the Public Health Insurance Model of Ogura and Irifune (1990) and includes the Public Pension Model that originated in Ogura and Nishimoto (1984). We have adopted this strategy primarily because, in Japan, public health insurance programs collectively have the most extensive coverage of all social insurance schemes. For instance, as of the end of March 1990, a simple sum of all individuals covered by any public health insurance program was 123,600,000, which was slightly greater than the entire population of Japan at the time. Moreover, availability of information on the economic, social, and other characteristics of participants in major public health insurance programs is far better than that for public pension programs. Finally, similarities exist between public health insurance programs and public pension programs, as shown in table 1.2.

Roughly speaking, the workers covered by Health Insurance Managed by Associations (HIMA) are employees of corporations large enough to form independent health insurance groups (interpreted as corporations with more than 700 employees), while those covered by Health Insurance Managed by Government (HIMG) are employees of the rest of the corporations. With respect to public pensions, both groups are covered by the Welfare Annuity Plan (WAP).

Table 1.1   **Projection of Age Composition of the Japanese Population (percent)**

Age Group	1960	1970	1980	1990	2000	2010	2020	2030	2040	2050
0–9	18.3	16.3	15.8	11.7	9.4	9.7	7.9	7.5	7.9	7.1
10–19	21.8	16.3	14.7	15.4	11.4	9.4	10.2	8.6	8.3	8.9
20–29	17.7	19.0	14.4	13.5	15.0	11.3	9.9	11.0	9.4	9.2
30–39	14.5	16.0	17.1	14.1	13.2	15.0	11.8	10.7	12.1	10.5
40–49	10.5	12.7	14.1	15.7	13.7	13.0	15.5	12.7	11.6	13.4
50–59	8.4	8.9	11.0	12.7	14.9	13.3	13.3	16.3	13.6	12.6
60–64	3.1	3.6	3.8	5.4	6.0	7.4	6.0	7.2	8.1	6.8
65–69	2.3	2.9	3.4	4.0	5.5	6.4	6.9	6.2	8.6	7.3
70–79	2.7	3.3	4.3	5.4	7.6	9.5	12.0	11.4	12.2	15.3
80–84	0.5	0.6	0.9	1.4	1.9	2.9	3.5	4.8	4.0	5.0
85+	0.2	0.3	0.5	0.7	1.5	1.9	2.9	3.6	4.3	3.9
Total	100.0	100.0	100.0	100.0	100.0	100.0	100.0	100.0	100.0	100.0

Sources: Ogura (1991) and author's computations.

Table 1.2   **Coverage of Public Health and Public Pension Plans (thousand individuals)**

Public Health Insurance Programs		Public Pension Programs	
Health Insurance Managed by		Welfare Annuity Plan	
Total	31,509		29,921
Associations (large firms)	14,173		
Government (small firms)	17,336		
Mutual Aid Associations		Mutual Aid Associations	
Health Insurance for		Pension Plan	
National Government	1,707		1,656
Local Governments	2,957		3,277
Private Schools	393		384
National Health Insurance		National Pension Plan	
All NHI Programs	43,789		17,799

Sources: Social Insurance Agency (1992) and author's computations.

Mutual Aid Associations (MAA) provide health insurance and pension insurance for workers in national government, local governments, and other public corporations. Municipal governments provide National Health Insurance (NHI) plans for self-employed residents and employees of unincorporated businesses, who are obligated to join the National Pension Plan (NPP).

Our model starts with the current allocation of participants in public health insurance programs and adjusts this number to obtain the allocation of participants in public pension programs. By comparing these two numbers, it is clear that only small adjustments are required as far as the WAP is concerned. The problem is the NPP, which is plagued by a high noncompliance ratio.

Allocation of labor force entrants. In the framework of our model, workers enter the labor market for the first time in the two five-year age groups 15–19 and 20–24. They are absorbed into one of three sectors, each of which represents a public health insurance plan, according to the rules in table 1.3.

The remainder of the cohort will either become self-employed, to be covered by the NHI/NPP, or be dependent family members of employed workers insured by the HIMA, HIMG, or MAA. To arrive at the number of those to be insured by the NHI/NPP, it is necessary to estimate the number of dependent family members of workers covered by the HIMA, HIMG, or MAA; then

NHI coverage = Cohort population
            − (HIMA workers + HIMG workers
            + MAA workers)
            − (HIMA dependents + HIMG dependents
            + MAA dependents).

Allocation of dependents of employed workers. Ogura and Irifune (1990) estimated the number of family dependents of employed workers from the cross-

Table 1.3   **Allocation of Labor Force Entrants**

Age Group	Sex	HIMA (%)	HIMG (%)	MAA
15–19	Male	4	5	59,000
	Female	6	6	3,000
20–24	Male	23	22	317,000
	Female	31	23	180,000

Source: Author's computations based on Ministry of Health and Welfare (1993).

tabulation of numbers and ages of dependents and workers using the latest available HIMA and HIMG data. These cross-tabulations are available for each of the four possible combinations of sexes for worker and dependent. For instance, in the given data, if we denote the number of female dependents in the kth age group supported by the sth age group as $f_m(k, s)$ and the number of male workers in the sth age group as $M(s; 0)$, the probability that a male worker in the sth age group supports a female family member in the kth age group, denoted as $\mu_{fm}(k, s)$, is computed as follows:

$$\mu_{fm}(k, s) = f_m(k, s) / M(s; 0).$$

Repeating the process for all possible s and k, we can obtain the support probability matrix $[\mu_{fm}(k, s)]$. We can then postmultiply this matrix by the age-group column vector of the number of male workers at time t, or $[M(s; t)]$, and obtain the age-group column vector of the number of female dependents supported by male workers in this system, or $[F_{fm}(k; t)]$. We can repeat this procedure for female-female, male-male, and male-female combinations to obtain $[F_{ff}(k; t)]$, $[M_{mm}(k; t)]$, and $[M_{mf}(k; t)]$. Female dependent vectors can then be added to yield the total number of family dependents in this system. This was the procedure adopted by Ogura and Irifune (1990).

The problem with this procedure is that the number of family dependents at a given time reflects family formation behavior such as marriage and fertility during the preceding years. Thus, in view of the fundamental changes that have been taking place in Japanese family structure, if we apply this method directly we will end up substantially overestimating the number of dependents of employed workers and hence substantially underestimating the population in the self-employed sector.

To avoid this problem, in this model we computed the share of dependents for each male and female worker; for instance, instead of computing $[f_m(k, s)/M(s; 0)]$, we computed $[(f_m(k, s)/F(k; 0))/M(s; 0)]$, where $F(k)$ is the female population of the kth age group. Postmultiplying this share matrix by the age-group vector of the number of male workers, or $[M(s; t)]$, we obtained the age-group vector of the proportion of the female population that will be supported by employed male workers in this system, or $[\theta_{fm}(k; t)]$. Multiplying each component of this vector by the female population in the appropriate age group, or $F(k; t)$, we obtained the new number of female dependents supported by male workers covered by each plan. This procedure takes care of the effect of changes in fertility, but not of the effect of changes in marital behavior. We have yet to adjust for the latter in the current version of our model.

Net quit rates. The labor force entrants absorbed in each system will move across the systems over time. The quality of available data on intersystem mobility is not sufficiently high to enable us to model such behavior, and in the past we used crude "net quit rates" (Ogura 1989; Ogura and Irifune 1990). The net quit rate of male workers in a system is simply the expected number of male workers of the $(k + 1)$-th age group in the next period per one male worker of the kth age group in the system. As such, the rate reflects both entry and exit behaviors of workers in the system in different age groups. We constructed these rates for male workers in both the WAP and the MAA, using the combined data of the HIMG and the HIMA during the 1980s, and assumed that they remain constant during the entire period of our simulation exercise.

As for female workers, in view of the upward trend in their labor force participation rates, we decided to incorporate the expected changes in their net quit rates. Currently, the labor force participation rates of Japanese women follow an M shape, with ages 20–24 as the first peak (about 75 percent) and ages 40–44 and 45–49 forming the second peak (about 70 percent). At present, the valley is located at ages 30–34, but it has been getting shallower every year. Most long-term economic forecasts predict that early in the twenty-first century the valley between the two peaks will virtually disappear, as it has in most Western industrialized countries. We adjusted our net quit rates in such a way that, by the year 2010, the labor force participation rate will assume a flat pattern at around 70 percent, as is the case in the United States.

1.2.3   Welfare Annuity Plan Sub-Model

Estimation of the average cost of benefits   We estimated the average cost of benefits separately for retired male and female workers in each cohort, as they become eligible for WAP benefits.

Special benefits before age 65.   For male employed workers covered by the WAP, we incorporated the four following full components (the parameters in **boldface** are those directly determined by laws or regulations, and those in *italics* are our estimates using WAP data up to 1990):

$$\text{Special benefit} = \text{Fixed benefit} + \text{Proportional benefit}$$
$$+ \text{ Spouse benefit} + \text{Special benefit},$$

where

$$\text{Fixed benefit} = \mathbf{1{,}388} \times \mathbf{Adjustment\ rate}\ (t)$$
$$\times \textit{Average months credited}\ (t),$$

Proportional benefit = **Coefficient** (*t*)
$\times$ *Average monthly earnings* $\times$ *Average months credited* (*t*),

Spouse benefit = **209,100** $\times \sum\limits_{n}$ *Dependent spouse ratio* (*n, t*),

Special spouse benefit = **Special benefits constant** (*t*)
$\times \sum\limits_{n}$ *Dependent spouse ratio)* (*n, t*).

For female employed workers covered by the WAP, however, only the first two components were incorporated in the computation. Those receiving partial benefits due to continued employment at ages 60–64 were assumed to receive 80 percent of full benefits.

WAP benefits. With respect to male retired workers over age 65, the average cost of a benefit was computed

WAP cost = Husband's basic pension + Wife's basic pension
+ WAP benefit,

where

Husband's basic pension = **725,300** $\times$ *Credited month ratio* (*t*),

Wife's basic pension = **725,300** $\times$ *Credit month ratio* (*t*)
$\times \sum\limits_{n}$ Dependent spouse ratio (*n, t*)
+ **Transfer benefit** (*t*),

Credit month ratio = *Average months credited* (*t*) /
Number of creditable months (*t*),

WAP benefit = Proportional benefit + Spouse benefit for wife less than 65 years old + Special spouse benefit for wife less than 65 years old.

Survivor benefit

Male receiving survivor benefit = *13,000* $\times$ 12,
Female reveiving survivor benefit = *75,000* $\times$ 12.

Intersystem benefit

Intersystem benefit = *0.2* $\times$ WAP benefit.

Credited months. On the basis of the 1981 and 1986 data on the distribution of workers according to the number of credited months in each age group, pub-

people covered by the NPP is about 75 percent of those in their twenties, about 50 percent of those aged 30–34, and over 90 percent of those aged 35 and up.

Number of credited months. Starting from the average number of credited months for each sex and age group contained in the 1990 official government forecast, we added the proportion of a period (namely, 60 months) that corresponds to the average NPP coverage ratio of the age group for each sex.

Average old-age pension benefit. The full old-age pension benefit for those who joined the NPP for the maximum possible months before age 60 is 725,000 yen per year. This is prorated according to the ratio of credited months to maximum possible months (480 months, except for those born before 1941).

Number of pension beneficiaries. We have assumed that 75 percent of those covered by the NHI in the 55–59 age group will become vested for an old-age pension benefit by accumulating at least 300 credited months before they reach age 60. This ratio is based on records for the past few years. Of those who become vested, we have again assumed that 11 percent of men and 18 percent of women will elect to receive reduced (50 percent) pension benefits when they reach age 60 but that the rest will wait until age 65 for full pension benefits.

Cost of other benefits. Since the disability benefit of the NPP is far more generous than the old-age benefit, its share of the total cost of the NPP exceeds that of the WAP disability benefit by a wide margin. We have not yet modeled the following benefits individually: partial credit benefits, survivor benefits, and disability benefits. We have added 40 percent of the cost of old-age benefits to account for the costs of these benefits.

1.3   Simulation Results of the Public Pension Model

1.3.1   Framework of Simulation

As our baseline case, we fixed the system parameters in the benefit equations and the wage structures at 1990 levels, as in our Social Insurance Model, and measured the effects of changes in population structure as well as in cohort-specific parameters in the benefit equations. Literally interpreted, this case reflects no growth in real wages in the next half-century. More realistically, however, it should be interpreted as a case in which all system parameters in the benefit equations are fully indexed to keep pace with changes in real wages. The advantage of our method is that by measuring everything in terms of units of labor, it is far easier for us to comprehend intuitively the sizes of benefits and burdens in the distant future and compare them with the present.

With respect to wage indexation, the present Japanese public pension laws require the government to reevaluate past earnings every five years to reflect changes in market wage rates. We should note that the laws have left room for the government to decide how closely past earnings should be indexed to changes in real wages. The government quietly took advantage of this loophole in the last evaluation (1989) and limited the long-run indexation of real wage rates to about 70 percent without any explanation.

1.3.2   Numbers of Recipients

By adding together the numbers of recipients of all the benefits, one may not obtain a good quantity index to indicate the cost of the public pension systems. In 1990, for the WAP, old-age benefits accounted for 50 percent of recipients but 70 percent of the cost. In contrast, survivor benefits accounted for 20 percent of the number of recipients but only 14 percent of the cost because the average cost of survivor benefits is only half that of old-age benefits. For this reason, in figure 1.4, we show only the numbers of old-age benefits recipients in the three systems through the first half of the next century (with the present system parameters). In 1990, there were 3.94 million recipients in the WAP; this number will increase to 7.59 million by 2000 and 14.39 million by 2020. There were 1.71 million recipients in the MAA.

1.3.3   Total Cost of Benefits

Figure 1.5 shows the total cost of benefits (in 10 billion yen) for the three systems in our baseline simulation case. According to our model, the total cost of WAP benefits, which stood at 9.2 trillion yen in 1990, will surpass 16 trillion yen in 2000, reach almost 23 trillion yen in 2010, and almost 28 trillion yen in 2020.

The total cost of the MAA, which stood at 5.6 trillion yen in 1990, will

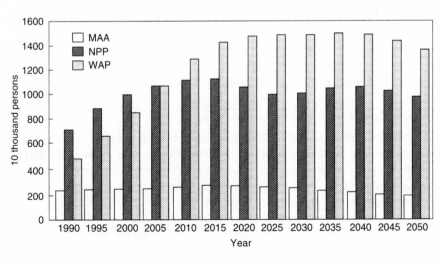

Fig. 1.4   Estimated number of old-age pension recipients

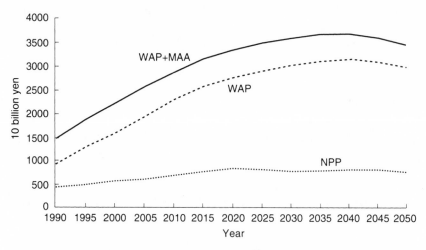

Fig. 1.5   Total costs of benefits

increase only moderately to 6.2 trillion yen in 2000, after which it will begin a slow decline. The combined costs of benefits for these two employee pension plans will increase at a rate of 3 trillion yen every five years, from 14.8 trillion yen in 1990 to 36 trillion yen in 2030, or 2.5 times the 1990 level.

As for the NPP, the cost of benefits, which stood at 4.3 trillion yen in 1990, will reach 5.6 trillion yen in 2000, 7 trillion yen in 2010, and 8.5 trillion yen in 2020, which will be the peak. The cost will remain around 8 trillion yen for some time afterward. Although the number of NPP recipients will increase by only 50 percent, costs will increase by 100 percent as a result of an increase in credited months.

To summarize, given the present parameters of our public pension systems, the total cost of public pensions was 19 trillion yen in 1990; this cost will increase to 28 trillion yen in 2000, 36 trillion yen in 2010, and 42 trillion yen in 2020, after which the rate of increase will become less sharp.

1.3.4   Cost of Basic Pension Benefits

Figure 1.6 shows how much of the total cost of public pensions is accounted for by the cost of basic pension benefits. The basic pension includes not only the basic pension costs themselves but also what are usually referred to as their "equivalents" in the WAP and MAA for the claims already existing when the basic pension was introduced. Currently, the basic pension accounts for slightly more than one-third of the total cost, but in 2015 it will account for almost one-half of the total. This implies that it will become much more difficult to reduce the cost of benefits in the next century.

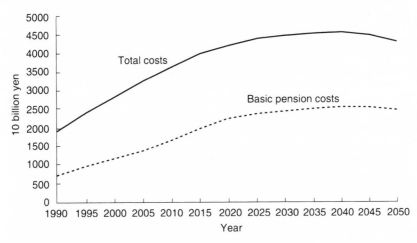

Fig. 1.6   Total costs and basic pension costs

1.3.5   Cost of Benefits Borne by Each System

Under the current Japanese public pension arrangement, each system does not automatically bear the full cost of its benefits, to be paid by either its own insurance taxes or income earned from accumulated funds, if any. Adjustments must be made for both the national government subsidy and the cross-subsidization involved in the Basic Pension Program. The national government subsidy is, however, tied to the Basic Pension Program, so we discuss only the structure of the Basic Pension Program here.

Under the program, the government first adds up the costs of the basic pension benefits for all three major systems. The total cost is then prorated to each system according to the number of insured individuals in the system (instead of the number of recipients) to arrive at the cost of the Basic Pension Program assessed to each system. For the WAP and the MAA, the number of insured individuals includes not only the workers themselves but also their dependent spouses. Thus, for each system,

Basic pension cost assessed = National cost of basic pension benefits
× Share of insured individuals
in the basic pension system.

The national government subsidizes one-third of this assessed cost for each system, and each system bears two-thirds of this assessed value as far as basic pension benefits are concerned. Therefore, the cost actually borne by each system is given by

Cost actually borne = Cost of benefits other than basic pension
+ (2/3) * Basic pension cost assessed.

1.3.6   Tax Bases

For the WAP and MAA, we can approximate the tax rates required to keep the systems solvent as a ratio of the costs actually borne to the size of the tax base. For these two systems, the tax base is essentially the annual payroll (excluding semiannual bonuses), which is primarily determined by the number of employed workers. For the NPP, which collects what is essentially a poll tax, the number of insured individuals is its tax base. Figure 1.7 shows the changes in the number of insured workers over time in each system as predicted by our model. Although our model is based on a set of very rigid and mechanical assumptions, it is nevertheless quite clear that, sooner or later, each system must face a declining number of insured workers.

Both the MAA and the NPP are already facing a long, slow decline in workers toward 2020, at which time they will begin to experience a rapid decrease. For the MAA, the number of workers will decline slowly from 5 million in 1990 to 4 million in 2020. As for the NPP, the number of insured individuals will decline from 15 million in 1990 to 13 million in 2020, after which the rate of decrease will accelerate.

In our scenario, the only short-run exception is the WAP, which will show a net increase of more than 2 million insured workers between 1990 and 2000. This will be brought about by a combination of two factors: the participation of the second baby boom generation in the labor market and the continued increase in female labor force participation. After the year 2000, the number of male workers in the WAP is expected to decline sharply, but the decline in the number of female workers will be more gradual. As a result, in 2020, compared to 1990, there will be 2 million fewer male workers but about the same

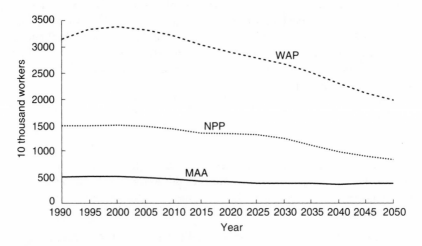

Fig. 1.7   Estimated number of insured workers

number of female workers. In the following 20 years, the number of both male and female workers will decline by more than 20 percent.

In addition to the number of employed workers, the size of the WAP and the MAA annual payrolls will be affected by their sex/age mixes. Figure 1.8 shows the changes in their tax bases, assuming that the sex/age profile of wages of WAP workers remains constant. The two curves decline rather sharply, reflecting decreasing employment. At the same time, however, figure 1.8 shows that we can maintain the current size of our tax bases if we secure a 1 percent annual increase in real wages in the next half-century.

1.3.7   Required Tax Rates

The required tax rates are computed by dividing the costs borne by the tax base for the WAP and the MAA separately and for them as a single system. In reality, the WAP in particular still holds a very substantial fund at this point, and this fund, as well as its interest income, could be used to pay for part of its costs. Therefore, calling the ratio a "required tax rate" may be inappropriate. Although this is a valid criticism, it is clear that this ratio gives the upper bound of taxes required to keep the systems solvent. Moreover, we feel strongly that the significance of the system's fund is blown out of proportion for the following two reasons.

First, although the nominal interest income seems to be very large, most of it is depreciation of capital due to inflation, and the real interest income is a small portion of it. In fact, at present, the real rate of interest is only about 1 percent. The accumulated fund of the public pension systems collectively

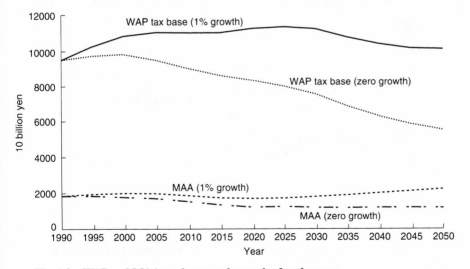

Fig. 1.8   WAP and MAA tax bases and growth of real wages

amounts to around 130 trillion yen, or about six years' cost of all benefits at the current rate. A real interest rate of 1 percent a year will pay only 1.5 months of benefits on a permanent basis, even if the cost of benefits remains the same. Second, in a public pension system that promises wage indexation of benefits, the whole real interest income cannot be used to pay for the benefits on a permanent basis; the relevant interest rate must be the difference between the nominal interest rate and the rate of increase in nominal wages, or the difference between the real interest rate and the rate of increase in real wages. Past experience suggests that this is very close to zero in Japan.

As figure 1.9 shows, we should expect the required tax rate of the WAP to keep increasing by almost 5 percent every five years, from 11 percent in 1990 to 17 percent in 2000, 23 percent in 2010, 28 percent in 2020, 33 percent in 2030, and 40 percent in 2040. In contrast, the tax rate of the MAA in 1990 was already very high, 31 percent, and we do not expect it to increase much more. Its peak will come around 2101 at 35 percent, and it will remain at about 33 percent for a long time. If the WAP and MAA are viewed as a combined system, something almost certain to become a reality in the near future, their tax rate was 14 percent in 1990, and we expect it to increase to 39 percent in 2040, following almost a straight line.

1.4 Three Policies to Alleviate Future Burdens

Given current public pension systems and demographic factors, we have shown that the pension tax burden on the working population in half a century will be almost three times higher than it is now. Furthermore, as the population continues to age, health care costs will increase rapidly, and most of these costs

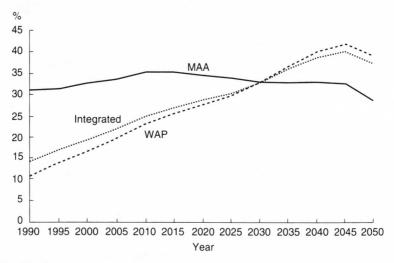

Fig. 1.9 Required tax rates for WAP and MAA

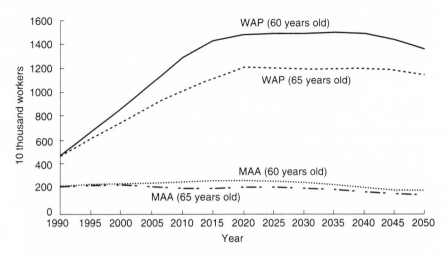

Fig. 1.10   Reduction in number of old-age pension recipients

will be borne by the future working population. To strike a proper balance in the burdens between generations, we must find a way to alleviate the burden of future generations effectively without eroding the confidence of the elderly in the pension systems. In this section, we measure the impacts of three alternative policies that could serve this purpose: (1) delay of the start of payments until age 65, (2) a form of indexation of pension benefits to the real disposable income of the working population, and (3) price indexation of pension benefits.

1.4.1   Delay of the Start of Pension Benefits

Number of recipients. Figure 1.10 shows the reduction in the number of pension recipients if the start of WAP and MAA benefits is delayed until age 65. The transition is assumed to start in 1995, at the rate of one biological year for every five years, and it is assumed to be completed in the year 2015. In terms of actual computation, the proportion of baseline case recipients who will actually receive benefits in the 60–64 age group is reduced by one-fifth every five years, until it reaches zero in 2015. Our results suggest that the total number of old-age WAP recipients will be reduced by about 2.5 million individuals once the transition is completed. This amounts to one-sixth of the baseline old-age benefit recipients.

Cost of benefits. In terms of the total cost of benefits, the delay in the start of payments will save about 3 trillion yen for the WAP and about 0.5 trillion yen for the MAA. These savings are much smaller than the reduction in the number of old-age pension recipients might suggest because survivor benefits will be affected very little by the measure.

Required tax rate. In figure 1.11, we show how the required payroll tax rate will evolve if we move to delay the start of pension payments. After 2015, this measure will reduce the required tax rate by 4–5 percent.

1.4.2   Indexation to Disposable Income or Taxation of Benefits

The most compelling reason to control the future cost of pension benefits is that if we leave the current system as it is now, it is quite possible that the net disposable income of the future working population will be reduced to less than that of the pension recipients. Considering this possibility, some argue that pension benefits should be indexed, not to wages, but to the disposable income of the working population, as in Germany (Takayama 1992). It is not easy to simulate this case, and know what this proposal will mean in terms of the required tax rate within the current framework, without modeling the entire public sector. Therefore, we consider an alternative scheme in which insurance taxes are collected from pension benefits. This alternative measure not only adequately captures the spirit of disposable income indexation but also has considerable merit on its own.

First of all, under this scheme, if an increase in the insurance tax reduces the disposable income of the working population, it will reduce the disposable income of retirees at exactly the same rate. Social insurance tax rates by themselves will not affect the relative amounts of disposable income between generations.

Second, the consequence of this measure is very predictable. Suppose that under the present scheme the total cost of the benefits program at time t is given by $B(t)$ and its tax base is given by $X(t)$. Under this measure, although the total cost of the benefits remains unchanged, the new tax base is the sum of the original tax base and the total cost of the benefits, or $B(t) + X(t)$. Thus,

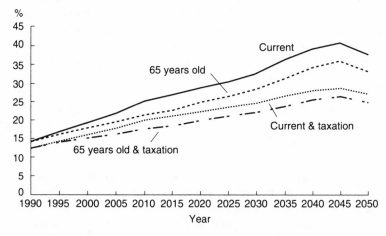

Fig. 1.11   Comparison of effects of delay of start (65) and taxation of benefits

if we denote the ratio of $B(t)$ to $X(t)$ as $b(t)$, the new (net) required tax rate, $\tau^*(t)$, will be given by

$$\tau^*(t) = b(t)/[1 + b(t)],$$

which is very simple to calculate. However, the government will pay part of the benefits, say $\lambda(t)B(t)$, where $\lambda(t)$ is the ratio of the government's subsidy to the total cost of the benefits. Thus, the cost charged to the unit tax base of the program is given by $[1 - \lambda(t)]b(t)$, and the required tax rate will be given by

$$\tau^*(t) = [1 - \lambda(t)]b(t)/[1 + b(t)].$$

To simplify the matter further, we will assume that each program can "tax" the benefits only up to the sum actually charged to it, or $[1 - \lambda(t)]B(t)$. Under these assumptions, the required tax rate will be given by

$$\tau^*(t) = [1 - \lambda(t)]b(t)/[1 + (1 - \lambda(t))b(t)],$$

or simply

$$\tau^*(t) = \tau(t)/[1 + \tau(t)],$$

where $\tau(t)$ is the required tax rate for the baseline case.

The relationship between the new required tax rate $\tau^*(t)$ and the baseline tax rate $\tau(t)$ is quite nonlinear; for example, if $b(t)$ is 30 percent, the new tax rate will be 23 percent, and if $b(t)$ is 40 percent, the new tax will still be only 29 percent. Figure 1.11 shows the path of the new tax rate. From the figure, we can see that even if we continue to start paying the old-age pension at age 60, we will still be able to keep the required tax rate under 30 percent in the 2040s, when it is at its peak. Delaying the start of the old-age pension by five years will shave off 2 percent more at the peak.

1.4.3 Price Indexation

In the baseline case, we have seen that if we try to index public pension benefits fully to wages, we must expect an unrealistically heavy burden on the future working population. The proposed delay of the start of old-age benefits by five years will help to reduce the burden, but only by about 5 percent, which hardly makes a dent in the problem. This is precisely the reason we have investigated the implication of disposable income indexation. In this section, as an alternative to disposable income indexation, we look at the effect of indexing benefits to the price level.

Every five years, public pension systems take account of changes in the wage level, reevaluate the historical wages of pension recipients, and recompute pension benefits. For the years in between, the benefits are indexed to the price level. In the baseline case, we have assumed that pension benefits are fully indexed to the wage index. This was the case until 1986, when the WAP law was revised.

Since the last revision of the WAP law, however, historical wages are no longer given an across-the-board full-wage indexation. In fact, the rates at which historical wages are reevaluated are decreasing functions of the time elapsed. That rate is 100 percent for the preceding five years and declines to around 70 percent for 30-plus years. Since this indexation is one of the most important parts of the public pension systems, it should not be left to the discretion of the government.

If there is no growth in real wages, it makes no difference whether we index benefits to the wage level or the price level. In what follows, we assume some growth in real wages. No one knows, however, what the rate of growth in real wages will be in the next 50 years, and all we can do is assume a reasonable rate of growth. In fact, we will assume that real wages will grow 1 percent per year, which is modest enough to be within the reach of our economy and yet sizable enough to make a real difference in the proposed scheme.

In figure 1.12, the curve at the top stands for standardized wages of male workers of different ages in 1990 who belonged to HIMG. The horizontal axis represents age in decreasing order, and the vertical axis represents wages expressed in terms of thousands of yen. We can interpret this curve as the reevaluated values of the historical wages a retiring worker will get at age 60 if he has worked in a small firm for most of his life and if his past wages are reevaluated by reflecting all the increases in wages until his retirement.

The second curve from the top stands for the results of reevaluation using the price level instead of the wage level. We are assuming a difference of 1 percent per year between the two indices. Because of the change in indexation, for a worker to whom the maximum 480 months are credited, the lifetime average of his monthly earnings will be about 86 percent of the average in

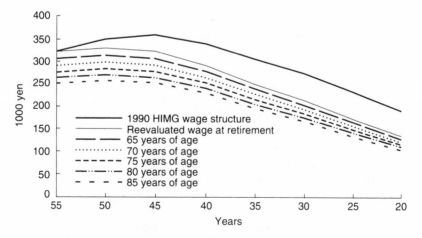

Fig. 1.12   Effects of reevaluation of wages, by private index (1 percent real wage growth assumed)

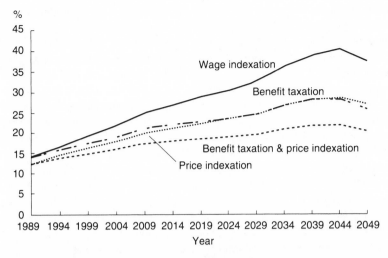

Fig. 1.13   Effects of price indexation on required tax rates (1 percent real wage growth assumed)

the wage indexation case. If he has only the minimum 300 months' credit, the lifetime average will be 95 percent of the baseline case.

After retirement, the worker will receive only the price indexation, not the wage indexation. The five bottom curves reflect the relative values of his reevaluated wages vis-à-vis the working population at subsequent ages. As a result, for a worker who has 480 months' credit, the lifetime average will be about 67 percent, or two-thirds, of the average in the full-wage indexation case.

Required tax rate. Figure 1.13 shows the path of the required tax rate if we start price indexation of all past earnings in 1995. It also shows the path for the case of benefit taxation combined with price indexation. For reference purposes, paths for the baseline case and for benefit taxation with wage indexation also are shown. By and large, price indexation alone has about the same effect as the taxation of benefits, and price indexation and taxation can keep the maximum tax rate below 25 percent.

1.5   Concluding Remarks

The results of our simulation of the baseline case clearly illustrate the instability of the Japanese public pension systems. The insurance tax rates of pension programs for employees will climb in an almost straight-line fashion until they reach 40 percent in the middle of the next century. The generation born in the 30 years after 2020 will have to bear about twice the burden of the preceding generation. It is very hard to justify such rapid changes in the distribution of income between generations. Under a reasonable set of circumstances, it is quite possible for the economic welfare of the future working population to fall below that of the retired population.

The most effective way to deal with this problem is to control the cost of future benefits. In the preceding analyses, we have investigated the effects of three possible measures: (1) delay of the start of old-age pensions, (2) indexation of benefits to disposable income or taxation of benefits, and (3) price indexation of benefits. We have seen that option 1 will reduce the required tax rate by 5 percent, option 2 by 10 percent, and option 3 by 10 percent, if they are implemented separately. Various combinations of these options will have greater effects but much less effect than the simple sum of all the options.

The JCER-NBER joint Hakone Conference on Aging, where this paper was first presented, was held in September 1993. In spring 1994, the Japanese government prepared a comprehensive WAP reform package and sent it to the Diet. The package had three major components: (1) minimization of work disincentive by redesigning partial benefits, (2) postponement of full benefits until age 65, and (3) formal adoption of disposable income indexation instead of wage indexation. With regard to the second point, under the government proposal, starting in 2013 those aged 60–64 who currently qualify for WAP special benefits would lose the equivalent of the basic pension. Retired employees and spouses would also have to wait until age 65 to receive basic pension benefits. With regard to the third point, the government formally proposed abandoning full indexing of past earnings to the current wage level, which it did de facto in 1990. The idea of disposable income indexation, however, invited another question: Whose disposable income should be chosen as the index?

The reform bill passed, and the government was able to get what it wanted—disposable income indexation and a reduction in the special benefit by an amount equal to the basic pension. The government has also prepared its official 1994 projections of public pension costs, but as the technical details of these projections are not made public, we cannot compare them with ours. The government is, in any case, constrained by its own unrealistic population projections, which must account for some of the difference with ours. The government's projections are substantially more optimistic than ours.

References

All works listed are in Japanese.

Ministry of Health and Welfare. 1990. *Official projection of public pension costs.* Tokyo: Government Printing Office.
———. 1993. *Report on the status of insured individuals in the public health insurance programs.* Tokyo: Government Printing Office.
———. Various years. *Vital statistics.* Tokyo: Government Printing Office.

Office of the Prime Minister. 1990. *Statistical yearbook of social security.* Tokyo: Government Printing Office.

Ogura, S. 1991. Projection of Japanese population up to 2020. JCER Discussion Paper no. 16. Tokyo: Japan Center for Economic Research.

———. 1992. Explaining the decline of fertility of Japanese women since the 1970s. In *Economic policies of the aging society,* ed. H. Kanamori et al. Tokyo: University of Tokyo Press.

Ogura, S., and R. Dekle. 1992. On the decline in fertility of Japanese women since the 1970s. *Nihon Keizai Kenkyu* 22:46–76.

Ogura, S., and T. Irifune. 1990. The effects of population aging on the finances of Japanese public health insurance programs. *Financial Review* (Institute of Monetary and Fiscal Research, Ministry of Finance) 17:51–77.

Ogura, S., and R. Nishimoto. 1984. Simulation analyses of the effects of welfare annuity pension reforms. *Gendai Keizai* 60:89–103.

Social Insurance Agency. 1992. *Annual report.* Tokyo: Government Printing Office.

Takayama, N. 1992. *On pension reforms.* Tokyo: Nihon Keizai Shinbun.

2 The Effects of Demographic Trends on Consumption, Saving, and Government Expenditures in the United States

Michael D. Hurd

2.1 Introduction

The developed countries are all forecast to experience a demographic shift to older populations as the combined result of the temporarily high fertility rates that produced the baby boom and falling mortality rates that have increased both the probability of living to age 65 and life expectancy at age 65. Table 2.1 shows the percentage of the population aged 65 or over (elderly) in seven developed countries for 1990 and projected percentages for 2000 and 2020. In the United States, the percentage is expected to increase from 12 percent in 1990 to 16 percent in 2020. Compared with some other countries, this change is rather modest: in Japan, for example, the percentage is expected to increase from 11 percent to 21 percent.

In the United States after 2020 the fraction of the population over age 65 is expected to increase further as the baby boom generation fully ages past 65. However, the growth in the oldest-old population (age 85 or over) is expected to be much larger: the percentage of the population age 85 or over is forecast to double by 2020 and to increase by 275 percent by 2040 (Advisory Council on Social Security 1991a).

These demographic changes may have profound effects on the economy because the economic behavior of the elderly is very different from that of the nonelderly. The most obvious difference is in labor force participation: an older population will have fewer workers per person, and so, ceterus paribus, the economy will have lower output per person. The elderly tend to dissave whereas the working-age population saves. Thus, an older population will have

Michael D. Hurd is professor of economics at the State University of New York, Stony Brook, and a research associate of the National Bureau of Economic Research.

Financial support from the Japan Foundation Center for Global Partnership is gratefully acknowledged.

Table 2.1   **International Population Aging (percentage of population 65 or older)**

Year	Canada	France	Germany	Italy	Japan	U.K.	U.S.
1990	11	14	16	14	11	15	12
2000	13	15	17	15	15	15	12
2020	19	20	22	19	21	16	16

Source: Advisory Council on Social Security (1991a).

a lower saving rate. The pattern of consumption by the elderly is different: they consume more medical services and less private transportation. To the extent that these goods are purchased in a normally functioning market, the economy should accommodate a change in the pattern of consumption. In the United States, however, the elderly are substantially supported by the government through the tax-and-transfer system, in particular, through Social Security (the public pension system in the United States), Medicare (the government health insurance system for the elderly), and Medicaid (the government health insurance system for the poor, whose primary users are the elderly). Therefore, part of their income and some of their consumption arise, not from market transactions, but rather from taxation and subsidized spending. Not only may there be deadweight losses from this system, but an aging population will require increasing taxation, which may strain the political consensus underlying the programs. Thus, for example, the future of the Social Security system has been questioned.

This development is especially troubling for the elderly because of the importance to them of Social Security income. Table 2.2 shows the sources of income of the elderly in the United States. Ninety-three percent of households in which an elderly person lived received Social Security income, compared with just 31 percent with income from private pensions.[1] Social Security accounts for 38 percent of the total income of the elderly, but the distribution of income is such that it is much more important to some households than this figure would suggest. The fraction of households that receive more than 20 percent of their income from Social Security is 0.82; the fraction that receive more than half of their income from Social Security is 0.55. That is, more than half the households receive more than half of their income from Social Security. These figures suggest than any uncertainty about the future of the Social Security system is a matter of concern to the elderly.

The goal of this paper is analyze some projections for the U.S. economy to the year 2020. The focus will be the effects of population aging arising from compositional effects and from increased life expectancy at age 65. However, in the United States, the effects of rapidly rising medical expenditures interact with an aging population and dominate the composition of consumption and

1. These pensions are almost all associated with previous employment in the private sector.

Table 2.2   **Sources of Income of Elderly Family Units, 1988**

	Earnings	Social Security	Other Public Pensions	Private Pensions	Assets	Public Assistance	Other
Fraction with income from source	0.22	0.93	0.16	0.31	0.72	0.05	
Fraction of total income from source	0.17	0.38	0.10	0.08	0.25	0.01	0.02
Fraction with more than 20% of total income from source	0.16	0.82	0.10	0.15	0.19	0.05	
Fraction with more than half of total income from source	0.09	0.55	0.05	0.02	0.06	0.02	

Source: Grad (1990).

government spending in the year 2020, so they will be the subject of considerable analysis. The analysis will find the effects on households, firms, and government and how the effects interact at the macrolevel.

2.2   Social Security Administration Forecasts

The Office of the Actuary of the Social Security Administration (SSA) makes detailed forecasts of the future of the Social Security system. The greatest effort is made for the demographic variables, principally fertility rates and mortality rates, because in the long run, trends in demographics have the greatest impact on the system. Earnings, unemployment, inflation, and other macrovariables are also forecast, and these variables enter a complicated forecasting model that incorporates the Social Security law. The results are forecasts of the income and expenditures of the Social Security system, as well as a great number of other variables. These forecasts will be the basis of the analysis in this section.

2.2.1   Demographic Aspects of the Social Security Forecasts

There are three groups of forecasts. Forecast I is a high-income, low-cost projection based on assumptions of high fertility and low increases in life expectancy. Forecast III is a low-income, high-cost projection based on low fertility and high increases in life expectancy. Forecast II, which is normally used, is a medium-level projection.

The forecasts depend critically on the assumptions about fertility and mortality. Table 2.3 summarizes the main assumptions. Between forecasts I and III, there is substantial variation in the assumptions, which has led many users

Table 2.3   Assumptions for Alternative SSA Demographic Projections

	Fertility Rate[a]			Age-Adjusted Death Rate[b]		
Year	I	II	III	I	II	III
1990	2.05	2.05	2.05	785	792	800
2000	2.12	2.00	1.87	754	723	739
2020	2.20	1.90	1.60	714	633	560
2040	2.20	1.90	1.60	679	573	475

Source: Board of Trustees of the Federal OASDI Trust Funds (1991).
[a]Births per woman.
[b]Deaths per 100,000.

Table 2.4   Life Expectancy at Age 65

	Males			Females		
Year	I	II	III	I	II	III
1990	15.2	15.3	15.3	18.9	19.0	19.0
2000	15.3	15.9	16.4	18.9	19.6	20.2
2020	15.6	16.7	18.0	19.1	20.4	21.9
2040	15.9	17.5	19.5	19.5	21.3	23.5

Source: Board of Trustees of the Federal OASDI Trust Funds (1991).

of the forecasts to assume that I and III bound the possible outcomes. However, there is no reason to suppose this. For example, Manton, Stallard, and Singer (1994) and Vaupel and Lundström (1994) have population-forecasting models that under some circumstances predict much larger elderly populations than the population under forecast III.

Table 2.4 has life expectancies conditional on reaching age 65. The fiscal stability of the Social Security system depends critically on conditional life expectancy: a 1 percent increase in life expectancy at age 65 increases expected costs by 1 percent. There is considerable variation between forecasts I and III: for example, the life expectancy of women in 2040 is 20 percent higher under III than under I. This implies that costs under III will be 20 percent higher than under I.

We cannot assess the reasonableness of the demographic assumptions that underlie the forecasts by comparing the predictions with actual outcomes because we have not observed the process for enough years. However, if the forecasts vary considerably from year to year, it would suggest that even small amounts of new information have large effects on the forecasts. This, in turn, would suggest that the forecasts are not very reliable. Table 2.5 compares two forecasts for the years 2000, 2020, and 2040 of life expectancy at age 65. The predictions were made in 1989 and 1993, so we can see how they evolved with

Table 2.5   **Forecasts of Life Expectancy at Age 65**

Relevant Year	Year of Forecast	I		II		III	
		Men	Women	Men	Women	Men	Women
2000	1989	15.0	18.9	15.6	19.6	16.2	20.4
	1993	15.0	18.8	15.4	19.4	15.8	19.9
2020	1989	15.3	19.2	16.4	20.5	17.8	22.0
	1993	15.2	18.9	16.3	20.2	17.4	21.5
2040	1989	15.7	19.6	17.1	21.4	19.3	23.7
	1993	15.5	19.2	17.1	21.1	19.0	23.2

Source: Board of Trustees of the Federal OASDI Trust Funds (1989, 1993).

Table 2.6   **Four-Year-Ahead Forecasts**

		Percentage			
Variable	Observations	Within[a]	On Boundary[b]	Outside[c]	Total
Unemployment	11	36	18	46	100
GNP change	11	18	0	82	100
Wage change	9	33	0	56	100
Inflation	11	36	9	55	100

Source: Advisory Council on Social Security (1991b).

[a]Between forecasts I and III.

[b]Equal to either forecast I or forecast III.

[c]Outside of range bounded by forecasts I and III.

new information. Especially for forecast III, there were rather large declines in predicted life expectancy. Take the year 2000 for example. The forecasted life expectancy of women 10 years in the future changed by about 3 percent in just four years.

Although we cannot compare the demographic forecasts with actual outcomes, we can compare some of the economic forecasts with outcomes because of the shorter time scale. Table 2.6 summarizes such a comparison for four-year-ahead forecasts of some economic variables. The table gives the number of observations (comparisons between predicted and realized outcomes), the percentage of the realizations that fell between forecasts I and III, the percentage that were exactly the same as either I or III (on the boundary), and the percentage that fell outside the range bounded by I and III. For example, there were 11 comparisons of the actual unemployment rate with the four-year-ahead forecast unemployment rate. Thirty-six percent of the realizations fell within the range bounded by forecasts I and III, 18 percent were equal to I or III, and 46 percent fell outside the range. Therefore, one would estimate that forecasts I and III form a 36 percent confidence interval for four-year-ahead forecasts of the unemployment rate. From this point of view, it is apparent that forecasts I and III do not bound high-level confidence intervals for forecasts of the economic variables. Whether this will prove to be true for the demographic variables as well will be seen in 20 or 30 years, but in the meantime we should probably not treat forecasts I and III as giving high-level confidence bounds. Although I will not repeat this caution later in this paper, it should be assumed that I have this in mind.

The assumptions about fertility and mortality, along with other economic and demographic assumptions, are used in a complicated forecasting model to find future income, costs, and so forth, and the number of Social Security beneficiaries and the number of workers paying into the system (covered workers). The ratio of beneficiaries to covered workers is important because it gives the number of retirees each worker supports through the Social Security tax-and-transfer system. Table 2.7 shows that even under forecast II, the intermediate forecast, the ratio rises from 0.30 to 0.41 in 2020 to 0.51 in 2040. Without any accompanying changes the implication is that the tax rate on each worker will have to be raised substantially. Under forecast III the ratio increases to 0.62 by 2040, implying that the tax rate would have to double.

2.2.2   Financial Aspects of the Social Security Forecasts

The Social Security system is composed of three funds:

> *The Old-Age Survivors Insurance and Disability Insurance Fund* (OASDI). This fund has two parts: Old-Age Survivors Insurance (OASI) and Disability Insurance (DI). OASI primarily supports retired workers and their spouses and widows. It provides the old-age public pensions in the United States, and it is what most people think of when they refer to Social Security. DI supports disabled workers. It is a much smaller program than OASI.

> *The Federal Hospital Insurance Fund* (HI). This is part A of the Medicare system, which provides health insurance to the elderly.

> *The Federal Supplementary Medical Insurance Fund* (SMI). This is part B of the Medicare system. It differs from HI in that the retired elderly

Table 2.7   **Beneficiaries per 100 Covered Workers**

Year	I	II	III
1991	30	30	30
2000	29	31	32
2010	31	33	36
2020	37	41	46
2030	43	49	56
2040	42	51	62
2050	41	52	67

Source: Board of Trustees of the Federal OASDI Trust Funds (1991).

Table 2.8   **Income Rate, Cost Rate, and Trust Fund Balance of OASDI**

	I			II			III		
Year	Income	Cost	Balance	Income	Cost	Balance	Income	Cost	Balance
1991	12.6	11.0	83	12.6	11.1	82	12.6	11.3	82
2000	12.6	9.7	303	12.7	10.9	229	12.7	12.3	139
2010	12.8	9.8	641	12.8	11.3	392	12.9	12.9	160
2020	12.9	11.8	769	13.0	14.0	387	13.1	16.1	60
2030	13.0	13.3	772	13.1	16.3	235	13.3	19.5	–
2040	13.0	12.8	844	13.2	16.6	40	13.4	21.1	–
2050	13.0	12.3	981	13.2	16.7	–	13.4	22.7	–

Source: Board of Trustees of the Federal OASDI Trust Funds (1991).

voluntarily pay a premium to be enrolled. The premium is normally set to cover 25 percent of the cost of the program, with the other 75 percent of the cost coming from general Treasury funds. Almost all elderly persons subscribe to SMI.

The financial status of OASDI and HI is generally stated in terms of the income rate and the cost rate. The income rate is the percentage of the taxable payroll paid into the funds through Social Security taxes.[2] The cost rate is the percentage of the taxable payroll paid out in Social Security benefits. These are good measures because they are invariant with respect to scale effects and, if they differ, they show directly how tax rates would have to change to balance the funds.

Table 2.8 presents income and cost rates under forecasts I, II, and III and the balance, which is the percentage of annual expenditures in the fund. In 1991 the income rate was 12.6 and the cost rate was 11.0, indicating that the OASDI fund was accumulating monies at the rate of 1.6 percent of taxable payroll. The balance in the fund was 83 percent of annual expenditures.

Over the next 60 years the income rate is forecast to be approximately stable, but the cost rate will increase. Under forecast I, which is based on assumptions of high fertility and high mortality, the fund remains positive over the forecast horizon, and even in 2040, when the baby boom generation is aged 80–90, the cost rate is only marginally greater than the income rate.

Under forecast II the cost rate exceeds the income rate sometime between 2015 and 2020 (not shown), but because of accumulations the fund has a positive balance until sometime between 2040 and 2045 (not shown). The changes required to bring the fund into balance are not particularly large: in 2020 the tax rate would have to be increased by 1 percent of taxable payroll to match income with cost.

2. The taxable payroll includes most earnings and has a maximum ($57,000 in 1993). The combined OASI and DI tax rate is 6.20 percent paid by the employee and 6.20 percent paid by the employer. A self-employed person pays both.

Table 2.9   **Cost Rate of HI**

Year	I	II	III
1991	2.59	2.61	2.65
2000	2.99	3.52	4.16
2010	3.28	4.56	6.43
2020	3.73	6.20	10.50
2030	4.17	7.84	14.95
2040	4.37	8.55	16.93
2050	4.46	8.72	17.29

Source: Board of Trustees of the Federal OASDI Trust Funds (1991).
Note: Income rate is 2.90.

Even under forecast III, which is based on assumptions of low fertility and low mortality, the tax increases in the early part of the forecast period are rather small: an increase of 3.0 in the income rate would make income and expenditures the same in 2020.

The long-run financial situation of the funds can be found from the summarized income and cost rates. These are the expected present values of the income and cost streams normalized by the expected present value of taxable payroll. Over the period 1991–2040, the summarized income rate under forecast II is 13.10, and the summarized cost rate is 13.80. This means that the fund would just be in balance in 2040 if today the tax rate were permanently increased by 0.7 percent of taxable payroll. Even under forecast III the summarized cost rate is just 2.3 percent of taxable payroll higher than the income rate. These figures indicate that as far as the retirement part of Social Security is concerned, the aging of the population will increase costs but the increase is manageable.

Table 2.9 shows the cost rates for HI, and they have a rather different time path than the cost rates for OASDI. (The income rate is constant under current law at 2.90.) Even under forecast II the cost rate more than doubles by 2020. Under forecast III, the increase is 7.9 percent of taxable payroll: this is larger than the increase under forecast III in OASDI, even though OASDI is a much larger program.[3]

The income and cost rates are normalized by taxable payroll, which is about 45 percent of GNP. Table 2.10 shows OASDI and HI expenditures under forecast II as percentages of GNP. What is striking is how large the increase in HI is forecast to be compared with the forecast for OASDI: by 2040, HI is forecast to consume an additional 2.4 percent of GNP. Even these forecasts are conservative, however, compared with some other expert forecasts that I will discuss below.

3. A comparison of the cost rates shows that HI is only about one-fourth the size of OASDI.

Table 2.10   Ratio of Expenditures to GNP under Forecast II

Year	OASDI	HI	Total
1991	4.8	1.2	6.1
2000	4.7	1.6	6.3
2010	4.8	2.0	6.8
2020	5.8	2.7	8.5
2030	6.7	3.3	10.0
2040	6.6	3.6	10.2
2050	6.6	3.6	10.1

Source: Board of Trustees of the Federal OASDI Trust Funds (1991).

2.3   Forecasts by the Expert Panel

The 1991 Advisory Council on Social Security convened a panel of economists and actuaries (the Expert Panel) to study the impact of population aging
on households, government, firms, and the macroeconomy. It was evident,
however, that such a study would be incomplete without considering the evolution of health care costs because of their high rate of growth and because of
the interaction between health care costs and population aging. This section
will analyze some of the findings of the Expert Panel.[4]

The panel requested that the Health Care Financing Administration (HCFA)
make four forecasts or scenarios of health care costs. These forecasts used the
main demographic and economic assumptions of the SSA's forecast II but used
assumptions about the evolution of health care costs different from those im-
bedded in forecasts I, II, and III. The four health care forecasts all were based
on estimating the future cost and use of 18 different types of health care resources. They all were based on use by age categories, so they included
changes in cost due to changes in age composition. The main differences in
the four scenarios come from differences in assumptions about the real rate of
inflation of medical services and about the rate of use and intensity of use
holding age constant.[5]

Table 2.11 gives examples of the differences in assumptions and use for the
four scenarios. Scenario 1 is the highest cost forecast. It assumes that the real
rate of health care inflation from 1970 to 1990 (1.4 percent) will continue until
2000 and then fall to 1.2 percent. The rate of increase in real consumption per
person will continue at the 1970–90 rate (4.7 percent per year). Scenario 2 is
the same as scenario 1 except that the rate of increase in per capita consumption falls to about 4 percent after 2000. Scenario 3 has lower rates of inflation

4. I was a member of the panel, and I did some of the calculations reported in this section,
particularly on the macroeconomy and saving rates.

5. Intensity of use refers to the cost of a specific encounter with the health care system. For
example, holding prices constant, a visit to a doctor may change because the visit takes longer or
because more procedures are used.

Table 2.11   Medical Expenditures: Sources of Growth, Historical and Projected

Period and Scenario	Real Medical Inflation (%)	Real Per Capita Medical Spending (%)	Percentage of GNP (end of period)
1970–80	0.3	4.1	9.1
1980–85	2.1	4.4	
1985–90	2.0	5.0	12.2
1990–2000			
1	1.4	4.7	17.4
2	1.4	4.7	17.4
3	1.2	4.2	16.4
4	0.0	1.8	13.1
2000–2020			
1	1.2	4.7	36.0
2	1.2	4.0–4.1	31.5
3	0.8–0.9	2.7–2.6	22.7
4	0.0	1.3–1.1	13.7

Source: Advisory Council on Social Security (1991a).

and increase in use than have been observed over the last 20 years. The assumptions about health care costs in scenario 3 are approximately the same as those in SSA forecasts I, II, and III, discussed in section 2.2. Scenario 4 has no real medical cost inflation and no increase in use or intensity given age. That is, it shows the effects of population aging only.

In 1990 about 12.2 percent of GNP was consumed in medical expenditures. By 2020 this is forecast to rise to 36.0 percent under scenario 1, 31.5 percent under 2, 22.7 percent under 3, and 13.7 percent under 4. A comparison of scenario 4 with the others shows that most of the increase in these scenarios comes from assuming that past increases in cost and use will continue into the future: holding real prices and age-adjusted use and intensity of use per person constant, spending for medical care will increase by just 1.5 percent of GNP. This is the ceterus paribus aging component. Of course, increasing prices and use of medical services along with population aging will have effects that are greater than the marginal increases because of interactions. Here, the increases are great enough that the interactions are not just second-order effects.

It is already clear that scenario 3 and possibly scenario 2 are not wildly improbable and that scenario 4 will be a substantial underestimate. The estimate of 1993 medical care expenditures is 14 percent of GNP, compared with 12.2 percent in 1990. If this rate of increase continues until 2000, medical care expenditures will be about 19 percent of GNP, which is larger than under any of the scenarios.

In the rest of the paper I will give outcomes under scenarios 2 and 3. Neither the panel nor I thought, however, that they necessarily bound the medical care expenditure outcomes. The other forecasting assumptions (unemployment, general inflation, demographics, and so forth) are those of SSA forecast II.

2.3.1   Impact on Government

Table 2.12 has OASDHI income and cost rates for the two scenarios. Income is roughly constant, but costs increase substantially: even under scenario 3 the tax rate would have to increase by 6.7 percent of payroll. As we have already seen, less than half of this is caused by OASDI (2.9 percent in table 2.8, forecast II).

The impact on governmental budgets from increasing health care costs and demographics is shown in table 2.13. It shows a decline in federal government purchases. This is caused by a decline in defense spending from 5.8 percent of GNP to 3.9 percent and some decrease in spending for education resulting from the changing age structure of the population. These decreases more than offset an increase in direct expenditures for health care by the federal government. Of course, the increases in OASDI and HI are much greater than the fall in government purchases so that the total federal budget as a percentage of GNP will increase. A larger fraction of the federal government budget will be transfers rather than direct purchases.

Under either scenario, state and local government spending will increase as a result of higher medical care expenditures even though there is some offset from reduced education expenditures.

2.3.2   Impact on Households

Average real income of elderly households is forecast to increase by 47 percent by 2020, mainly due to increases in Social Security benefits and pension

Table 2.12   OASDHI Income and Cost Rates

		2020	
Rate	1989	Scenario 2	Scenario 3
Income	15.5	15.9	15.7
Cost	13.7	22.9	20.4

Source: Advisory Council on Social Security (1991a).

Table 2.13   Government Expenditures (percentage of GNP)

		2020	
Expenditure	1989	Scenario 2	Scenario 3
Federal	14.3	20.4	15.8
Purchases	7.7	6.5	6.2
HI and SMI	2.0	8.1	5.8
OASDI	4.6	5.8	5.8
State and local	12.0	13.7	12.7

Source: Advisory Council on Social Security (1991a).

Table 2.14   **Out-of-Pocket Medical Expenditures by the Elderly (percentage of median income)**

	1989	2020	
		Scenario 2	Scenario 3
Couples	17	30	23
Singles	21	40	29

Source: Advisory Council on Social Security (1991a).

income. Income of nonelderly households is forecast to increase by 39 percent. When combined with the growing elderly population, these forecasts imply that a substantially greater fraction of the income in the economy will go to elderly households, about 10.6 percent, compared with 7.4 percent in 1989.[6]

Medical expenditures by households will rise substantially under either scenario 2 or 3. Table 2.14 shows out-of-pocket medical care expenditures expressed as a percentage of median before-tax income. In 1989 a couple with median income would have spent about 17 percent of its income on out-of-pocket medical expenses. As the table shows, this percentage is expected to grow substantially, to 30 percent under scenario 2 and 23 percent under scenario 3. Expenditures are expected to grow even more for singles.

A major component of medical care expenditures by households is the premium for SMI, even though the premium is only 25 percent of actual cost. Current law establishes the SMI premium for each year until 1995. Panel A of table 2.15 shows what the premium would be in 2020 if there is no change in the law; in this case, the premium would cover a small fraction of actual costs. Because the historical aim has been for the premium to cover 25 percent of costs, as it did in 1989, the second part of the table shows the premium necessary to cover 25 percent of SMI costs. This is probably more relevant. The premium will increase under scenario 3 by 359 percent in real dollars and will require 7 and 9 percent of the median incomes of couples and singles, respectively. If this expenditure is added to the out-of-pocket medical expenditure in table 2.14, under scenario 3 costs for couples will increase from 20 percent of median income to 30 percent and for singles from 25 percent to 38 percent. This seems like a large burden indeed.

2.3.3   Impact on Firms

Firms will have increased liabilities for pensions because of the demographic changes, but unless coverage expands greatly the increased burden should be no more than what we have seen for OASDI. Furthermore, pension

6. Note that these figures cannot be used to make utility comparisons because elderly households are considerably smaller than nonelderly households and because no accounting is made of nonmoney income.

Table 2.15   **SMI Premiums**

		2020	
Case	1989	Scenario 2	Scenario 3
A. *Current law*			
Annual premium (1988$)	298	377	377
Percentage of SMI cost	25	7	10
B. *Premium covers 25 percent of cost*			
Annual premium (1988$)	298	1450	1070
Percentage of median income			
Couples	3	9	7
Singles	4	12	9

Source: Advisory Council on Social Security (1991a).

Table 2.16   **Health Expenditure Paid by Private Insurance**

		2020	
Expenditure	1989	Scenario 2	Scenario 3
Total amount (billion 1990$)	222	866	618
Per capita (1990$)	854	2,707	1,930

Source: Advisory Council on Social Security (1991a).

growth has been in defined-contribution plans, which place no liability on the firm once the contribution has been earned.

However, firms will have substantial exposure to risks associated with medical care expenditures. Table 2.16 shows estimated medical care expenditures paid for by private insurance: per capita, the increase under scenario 3 is 226 percent. In that about 80 percent of medical insurance is associated with employment, firms can expect sharply higher expenses for medical insurance. Of course, under this scenario, workers can expect that most, if not all, of growth in total compensation will be in fringe benefits to cover medical expenses.

2.3.4   Impact in the Aggregate

Sources of financing medical care expenditures should change. According to table 2.17, the percentage paid by Medicare will increase from 16.5 percent to 25.5 percent under scenario 3, mainly because of the demographic changes. This rise is equivalent to an increase from 2 percent of GNP to 5.8 percent of GNP. Similarly, Medicaid will increase to 3 percent of GNP. Even though the fraction of total expenses paid by private insurance and out-of-pocket payments will fall, they will still increase as a fraction of GNP because of the rapid increase in total medical costs. For example, private insurance will pay 6.7 percent of GNP in medical care expenditures, up from 4 percent in 1989.

The fraction of personal consumption by the elderly will change because of

Table 2.17   Sources of Funds for Medical Spending (percentage distribution)

Source	1989	2020 Scenario 2	2020 Scenario 3
Medicare	16.5	25.8	25.5
Medicaid	11.2	13.4	13.3
Other government	14.4	11.2	11.8
Private insurance	33.1	29.7	29.4
Out-of-pocket	20.5	16.2	16.3
Other private	4.4	3.7	3.6
Total	100.0	100.0	100.0
Total medical (% of GNP)	12.2	31.5	22.7

Source: Advisory Council on Social Security (1991a).

demographic changes, income changes, and other reasons. To get a rough idea of the magnitude, the panel divided the population into the elderly and nonelderly. The 1988 Consumer Expenditure Survey was used to find differences between the consumption patterns of the two groups. If incomes do not change and consumption patterns are fixed, the population changes will indicate how consumption of different commodities will change. For example, the nonelderly consume more motor vehicles than the elderly, so aggregate consumption of motor vehicles should fall as the population ages. To account for income changes, the panel assumed the income elasticity of each commodity group was 1.0. Therefore, consumption by commodity group for each age group can be projected from the SSA II income and demographic forecasts. Consumption of medical services is not forecast in this way; it comes from the scenarios furnished by HCFA.

Table 2.18 shows the shares of personal consumption by the nonelderly and by the elderly. In 1989, nonhealth consumption by the elderly was 12 percent of the total, which was just their share in the population. However, they consumed 36 percent of the health care services, mainly through the transfers in Medicare and Medicaid. These transfers are, of course, not recorded as income; were they to be, the elderly would have a much larger share of total income than indicated by money income. In total, the elderly accounted for 15 percent of private consumption in 1989.

In 2020 the elderly are forecast to be 16 percent of the population. They will consume 15 percent of nonhealth personal consumption but 45 percent of the health care services. This increase is due to the demographic changes. In total, under scenario 3 the elderly will consume 21 percent of total personal consumption even though they will be just 16 percent of the population.

With such large predicted increases in medical care expenditures, it is natural to wonder where the increased consumption will come from. To understand the magnitude of the adjustment that would be required, the demands of gov-

Table 2.18 **Shares of Personal Consumption (percent) by Age**

	1989	2020	
		Scenario 2	Scenario 3
Nonhealth			
Under 65	88	85	85
65 or over	12	15	15
Health			
Under 65	64	55	55
65 or over	36	45	45
Total			
Under 65	85	77	79
65 or over	15	23	21

Source: Advisory Council on Social Security (1991a).

ernment, consumption, investment, and the foreign sector were either forecast or assumed. For example, as mentioned above, it was assumed that federal government purchases would fall from 7.7 percent of GNP to 6.2 percent (table 2.13, scenario 3). Personal consumption except for health care expenditures were calculated from the assumption of an income elasticity of 1.0. Health care expenditures come from the HCFA scenarios. The foreign sector is assumed to be in balance, and gross investment is assumed to return to its historic level of 13 percent of GNP.

Table 2.19 presents the result of these forecasts and assumptions. Personal consumption was 66.3 percent of GNP in 1989. Of this, 30.9 percent was in goods and 35.5 percent in services. Among consumption of services, consumption of housing was 14.3 percent of GNP and consumption of medical services was about 8.4 percent. Government purchases were 19.7 percent, gross investment was 14.8 percent, and exports were −0.9 percent. Under scenario 3, personal consumption will increase to 77 percent of GNP, with most of the increase coming from higher medical care expenditures. Government purchases and gross investment will fall slightly. Because there is no residual category that makes total demand equal total supply, demand does not have to equal supply, and indeed scenario 3 shows total demand at 108.9 percent of supply. Under scenario 2 demand will be 116.6 percent of supply.

Of course, adjustments will bring supply and demand into equality. One way to see the magnitude of the adjustments that will be required is to suppose that medical care expenditures, investment, government spending, and foreign sector demands are met; then all the adjustment will have to come from nonhealth personal consumption. Table 2.20 shows the allocation of per capita GNP under this assumption. Total per capita GNP increases from $20,340 to $27,890. Under scenario 2, $8,790 will be spent on health care expenses, $1,450 on education, and so forth. Nonhealth personal consumption, the residual category, will be $10,990, which is less than the 1989 level. That is, all the

Table 2.19   Components of GNP (percentage of GNP)

		2020	
Component	1989	Scenario 2	Scenario 3
Personal consumption	66.3	83.8	77.0
Goods	30.9	31.5	31.5
Durable	9.1	9.7	9.7
Nondurable	21.7	21.8	21.8
Services	35.5	51.8	45.5
Housing	14.3	15.2	15.2
Medical	8.4	22.6	16.3
Other	12.9	14.1	14.1
Government purchases	19.7	20.2	18.9
Federal	7.7	6.5	6.2
Health	0.4	1.1	0.8
Other	7.3	5.4	5.4
State and local	12.0	13.7	12.7
Health	1.4	3.7	2.6
Other	10.6	10.0	10.1
Gross investment	14.8	13.0	13.0
Net exports	−0.9	0.0	0.0
Total	100.0	116.6	108.9

Source: Advisory Council on Social Security (1991a).

Table 2.20   Adjustment in Personal Consumption: Per Capita Allocation (1989$)

		2020	
Demand	1989	Scenario 2	Scenario 3
Health	2,360	8,790	6,330
Education	1,220	1,450	1,450
Government (excl. medical)	2,600	3,040	3,040
Investment	3,010	3,630	3,630
Nonhealth personal consumption	11,080	10,990	13,450
Total	20,340	27,890	27,890

Source: Advisory Council on Social Security (1991a).

growth in per capita GNP between 1989 and 2020 (38 percent) will be used to finance increases in medical care expenditures. It is hard to believe that this outcome will be desired by the general population. Even under scenario 3, nonhealth consumption grows at a much smaller rate than GNP.

From two perspectives an older population could be expected to have a lower average saving rate than a younger population. In the first perspective, increasing the fraction of the population that is aged will increase the asset holdings of the aged population. At a constant rate of asset decumulation, a

Table 2.21   **Asset Decumulation and the Saving Rate**

	1989		2020	
	Amount	Source	Amount	Source
Assets of elderly	1.6×10^{12}	A.C.	3.7×10^{12}	Calculation[a]
Asset decumulation	0.04×10^{12}	Calculation: 2.9% rate of decumulation (Hurd 1991)	0.107×10^{12}	Calculation: 2.9% rate of decumulation (Hurd 1991)
After-tax earnings	2.1×10^{12}	A.C.	3.6×10^{12}	A.C.
Asset decumulation out of after-tax earnings (%)	2.2	Calculation	3.0	Calculation
Household saving rate (%)	4.6	A.C.	3.8	Calculation

Source: A.C. = Advisory Council on Social Security (1991a).
[a]Calculated as the product of 1989 assets, real per capita GNP growth of 1.01 percent per year, and 1.8 percent growth in the elderly population.

greater fraction of the savings of the working-age population will be used to purchase the assets that the elderly are selling. Thus, the average saving rate will fall.[7] In the second perspective, the life-cycle hypothesis of consumption implies that the working population saves and the retired population dissaves; therefore, ceteris paribus, increasing the fraction of the population that is elderly should reduce the saving rate out of income. Of course, these two perspectives are really two ways of saying the same thing.

Table 2.21 shows estimates of the assets of elderly in 1989 and 2020 and the resulting levels of asset decumulation. The most important assumption is about the rate of dissaving: it is taken to be 2.9 percent of bequeathable nonhousing wealth. This figure is estimated from observed wealth changes of elderly households in the 1984 Survey of Income and Program Participation (SIPP), Waves 4 and 7 (Hurd 1991). The economy was rather stable during the mid-1980s, so the rate of wealth change may well represent the desired long-run rate of change. Furthermore, the 10-year averages from the Retirement History Survey (3.2 percent) are very similar to the averages from SIPP even though the economic conditions during the years of the Retirement History Survey (1969–79) were quite different. Other panel data sets give estimates that overall are about this magnitude (for other estimates, see Hurd 1992).

In 1989, the elderly held about $1.6 trillion of nonhousing bequeathable wealth. At a rate of dissaving of 2.9 percent, they sold $46 billion of assets, which was 2.2 percent of after-tax earnings. Under the assumptions given in the table, nonhousing assets of the elderly will grow to $3.7 trillion by 2020, and the elderly will decumulate at a rate of $107 billion per year. This amount is 3.0 percent of after-tax earnings, requiring 0.8 percent more of household

---

7. It is of independent interest to estimate the increase in the stock of assets that will be put on the market as the population ages.

saving. Thus, the household saving rate is projected to fall from 4.6 percent to 3.8 percent.

An alternative calculation based on saving rates out of income is the following: The average one-year rate of wealth decumulation in SIPP was 2.9 percent from mean wealth of $75,900, implying an excess of consumption over income of $3,800. Net income of the elderly in 1984 was $13,200 (Bureau of Labor Statistics 1989), so the rate of saving out of income by the elderly was −16.6 percent. I will take this to be the desired, or steady state, rate of saving by the elderly. By assuming that the saving rates of the elderly and nonelderly are stable over time, the effects of population aging on the aggregate saving rate can be found simply by changing the weights on the saving rates of each group. In 1989 the elderly were 12 percent of the population, and their average household income was 62.3 percent of average household income of the population. The household saving rate out of after-tax income was 4.6 percent. Therefore, the saving rate of nonelderly households was 6.3 percent. In 2020 the elderly are forecast to be 16 percent of the population. Under the assumption that the average income of elderly households grows by 47 percent and the income of nonelderly households by 38 percent (Advisory Council on Social Security 1991b), the aggregate household saving rate will fall by 0.7 percentage points to 3.9 percent of after-tax household income. This is very close to the estimate from the method based on the change in asset holdings.

In view of the large variation over time in the household saving rate and the large international variation, the fall in the household saving rate from 4.6 percent to 3.8 or 3.9 percent does not seem like a large change.

2.4 Conclusion

Excluding increases in medical care expenditures, at least to the year 2020, the aging of the population in the United States seems to have effects that are manageable: the necessary increases in Social Security retirement benefits will require some tax increases, but not large ones; the change in the mix of consumption is rather modest; the estimated effects on the aggregate saving rate are within the bounds of historical variation. The effects beyond 2020 are greater, but they are not of crisis proportions. These demographic changes and the increased requirements for retirement income are dominated by increases in spending for health care. Even the forecasts to 2020 probably cannot be realized because of the required reduction in other spending.

Some of the reduction in other spending may be in saving and investment. We do not know enough about saving determination at the household level to predict how a large increase in medical care expenditures financed through Social Security taxation, out-of-pocket payments, and employers contributions will affect saving rates; but it may noted that the fall in the U.S. saving rate coincided with the large increase in health care spending.

References

Advisory Council on Social Security. 1991a. Income security and health care: Economic implications 1991–2020. Washington, D.C.: U.S. Department of Health and Human Services, Social Security Administration.

———. 1991b. The Social Security Technical Panel report to the 1991 Advisory Council on Social Security. Washington, D.C.: U.S. Department of Health and Human Services, Social Security Administration.

Board of Trustees of the Federal OASDI Trust Funds. 1989. *The 1989 annual report.* Washington, D.C.: U.S. Government Printing Office.

———. 1991. *The 1991 annual report.* Washington, D.C.: U.S. Government Printing Office.

Bureau of Labor Statistics. 1989. Consumer Expenditure Survey: Integrated survey data, 1984–86. Bulletin 2333. Washington, D.C.: U.S. Department of Labor.

Grad, Susan. 1990. Income of the population 55 or older, 1988. Washington, D.C.: U.S. Department of Health and Human Services, Social Security Administration.

Hurd, Michael D. 1991. The income and savings of the elderly. Stony Brook, N.Y.: State University of New York, Department of Economics. Typescript.

———. 1992. Wealth depletion and life-cycle consumption by the elderly. In *Topics in the economics of aging,* ed. David Wise, 135–60. Chicago: University of Chicago Press.

Manton, Kenneth, Eric Stallard, and Burt Singer. 1994. Methods for projecting the future size and health status of the U.S. elderly population. In *Studies in the economics of aging,* ed. D. Wise, Chicago: University of Chicago Press.

Vaupel, James, and Hans Lundström. 1994. Longer life expectancy? Evidence from Sweden of reductions in mortality rates at advanced ages. In *Studies in the economics of aging,* ed. D. Wise, Chicago: University of Chicago Press.

3 Population Aging and the Savings-Investment Balance in Japan

Naohiro Yashiro and Akiko Sato Oishi

The main purpose of this paper is to analyze the major effects of population aging on the macroeconomic savings and investment balance in Japan and to discuss their major policy implications. Although population aging is a phenomenon common to many OECD countries, Japan's case is striking because of the high rate at which it is progressing. The rapid aging process in Japan is a product of the high rate of economic growth and associated changes in family and social structures in the postwar period, which has resulted in a large decline in the fertility rate and a marked lengthening of the average life expectancy.

The rapid aging of the population has important macroeconomic effects. The first effect is the impact on the labor market through a shrinking labor force and an increasing share of older workers in the labor force. The second is the impact on the capital market due to falling household and national savings ratios, coupled with the rising ratio of retired people to working-age people. In addition, a shrinking labor force will affect investment and thus the financing of capital. The third effect is the fiscal impact, with an increasing share of the elderly causing substantial transfers of income from the working to the retired generation through the tax and social security systems. These impacts eventually affect both investment and savings, and thus the current external account.

In this paper, we focus on the impact of population aging on macroeconomic savings and investment balances mainly through the labor market. While Ja-

Naohiro Yashiro is professor of economics at the Institute of International Relations, Sophia University. Akiko Sato Oishi is an economist at the Japan Center for Economic Research.

The authors are grateful to the Japan Foundation Center for Global Partnership for financial support. They appreciate comments on the preliminary paper by Yutaka Kosai, Yukio Noguchi, and other conference participants. They would also like to thank Katsuhisa Uchiyama for his valuable assistance.

pan's huge trade surplus is the cause of various economic frictions, a trade deficit could bring about another problem, adversely affecting not only Japan but the world economy as well through the curtailment of Japan's capital exports. In the sections that follow, we look at the development of the population structure and the labor force in the coming decades. This overview is followed by a review of previous empirical studies of the economic impacts of population aging, most of which have reached pessimistic conclusions, and an attempt to identify the major factors behind these conclusions. We also explore various alternative conclusions under different assumptions. Finally, we discuss the policy implications of population aging.

3.1   Aging of the Population and Labor Force

Japan's strong economic performance in the past may be explained partly by its low dependency ratio—that is, the ratio of the population younger than 15 years (young) or older than 64 years (elderly) to the total population. In the early phase of the population aging process, the rapid decline in the fertility rate resulted in a decrease in the young population that exceeded the increase in the elderly population, thus lowering the total dependency ratio. It is not a coincidence that Japan and Germany (the former Federal Republic of Germany), which had the lowest total dependency ratios of the major OECD countries, also had the best economic performance until very recently (fig. 3.1A). For this reason, the rapidly progressing aging of the population will be a major challenge for Japan in the coming decades.

There are two aspects to population aging: one is the increase in the proportion of the elderly in the total population, and the other is the slower growth of the population coupled with a decrease in the labor force arising directly from the falling fertility rate. While the former affects economic performance mainly through redistribution of income, for example, by increasing the social security burden and benefits, the latter has a more direct impact on economic growth by reducing the labor force, a major factor in production.

3.1.1   Increasing Ratio of the Elderly

Two major factors fostering population aging are declining fertility rate and extension of life expectancy. In Japan, the total fertility rate (i.e., the average number of births per woman in her lifetime) rapidly fell from 4.5 in 1950 to 2.1 in the 1970s. After stabilizing temporarily, it fell again during the 1980s to 1.50 in 1994. The falling fertility rate will soon be reflected in a decreasing working-age population (i.e., those between 15 and 64 years of age), which is likely to begin falling in 1995. Although the Institute of Population Problems (IPP) of the Ministry of Health and Welfare projects that the fertility rate will recover after reaching its low in 1995, there are more pessimistic views of the recovery of fertility (Ogura, chap. 1 in this volume). If the fertility rate stays at the current low level through the 1990s, the process of population aging will accelerate even faster than currently projected.

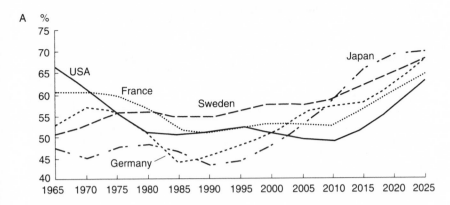

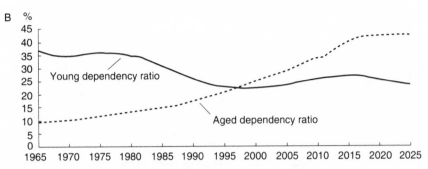

Fig. 3.1 *A,* **International comparison of dependency ratios, 1965–2025;** *B,*
Japanese dependency ratios by age group, 1965–2025
Sources: A, Bos et al. (1992); *B,* Ministry of Health and Welfare (1992).

Life expectancy for 65-year-olds has risen by 4.51 years for males and 6.37
years for females over the past four decades.[1] Japan's life expectancy growth
and the level attained in 1994 were the highest in the world. Improvement in
medical services and in the incomes of the elderly contributed to the longer
lives of the Japanese. This extension in life expectancy for 65-year-olds since
1955 raised the proportion of the elderly (defined as those aged 65 years and
over) in the total population in 1990 by over 2 percent and accounts for approximately one-fifth of the increase in the ratio projected for 2025.[2]

With falling fertility and rising life expectancy, the ratio of the elderly to the
working-age population is expected to double from the current level by the
year 2025 (fig. 3.1*B*). The extent to which population aging will have negative
impacts on the economy is a matter of great concern.

1. The extension of life expectancy at birth during the same period is more significant because
of a large fall in infant mortality: 14.35 years for males and 16.81 years for females.
2. If we assume that the life expectancy for 65-year-olds is unchanged—i.e., that the probability
of survival in each age cohort has been unchanged since 1955—the old-age dependency ratio
would have been 10.1 percent instead of 12.1 percent in 1990, and it would be 20.6 percent instead
of 25.8 percent in 2025.

Table 3.1   **Projection of the Labor Force (million)**

						Growth Rate per Annum (%)		
Population	1970	1980	1990	2000	2010	1970–1990	1990–2000	2000–2010
Total	51.7	56.7	63.8	67.4	66.0	1.06	0.55	−0.21
Male	31.4	34.8	37.9	39.8	38.5	0.95	0.49	−0.33
Female	20.3	21.9	25.9	27.6	27.5	1.23	0.64	−0.04
Aged 15–24	11.6	7.3	8.3	7.4	5.9	−1.66	−1.14	−2.24
Aged 55–64	5.6	6.5	9.3	10.4	11.6	2.57	1.12	1.10

Source: Economic Planning Agency (1991a).

Note: Projections beyond the year 1990 are made assuming an increase in the female labor force participation rate.

3.1.2   Decreasing Labor Force

The effects of a decrease in the working-age population in Japan will be partly offset by higher female labor force participation. Japan's female labor force participation rate was 50.0 percent in 1995, low by international standards. A major characteristic of the female participation rate in Japan is its M-shaped pattern, produced by a sharp decline in women's participation during their childbearing years, between the ages of 25 and 40. However, the ratio of those who wish to work to those who do not work is highest in this age group, indicating that this will be a large source of labor in the near future. Toward the year 2025, this potential labor force is likely to find work under tightening labor market conditions and will raise the working-age female participation rate.

According to the projection of the Economic Planning Agency (1991a), however, even accounting for higher female labor force participation, the growth rate of the labor force will decline from 1.1 percent per annum in 1970–80 to 0.6 percent on average in the 1990s and will turn negative in the following decade. Beyond the year 2000, the decrease in the male labor force will be more significant, particularly in the younger generation, indicating a rapid change in the structure of the labor force (table 3.1).

3.2   Review of Previous Studies on the Savings-Investment Balance

Several long-term projections of macroeconomic developments in Japan have been made. Some major methods used to project the economic effects of population aging are the Multi-Country Macroeconomic Model, the Neoclassical Model, the Overlapping Generations Model, and the Turnpike Model.[3] Although the techniques of these models differ widely, how they deal with the

---

3. For a detailed survey on the impact of demographic changes on long-term trends in the savings rate, see Horioka (1992).

following points is worth noting when evaluating the results: profitability of capital, endogenous technological change, and labor supply responses to aging. Conclusions about the effects of aging depend on whether a model takes into account these effects associated with population aging. In the following paragraphs, we review previous studies, centering our attention on differences in their assumptions about the labor force and technological changes, as well as forces counteracting population aging.

Masson and Tryon (1990) used the IMF Multi-Country Macroeconometric Model to determine the effect of population aging on the current external accounts of seven major OECD countries. The effects of population aging are captured by the following path: first, consumption expenditure is stimulated by a falling savings rate; then the reduction of the labor force leads to a proportionate contraction of capital stock and potential output, leaving capital stock per worker constant; finally, increases in government expenditures expand aggregate demand. The combined effects of the demographic shifts will be as follows: The share in GNP of Japan's private savings will fall by 4.3 percent from baseline during the 1995–2025 period, while that of gross private investment will fall by 1.8 percent, resulting in persistent falls in the net external surplus. As population aging occurs earlier in Japan than in the United States, the U.S.-Japan trade balance should move in favor of the United States in the coming decades. Although the model by Masson and Tryon accounts for interactions between countries with different rates of aging, it assumes no changes in the labor force participation rate and no technological changes. Also, it is basically a Keynesian-type model in the sense that increases in government expenditures lead to large aggregate demand, which is not an appropriate property for a long-term projection model.

Auerbach et al. (1989) developed a general equilibrium-type Overlapping Generations Model for four OECD countries (United States, Japan, Germany, and Sweden). Given the underlying life-cycle framework of the model, population aging will result in a general decline in the national savings rates; the speed of decline will be most noticeable in Japan and will approach zero in the year 2025, when the ratio of the aged to the total population will reach a plateau. However, with the "open economy" assumption of the paper—that is, perfect international capital mobility—an increase in the capital-labor ratio arising from the rapid demographic shift in Japan will stimulate an outflow of capital to maintain the preexisting return on capital, resulting in an increasing current account surplus. In other words, the declining labor supply will lead to a proportionate reduction of domestic investment and thus will not bring about a deterioration of the external current account.

Noguchi (1990) explored the Neoclassical Model, based on the life-cycle theory of savings and the Cobb-Douglas production function. The basic scenario of the paper is that, while national savings will decline gradually, so will business investment, as the return on capital falls with increasingly scarce labor. Although Noguchi accounted for labor-augmenting technological change, he assumed that the rate will remain unchanged despite the decrease in the labor force. In addition, he did not account for labor supply responses to population aging in the model. Based on this model, the current external surplus in Japan is expected to remain unchanged through the 1990s, to increase in the 2000–2010 period, and to decline only after the year 2010.

Horioka (1991, 1992) made a single-equation analysis of Japan's savings rate in conjunction with the age structure of the population and used the estimated regression coefficients to project its future trends. Explanatory variables are the old-age dependency ratio (AGE) and the young-age dependency ratio (DEP), which are the ratios of the population aged 65 years and over and the population aged 19 years and under to the population aged 20–64 years, respectively. A major conclusion of Horioka's projection is that Japan's private savings ratio (both household and corporate sector) will become negative after the year 2007 with rapid population aging.

The Economic Planning Agency (1991b) published a long-term projection of the Japanese economy based on a Turnpike "optimal growth" Model.[4] The national savings rate will decline gradually, with changes in time preferences due to the demographic shift. Aggregate investment also will decline in the 1990s but will stay at the same level during the 2000–2010 period. These results arise mainly because, based on the assumption of free mobility of labor across industries, the efficiency of labor will improve with increasing labor scarcity, particularly in the service sector, where relative labor productivity is particularly low. As a result, the current external balance will remain a surplus in the 1990s but will sustain a deficit from the year 2000. Given the projected stable growth in labor productivity, the decrease in the labor force will lead directly to a falling rate of economic growth; GDP growth is projected to fall from 4.2 percent in the 1980s to 3.75 percent in the 1990s and 2.75 percent in the period 2000–2010 (Yoshitomi and Yashiro 1992).

Many previous studies agree that both savings and investment ratios to GNP are likely to fall as the population ages and that the relative speed is critical in determining the future path of the current external balance. Although the structures and assumptions of the models discussed above differ significantly, the differences in the projections of savings, investment, and GNP depend on the extent to which these models account for feedback effects of the demographic shifts.

3.3 Feedback Effects of Population Aging

The extent to which key macroeconomic variables, such as labor productivity, savings, and investment, are affected by an aging population and the associated decline in the growth rate of the labor force is crucial in forecasting eco-

---

4. This is the Multi-Industry Linear Programming Model, which maximizes long-run household consumption subject to labor supply and technological constraints. Capital-labor ratios and input-output coefficients of respective industries are given exogenously, but they change over time, reflecting technological progress. See Economic Planning Agency (1991b) for details of the model.

nomic performance in the coming decades. Pessimistic views that population aging will greatly discourage the currently high savings and investment rates in Japan are often founded on the historical relationship between savings and investment, on one hand, and demographic changes, on the other. Those studies implicitly assume that both labor force participation and technological change are independent of population aging.

However, past Japanese experiences with oil price hikes in the 1970s and the substantial yen appreciation in the 1980s indicate that the economy readily adapts to external shocks. In this sense, whether or not mechanisms counteracting external shocks are incorporated in the model will result in an entirely different picture of the coming "aged society" in Japan. As the labor supply becomes scarce with a declining fertility rate, more rapid technological change might be induced, partly offsetting the negative impact of population aging on savings and investment. Thus, treating the labor supply and technological change factors as endogenous rather than exogenous will alter the projections of savings and investment trends.

3.3.1 Alternative Definition of the Elderly

The projections for an economy under population aging are often pessimistic because with a decreasing labor force, the old-age dependency ratio will double between 1990 and 2025. However, this pessimistic picture is partly based on the conventional definition of the elderly—those who are 65 years of age or older. The implicit assumption is that the labor force participation rates of older men and women will remain unchanged throughout the aging of society. This assumption may not be appropriate for Japan's economy in the coming decades.

The rate of labor force participation among the elderly in Japan has been high by international standards. Participation rates for men aged 65–69 and aged 70 and over were 56.5 percent and 26.6 percent, respectively, which are much higher than the rates in the United States (table 3.2). Although most large Japanese firms set the age of mandatory retirement, which is not against the

Table 3.2   **Labor Force Participation of the Elderly in Japan and the United States, 1992**

Age	Japan			United States		
	Total	Men	Women	Total	Men	Women
Average (all ages)	64.0	77.9	50.7	66.3	75.6	57.8
55–59	74.2	93.6	55.6	67.4	78.9	56.8
60–64	57.2	75.0	40.7	45.0	54.7	36.5
65–69	41.4	56.5	29.3	20.7	25.9	16.2
70+	16.6	26.6	10.7	7.1	12.1	6.3

Sources: For Japan, Management and Coordination Agency, *Annual Report on the Labor Force Survey* (Tokyo: Government Printing Office, 1992); for the United States, U.S. Department of Labor, *Employment and Earnings* (Washington, D.C., January 1993).

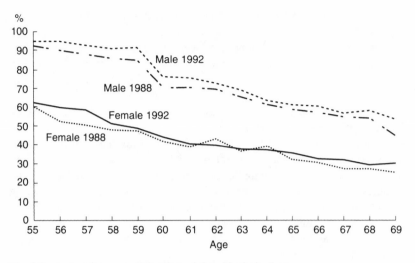

Fig. 3.2   Labor force participation of the elderly in Japan
Source: Ministry of Labor, *Survey of Employment Conditions of Older Persons* (Tokyo, 1988, 1992).

law in Japan, at 60 or under, many workers continue to work beyond retirement age by moving to smaller firms. Thus, there is only a small decline in participation at age 60, and the rate falls gradually through the sixties (fig. 3.2).[5]

Early retirement has increased in Japan. The labor force participation rate of men aged 60–64 declined from 81 percent in 1960 to 71 percent in 1988. Major factors behind this are the following: (1) The share of self-employed men in the age group 60–69, among whom labor force participation is higher than the average, has fallen over time with contractions in the agriculture and distribution sectors, and this decrease contributes to a lower participation rate for the elderly. (2) Improvements in pension benefits have stimulated retirement (for details, see Seike 1993).

However, these factors encouraging early retirement are weakening. Indeed, the labor force participation rate of those 60 years of age or older has risen since 1988, reflecting tighter labor market conditions. The tendency is more prominent among those who are in employee households; their participation rate rose from 37 percent in 1986 to 42 percent in 1991. The change in the age of eligibility for public pensions from the current 60 years to 65 as of the year

5. One of the major factors affecting this high level of labor force participation of those who are 60 years of age or older is the relatively large share of the self-employed in Japan. In 1991, the labor force participation rate of those who were 65 years old or over was 74 percent in self-employed households and 42 percent in employee households. In 1993, self-employed and family workers accounted for 19 percent of the labor force, and the share rose to 47 percent for those aged 60 or older.

2000 should aggravate this tendency.[6] This is, in a sense, a rational reaction by Japanese employees to their increased life expectancy and is likely to continue during the 1990s.

For this reason, the conventional definition of the elderly, which fixes the "cutoff age" between the elderly and the nonelderly at 65, is misleading because it implicitly assumes that the labor force participation of older workers will be unchanged despite longer life expectancy and an increasing need to finance prolonged retired lives. Although the speed of population aging in Japan (which was far below the OECD level in the 1960s but is projected to be among the highest levels in 2025) is a major characteristic of the country, the rapid increase in this rate overstates the "true" aging process because the conventional definition, which considers everyone aged 65 or over as dependent elderly, accounted for only a minor portion of the true elderly in the 1960s, when average life expectancy was close to 65 years of age. Also, it overstates the effects of aging in the twenty-first century because those aged 65 will be the "relatively young elderly" in 2025, when their life expectancy is further extended.

The life expectancy of the weighted average of males and females is projected to rise from 79 years in 1990 to 82 years in 2025.[7] Thus, we can set an alternative definition of "elderly" by shifting the boundary vis-à-vis the nonelderly to take into account the extension of life expectancy at age 65.[8] This new definition of the elderly applies what was the economic capability of a 65-year-old in 1955 to other periods that have increased life expectancy. If we apply the new definition to find the boundary of the elderly population, the elderly in 1990 were those aged 67 or over and in 2025 will be those aged 70 or over. According to this definition, the ratio of the elderly to the total population in the year 2025 will be 20.6 percent rather than the 25.8 percent conventionally used (fig. 3.3). An economic implication of the alternative definition is the approximate ratio of the dependent population to the total population when the elderly are free to choose between work and retirement without the distortions of the tax and social security systems. Whether we apply a conventional definition of the elderly based on the current institutions or an alternative one assuming changes in social practices under the pressure of an aging population has important implications for the projection of the economic impact of population aging.

6. In 1995, the government decided to gradually extend the pensionable age for Employees' Pension Insurance from the current 60 years to 65, as of the year 2000.

7. The average life expectancies of males and females in Japan were 75.92 and 81.90 years, respectively, in 1990 and are projected to rise to 78.27 and 85.06 years, respectively, in 2025 (Ministry of Health and Welfare 1992).

8. If we assume that the probability of survival for those aged 65 or older has been unchanged since 1955, we can calculate the "would have been" old-age dependency ratio. The discrepancy between the conventional old-age dependency ratio and the one we calculated indicates the impact of the extension of life expectancy. Under the alternative definition of the elderly, the boundary age of the elderly population will shift to offset the impact of the extension of life expectancy.

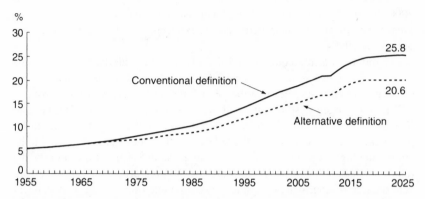

Fig. 3.3   Elderly as a percentage of total population under conventional and alternative definitions of the elderly

Applying the alternative definition of the elderly also affects the projection of savings with an aging population. The life-cycle theory predicts that the household savings rate will decline as the proportion of the elderly in the total population increases because individuals save while they are employed and dissave after retirement.[9] Based on a cross-sectional analysis of the relationship between the rate of household savings and the old-age dependency ratio in OECD countries in the 1980s, the current household savings rate in Japan will fall by more than one-half in response to the projected doubling of the old-age dependency ratio (see OECD 1990, 75). Because the high level of household savings in Japan has been considered one of the major sources of Japan's high economic growth, the falling savings rate may become a major constraint on economic growth.

Applying our definition of the elderly, which shifts according to changes in life expectancy, to Horioka's projections of the future savings rate results in a significant difference in the projection of the private savings rate. The critical year when Japan's private savings rate turns negative is later, and the double-digit private savings rate is maintained for another decade (fig. 3.4). These results are due mainly to a slower increase in old-age dependency resulting from a longer working life.

3.3.2   Labor-Augmenting Technological Progress

Demographic changes affect labor productivity by causing changes in capital intensity, holding the rate of technological change constant. If we take the

---

9. It seems at first glance that the life-cycle theory of savings may not be applicable to Japan because households headed by the elderly do save significantly. However, there are various statistical biases in this result: first, savings in a self-employed household may incorporate profits from business; second, elderly people who live alone are often excluded from the sample; third, the rate of coresidence of the Japanese elderly with their children or other relatives is not only high but

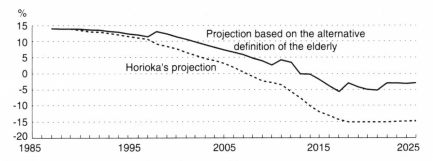

Fig. 3.4   Future trends in Japan's private savings rate: effect of the longer working period

Sources: Horioka (1991); Ministry of Health and Welfare (1992).

Note: Savings rates are calculated using the estimated coefficients in Horioka (1991). Projections beyond the year 2011 are authors' calculations based on the new population estimates of the IPP.

capital stock as given, reduced population growth would raise the capital-labor ratio, leading to higher labor productivity. Alternatively, a falling labor supply would indicate less need for investment to maintain a certain level of labor productivity and thus would increase the share of output available for consumption, assuming an optimum capital-labor ratio in the economy. This "consumption dividend," associated with population aging, would counteract the negative effects on per capita consumption resulting from the burden of the increased old-age dependency ratio and of the lower average quality of the labor force due to an increasing proportion of older workers.

A cross-country comparison among the major OECD countries implies that a significant negative relationship exists between growth of the labor force and total factor productivity (fig. 3.5). That is, with a 1 percent decline in labor force growth, total factor productivity growth of 0.4 percent is induced mainly through labor-augmenting technological change or the more efficient use of scarcer labor. Whether this relationship in the cross section of the OECD countries may apply to future developments in Japan is discussed below.

Historical evidence in Japan suggests that the growth of labor productivity has largely exceeded that of the labor force; the labor force grew an average of 1.1 percent a year in the 1970–90 period, while productivity grew 3 percent a year. The greater growth in productivity is the result of a consistent rise in the capital-labor ratio over the same period, with the capital stock growing at a rate exceeding the growth of the labor force. As a result of the improvement in labor productivity, the average real wage in Japan rose continuously (fig. 3.6A).

Such a continuous increase in the capital-labor ratio is often attributed to

---

rises with age, thus the relatively poor elderly are dropped from statistics that are measured on a household basis (for details, Horioka 1991; Yashiro, chap. 4 in this volume).

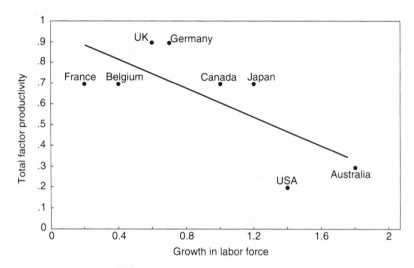

Fig. 3.5   Total factor productivity and labor force growth, 1980–91
Source: OECD, *National Accounts 1979–1991* (Paris, 1993); OECD, *Main Economic Indicators* (Paris, various issues).
Note: TFP = 0.954 − 0.347 Labor, R^2 = 0.532.
        (5.04) (−2.61)

labor-saving investment, which is stimulated by the increasing scarcity of labor and the reduction of working hours. That is, given an output level, higher wages relative to the return on capital would lead to the application of more capital-intensive production. However, while the higher capital-labor ratio would raise labor productivity, it should also lower capital productivity, leading to a falling rate of return on capital. This adverse effect of accumulated labor-saving investment would naturally discourage business investment in the long run, and labor productivity would eventually stop increasing. This is the "steady-state equilibrium" in which there is no productivity growth since net capital stocks are growing at the same rate as the labor force. Nevertheless, the return on capital (approximated by the real long-term interest rate) has been relatively stable in postwar Japan, despite a continuous increase in the capital-labor ratio (fig. 3.6*B*). This stability implies that technological changes have prevented the profitability of capital from falling.

The divergent movements of the returns on labor and capital can be explained in the following way: In the Cobb-Douglas production function, labor productivity is expressed as a function of the capital-labor ratio, where labor is expressed in efficiency units:

$$Y/L = A*F(K/AL),$$

where Y is GNP, L is labor, K is capital, and A is efficiency of labor. With capital stocks growing at the same rate as efficiency of labor, the return on

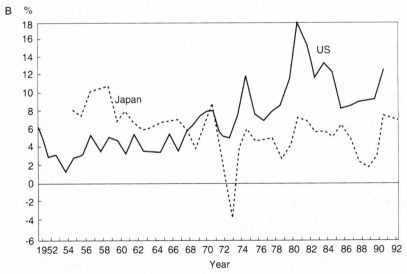

Fig. 3.6 *A*, Change of real wage in Japan and the United States; *B*, Return on capital in Japan and the United States

Source: Shimpo (1991, 160–61).

capital would be at the steady-state level. Whereas labor productivity in efficiency units would be stable, the return on labor would increase at a rate equivalent to changes in labor efficiency. Thus, the historical movements of real wages and profitability of capital in Japan can be fully explained by the introduction of labor-augmenting technological progress.

The existence of labor-augmenting technological change does not necessarily indicate causality vis-à-vis changes in the labor supply associated with demographic shifts. On the one hand, given technological change, the labor supply may be adjusted to maintain the rate of real wage increase at the historical average. The fact that working hours fell most dramatically in the period when wage growth was high with tightening labor market conditions may support this view. On the other hand, labor-augmenting technological change may be induced by a decline in the labor supply. The relative importance of these mechanisms can only be assessed empirically.

There are contradicting views regarding the effects of the demographic shift on technological change in the coming decades. The pessimistic school holds that the growth of business investment is likely to slow as the population ages because a society with a larger proportion of older people loses some of its dynamism, and the slower population growth and the lackluster consumption market will discourage innovation (see Cutler et al. 1990). By contrast, the optimistic school argues that an increasing labor shortage accompanying the aging process will stimulate incentives to use more efficiently existing human resources, particularly older and female workers, who have been assigned somewhat peripheral roles under current Japanese employment practices.

3.4 Empirical Studies

3.4.1 Structure of the Model

The model consists of equations for savings, investment, labor productivity, and the long-term interest rate, which are estimated by ordinary least squares and are based on annual data from 1958–92. The exogenous variables are population and its age composition. The rate of inflation during the simulation period is assumed to be 1.7 percent a year, which is the average for the period 1980–92.

The ratio of savings to GNP is a function of the young-age and old-age dependency ratios and of real per capita GNP growth, which is based on Horioka's (1991) formulation (see below for details). The ratio of business investment to GNP is a Solow-type formulation based on the growth of the working-age population (20–64 years of age) and the interest rate, which is a proxy for the return on capital. Labor productivity is expressed as a function of the capital-labor ratio. The long-term interest rate is determined by changes in the savings-investment balance. A detailed explanation of each equation follows.

Savings

The savings function is based on a modified life-cycle model, explaining the national savings rate by old-age and young-age dependency ratios and per capita economic growth. Also, the life cycle model is applied to the national savings rate, instead of the household savings rate. This is based on the assumption that households consider their savings substitutable for those of the corporate and government sectors, which is an awkward assumption in the short run but less so in long-term projections. Higher income growth raises the savings rate mainly because savings for future consumption are considered a "luxury good" and the capacity to save increases with income level. Savings are in gross terms, including depreciation of corporate and housing stocks. This may not be appropriate for examining the international comparison of savings rates per se, as already pointed out by Horioka (1991), but our major interest here is to focus on the savings-investment balance in the conventional definition, which is consistent with the current external balance.

Business Investment

Gross investment consists of business, housing, government, and inventory investment, the last two of which are set unchanged in the projection period. The long-run trend of business investment is based on labor force growth, given an optimal capital-labor ratio, and return on capital. We assume the following Cobb-Douglas production function:[10]

$$Y = L*(K/L)^e$$

where Y is real GNP, L is the working-age population (20–64 years of age), K is gross capital, and e is a parameter representing the share of capital income. Assuming that the long-term real interest rate (r) equals the marginal return on capital, the following equation is derived:

$$r = \frac{e}{(K/L)^{1-e}}.$$

In the "steady-state equilibrium," the growth of capital stocks equals that of labor in efficiency units:

$$dK/K = n + t,$$

where n is the growth of the population aged 20–64 and t is the rate of labor-augmenting technological change.

Based on the above equations, the ratio of business investment to GNP is expressed by the following:

---

10. The estimation of the long-run business investment function derived from the production function is based on Noguchi (1987, 1989, 1990).

$$\frac{IO}{Y} = \frac{dK}{L*(K/L)^e}$$

$$= \frac{dK/K}{(L/K)\,(K/L)^e}$$

$$= \frac{dK/K}{(K/L)^{-1}(K/L)^e}$$

$$= \frac{dK/K}{(K/L)^{e-1}}$$

$$= \frac{e(dK/K)}{e(K/L)^{e-1}}$$

$$= \frac{e(n+t)}{r}.$$

Using this equation, we can estimate the capital share parameter (e) and labor-augmenting technological changes (t):[11]

$$IO/Y = e*(n/r) + et*(1/r).$$

The estimates of the capital share (e) and the average rate of increase of the labor efficiency unit are 26.4 and 4 percent, respectively, which seem to be within the plausible range.[12] The rate of return on capital (r) is a function of the savings-investment balance (see below for details).

Residential Investment

Residential investment is considered to be affected mainly by the population of young adults and the cost of financing. We use the population aged 20–34, which represents potential purchasers of houses. The indicator of the cost of financing for housing is the interest rate, which is set to be the same as the rate of return on capital in the previous equation. We formulate the residential investment equation as follows:

$$IH/Y = f(PT2034, r),$$

where IH/Y is the ratio of residential investment to GNP, PT2034 is the population aged 20–34, and r is the interest rate.

---

11. Theoretically, $n(t)$ rather than $n(t-1)$ should be used in the estimation. However, as Noguchi (1990) pointed out, estimation with $n(t)$ provides poor R^2, so the equation with $n(t-1)$ is adopted.

12. This is comparable to the results by Noguchi (1990), which were 24.6 and 3.55 percent, respectively. The difference between Noguchi's results and ours is mainly due to the longer estimation period that we used.

Interest Rate

Many previous studies assumed that interest rates are exogenous in long-term projections based on the "small country" model. However, Japan is no longer a small country, particularly in international financial markets, and the decline in Japan's net capital exports should affect both domestic and world interest rates. In our model, the interest rate is set as a function of net external surplus in Japan; thus, the excess savings over investment (i.e., the current external surplus) tends to lower the interest rate. Historical evidence implies that an increase in the net external surplus of 1 percent of GNP translates into a 0.55 percent decline in the long-term interest rate. This interest rate function constitutes one of the feedback mechanisms in our model, where excess investment over savings raises the interest rate to discourage domestic investment, thereby restoring the equilibrium.

3.4.2   Simulation Results

The major results of the estimated equations and their explanations are summarized in the appendix. These equations do not necessarily track the fluctuations in the actual variables, reflected in low Durbin-Watson statistics, mainly because these are very simple equations neglecting several important variables explaining cyclical fluctuations. However, a major aim of this model is to explain the long-run trends of savings and investment and to see the net effects of changes in the assumptions or in exogenous variables, rather than pinpointing the economic growth rates or savings rates in a particular year, as we would do in short-term projections. In addition, including many economic variables would require projections of their long-term changes, which causes various difficulties. Using population variables, estimates of which are available up to the year 2025 and are on average more reliable than long-term projections of other economic variables, avoids this problem to some extent. For the projection of the population and its age structure, we use the medium estimates by the IPP, mainly to compare the results of our simulation with those in earlier studies.

These equations are solved simultaneously to maintain consistency between the interactions of the variables. When we use these estimated equations for long-term projections, several procedures concerning the labor supply and labor-augmenting technological change are included. Many previous studies took these economic variables to be unchanged despite the rapid pace of population aging. However, treating these key variables as exogenous often leads to "extreme results," mainly due to the lack of adjustment mechanisms in the projection period. In the following sections, major simulation results based on the above model are shown (table 3.3). Care must be taken in interpreting the results because the "baseline case" here is *not* the most plausible one, as in most other macroeconomic simulations. On the contrary, here "baseline" indi-

Table 3.3 Simulation Results (period average)

Period	Growth in Per Capita Real Income (% per annum)				Growth in Real GNP (% per annum)				Gross Saving (% of GNP)			
	Baseline	Sim. 1	Sim. 2	Sim. 3	Baseline	Sim. 1	Sim. 2	Sim. 3	Baseline	Sim. 1	Sim. 2	Sim. 3
1980s	3.6	3.6	3.6	3.6	4.2	4.2	4.2	4.2	31.7	31.7	31.7	31.7
1990s	2.1	2.0	2.0	1.7	2.4	2.3	2.3	2.3	31.3	31.3	31.0	31.1
2000s	0.8	1.0	1.2	0.7	1.0	1.3	1.4	1.0	22.9	23.1	23.6	22.9
2010s	0.0	0.5	0.7	0.2	−0.1	0.3	0.6	0.2	10.4	10.7	12.6	10.5
2020–2025	0.6	0.5	0.8	0.3	0.2	0.1	0.4	0.0	5.9	5.9	9.1	5.8

Period	Interest Rate (%)				Gross Nonresidential Fixed Investment (% of GNP)				Gross Investment (% of GNP)			
	Baseline	Sim. 1	Sim. 2	Sim. 3	Baseline	Sim. 1	Sim. 2	Sim. 3	Baseline	Sim. 1	Sim. 2	Sim. 3
1980s	6.6	6.6	6.6	6.6	18.1	18.1	18.1	18.1	29.6	29.6	29.6	29.6
1990s	7.0	7.0	7.1	7.4	18.5	18.3	18.3	17.8	30.2	30.1	29.9	30.8
2000s	8.0	8.2	8.3	9.2	12.4	13.0	13.7	11.7	23.5	24.1	24.8	25.6
2010s	10.1	10.7	10.3	12.2	8.3	9.9	10.9	8.8	15.1	16.5	17.6	19.1
2020–2025	12.2	12.3	11.4	14.1	8.3	8.6	9.7	7.5	13.8	14.0	15.4	17.0

	Saving-Investment Balance (% of GNP)				Growth in Working Population (% of GNP)				Retired/Working Population			
Period	Baseline	Sim. 1	Sim. 2	Sim. 3	Baseline	Sim. 1	Sim. 2	Sim. 3	Baseline	Sim. 1	Sim. 2	Sim. 3
1980s	2.2	2.2	2.2	2.2	0.8	0.8	0.9	0.9	0.168	0.168	0.168	0.168
1990s	1.1	1.2	1.1	0.2	0.4	0.4	0.6	0.6	0.230	0.230	0.185	0.221
2000s	−0.6	−1.0	−1.2	−2.8	−0.5	−0.5	−0.4	−0.4	0.317	0.317	0.243	0.299
2010s	−4.7	−5.8	−5.0	−8.6	−0.9	−0.9	−0.7	−0.7	0.428	0.428	0.317	0.395
2020–2025	−7.9	−8.1	−6.4	−11.2	−0.2	−0.2	0.0	0.0	0.479	0.479	0.346	0.436

Sources: Ministry of Health and Welfare (1992); Economic Planning Agency, *Report on National Accounts from 1955 to 1969* (Tokyo: Government Printing Office, 1988), *Report on National Accounts from 1955 to 1989* (Tokyo: Government Printing Office, 1991), *Report on Revised National Accounts on the Basis of 1985* (Tokyo: Government Printing Office, 1990), *Annual Report on National Accounts* (Tokyo: Government Printing Office, various issues).

Notes: Simulation 1 assumes that there will be labor-augmenting technological progress (0.8 percent for each 1 percent decline in working population). Simulation 2 includes the influence of longer working life, assuming the same equation for technological progress as in Simulation 1. Simulation 3 considers the effect of the increase in foreign workers, assuming the same equation for technological progress as in Simulation 1.

cates conventional cases applied in previous studies, which often report extreme results for their projections. We consider simulation case 2 to show the most plausible picture because it takes into account various counteracting effects that would be induced as a result of population aging.

Baseline Projection

The major characteristics of the baseline projection using conventional methods are as follows: First, the projected national savings ratio will fall with a sharply increasing dependency ratio and slower economic growth. While the savings ratio will decline only slightly during the 1990s (from an average of 31.7 percent in the 1980s to 31.3 percent in the 1990s), it will start to decline rapidly after the year 2000 and reach a historical low after the year 2020 (the baseline case in table 3.3). This baseline projection of the national savings ratio is basically consistent with that of Horioka because both are based on the conventional definition of the elderly (65 years of age and over).[13]

Second, the fall in the ratios of business investment and national savings to GNP in the baseline projection is due to the following factor: the decline in the labor supply beyond the year 2000 with no offsetting movements in technological change should lower the amount of capital needed to maintain the optimum capital-labor ratio. Because the decline in the investment rate will be less rapid than that in the savings rate, the external account will show a deficit beyond the year 2000, and the deficit will continue to widen, mainly as a result of the sharp decline in the savings rate.

Third, the widening current external deficit will boost interest rates to absorb foreign capital so that it can be financed. Even if we assume that these huge inflows of foreign capital are sustainable, GNP in real terms will begin declining after the year 2010. This rather unrealistic situation often leads to the pessimistic view that the current excellent macroeconomic performance in Japan cannot be sustained under population aging.

Alternative Simulations

The above picture of population aging will be modified by introducing endogenous labor-augmenting technological progress and increases in the elderly labor supply. First, accounting for labor-augmenting technological change in simulation 1 would stimulate investment. We assume that the past relationship in Japanese industries, in which a 1 percent decline in labor supply has induced a 0.8 percent increase in labor productivity,[14] after accounting for an increase

---

13. Care must be taken when comparing the results of our baseline projection with those of Horioka's in the following two points: First, our baseline projection is on the national savings rate, while Horioka's published one is on the private savings rate, excluding government savings. Second, our results are based on simultaneous equations of savings, investment, labor productivity, and so on, while Horioka's are based on a single equation.

14. This is based on the following equation using cross-sectional data for 21 industries on the average labor productivity growth between 1961 and 1990 for six periods:

in capital stocks and initial productivity level, will basically hold in coming decades.[15] As the increase in capital stocks and initial differences in productivity levels by industry are accounted for, this increase in labor productivity is approximated as labor-augmenting technological change, which is induced by the scarcity of labor. With the assumption of endogenous technological change, the investment ratio will fall more moderately through the 1990s and beyond, with higher growth in labor productivity and GNP.

Second, the sharp fall in the national savings ratio in the baseline projection depends critically on how the elderly population, a key explanatory variable for the savings equation, is defined. In other words, this baseline projection is limited to the case in which the elderly's working years remain unchanged despite the extension of their life expectancy. In simulation 2, we apply an alternative definition of the elderly in which the cutoff age between working population and elderly shifts upward as life expectancy increases. In this case, it is assumed that people will adjust their working years in anticipation of longer life expectancy. Thus, the old-age dependency ratio will rise more slowly (see fig. 3.3), and the decline in the working population will be offset by about 26 percent due to this increase in the labor force throughout the projection period. With the additional labor supply and the smaller size of the retired population, the national savings ratio will fall more gradually, resulting in a national savings rate of 9.1 percent rather than 5.9 percent for the period 2020–25. This result is more reasonable than the baseline projection in the sense that the effects from tightening labor market conditions and improvements in the health, educational attainment, and skills of the elderly are accounted for.[16] Also, the projected deficit in the current external account will be less drastic, and the interest rate levels needed to finance the external deficit will be lower than in the baseline projection.

Third, we simulate the effects of an increase in the labor supply through the importation of foreign workers, which is often suggested as an alternative means to offset the negative impacts of population aging. In simulation 3, the

---

$$\ln(Y/L) = -2.150 - 0.817 \ln L + 0.056 \ln(Y^*/L^*) + 0.420 \ln K,$$
$$(-9.246)(-9.078) \qquad (4.042) \qquad\qquad (3.839)$$
$$\hat{R}^2 = 0.583,$$

where Y is real GNP, K is capital, and L is labor. An asterisk indicates the initial period.

15. The ratio of induced labor-augmenting technological change may well be overestimated, as it includes the autonomous improvement in quality of labor and capital in the past. Also, the possibility of an increase in foreign direct investment induced by a labor shortage is not accounted for. However, the rationale behind this assumption of continuous labor-augmenting technological change toward the year 2025 is that there is still plenty of room for improving labor productivity in Japanese industries, particularly in the service sector; thus, the reduction in the labor supply is likely to improve average labor productivity, as we see in the cases of major European countries.

16. The rate of college enrollment, including junior colleges, has been at a plateau of 40 percent since the late 1970s. Assuming a constant enrollment rate at the present level in the coming decades, the share of college graduates in the total population will rise from the current 20 percent to 40 percent.

number of foreign workers is assumed to be equivalent to the number of additional older workers in simulation 2, simply to compare the results.[17] In this case, although the additional supply of workers is the same as in simulation 2, the ratio of the retired population to the working population will be higher because older workers will have to compete for job opportunities with foreign workers and some of them will be driven out of the labor market. In addition, foreign workers are assumed to transfer their savings to their home country, resulting in a lower national savings rate than in simulation 2. This effect is measured by not counting additional foreign workers in the savings equation. Major implications from this simulation are that, although importing foreign workers will partly relieve the labor shortage, a higher old-age dependency ratio will reduce national savings, leading to a rise in the interest rate.

Finally, if we modify the model by fixing the real interest rate for the projection period at 5 percent, the net external deficit beyond the year 2015 will expand to unrealistically high levels. This result indicates the importance of the feedback channel, which prevents the widening of savings-investment imbalances arising from decreasing national savings.

3.5 Policy Implications

Although major challenges to the Japanese economy will result from the shrinking labor force and the increasing share of the elderly in the total population in the coming decades, they can be overcome with appropriate policies. The major policy implications of the above simulations follow.

First, the key to overcoming the increasing labor shortage in the coming "aged society" is to stimulate labor-augmenting technological change. Average labor productivity in Japanese industry (GDP per person employed), measured at purchasing power parity in 1990, is still lower than that of the United States by 26 percent and lower than that of France and Germany by 28 and 12 percent, respectively. Accounting for differences in working hours further increases the gap between Japan and other countries (Japan Productivity Center 1992). With the low level of average labor productivity in Japan, there is much room to improve the efficiency of the existing labor force, particularly in the service sector. In addition, the quality of the labor force will continuously improve through the 2010s as long as the current high level of college enrollment is maintained. Relaxing regulations that keep excess labor in less efficient sectors of the economy would be an effective policy to stimulate labor-augmenting technological change.[18] In this respect, the further opening of the domestic

17. The accumulated increase in the working-age population from the baseline case in 2025 would be 6.9 million (5 percent of the total population).

18. An example of restricting competition in the distribution sector is the Large Scale Retailer Law, which de facto requires supermarkets and department stores to obtain the agreement of small retailers in the neighborhood in order to open or to extend operating hours. The law effectively deters new entries, and rescinding it should improve the efficiency of the distribution sector.

market to foreign firms, raising the ratio of manufactured imports to GNP, is an important way to stimulate competition with Japanese firms, as well as import foreign labor in the form of foreign manufactured products.[19]

Second, the higher labor force participation and longer working life of the elderly will be important factors in determining the growth of the labor force and savings rate in the coming decades. Current labor market institutions and practices have important implications in this respect. In Japan, most large firms set the mandatory retirement age at 60 years, although reemployment is possible for a few additional years. "Retirement" in Japan does not necessarily mean withdrawal from the labor market; it often means a move to a different firm at lower wages and with less favorable working conditions. Indeed, the rate of unemployment is particularly high in the 55–64 age group.[20]

There are two ways to cope with the problem of unemployment in this age group. One is by extending the mandatory retirement age, particularly since the pensionable age for Employees' Public Insurance is to be raised to 65 years. However, with a continuously rising share of older workers in the labor market, an increase in wage costs under the seniority-based wage structure will be inevitable, leading to the letting go of older workers even before the current mandatory retirement age.[21] Another solution is to modify Japanese employment practices so that they accommodate increasing mobility across firms. Because mandatory retirement is an inevitable consequence of rigid employment security and the seniority-based wage structure, measures to mobilize the existing labor force would increase efficiency in Japanese labor markets, particularly for older workers.

In summary, although the rapidly proceeding aging of the Japanese population is a major challenge to the Japanese economy, its negative impacts on savings and investment can be largely reduced by stimulating labor-augmenting technological change and extending the working life of the elderly. Projections of the Japanese economy differ largely depending on whether these forces offsetting population aging are accounted for. Many previous studies neglecting these counteracting effects produced a pessimistic picture of Japan's economy under population aging, but if appropriate policies are implemented the future need not be dark.

19. Assuming that capital-labor ratios in the 13 Japanese manufacturing industries were fixed at their 1960 levels, the increase in the import ratio (manufactured imports to value-added imports) in the respective industries between 1960 and 1990 should have reduced the demand for labor by 1.26 million workers (9.6 percent of total manufacturing employment) through an increase in imports from labor-intensive industries and a relative decline in the share of those industries in total manufacturing.

20. While the average rate of unemployment in Japan was 2.1 percent in 1992, that in the elderly group was particularly high; the rate of unemployment for men in the 55–64 age group was 3.2 percent. Unemployment rates of the elderly are higher than those of youth, which is a cause of friction in Japan.

21. One way to let go of employees before the mandatory retirement age is to transfer them to subsidiary companies by order of the parent company. Another is to encourage them to quite voluntarily by offering large lump-sum severance payments (for details, see Seike 1993).

Appendix
Model Description

Endogenous Variables

IO%	Gross nonresidential fixed investment (percentage of GNP)
IH%	Gross residential investment (percentage of GNP)
STOT%	Gross national saving (percentage of GNP)
RMAA%	Average interest rate on loans and discounts of all banks (percent)
RGNPPMH	GNP per man-hour (1985 yen)
RGNPPC	GNP per capita (1985 yen)
GRGNPPC%	Annual growth rate of real GNP per capita (percent)
KR	Gross capital stock (million yen)
IFIX	Gross fixed investment (billion yen)
NGNP	Gross national product (billion yen)
RGNP85	Gross national product (billion 1985 yen)
ITOT%	Gross national investment (percentage of GNP)
BALANCE	Savings-investment balance (percentage of GNP)
PRRATIO	Ratio of annual growth rate of working population (percent) to the average interest rate on loans and discounts of all banks
INVRMAA%	Reciprocal of average interest rate on loans and discounts of all banks
OLD	Ratio of old-age population to working population
YOUNG	Ratio of population 0–19 years old to working population
BALANCEA	Savings-investment balance (percentage of GNP, three-year average)
IO	Gross nonresidential fixed investment (billion yen)
IO85	Gross nonresidential fixed investment (billion 1985 yen)
IOP85	Gross private nonresidential fixed investment (billion 1985 yen)

Exogenous Variables

POPTOTR	Population, total (thousand persons)
PT019	Population, 0–19 years old (thousand persons)
PT2034	Population, 20–34 years old (thousand persons)
PT2064	Working population (thousand persons)
PT65OV	Retired population (thousand persons)
PGNP	GNP deflator (1985 = 100)
PIO	Deflator for gross nonresidential fixed investment (1985 = 100)

IG	Government investment (billion yen)
IV	Change in inventories (billion yen)
UTRATE	Utilization rate (1990 = 1)
HOUR	Hours worked (hours per month)
DEPR	Depreciation rate (in real terms, percent)
ALPHA	Ratio of gross private nonresidential fixed investment to gross nonresidential fixed investment

Estimated Equations

Investment (nonresidential) rate equation
Sample period: 1956–92

$$(A1)\ IO\% = 26.3524*PRRATIO\ (-1) + 106.637*INVRMAA\%\ (-1),$$
$$\qquad\qquad (5.56) \qquad\qquad\qquad (15.15)$$
$$\qquad\qquad Adj.\ R^{\,2} = 0.234, \qquad D.W. = 0.988.$$

Residential investment rate equation
Sample period: 1958–92

$$(A2)\ \ IH\% = -9.81875 + 0.0006924*PT2034 - 0.32088*RMAA\%,$$
$$\qquad (-7.52) \qquad (13.47) \qquad\qquad\quad (-3.61)$$
$$\qquad\qquad Adj.\ R^{\,2} = 0.841, \qquad D.W. = 0.815.$$

Savings rate equation
Sample period: 1958–92

$$(A3)\ \ STOT\% = 65.96 - 91.967*OLD - 41.917*YOUNG$$
$$\qquad\qquad (12.20)(-5.19) \qquad\quad (-7.25)$$

$$\qquad\qquad + 0.6364*GRGNPPC\%\ (-1),$$
$$\qquad\qquad (6.07)$$
$$\qquad\qquad Adj.\ R^{\,2} = 0.688, \qquad D.W. = 1.092.$$

Production function
Sample period: 1970–92

$$(A4)\ \ \ln RGNPPMH = -5.96263 + 0.57536*\ln ((KR*UTRATE)\ /$$
$$\qquad\qquad (-199.69) \qquad (55.89)$$

$$\qquad\qquad (POPTOTR*HOUR)),$$
$$\qquad\qquad Adj.\ R^{\,2} = 0.993, \qquad D.W. = 1.515.$$

Interest rate equation
Sample period: 1958–92

$$(A5)\ \qquad RMAA\% = 7.83246 - 0.55126*BALANCEA,$$
$$\qquad\qquad (63.55) \quad (-7.53)$$
$$\qquad\qquad Adj.\ R^{\,2} = 0.621, \qquad D.W. = 1.012.$$

Investment (nonresidential) rate equation for simulation 2
Sample period: 1956–92

(A6) IO% = 20.9038*PRRATIO (-1) + 111.611*INVRMAA% (-1),
        (4.22)   (14.09)
              Adj. R^2 = 0.125,   D.W. = 1.125.

Savings rate equation for simulation 2
Sample period: 1958–92

(A7)   STOT% = 65.444 -126.83*OLD $- 36.781$*YOUNG
            (10.47) (-4.46) (-6.41)

            + 0.73158*GRGNPPC% (-1),
            (6.50)
            Adj. R^2 = 0.637,   D.W. = 1.244.

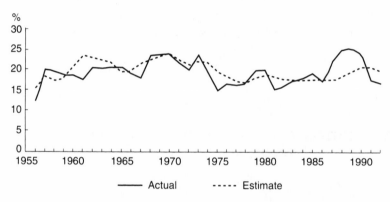

Fig. 3A.1   Gross nonresidential fixed investment (as percentage of GNP)

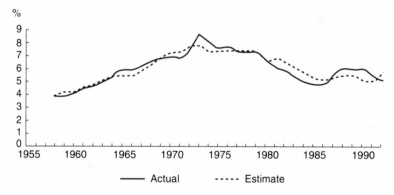

Fig. 3A.2   Gross residential investment (as precentage of GNP)

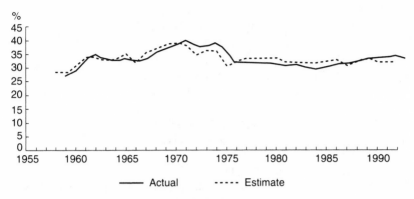

Fig. 3A.3   Gross saving (as percentage of GNP)

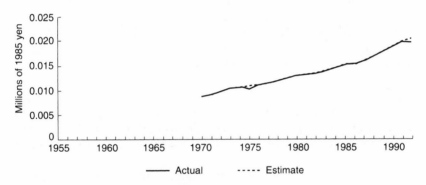

Fig. 3A.4   GNP per man-hour (million 1985 yen)

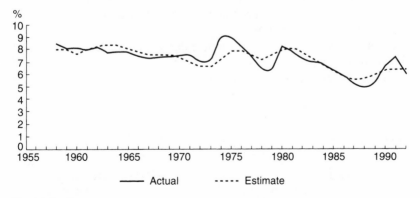

Fig. 3A.5   Interest rate

Identities

IDENT EQI1	RGNPPC = RGNP85/POPTOTR
IDENT EQI2	GRGNPPC% = RGNPPC/RGNPPC (-1)∗100 $-$ 100
IDENT EQI3	KR = KR (-1) + IOP85∗1000 $-$ DEPR/100∗KR (-1)
IDENT EQI4	IFIX = IO%∗NGNP/100 + IH%∗NGNP/100 + IG
IDENT EQI5	NGNP = RGNP85∗PGNP85/100
IDENT EQI6	RGNP85 = RGNPPMH∗POPTOTR∗HOUR
IDENT EQI7	ITOT% = (IFIX + IV)/NGNP∗100
IDENT EQI8	BALANCE = STOT% $-$ ITOT%
IDENT EQI9	IG = NGNP∗0.052
IDENT EQI10	IV = NGNP∗0.005
IDENT EQI11	PRRATIO = [(PT2064/PT2064 (-1))∗100 $-$ 100]/RMAA%
IDENT EQI12	INVRMAA% = 1/(RMAA%)
IDENT EQI13	OLD = PT65OV/PT2064
IDENT EQI14	YOUNG = PT019/PT2064
IDENT EQI15	BALANCEA = (BALANCE + BALANCE (-1) + BALANCE (-2))/3
IDENT EQI16	IO = IO%/100∗NGNP
IDENT EQI17	IO85 = IO/(PIO/100)
IDENT EQI18	IOP85 = IO85∗ALPHA

Assumptions

Data on future population are computed from data on the medium estimates of population by age group presented in Ministry of Health and Welfare (1992).

IG (government investment) is set at 5.2 percent of GNP during the simulation period.

IV (change in inventories) is set at 0.5 percent of GNP during the simulation period.

Inflation rate is assumed to be 1.7 percent a year.

PIO is assumed to rise 0.1 percent a year.

UTRATE (utilization rate) is set at 0.945 during the simulation period.

Future values of HOURS (hours worked) are calculated based on Economic Planning Agency (1991a, 1991b).

DEPR (depreciation rate in real terms) during the simulation period is assumed to be 4.89 percent a year.

ALPHA is set at 0.91 during the simulation period.

References

Auerbach, Alan J., Laurence J. Kotlikoff, Robert P. Hagemann, and Giuseppe Nicoletti. 1989. The economic dynamics of an aging population: The case of four OECD countries. *OECD Economic Studies* 12 (Spring): 28–29.

Bos, Eduard, My T. Vu, Ann Levin, and Rodolfo Bulatao. 1992. *World population projections, 1992–93 edition.* Baltimore: Johns Hopkins University Press.

Cutler, David M., James M. Poterba, Louise M. Sheiner, and Lawrence H. Summers. 1990. An aging society: Opportunity or challenge? *Brookings Papers on Economic Activity* 1:1–73.

Economic Planning Agency. 1991a. *2010 Nen heno Sentaku* (Japan in the year 2010). Tokyo: Government Printing Office.

———. 1991b. *2010 Nen no Sangyo Keizai* (Simulation of the industry and economy in 2010). Tokyo: Government Printing Office.

Horioka, Charles Yuji. 1991. The determinants of Japan's saving rate: The impact of the age structure of the population and other factors. *Economic Studies Quarterly* 42 (3): 237–53.

———. 1992. Future trends in Japan's saving rate, and the implications thereof for Japan's external imbalance. *Japan and the World Economy* 3 (4): 307–30.

Japan Productivity Center. 1992. *Roudouseisansei no Kokusaihikaku* (A cross-national comparison of labor productivity). Tokyo: Japan Productivity Center.

Masson, Paul R., and Ralph W. Tryon. 1990. Macroeconomic effects of projected population aging in industrial countries. *International Monetary Fund Staff Papers* 37 (3): 453–85.

Ministry of Health and Welfare. Institute of Population Problems. 1992. *Population projections for Japan: 1990–2090.* Tokyo: Ministry of Health and Welfare.

Noguchi, Yukio. 1987. Koteki Nenkin no Shorai to Nihon Keizai no Taigai Pafomansu (The future of public pensions and the external performance of the Japanese economy). *Financial Review* (Institute of Fiscal and Monetary Policy, Ministry of Finance) 5 (June): 9–19.

———. 1989. Macroeconomic implications of population aging. Paper presented at the Conference on the Economics of Aging jointly sponsored by Japan Center for Economic Research and the National Bureau of Economic Research, Tokyo, 8–9 September.

———. 1990. Jinko Kozo to Chochiku/Toshi: Kakkoku Hikaku ni yoru Bunseki (The age structure of the population and saving/investment: An analysis based on cross-country comparisons). *Financial Review* (Institute of Fiscal and Monetary Policy, Ministry of Finance) 17 (August): 39–50.

OECD (Organisation for Economic Cooperation and Development). 1990. *The economic survey on Japan 1989/1990.* Paris: Organisation for Economic Cooperation and Development.

Seike, Atsushi. 1993. *Koreika Shakai no Rodo Shijo* (The labor market in the aging society). Tokyo: Toyokeizai Shimposha.

Shimpo, Seiji, ed. 1991. *Zeminaru Makuro Keizaigaku Nyumon* (Introduction to macroeconomics). Tokyo: Nihon Keizai Shimbun.

Yoshitomi, Masaru, and Naohiro Yashiro. 1992. Long-term economic issues in Japan and Asia Pacific region. In *The long-term prospects for the world economy.* Paris: Organisation for Economic Cooperation and Development.

4 The Economic Position of the Elderly in Japan

Naohiro Yashiro

Japan's economy and society face a rapid aging of the population. The proportion of the elderly (defined here as those 65 years of age or older) in the total population, which was 4.9 percent in 1950—very low by international standards—rose to 14.8 percent in 1995. The ratio is projected to rise further, to over 25 percent by 2020, which would make it among the highest in the major OECD countries.[1] The rapid aging of the Japanese population reflects the high rate of economic growth during the postwar period and associated structural changes in industry and society, particularly in family structure.

This paper focuses on the economic status of the elderly, with specific reference to their family relationships. First, the transformation of the Japanese household structure in the postwar period is reviewed. Second, the income of elderly households under both conventional and alternative definitions is compared with that of average households for a better understanding of their relative economic status. The distribution of the income and wealth of elderly households is a major concern here. Third, the high proportion of the elderly living with their children, though declining steadily over time, has been a particular characteristic of the Japanese family. Major factors determining the coresidence of the elderly with their children are analyzed based on cross-sectional data by prefecture. Finally, we arrive at some policy conclusions from the above discussions.

Naohiro Yashiro is professor of economics at the Institute of International Relations, Sophia University.

Financial support from the Japan Foundation Center for Global Partnership and technical assistance from the Japan Center for Economic Research are gratefully acknowledged.

1. The relatively fast aging process in Japan is evident when we compare the time required to double the share of the elderly from 7 percent to 14 percent in various countries. In Japan, this doubling is projected to take only 25 years, compared with 70 years in the United States, and 130 years in France. For an overview of the economic aspects of the aging of the Japanese population, see OECD (1990) and Takayama (1992).

4.1 Changes in Living Arrangements of the Elderly

The aging of the Japanese population has been due largely to the gradual aging of the postwar baby boom cohort (born between 1947 and 1949), which will become elderly toward the year 2020. The rapidity of the aging is due mainly to the continuous decline of the birthrate, from 4.5 in 1947 to 1.43 in 1995. In addition, an increase in life expectancy has contributed to an increase in the average age of the population; the average life expectancy of those reaching age 65 rose from 11.5 years in 1950 to 16.7 years in 1994 for males and from 13.9 years to 21.0 years for females. This extension of life expectancy has greatly affected the living arrangements of the elderly in Japan. In 1990, 85 percent of elderly men lived with their wives (including those who also lived with other family members), while only 42 percent of elderly women lived with their husbands, reflecting the large difference in life expectancies and the low divorce rate.[2]

A major characteristic of Japan's family structure is the high proportion of the elderly who live with their children or other relatives, indicating the important role of extended families in securing a comfortable life for the retired elderly. For example, only 15 percent of all elderly women in Japan lived alone in 1989—much lower than the 41 percent in the United States (table 4.1).[3] In addition, the more aged the elderly become, the more likely they are to live with their extended families.

Moreover, the likelihood of coresidence of elderly women is relatively high; 62 percent of "very elderly" (those aged 75 or over) men and 77 percent of very elderly women live with their families in Japan, compared to 9 and 22 percent in the United States, respectively. While the greater likelihood for women is partly due to the fact that elderly women are on average older than elderly men, the incidence of elderly women living with their children is consistently higher than that of elderly men in the same age groups; for example, over 80 percent of Japanese women aged 80 or over live with their children, compared with 70 percent of men in the same age group. This high rate of coresidence of elderly women with their children helps to reduce the incidence of poverty among the elderly in Japan.

The living arrangements of the elderly, which have important implications for their economic position, have continuously changed over time. The share of the elderly who live with and are supported by their children in the total number of elderly declined from 56 percent in 1977 to 39 percent in 1991, consistent with the decline in the share of extended families in total house-

2. In 1993, Japan's divorce rate (the number of divorces per 1,000 population) was 1.53. This compares with 1990 divorce rates of 4.73 in the United States, 2.88 in the United Kingdom, and 2.20 in Sweden.

3. These figures do not include the elderly who are institutionalized. According to the Census of the Population in 1990, 4.3 percent of the total elderly population was institutionalized.

Table 4.1   Distribution of Living Arrangements of the Elderly (percent)

	Men					Women				
Age	With Spouse	Alone	All Relatives	Children's Family	Nonrelatives	With Spouse	Alone	All Relatives	Children's Family	Nonrelatives
Age 65+										
Japan	37	5	57	36	0	18	15	67	47	0
United States	75	16	7	–	2	40	41	17	–	2
Age 65–74										
Japan	41	5	54	31	0	24	16	60	39	0
United States	80	13	5	–	2	51	33	14	–	2
Age 75+										
Japan	32	6	62	45	0	8	15	77	58	0
United States	67	22	9	–	2	24	51	22	–	3

Sources: For Japan, Ministry of Health and Welfare (1989); for the United States, Hurd (1990).

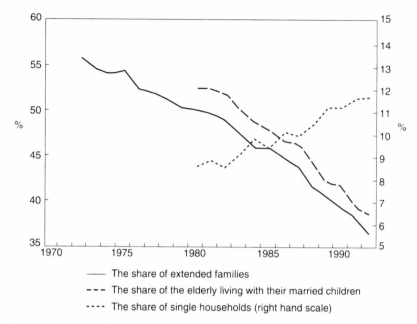

Fig. 4.1   Historical development of living arrangements of the elderly
Source: Ministry of Health and Welfare (1989).

holds. At the same time, the share of the elderly living alone rose from 8 percent to 12 percent (fig. 4.1).

Various signs suggest that this trend is likely to continue in the coming decades. First, the share of extended families in total households in rural areas is consistently higher than the share in urban areas and is inversely related to the size of the city; the share of extended family households in small cities is twice as large as that in large cities. Second, nearly half of farming households are extended families, in both urban and rural areas; this share is much higher than the shares among nonfarm self-employed and employee households (fig. 4.2). Both continued urbanization—migration from rural to urban areas, particularly large cities—and the associated contraction of the agricultural sector as it is replaced by the manufacturing and service sectors should contribute to a further decrease in the share of extended family households and an increase in the incidence of single elderly households.

Improvements in the social security and welfare systems have also contributed to the increased incidence of the elderly living alone and have allowed for other, diversified living arrangements. Instead of the traditional type of extended family in which household members' incomes are pooled, the elderly can live economically independent from their children while sharing the house

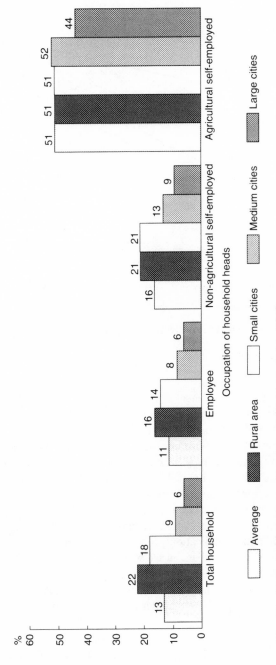

Fig. 4.2 Extended families as a fraction of total households, 1989
Source: Ministry of Health and Welfare (1989).

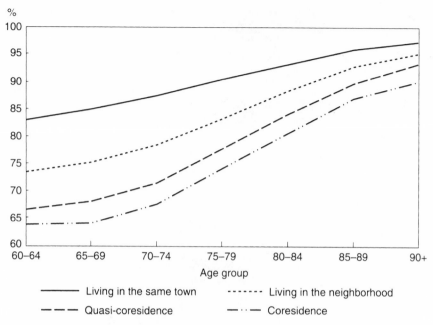

Fig. 4.3   Incidence of various types of living arrangements of the elderly, 1989 (accumulated basis)

Source: Ministry of Health and Welfare (1989).

or housing space ("quasi coresidence"),[4] or they can live alone in either the same neighborhood or the same town as their children. Indeed, the pattern of living arrangements evolves from the elderly living apart from their children but in the same neighborhood toward coresidence as they age. As a result, the accumulated level of the various types of elderly living arrangements (fig. 4.3, *solid line*) is flatter than the closer coresidence type (i.e., living together in the same house) across various age groups (fig. 4.3).

The wide divergence in the living arrangements of the elderly between Japan and the United States and how these arrangements have evolved over time has various analytical and policy implications. In an extended family, the economic independence of household members varies with age: Of males aged 40–59, over 90 percent earn the largest incomes in the household; they are normally heads of household. However, the ratio declines steadily with age, to 23 percent of males aged 80 or over; the remainder are economically dependent on their children.

4. In typical examples of quasi coresidence the child's family lives in a small house built in what was a yard next to the parents' house, or the extended family occupies a multilevel dwelling in which parents and children maintain separate households by living on different floors of the same building.

4.2   Income, Consumption, and Wealth of the Elderly

4.2.1   Income of the Elderly

The economic status of the elderly vis-à-vis the nonelderly has important implications for social policy and the system of transfers from the nonelderly to the elderly. Comparing ordinary household income (excluding single households) by age of household head indicates that elderly households (defined here as those 70 years of age or older) have incomes equivalent to 79 percent of average household income (table 4.2). If we exclude the self-employed, whose reported incomes are less accurate than those of salaried employees, the relative income of the elderly household falls further, to 60 percent of the income of the average employee household. The incomes of single elderly households, which usually belong to the poor group, were approximately 60 and 70 percent of the average, for males and females, respectively.

The large income difference between households headed by the elderly and average households, however, is subject to the following qualifications: First, elderly households are smaller; the average number of members in elderly households was 2.9 compared with 3.8 in all households in 1989. Accounting for the difference in family size, the per capita income and consumption of the elderly household exceeded those of the average household, though scale economies of household consumption should be accounted for.[5] Second, self-employed incomes may not be fully declared, particularly by farming households. Elderly workers are found most often in the self-employed sector; close to 60 percent of elderly workers are self-employed, though self-employed workers account for less than 30 percent of all workers. This high incidence of self-employment among elderly workers may well lead to an underestimation of average elderly income.

Finally, the income gap between the elderly and the nonelderly would be even smaller if imputed incomes from nonmonetary sources were accounted for as follows: First, the ratio of homeownership for elderly households is generally higher than the national average (80 percent vs. 60 percent in 1989). In addition, elderly people who bought their houses in the past have more unrealized capital gains from continuous land price hikes. Both factors result in larger housing and land assets for the elderly, on average two times those of the nonelderly (see table 4.2). Second, the elderly are intensive users of medical benefits, and most such use takes the form of in-kind transfers from the government; the average per capita medical expenses of the elderly are approximately five times as large as those of the nonelderly. Accounting for these

---

5. To compare per capita household income and consumption by family size, a family of two has 5 percent lower per capita income than a single person and 12 percent lower per capita consumption, implying a scale merit of household consumption of 7 percent. A family of four has 30 percent lower per capita income than a single person and 49 percent lower per capita consumption (Ministry of Health and Welfare 1989).

Table 4.2   **Relative Economic Position of the Elderly (average household = 100)**

Age	Total Ordinary Household			Total Excluding Self-Employed		
	Annual Income	Consumption	Housing Assets	Annual Income	Consumption	Housing Assets
Age 60–69	92.3	91.8	140.9	82.7	90.8	142.5
(per capita)	(112.2)	(111.7)		(113.3)	(124.3)	
Age 70+	79.1	77.2	183.1	59.7	66.9	179.1
(per capita)	(102.9)	(100.4)		(93.9)	(105.2)	

	Single Household					
	Males			Females		
	Annual Income	Consumption	Housing Assets	Annual Income	Consumption	Housing Assets
Age 60–69	73.8	81.2	487.6	94.6	91.3	110.3
Age 70+	60.5	76.3	201.6	72.3	91.0	235.3

Source: Ministry of Health and Welfare (1989).

sources of imputed income would significantly improve the relative economic position of the elderly.

4.2.2   Distribution of Income and Wealth of the Elderly

The comparison of income and wealth between the elderly and the nonelderly indicates that the economic position of the *average* elderly household is no less advantageous than that of the average nonelderly household. However, as in other industrial countries, the income and wealth of the elderly appear to be less equally distributed than those of the nonelderly (Tachibanaki 1989). While the elderly head 18 percent of households, 35 percent of elderly households are in the lowest income quartile, compared with 13 percent of nonelderly households. Moreover, the income distribution of the elderly is U-shaped, contrary to the traditional normal distribution pattern (fig. 4.4).

There are various reasons why income distribution among the elderly is inequitable in Japan. First, while public pensions account for nearly half of average elderly income, labor income still accounts for one-quarter, implying that whether one can continue working beyond retirement age, subject to health as well as employment opportunities, is an important factor (table 4.3). Second, under the seniority-based wage structure prevalent in the Japanese labor market, not only does the average wage of employees grow with age but the dispersion of wages in the same age group becomes wider. Because the size of the firm pension or lump-sum severance payment is proportional to a person's wage at the time of retirement from the firm, differences in wages continue to be reflected in income differentials after retirement. Third, because many elderly women were either homemakers or unpaid family workers, their eco-

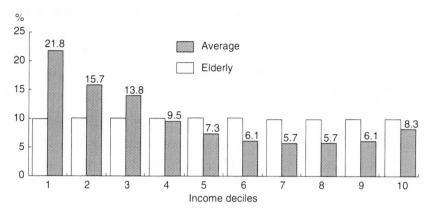

Fig. 4.4   Distribution of elderly household incomes, 1989
Source: Management and Coordination Agency (1989).

nomic positions often depend on family situations, such as whether they live with their extended families, with their spouses, or alone. In 1989, the average income of an elderly man living alone was 40 percent of that of an elderly couple (without children), while that of an elderly woman living alone was 36 percent that of an elderly couple.[6]

Housing assets are even less equitably distributed than household income. While housing and land assets account for much of the wealth of the elderly, the value depends on accumulated potential capital gains in previous periods. The median housing asset of the elderly (those 70 years of age or older) is 50 percent larger than that of the average household, and the gap widens in the third quartile to 150 percent, indicating that the housing asset distribution by age group is wider in the higher asset-holding class. In addition, even among the elderly, the distribution of housing assets varies across regions, particularly between large cities and rural areas. For example, the average value of housing of the elderly in the Tokyo area was twice the national average in 1989 (Management and Coordination Agency 1989).

4.2.3   Savings of the Elderly

One of the major issues concerning Japanese household behavior is how to explain its high rate of savings. Numerous studies have been published giving possible reasons for the difference in the average rate of savings between Japan and the United States.[7] One of the factors that raises average Japanese household savings is the relatively high rate of savings of the elderly, who are ex-

6. Here, the single elderly are defined to be those aged 60 or over, and elderly couples are defined to be those families in which the husband is aged 65 or over and the wife is aged 60 or over (Ministry of Health and Welfare 1989).

7. See Horioka (1990b) for a survey of the major literature on Japan's high savings rate.

Table 4.3   International Comparison of Major Sources of the Elderly[a] Income (percent)

Major Sources of Income	Japan 1981	Japan 1986	Japan 1990	United States 1981	United States 1986	United States 1990	United Kingdom 1981	United Kingdom 1990	Korea 1981	Korea 1990
Wages	31.3	24.5	23.8	15.2	14.1	10.7	6.5	5.5	16.2	31.9
Public pension	34.9	53.4	54.3	53.9	53.0	55.2	64.0	68.8	0.8	2.5
Private pension	3.8	1.9	1.9	10.0	10.4	13.6	13.5	18.0	0.0	0.3
Deposit	2.1	2.2	2.0	1.7	1.8	1.8	1.6	1.3	2.2	1.9
Other wealth income	5.3	5.6	4.0	14.5	17.4	11.0	2.2	1.9	3.3	4.6
Support from children	15.6	9.0	5.7	0.3	0.2	0.7	0.5	0.1	72.4	54.8
Income maintenance	1.2	1.1	0.9	0.7	0.4	1.4	3.1	2.3	1.2	2.2
Others	3.1	1.9	1.8	3.5	2.4	2.7	2.6	0.9	3.2	1.6
None of the above	2.7	0.4	5.7	0.2	0.3	3.0	6.1	1.3	0.6	0.2

Source: Management and Coordination Agency, *Life and View of the Elderly* (in Japanese; Tokyo; Government Printing Office, 1992).

[a]Age 60 or older.

pected to be dissavers. Major explanations for the high rate of elderly household savings in Japan are later retirement from the labor market, greater incentive to leave bequests to their children, significant imputed incomes, and absorption of the poor elderly into their children's households (Horioka 1990a).

First, the life-cycle theory states that people start to dissave after retirement. A simple explanation of the high savings rate of the Japanese elderly is that many of them continue to work after normal retirement age. Though labor force participation rates of the male elderly fall with age, the decline at age 60—the normal retirement age from a company—is relatively small, and beyond age 60 the participation rate falls only gradually; the average participation rates for those aged 60–64 and 65–69 in 1992 were 72 and 59 percent, respectively (fig. 4.5). Moreover, declining labor force participation rates bottomed out and then rose from 1988 to 1992, partly reflecting tightening labor market conditions. If this new trend toward later retirement continues, it may have a significant impact on Japanese household savings.

If Japanese household savings rates are examined by age group in employee household data (the most readily available and thus the most often cited statistic), elderly household savings rates are found to be as high as 50 percent (fig. 4.6). This surprisingly high rate of savings is attributable to the fact that only the rich elderly remain employed while continuing to be household heads; they accounted for 15 percent of those aged 65–69 and only 5 percent of those aged 70 or older. On the other hand, the retired elderly (those who do not work) do dissave in Japan as the life-cycle theory predicts. Combining these employee and retired households results in a falling savings rate for elderly households,

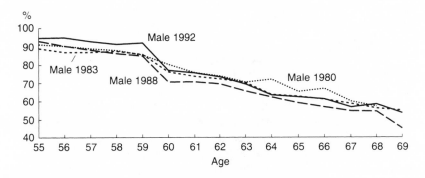

Fig. 4.5   Labor force participation of the elderly by age, 1992
Source: Ministry of Labor, *Basic Survey on the Elderly's Employment* (Tokyo, 1992).

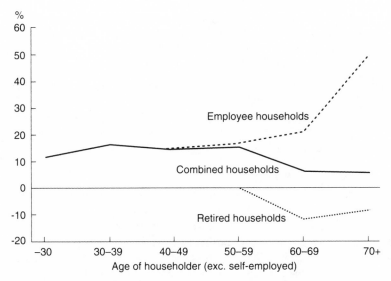

Fig. 4.6   Household savings rates (employee vs. retired households)
Source: Management and Coordination Agency (1989).

though not to a negative level, which is similar to what occurs in the United States.

A principal factor behind longer retirement life is the continuous extension of Japanese life expectancy; expected life remaining at age 65 increased by 4.9 years for males and 6.7 years for females between 1950 and 1993. This increase forces the elderly to save more in order to finance their longer lives. Another factor accounting for the large aggregate household savings (National Account basis) is the large fraction in the elderly labor force of the self-employed,[8] whose business profits are often mixed with household savings and for whom retirement is quite flexible, unlike the case of employees subject to mandatory retirement.[9]

Second, the desire of the Japanese elderly to leave bequests to their children is also important in explaining their later retirement and relatively high rate of savings. A survey by the Bank of Japan in 1990 indicated that the majority of Japanese parents who have financial and real assets want to leave bequests to their children. The share is higher among the older generation and among self-employed, particularly farming, households. The bequest motive, however, can be altruistic or strategic. While 60 percent of the elderly responded that they would leave the bequest unconditionally, the remainder said that they would do so only if their children agreed to take care of them in their retired life (Management and Coordination Agency 1992).

Third, the significant imputed income of the elderly raises their savings rate as conventionally measured. When we account for estimated imputed income and consumption from housing and land, as well as medical benefits, the savings rate of the elderly falls, resulting in a consumption pattern resembling the life-cycle pattern. In addition, if household expenditure for education, which is conventionally defined as consumption, is reclassified as savings for human capital investment in the family, it raises the savings rate of the nonelderly, while having little effect on the rate for the elderly. Also, by so doing, the mysterious decline in the household savings rate for those aged 40–49 (when the household's burden of educational expenditure is largest) disappears, and we are left with a smooth life-cycle pattern of savings in Japan (fig. 4.7).

4.2.4   Age Selectivity Bias

The sharp decline in the economic independence of the Japanese elderly as they age is a major source of the "age selectivity bias" in Japanese household statistics concerning the income and savings of the elderly that makes it difficult to compare the economic position of the elderly in Japan with that of the elderly in the United States. The extent of this age selectivity bias can be approximated by the gap between the age composition of the population and the age composition of heads of households. For example, 70-year-olds account for 13.2 percent of the population above age 30, but only 7.8 percent of household heads (table 4.4). This age composition gap is much smaller in the United States.

The likelihood that the Japanese elderly will be economically dependent on

8. The rates of labor force participation of the male elderly (those aged 65 years or older) in self-employed and employee households in 1991 were 72 and 40 percent, respectively. However, with a declining self-employed elderly population, mainly concentrated in agriculture, the average labor force participation rate of the elderly is likely to fall in the long run.

9. The age of mandatory retirement from a firm practicing long-term employment is set on a firm-by-firm basis. In 1991, over 90 percent of Japanese firms had this system, and half of them set retirement age at 60 or older. Unlike in the United States, this mandatory retirement system is a perfectly legal practice in Japan.

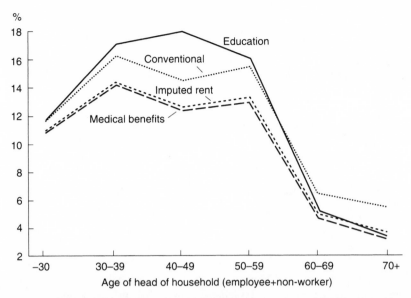

Fig. 4.7   Alternative definitions of household savings rates (excluding the self-employed)
Source: Management and Coordination Agency (1989).

Table 4.4   Comparison of Age Compositions of the Population and of Heads of Households between Japan and the United States, 1989

Japan			United States		
Age	Population	Households	Age	Population	Households
30–39	22.7	27.0	25–34	27.9	23.9
40–49	26.6	29.3	35–44	23.1	22.9
50–59	21.4	21.2	45–54	15.8	16.0
60–69	16.0	14.7	55–64	13.7	14.6
70+	13.2	7.8	65–74	11.5	13.3
			75+	8.1	9.3
Total	100.0	100.0	Total	100.0	100.0

Sources: For Japan, Management and Coordination Agency (1989); for the United States, U.S. Bureau of the Census, *Current Population Reports* (Washington, D.C., 1989).

their children or relatives, and will thus be omitted from statistics compiled on a household basis, is closely related to their income level. Three-quarters of the elderly who have annual incomes of less than 400,000 yen live with their children, which results in an *upward* bias in the perceived elderly household income because it is the relatively rich elderly who can afford to remain heads of households. However, the negative correlation between elderly individual

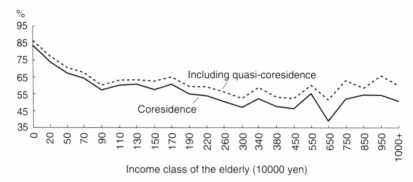

Fig. 4.8   Incidence of coresidence of the elderly (percentage of the total elderly population)
Source: Ministry of Health and Welfare (1989).

income level and incidence of coresidence with children disappears when income level exceeds 2 million yen, implying that the decision of the elderly to live with their children may be independent of their income level unless their income is so low that they have few choices. There is even a positive correlation between elderly income level and incidence of quasi coresidence (shown by the gap between the two lines in fig. 4.8). Thus, while coresidence is more prominent for the poor elderly, quasi coresidence, which assures privacy while maintaining the benefits of coresidence, is more associated with the rich elderly.

There are various ways to cope with this age selectivity bias (Ando, Yamashita, and Murayama 1986; Hayashi 1986). Hayashi (1986) estimated the income and consumption of the elderly living with their children as the difference between the income and consumption of extended families taking care of elderly members and those of nuclear families. We basically follow this method with various modifications, such as estimating the savings rate of the "hypothetical" elderly group, who are actually absorbed in their children's families, by equating the age compositions of the population and of household heads (Yashiro and Maeda 1994).[10] With this adjustment, the savings rate of elderly households (aged 70 or older) is estimated to be −93 percent—that is, they consume nearly twice their own incomes. The large negative savings of the elderly living with their children is not surprising, given their low incomes.[11]

10. This assumes that the elderly who depend economically on their children are statistically independent household heads. Including these hypothetical household heads with low savings greatly lowers the average elderly household savings rate.

11. The large negative savings rate of the elderly living with their children is consistent with the following estimates of a loglinear equation based on the income and consumption data of nonearning households in 1989 (Yashiro and Maeda 1994):

This result has two implications. First, the savings behavior of the Japanese elderly is not necessarily different from that of the U.S. elderly, but the large gap in rates of coresidence with children tends to overstate the difference. Second, the falling incidence of coresidence with children among the Japanese elderly is likely to lower their savings rate in household-based statistics and thus narrow the gap with the United States.

4.3   Determinants of Living Arrangements of the Elderly

The living arrangements of the elderly play a key role in determining their economic position as well as their household savings. We already observed in section 4.1 that the percentage of the elderly who live with their children rises with age. Also, the percentage of coresidence is higher for women, those who are without a spouse, those in farming households, and those living in rural areas; since the very old are more likely to be women and spouseless, these variables are not mutually exclusive.

Various studies indicate that the effect of economic factors, particularly the income level of the elderly, on their living arrangements is indecisive. Many previous studies attribute the increasing ratio of elderly persons living alone to their rising income level. According to this view, the poor elderly must live with their children for financial reasons, even though they do not wish to do so. In contrast, the school of the strategic bequest motive argues that many adult children live with their elderly parents for financial reasons—they cannot afford to buy their own homes. In return, the elderly parents expect in-kind services as well as monetary support from their adult children. For this reason, it may well be the rising income of children that will lower the likelihood of shared living arrangements.

4.3.1   Review of Previous Studies

Kotlikoff and Morris (1988) presented a model of family living arrangements in which the joint utility maximization between elderly parents and their adult children was explored. In the model, the economic gain from shared housing was compared with its disutility in determining whether the parent and child would live together. For example, when parents would like to coreside, but their children would not, the parents were able to bribe their children to coreside if their income, including housing services, was high enough relative to their children's income. A major conclusion of this study was that nonmonetary characteristics of children (such as gender and education) are

---

$$\ln \text{PTC} = 3.63 - 0.282 \ln \text{DI}, \qquad R^2 = 0.791,$$
$$(41.03) \quad (5.50)$$

where PTC is propensity to consume, DI is disposable income, and figures in parentheses are t-values.

more important than income differences as determinants of living arrangements.

With specific reference to Japan, Ando et al. (1986) compared the behavior of extended nonelderly families and nuclear nonelderly families. Their conclusion was that the larger the assets of the elderly, the lower their probability of living with their children, because the rich elderly tended to live alone. In contrast, Otake (1991) indicated that both the assets and the income of elderly parents increased the probability of coresidence with their children, mainly because of the parents' strategic bequest motive. The implications of these two results differ widely: Ando et al. implied that the current tendency of elderly incomes to rise, partly as the result of improved social security benefits, would lower the probability of coresidence, while Otake's conclusion was exactly the opposite.

4.3.2 Empirical Specification

The living arrangements of the elderly are explained by the incomes of the elderly and their adult children, housing services, and other family characteristics. The source of the data examined in this paper is the Basic Survey on the People's Life (BSPL), which was conducted nationwide by stratified random sampling in 1986 and 1989 by the Japanese Ministry of Health and Welfare. The 1986 and 1989 BSPL were based on about 40,000 randomly selected households. Because microdata were not available, the pooled data for 47 prefectures in 1986 and 1989 were used instead.

Table 4.5 shows the estimates of the living arrangements of the elderly. The dependent variable is the ratio of the elderly living with their married children and sharing income and consumption to the total elderly.[12] The elderly living with unmarried children were removed from the sample to eliminate cases of unmarried youths living with their parents until marriage. Elderly people living with their married children are classified by age group. Almost 30 percent of the elderly (those 65 years of age or older) in 1990 were self-employed. Since self-employment incomes are difficult to measure, household consumption is used as a proxy for permanent income. Consumption in households where the head is aged 40–49 is used as a proxy for children's income. Housing services are represented by the area of the house divided by the number of "tatami" mats (about 1.7 square meters each) per household member.

Major findings are the following: First, the higher the income (approximated by household consumption) of the elderly, the greater the probability of coresidence, which is consistent with the result obtained by Otake (1991). The extent of this income effect, however, declines with age, implying that the effect of

---

12. This is the narrowest definition of coresidence and is different from quasi coresidence (i.e., living together in the same living unit but maintaining independent family budgets) used in Otake (1991).

Table 4.5   Determinants of Coresidence[a]

Age Group	Constant	Consumption of the Eldrely	Consumption of Supporters[b]	Housing Spaces[c]	1989 Dummy	R^2
60–69	−5.187	2.984	−2.31	1.564	−0.345	0.583
	(0.293)	(5.446)	(−3.580)	(4.540)	(−5.32)	
70+	0.315	1.263	−0.89	0.648	−0.201	0.718
	(0.130)	(8.034)	(−3.983)	(4.032)	(−5.349)	

Sources: Ministry of Health and Welfare (1989).

Note: Figures in parentheses ate *t*-values.

[a]The ratio of the elderly living with children to the total number of elderly having children.

[b]Average consumption of the age group 40–49 (10,000 yen per month).

[c]1.7 m² per household number.

higher elderly income used to bribe children into coresidence diminishes with age, mainly because elderly income levels fall with age. Second, the higher the children's income, the *lower* the probability of their living with parents, which is consistent with what Kotlikoff and Morris (1988) implied. The greater independence of children with higher incomes would encourage their living alone, particularly in present-day Japan, where values differ widely between generations, in part, because of the vastly different societies in which the generations grew up. However, the extent of this negative income effect also declines with the age of the elderly, partly because the deteriorating health of a parent may depress economic incentives. Finally, better housing services, measured by larger space per household member, result in less congestion and more privacy, thereby stimulating coresidence. The effect again becomes relatively small as the age of the elderly increases.

The conclusion, based on prefectural data, that higher income of the elderly raises the probability of coresidence with their children could be subject to sample selection bias because the elderly who are economically independent tend to be richer in prefectures with a higher incidence of coresidence. However, the level of elderly consumption by prefecture is negatively correlated with the ratio of elderly household heads to the total elderly population.[13] This effect is mainly due to the fact that prefectures with a relatively high ratio of elderly household heads are generally poor regions in Japan, indicating that this sample selection bias is not necessarily significant when prefectural data are used.

---

13. Consumption of elderly households (C) is explained by the ratio of elderly household heads to total elderly (H) using data from 47 prefectures in both 1989 and 1990 as follows:

$$\ln C = 4.012 - 0.262 \ln H - 0.100 \, D, \qquad R^2 = 0.183,$$
$$\qquad (32.10) \quad (4.38) \qquad (3.37)$$

where D is a dummy for the year 1990. Figures in parentheses are *t*-values.

4.5   Summary and Conclusion

The pattern of Japanese family structure has been marked by a high number of extended families living together. This characteristic indicates that the role of the family in securing a comfortable retired life for the elderly is quite important in Japan and is a major source of "age selectivity bias" in household-based statistics. The economic position of the elderly and their savings rate as conventionally measured are largely overstated because these data tend to exclude the poor elderly who are economically dependent members of their children's families. This not only explains why the savings rate of the Japanese elderly is so much higher than that of the U.S. elderly but also predicts a decline in savings rate in the near future given the persistent increase in elderly persons living alone.

The economic position of the Japanese elderly on average is almost equivalent to that of the nonelderly. In addition, accounting for imputed income further narrows the gap between the elderly and the nonelderly. While the income of the majority of households headed by the elderly may be low, their asset level is significant, thanks to past asset inflation in Japan, so that the elderly may persuade their children to live with them by offering rich housing services. Empirical estimates suggest that this strategic bequest motive may well be important in determining the living arrangements of the elderly, despite their children's feelings about shared living.

Finally, the income and wealth distribution of the elderly is much wider than that of the nonelderly and is more concentrated in the lower income classes. This implies that welfare policy targeting the elderly *per se* would be inefficient, particularly given increasing fiscal constraints. The policy of concentrating welfare resources on the *poor* elderly, rather than on the elderly population as a whole, would be effective.

References

Ando, A., M. Yamashita, and J. Murayama. 1986. An analysis of consumption and saving behavior based on the life-cycle hypothesis (in Japanese). *Keizai Bunseki,* no. 101: 25–139.

Hayashi, Fumio. 1986. An extension of the permanent income hypothesis and the examination (in Japanese). *Keizei Bunseki,* no. 101: 1–23.

Horioka, Charles Y. 1990a. The importance of life-cycle saving in Japan. Discussion Paper no. 225. Osaka: Osaka University, Institute of Social and Economic Research.

———. 1990b. Why is Japan's household saving rate so high? A literature survey. *Journal of the Japanese and International Economies* 4 (1): 49–92.

Hurd, Michael D. 1990. Research on the elderly: Economic status, retirement, and consumption and saving. *Journal of Economic Literature* 28: 565–637.

Kotlikoff, Laurence J., and John Morris. 1988. Why don't the elderly live with their children? A new look. NBER Working Paper no. 2734. Cambridge, Mass.: National Bureau of Economic Research.

Management and Coordination Agency. 1989. *National survey of family income and expenditure.* Tokyo: Government Printing Office.

———. 1992. *National survey of family income and expenditure.* Tokyo: Government Printing Office.

Ministry of Health and Welfare. 1989. *Basic survey on people's life.* Tokyo: Ministry of Health and Welfare.

OECD (Organisation for Economic Cooperation and Development). 1990. *The economic survey on Japan 1989/1990.* Paris: Organisation for Economic Cooperation and Development.

Otake, Fumio. 1991. Bequest motives of aged households in Japan. *Ricerche Economiche* 45 (2–3): 283–306.

Tachibanaki, Toshiaki. 1989. Japan's new policy agenda: Coping with unequal asset distribution. *Journal of Japanese Studies* 15 (2): 345–69.

Takayama, Noriyuki. 1992. *The graying of Japan: An economic perspective on public pensions.* Tokyo: Kinokuniya; New York: Oxford University Press.

Yashiro, Naohiro, and Yoshiaki Maeda. 1994. Applicability of the life-cycle hypothesis in Japan (in Japanese). *JCER Economic Journal* 27: 57–76.

II   Aging and Asset Markets

5 The Consequences of Population Aging for Private Pension Fund Saving and Asset Markets

Sylvester J. Schieber and John B. Shoven

5.1 Background

In the United States the group of people born between 1946 and 1964 have come to be known as the "baby boom generation." After the end of World War II, birthrates in the United States jumped to a level significantly above long-term trends and stayed above generally expected levels until the mid-1960s. Because of the high birthrates over this period, the number of people born from 1946 to 1964 constitute an unusually large segment of the total U.S. population. Because of its size, the baby boom generation has had a more significant effect on various facets of the social structure during its lifetime than other birth cohorts represented in the population.

For example, as the baby boomers entered the education system they placed new demands on it. Between 1951 and 1954, the number of five- and six-year old children in the primary education system jumped by 70 percent. From 1950 to 1970, when the last of the baby boomers were in school, primary school enrollments jumped from 21 to 34 million students (U.S. Bureau of the Census 1975, 368). Then, as smaller cohorts of children reached school age, school enrollments began to fall off, dropping to 28 million students by 1975, and then stabilizing at around 28 million by 1980 (U.S. Bureau of the Census 1991, 132). As they came into the primary school system, the baby boomers created a fantastic demand for expanded educational services. As they exited the system,

Sylvester J. Schieber is a vice president of and director of the research and information center at The Wyatt Company. John B. Shoven is the Charles R. Schwab Professor of Economics and dean of the School of Humanities and Sciences at Stanford University and a research associate of the National Bureau of Economic Research.

The authors would like to thank Dean Maki and Linda Moncrief for their valuable research assistance and Henry Aaron and Tatsuo Hatta for their helpful comments. Any remaining errors are the authors' responsibility.

staffing positions were eliminated and schools were closed as student bodies were consolidated.

Counting kindergarten, the typical primary and secondary education program in the United States takes 13 years. For the baby boomers who did not go beyond secondary education, the leading edge of the group began to enter the workforce in significant numbers by 1964. The Vietnam conflict slowed the entrance of the oldest baby boom males, as many of them had a period of military service prior to entering the civilian workforce permanently. Of course, many of the baby boomers also pursued a college education. Thus, the baby boomers began to enter the workforce in earnest toward the end of the 1960s and throughout the 1970s. Between 1970 and 1986, the U.S. labor force grew at a compound rate of 2.60 percent per year. By 1985, the youngest of the baby boomers were 21 years of age, and most of those who were going to enter the workforce had done so. In the latter half of the 1980s, the U.S. workforce grew at an annual rate of 0.45 percent per year (U.S. Bureau of the Census 1975, 127; 1991, 384).

Given the predictability of the aging process and the evolving patterns of retirement behavior among workers, it is possible to begin to anticipate the retirement of the baby boom generation. Given its earlier disruptive effects on other aspects of the socioeconomic fabric, it is important to consider the implications of the baby boomers' retirements on existing social and economic institutions as far in advance of their retirements as possible. The two largest sources of cash income for retirees today are Social Security and employer-sponsored tax-qualified retirement plans. The extent to which policymakers have focused on the long-term status of the Social Security system and the employer-sponsored pension system varies significantly.

5.1.1 Social Security Funding and the Baby Boom Generation

For some time, policymakers have been aware that the baby boom generation will pose a particular set of challenges for the Social Security program. Traditionally, the Social Security program in the United States had been run largely on a pay-as-you-go basis. The 1983 Social Security Amendments, anticipating the special burden that baby boomers' retirements would place on workers in the future, included provisions for accumulating a substantial trust fund to prefund some of the benefits promised to the boomers. In other words, the baby boom generation was expected to prefund a larger share of its own benefits than prior generations had prefunded their own Social Security retirement income. The 1983 amendments also reduced the benefits promised to the baby boom generation by gradually raising the age at which full benefits would be paid, to age 67 after the turn of the century.

Shortly after the passage of the 1983 amendments, Social Security actuaries estimated that the Old-Age, Survivors, and Disability Insurance (OASDI) trust funds would grow from around $27.5 billion in 1983 to about $20.7 trillion in 2045 (see fig. 5.1). The trust funds were expected to have resources available

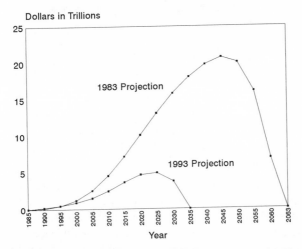

Fig. 5.1   Projected OASDI trust fund accumulations in current dollars
Sources: Ballantyne (1983) and Board of Trustees of the Federal OASDI Trust Funds (1993, 185).

to pay promised benefits until the youngest of the baby boomers reached 100 years of age. In the first projections after the passage of the 1983 amendments, OASDI trust funds were projected to be solvent until at least 2063.

In almost every year since 1983, the estimates of the accumulations in the OASDI trust funds have been revised downward. The most recent projection published in April 1993, also shown in fig. 5.1, suggests that the trust funds will accumulate to only about $5 trillion dollars around 2025 and will then decline to a zero balance in 2036. At that time the baby boomers will range in age from 72 to 90. Although their numbers will be declining there will still be significant numbers of them depending on their retirement benefits to meet their ongoing needs.

An alternative way to look at the financing of Social Security is to segment it into periods. Table 5.1 reflects the Social Security actuaries' April 1993 long-term OASDI financing projections broken into three 25-year periods. For the most part, the first 25-year period, from 1993 to 2017, will precede the bulk of the baby boom's claim on the program. The baby boomers first will be eligible for early retirement benefits in 2008, and only about half of them will have attained age 62 by 2017. In addition, if the increases in the actuarial reductions for early retirement benefits and the increases in actuarial adjustments for delayed retirement have any effect, the baby boomers will proceed into retirement somewhat more slowly than prior generations. Even on a purely pay-as-you-go basis, the tax revenues funding OASDI benefits are expected to exceed outgo as late as 2015. Over the next 25 years starting in 1993, OASDI has projected revenues that are about 7 percent above projected outlays.

As the baby boom moves fully into retirement, the projected financing situa-

Table 5.1   Social Security Income and Cost Rates as Projected under Current Law

Period	Income Rate	Cost Rate	Over or Under (−) Funding as a Percentage of Income Rate
1993–2017	12.72	11.87	6.76
2018–42	13.10	15.73	−20.08
2043–67	13.18	17.28	−31.11

Source: Board of Trustees of the Federal OASDI Trust Funds (1993, 26).

tion for Social Security turns decidedly negative. During the second 25-year period reflected in table 5.1, when the majority of the baby boomers expect to get the bulk of their lifetime benefits, the projected OASDI outlays exceed revenues by 20 percent. In other words, every bit of evidence available to national policymakers today indicates that Social Security will not be able provide the benefits currently being promised to the baby boom generation on the basis of inherent benefit promises now being held out to them and existing funding legislation. While it is impossible to anticipate exactly how OASDI projections might change over the next 5 or 10 years, assuming no change in legislative mandates, the recent history of continual deterioration in the projected actuarial balances of the program leads us to conclude that the future may turn out even worse than we now officially anticipate.

The recent history of major Social Security legislative adjustments, specifically including the 1977 and 1983 amendments, suggests that when benefit promises exceed program revenues, at least part of the rebalancing of the program comes in the form of reduced benefits for retirees. Given the size of the baby boom generation and the potential adjustment that may be required in their Social Security benefit expectations, it seems imperative that policymakers begin to address the funding of the baby boomers benefits as soon as possible so they will have the maximum amount of time to adjust their other retirement savings relative to more realistic Social Security promises.

5.1.2   Employer-Sponsored Retirement Plan Funding and the Baby Boom Generation

In the general context of retirement policy it is interesting that there is so much consternation about the long-term prospects of Social Security and the potential underfunding of benefits for the baby boom generation when there is hardly any concern about the long-term prospects of the funded pension system. A review of the effects of recent legislation and contributions to employer-sponsored retirement plans suggests there may be reason for concern on the pension front as well.

Employer-sponsored retirement programs typically operate in a significantly different environment than the federal Social Security program. While the federal government operates its own employer-sponsored retirement programs largely on a pay-as-you-go basis, most state and local governments prefund retirement obligations on some basis, and private employers are required to fund their retirement obligations on the basis of rules laid out in the Employee Retirement Income Security Act (ERISA) and the Internal Revenue Code (IRC).

ERISA became law in 1974. Its purpose was to provide more secure retirement benefits for all the participants in tax-qualified plans. Among other things, ERISA established rules for including workers in plans, rules for vesting or guaranteeing benefits, and requirements that benefits be funded on a scheduled basis. In order for a plan to qualify for retirement plan tax preferences in the IRC, it must meet certain requirements to assure that the benefits being promised are actually provided. For all plans there are fiduciary requirements seeking to assure that the assets are prudently invested solely for the purpose of providing benefits promised by the plans. In addition, ERISA requires that plan trustees disclose relevant financial and participation data to the government on a periodic basis so that the ongoing viability and operation of the plan can be assured.

For defined-contribution plans, the funding requirements are straightforward. On the date that a contribution to the plan is required by the plan rules the employer makes a contribution to the plan equal to the obligation. In this case, the employer is not obligated to make any additional contributions for prior periods. The ability of the plan to provide an adequate retirement benefit will depend heavily on the size of the periodic contributions and the investment returns to the assets in the plan.

For defined-benefit plans the funding requirements are somewhat more complicated because defined-benefit plans promise future benefits. If a worker enters a firm at age 25 and works until age 65 and he is retired under the plan for 20 years before dying, his span of life under the plan is 60 years. The essence of the ERISA funding requirements for defined-benefit plans is that the employer gradually contribute enough to the plan so that the promised benefits will be fully funded at the point a worker retires. The annual contribution to the plan is determined on the basis of an actuarial valuation of the plan's obligations and assets and specific funding minimums and maximums specified in the law. The funding minimums in the law are to assure that employers are laying aside money to pay promised benefits. The funding maximums are in the law to assure that extraordinary contributions are not made to the plan simply to avoid paying federal taxes.

It may seem odd to worry about the funding of employer-sponsored pension obligations, at least those of private plan sponsors, when the federal government has seemingly established strong funding and disclosure standards to assure that promised benefits will ultimately be delivered. The problem is that there is an inherent neurosis in federal law governing pensions between the provisions aimed at providing retirement income security, on the one hand, and those limiting the value of the preferences accorded pensions in the federal tax code, on the other. From the passage of ERISA in 1974 until the early 1980s concerns about benefit security held the upper hand in driving federal policy toward pensions. Since 1982, policies aimed at limiting tax leakages related to employer-sponsored retirement plans have played the dominant role. While a number of tax law changes have had an effect on defined-contribution plans since 1982, the effects on defined-benefit plans have been considerably more profound. This was especially true of the Omnibus Budget Reconciliation Act of 1987 (OBRA87).

Defined-benefit plans have a special appeal for workers because they ensure a promised level of benefits regardless of the gyrations in financial markets. Over the years, defined-benefit plans have had a special appeal for employers because they have provided the flexibility to fund promised benefits actuarially over the working lives of their employees. Traditionally, actuarial funding allowed employers to advance fund for benefits that increase steeply at the end of workers' careers. Through 1987 employers were allowed to fund up to 100 percent of the projected benefits that would be paid to a worker at retirement based on his or her current tenure, age, and actuarial probabilities of qualifying for a benefit in the future. OBRA87 dropped the full funding limits for defined-benefit plans from 100 percent of ongoing plan liability to 150 percent of benefits accrued to date.

The net effect of the new funding limits under OBRA87 was to delay the funding of an individual's pension benefit relative to prior law. Table 5.2 helps to show the implications of the revised funding standards. For purposes of developing this example, we assumed that a worker begins a job at a firm at age 25 earning $25,000 per year. We assumed that the worker's pay would increase at a rate of 5.5 percent per year throughout his or her career. This individual participates in a defined-benefit plan that pays 1.25 percent of final average salary per year of service at age 65. We assumed that accumulated assets in the plan would earn a return of 8 percent per year.

The column of the table labeled "Projected Unit Credit Contribution Rate" shows the contribution rate, as a percentage of the worker's salary, that would be required to fund this individual's benefit at retirement under the projected unit credit funding method. The other four contribution rates in the table show what the effect of imposing a funding limit of 150 percent of accrued benefits would have on workers affected at four different points in their careers. The column labeled "Age 25" was developed assuming that the worker is covered by the more restrictive funding limit throughout his or her career. The "Age 35," "Age 45," and "Age 55" columns were developed assuming that the new funding limit was not imposed until the individual had already participated in the plan for 10, 20, and 30 years, respectively.

For the worker who is covered by OBRA87 throughout his or her career, the full funding limits mean that the plan sponsor's contributions to the plan during the first half of the worker's career, until age 45, will be less than if the plan

Table 5.2   **Effects of OBRA87 Full Funding Limits on Contribution Rates for Workers at Ages when Implemented**

Age	Pay ($)	Projected Unit Credit Contribution Rate	Contribution Rates at Various Ages under Funding Limit of 150 Percent of Accrued Benefit			
			Age 25	Age 35	Age 45	Age 55
25	25,000	4.2	0.9	4.2	4.2	4.2
26	26,375	4.3	0.9	4.3	4.3	4.3
27	27,826	4.4	1.0	4.4	4.4	4.4
28	29,356	4.5	1.1	4.5	4.5	4.5
29	30,971	4.6	1.2	4.6	4.6	4.6
30	32,674	4.7	1.4	4.7	4.7	4.7
31	34,471	4.8	1.6	4.8	4.8	4.8
32	36,367	4.9	1.8	4.9	4.9	4.9
33	38,367	5.0	2.0	5.0	5.0	5.0
34	40,477	5.2	2.3	5.2	5.2	5.2
35	42,704	5.3	2.6	0.0	5.3	5.3
36	45,052	5.4	2.9	0.0	5.4	5.4
37	47,530	5.5	3.2	0.0	5.5	5.5
38	50,144	5.7	3.5	0.0	5.7	5.7
39	52,902	5.8	3.9	0.0	5.8	5.8
40	55,812	5.9	4.4	0.0	5.9	5.9
41	58,882	6.1	4.9	0.0	6.1	6.1
42	62,120	6.2	5.4	0.0	6.2	6.2
43	65,537	6.4	6.0	0.0	6.4	6.4
44	69,141	6.5	6.7	1.8	6.5	6.5
45	72,944	6.7	7.4	7.4	0.0	6.7
46	76,956	6.8	8.2	8.2	0.0	6.8
47	81,188	7.0	9.1	9.1	0.0	7.0
48	85,654	7.2	10.0	10.0	0.0	7.2
49	90.365	7.3	11.1	11.1	0.0	7.3
50	95,335	7.5	12.3	12.3	0.0	7.5
51	100,578	7.7	13.5	13.5	1.5	7.7
52	106,110	7.9	15.0	15.0	15.0	7.9
53	111,946	8.1	16.5	16.5	16.5	8.1
54	118,103	8.2	18.2	18.2	18.2	8.2
55	124,599	8.4	16.2	16.2	16.2	0.0
56	131,452	8.6	14.6	14.6	14.6	10.8
57	138,682	8.8	13.4	13.4	13.4	10.5
58	146,309	9.1	12.6	12.6	12.6	10.3
59	154,356	9.3	12.0	12.0	12.0	10.3
60	162,846	9.5	11.5	11.5	11.5	10.2
61	171,802	9.7	11.3	11.3	11.3	10.3
62	181,251	9.9	11.2	11.2	11.2	10.4
63	191,220	10.2	11.1	11.1	11.1	10.5
64	201,737	10.4	11.1	11.1	11.1	10.7

Source: Wyatt Company (1987).

were being funded on an ongoing basis. Of course, lower contributions in the early part of the worker's career mean that contributions in the latter half of the career would have to be higher to fund the promised benefits under the plan. In this particular example, the contribution rate to the plan during the worker's early to mid-fifties would have to be more than twice the contribution rate under the projected unit credit funding method.

For the worker not hit by the contribution limits until he or she is 10 years into the career, the imposition of the contribution limit implies that the employer would have a nine-year contribution holiday when no contributions would be made. In this case, the accrued benefit would have to catch up with the level of funding accomplished early in the career. Again, the contribution rate in the mid-fifties would be more than twice what it was under projected unit credit funding. For the worker not hit until age 45, the contribution holiday would be shorter, but the same general effect of delaying retirement funding would significantly increase late career contribution requirements given the level of promised benefits. Finally, for the worker not hit until age 55 by the new funding limit, the contribution holiday would only be one year, and while contributions during the remaining career would be higher than under projected unit credit funding, the implications are far less significant than in the previous cases.

In 1988, when OBRA87 funding limits took effect, the leading edge of the baby boom generation was 42 years of age. The trailing edge was 24 years of age. The gross effect of OBRA87 is that it has significantly delayed the funding of the baby boom generation's defined-benefit retirement promises. Given the significant numbers of workers falling within the baby boom cohorts of workers, OBRA87 has meant an overall slowdown in pension funding. As this legislation was being considered, The Wyatt Company analyzed its 1986 survey of actuarial assumptions and funding covering 849 plans with more than 1,000 participants to estimate the effects of the new funding limits. They found that 41 percent of the surveyed plans had an accrued benefit security level of 150 percent or greater. All of these plans would have been affected by the new limit and could not have received deductible contributions had the proposed limit been in effect for 1986. For a subset of 664 plans where they could estimate the marginal effects of the new limits, they found that 40 percent would be affected by the new proposal, compared with only 7 percent under prior limits (Wyatt Company 1987, 4).

In its 1987 survey of actuarial assumptions and funding, The Wyatt Company reported that 48 percent of the plans had an accrued benefit security ratio of 150 percent or more. Because plans at this funding level cannot make deductible plan contributions, the percentage of plans overfunded by this measure should decline over time. In its 1992 survey, Wyatt found that 37 percent of large defined-benefit plans still had accrued benefit security ratios of 150 percent or greater (Wyatt Company 1992, 4).

While OBRA87 significantly limited the funding of defined-benefit plans, it was only one piece of legislation out of several that affected the funding of tax-qualified retirement plans after 1982. In 1982, the Tax Equity and Fiscal Responsibility Act (TEFRA) reduced and froze for a period of time the dollar funding and contribution limits for both defined-benefit and defined-contribution plans. TEFRA also established new discrimination tests that had the practical effect of lowering contributions for many plans. The next year, the Deficit Reduction Act extended the freeze in the funding and contribution limits established by TEFRA. The Tax Reform Act of 1986 again reduced and froze funding and contribution limits for tax-qualified plans. Finally, the Omnibus Budget Reconciliation Act of 1993 (OBRA93) included provisions that reduce the level of individual employee's compensation that can be considered in funding and contributing to tax-qualified plans. The practical effects of the OBRA93 provisions will be to further limit the funding of employer-sponsored retirement programs.

Figure 5.2 shows annual employer contributions to private pension and profit-sharing plans dating back to the period just after the end of World War II. There was a gradual increase in contributions up through the early 1970s, and then an escalation in contribution levels as ERISA was passed and implemented. But right around the time that the federal government started passing the various restrictive tax measures affecting employer-sponsored retirement plans, contributions began to decline. By 1990, employer contributions to these plans were about 15 percent below contribution levels in the early 1980s. On an inflation-adjusted basis, contributions in 1990 were at about the same level they had been in 1970, four years before the passage of ERISA.

Most of the pension legislation passed in the past decade has evolved within the context of short-term fiscal considerations. The need to raise revenues to reduce the federal government's deficit has delayed the funding of the baby boom generation's pension benefits with virtually no consideration of the long-term impact on the cost or viability of those benefits. While the Social Security Act established a Board of Trustees to oversee the financial operations of the OASDI programs and requires that the board report to the Congress on the financial and actuarial status of the programs, there is no similar oversight body to identify pending problems with the funded pension system and to warn policymakers about them. Retirement plan sponsors are individually required to disclose the current funding status of their plans on a periodic basis, but the evolving policy focus pushing plan sponsors to fund for only current obligations hardly encourages planning for longer-term contingencies. In the aggregate, public policymakers have completely ignored the long-term implications of tax policy on pension funding in an attempt to minimize the short-term structural imbalances underlying federal fiscal policy. In the following sections of this paper we attempt to lay out a longer-term view of pension funding.

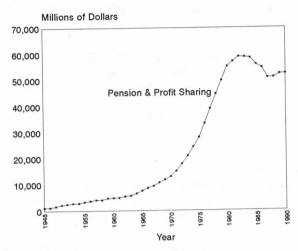

Fig. 5.2   Employer contributions to private pension and profit-sharing plans
Source: National Income and Product Accounts

5.2   Methodology of Current Study

This section gives a brief outline of the underlying methods, assumptions, and inputs that were used to develop the estimates that are presented in the next section of the paper. Projections of the U.S. pension system require a long-term projection of the population and workforce and their respective characteristics. For purposes of this exercise, we were not interested in developing a long-term demographic and labor force projection model. First of all, to develop such a model would have been a more herculean undertaking than we were prepared to commit to in the time frame we had. Second, we felt the nature of the projection we were making might lead to comparisons with the long-term Social Security projections and thought that it would make sense to have the same underlying demographic and workforce characteristics as utilized in developing those projections. Thus we began with the Social Security Administration's 75-year projections of the U.S. population, which gave us estimated numbers of people by single year who had attained ages between 0 and 99 for each of the projection years. We also started with their projections of the workforce in each year, distributed in five-year age cohorts.

We utilized published data and our own computations developed from the Department of Labor's Form 5500 pension reporting forms plus computations from the March 1992 Current Population Survey (CPS) and the 1991 Survey of Income and Program Participation (SIPP) to develop age- and sex-specific participation and vesting in and receipt of benefits from defined-benefit and defined-contribution plans. We developed age- and sex-specific distributions of tenure in current job, which is important for projecting the vesting rates of participants in pension plans. We developed estimates of total wages for the private, state and local, and federal sectors of the economy from data published by the Bureau of Economic Analysis in the National Income and Product Accounts. Estimates of age- and sex-specific pay levels were developed.

We used the Labor Department's Form 5500 files in conjunction with data from the Employee Benefit Research Institute's *Quarterly Pension Investment Report* (QPIR) to estimate the starting total distribution of assets and contributions between defined-benefit and defined-contribution plans. We also used the QPIR data to estimate the distribution of financial assets held by plans across various forms of investments. The resulting distribution of assets by plan type is shown in table 5.3. We are focusing on the private-defined benefit and defined-contribution plans in this paper. We note with interest the relatively large amount of cash and other short-term investments held by these pension funds, despite the long-run nature of the funds themselves. Equities, which have a superb track record over long holding periods, amount to only 36 or 41 percent of the total portfolio. Given historic returns, the pension funds would be better off with a larger stake in stocks. Our assumed real rates of return for the different asset categories are also shown in table 5.3. The numbers are loosely based on the information in Ibbotson (1993), although we are admittedly conservative. Ibbotson reports that the geometric average real rate of return for the Standard and Poor's 500 stock portfolio over the years 1926–92 was 7.0 percent. The corresponding average real rate of return on long-term corporate bonds was 2.3 percent, while it was 0.5 percent for short-term Treasury bills. We do not have any corresponding data for guaranteed investment contracts, which are fixed-income contracts, typically issued by insurance companies, and featuring a somewhat shorter maturity than long bonds. As the

Table 5.3   **Asset Allocation of Pension Plans as of July 1992 (percent)**

Type of Plan	Equities	Bonds	Guaranteed Investment Contracts	Real Estate	Cash
Private defined benefit	36	33	0	15	16
Private defined contribution	41	14	13	6	26
Federal defined benefit	44	44	1	6	5
Federal defined contribution	30	70	0	0	0
State and local defined benefit	44	44	1	6	5
State and local defined contribution	33	49	5	8	5
Real rate of return	5	2	1.2	2	0

Blended real rate for private DB plans: 2.76
Blended real rates for private DC plans: 2.646

Source: For asset allocation, Employee Benefit Research Institute, *Quarterly Pension Investment Report;* for rates of return, authors' assumptions.

reader can see, we have consistently assumed rates of return somewhat below the long-run averages calculated by Ibbotson.

The Social Security population projection was distributed by age, sex, and workforce participation for each year of the projection. Our analysis distributed the workforce into three separate sectors, the private employment sector, the state employment sector, and the federal employment sector. The working population was further distributed by tenure and pension participation status. In each year of the projection, the population and workforce were rolled forward one year with appropriate mortality decrements and workforce adjustments to account for job leavers, entrants, and changers. We had an underlying assumption that there was 14 percent turnover of workers between jobs each year.

The projections were developed separately for private employer plans, state and local defined-benefit plans, and the federal employee thrift plan. In each case, separate projections were developed for defined-benefit and defined-contribution plans and then aggregated. For example, in the case of the projection for the private sector, we estimated that total employer contributions to private plans were 2.8 percent of payroll, approximately 30 percent of which has been going into defined-benefit plans in recent years. Employee contributions to private plans were estimated to be 1.75 percent of payroll, with slightly less than 2 percent of that going to defined-benefit plans. Based on estimates from the Form 5500 files of plans with 100 or more participants, we estimated that employer contributions to defined-contribution plans were 1.13 times employee contributions to those plans.

In the initial year, benefits were estimated from the Form 5500 files and the QPIR data. Going forward, benefits were estimated on the basis of workers being covered by a pension and passing into immediate retirement starting at age 54. At that age, we assumed 3.7 percent of existing workers would retire. By age 80, we assumed all remaining workers would retire. For workers who terminated their employment under a defined-benefit plan, if they were vested we assumed they would be paid a deferred benefit at age 65. The accrual rate of the benefit formula for people working up until retirement calculated out to be 1.25 percent of final salary per year of service on average. For people receiving a deferred benefit it was 1.00 percent of final salary per year of service. For people participating in a defined-contribution plan, we assumed that 40 percent of the workers who terminated prior to retirement would take a lump-sum benefit and use it for some purpose other than meeting their retirement needs. For defined-contribution plans generally, benefits commence at retirement and are paid out as an annuity over a maximum of 30 years.

Future contributions and trust fund accumulations are driven in large part by economic assumptions. Our assumptions on inflation, 4.0 percent per year, and wage growth, 5.1 percent per year, correspond with those used in the Alternative II Social Security projections.

5.3   Projections for the Private Pension System

The current dollar figures of our projections for the combined defined-benefit and defined-contribution private pension plans are shown in table 5.4. Under the assumptions of our forecast, the assets of the total private pension system are shown to continue to grow in nominal terms for the next 60 years. However, this growth is almost continuously slowing. For instance, in 1993 the benefits (payouts) of the defined-benefit and defined-contribution private plans combined are 82.3 percent of total contributions. This means, of course, that there is a net inflow of funds into the total system, even without taking into account the investment return on the $3 trillion asset pool. However, by the year 2006, benefits are projected to be 102.4 percent of contributions, and we expect that aggregate benefits will continue to outstrip contributions for the entire remaining period through 2065. By 2025 benefits are projected to be 163 percent of contributions.

If inflation and asset returns match our assumptions, the value of pension assets will continue to climb, albeit at slowing rates until peaking (in nominal terms) in 2052. In real or relative terms, however, pension assets are projected to peak and begin to fall much earlier. Our model indicates that the ratio of pension assets to total payroll (now at 1.245) will climb modestly until reaching a peak of 1.362 in 2013 and 2014. The ratio is projected to fall after that and drop below 1.0 for the first time in 2038. Real inflation-adjusted pension assets would peak in 2024 with our set of assumptions.

The important story coming from our analysis is that private pensions will gradually cease being the major engine of aggregate saving that they have been for the past 20 years or more. This projected occurrence is shown in figure 5.3. Here we show the total real saving of the private pension system (projected contributions less benefits plus real inflation-adjusted asset returns) relative to the projected total private payroll in the economy for 1992 to 2065. We use total private payroll as the scaling factor simply because it is a readily available by-product of the Social Security forecasting operation. What figure 5.3 shows is that under our assumptions the pension system continues to generate significant investable funds for the American economy for the next 20 years or so. In fact, the decline is very minor for about the next 10 years and then it steepens considerably. By 2024 the pension system is projected to cease being a net source of saving for the economy. In fact, the pension system will then become increasingly a net dissaver. By 2040 the net real dissaving is more than 1.5 percent of payroll, and by 2065 the negative saving is projected to reach almost 4.0 percent of payroll. This change of the pension system from a large net producer of saving to a large absorber of saving or loanable funds will likely have profound implications for interest rates, asset prices, and the growth rate of the economy.

It should be emphasized that the timing of the prediction of the change in

Table 5.4 Combined Private Defined-Benefit and Defined-Contribution Projections

Year	Assets	Benefits	Contributions	Investment Income	Net Inflow	Real Net Inflow	Total Payroll	Saving/Payroll
1992	2,869,606	86,292	105,355	181,452	200,515	85,731	2,313,253	0.03706
1993	3,070,121	92,537	112,479	194,062	214,004	91,199	2,465,286	0.03699
1994	3,284,126	99,252	120,008	207,267	228,023	96,658	2,625,930	0.03681
1995	3,512,149	107,211	127,891	221,313	241,993	101,507	2,794,001	0.03633
1996	3,754,143	115,610	136,183	236,196	256,769	106,603	2,970,726	0.03588
1997	4,010,912	124,926	144,899	252,071	272,044	111,608	3,156,614	0.03536
1998	4,282,957	134,903	154,006	268,813	287,916	116,598	3,351,017	0.03479
1999	4,570,973	144,808	163,563	286,404	305,159	122,320	3,565,269	0.03431
2000	4,876,032	154,379	173,631	304,210	323,462	128,421	3,770,616	0.03406
2001	5,199,494	169,280	184,215	324,054	338,989	131,009	3,997,943	0.03277
2002	5,538,484	182,849	195,147	344,368	356,666	135,127	4,233,018	0.03192
2003	5,895,150	197,579	206,582	366,077	375,080	139,274	4,479,204	0.03109
2004	6,270,231	213,535	218,612	388,881	393,958	143,149	4,738,435	0.03021
2005	6,664,189	231,002	231,308	412,906	413,212	146,644	5,013,158	0.02925
2006	7,077,402	250,492	244,540	437,620	431,668	148,572	5,300,866	0.02803
2007	7,509,070	272,198	258,213	463,764	449,779	149,416	5,598,777	0.02669
2008	7,958,850	295,578	272,447	491,042	467,911	149,557	5,909,334	0.02531
2009	8,426,761	320,357	287,389	519,242	486,274	149,204	6,235,716	0.02393
2010	8,913,036	346,804	303,087	548,865	505,148	148,627	6,580,062	0.02259
2011	9,418,184	375,792	319,368	579,169	522,745	146,018	6,937,680	0.02105
2012	9,940,929	407,643	336,274	610,570	539,201	141,564	7,309,161	0.01937
2013	10,480,130	441,887	353,901	643,137	555,151	135,946	7,695,870	0.01766
2014	11,035,281	477,858	372,472	676,251	570,865	129,454	8,103,981	0.01597
2015	11,606,146	516,572	391,934	709,685	585,047	120,801	8,532,145	0.01416
2016	12,191,193	557,943	412,230	744,651	598,938	111,290	8,977,996	0.01240
2017	12,790,132	601,942	433,550	780,449	612,057	100,452	9,446,231	0.01063

2018	13,402,189	648,802	455,956	817,384	624,538	88,450	9,938,106	0.00890
2019	14,026,726	698,513	479,462	854,776	635,725	74,656	10,453,567	0.00714
2020	14,662,451	751,265	504,115	891,036	643,886	57,388	10,993,210	0.00522
2021	15,306,337	806,645	529,997	930,136	653,488	41,235	11,558,981	0.00357
2022	15,959,825	864,634	557,153	969,236	661,755	23,362	12,151,004	0.00192
2023	16,621,581	925,853	585,757	1,008,436	668,340	3,477	12,774,036	0.00027
2024	17,289,921	989,525	615,875	1,047,991	674,341	−17,256	13,429,026	−0.00128
2025	17,964,262	1,055,792	647,722	1,087,816	679,746	−38,824	14,121,320	−0.00275
2026	18,644,009	1,125,128	681,415	1,127,603	683,890	−61,870	14,852,756	−0.00417
2027	19,327,899	1,197,367	717,166	1,167,947	687,746	−85,370	15,627,696	−0.00546
2028	20,015,646	1,271,896	755,176	1,206,796	690,076	−110,550	16,451,511	−0.00672
2029	20,705,722	1,349,723	795,427	1,247,233	692,937	−135,292	17,324,066	−0.00781
2030	21,398,659	1,430,323	837,850	1,286,751	694,278	−161,668	18,243,015	−0.00886
2031	22,092,937	1,512,302	882,678	1,326,998	697,374	−186,343	19,212,820	−0.00970
2032	22,790,312	1,597,600	930,321	1,365,657	698,378	−213,234	20,244,774	−0.01053
2033	23,488,690	1,685,872	980,469	1,405,971	700,568	−238,980	21,329,161	−0.01120
2034	24,189,257	1,778,429	1,033,426	1,444,936	699,933	−267,637	22,476,016	−0.01191
2035	24,889,191	1,875,903	1,089,114	1,482,187	695,398	−300,170	23,683,343	−0.01267
2036	25,584,589	1,977,573	1,147,554	1,519,897	689,878	−333,506	24,948,948	−0.01337
2037	26,274,467	2,082,637	1,209,295	1,554,827	681,485	−369,494	26,286,980	−0.01406
2038	26,955,952	2,192,273	1,274,318	1,588,186	670,231	−408,007	27,696,937	−0.01473
2039	27,626,183	2,306,337	1,342,526	1,624,502	660,691	−444,356	29,176,895	−0.01523
2040	28,286,875	2,426,835	1,413,861	1,659,771	646,797	−484,678	30,725,273	−0.01577
2041	28,933,672	2,552,646	1,488,587	1,693,501	629,442	−527,905	32,348,308	−0.01632
2042	29,563,114	2,686,159	1,566,938	1,724,462	605,241	−577,284	34,051,585	−0.01695

(continued)

Table 5.4 (continued)

Year	Assets	Benefits	Contributions	Investment Income	Net Inflow	Real Net Inflow	Total Payroll	Saving/Payroll
2043	30,168,355	2,828,664	1,648,874	1,754,856	575,066	−631,668	35,833,093	−0.01763
2044	30,743,421	2,979,900	1,734,528	1,782,782	537,410	−692,327	37,693,201	−0.01837
2045	31,280,831	3,139,932	1,823,985	1,806,726	490,779	−760,454	39,643,201	−0.01918
2046	31,771,610	3,308,622	1,917,650	1,827,904	436,932	−833,932	41,681,502	−0.02001
2047	32,208,542	3,487,113	2,015,964	1,844,202	373,053	−915,289	43,820,980	−0.02089
2048	32,581,595	3,675,560	2,119,188	1,856,193	299,821	−1,003,443	46,067,832	−0.02178
2049	32,881,416	3,875,283	2,227,452	1,863,022	215,191	−1,100,006	48,425,244	−0.02272
2050	33,096,607	4,087,847	2,340,741	1,865,432	118,326	−1,205,538	50,891,965	−0.02369
2051	33,214,933	4,312,374	2,459,466	1,862,594	9,686	−1,318,911	53,475,702	−0.02466
2052	33,224,620	4,548,513	2,584,327	1,853,173	−111,013	−1,439,998	56,192,914	−0.02563
2053	33,113,607	4,798,158	2,715,652	1,835,601	−246,905	−1,571,449	59,050,927	−0.02661
2054	32,866,701	5,062,265	2,853,699	1,807,621	−400,945	−1,715,613	62,055,455	−0.02765
2055	32,465,756	5,344,679	2,998,678	1,765,939	−580,062	−1,878,692	65,211,909	−0.02881
2056	31,885,693	5,641,642	3,150,628	1,716,488	−774,526	−2,049,954	68,512,928	−0.02992
2057	31,111,167	5,950,656	3,311,404	1,650,758	−988,494	−2,232,941	72,009,968	−0.03101
2058	30,122,673	6,274,655	3,480,657	1,570,040	−1,223,958	−2,428,865	75,689,196	−0.03209
2059	28,898,715	6,615,627	3,659,028	1,469,293	−1,487,306	−2,643,255	79,566,775	−0.03322
2060	27,411,408	6,972,036	3,846,599	1,363,427	−1,762,010	−2,858,466	83,640,683	−0.03418
2061	25,649,398	7,347,019	4,044,539	1,220,242	−2,082,238	−3,108,214	87,942,578	−0.03534
2062	23,567,160	7,741,093	4,252,689	1,074,337	−2,414,067	−3,356,753	92,463,750	−0.03630
2063	21,153,092	8,152,261	4,472,002	891,500	−2,788,759	−3,634,883	97,230,372	−0.03738
2064	18,364,332	8,584,350	4,702,640	689,624	−3,192,086	−3,926,659	102,242,424	−0.03841
2065	15,172,245	9,037,520	4,945,204	462,211	−3,630,105	−4,236,995	107,513,489	−0.03941

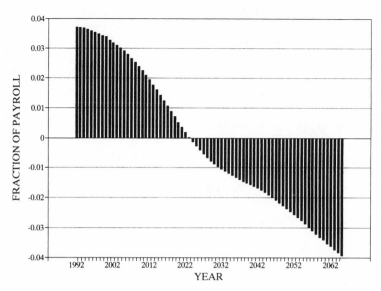

Fig. 5.3   Real saving of private pensions relative to total private payroll, 1992–2065

pensions from a net buyer of assets to a net seller is very sensitive to our assumptions about the rates of return earned on pension investments as well as to the assumed level of pension contributions. However, we feel that the pattern of figure 5.3 is almost inevitable; only the timing could be somewhat different than pictured. If investment returns exceed our fairly conservative assumptions, then the decline of the saving contribution of pensions will be delayed in time. Still, the demographic structure is such that the decline will by necessity occur. Higher investment returns would result in more saving in the early years and even more dissaving in the later years of our analysis. It is not even correct to think of the dissaving as a negative development. After all, pension assets are accumulated to provide the resources needed by the elderly in retirement. It is only natural that when we have an extraordinarily large number of retirees, the real assets of the private pension system will shrink and the system will at least temporarily cease to be a source of new investment funds for the economy.

One concern that all of this may raise is the impact on the prices of pension assets, mainly stocks and bonds. We share that concern to some degree but cannot predict the size or timing of any effect. One thing to note in this regard is that, while the pension system will become a less important purchaser of securities, it will not become a net seller for quite a while. As noted earlier, our model predicts that benefits will first exceed contributions in 2006. However, at that point the annual investment income (dividends, interest, and capital gains) on the $7 trillion dollar portfolio should approximate $450 billion in nominal terms and $170 billion in real terms. Needless to say, there would be no reason to be net sellers of assets at that point in time, and in fact, we would suppose that pensions will still be accumulating assets then. The period of time when the pension system begins to be a net seller is more likely in the early part of the third decade of the next century under our conservative assumptions. This could depress asset prices, particularly since the demographic structure of the United States does not differ that greatly from those of Japan and Europe, which also will have large elderly populations at that time. Another comment about the asset price effect is that if it occurs, it would likely affect all long-term assets. What we think may happen is high real interest rates that could depress the prices of stocks, bonds, land, and real estate. While this might suggest that a good investment for this period would be short-term Treasury bills, the effect if it occurs is likely to be gradual and to last for decades. In the twentieth century the longest stretch of time over which Treasury bills outperformed equities was about 15 years. We have little else to go on, but we certainly are not advocating that long-term investors invest in short-term instruments to ride out this demographic tidal wave. In fact, it is our opinion that far too many people invest in short-term instruments for long-term accumulations.

With our assumptions, the private defined-benefit plans are the ones that experience net outflows (dissaving) the earliest. These plans are already in a situation where benefits exceed contributions. In fact, benefits are roughly three times contributions. The robust investment returns of the past decade or so have permitted this and in fact forced it to be true. If investment returns drop to our conservative figures and if firms contribute a total of 2.8 percent of payroll to pension plans, then the real assets of the defined-benefit plans begin to fall immediately. Defined-benefit pension assets (which are now 88 percent of the total payroll in the economy) would fall to 77 percent of total payroll by 2000, 66 percent by 2010, and 42.5 percent by 2025. The net flow of funds into the defined-benefit plans (or savings) would be positive, but only in nominal terms. Even nominal defined-benefit saving becomes negative by 2025, and the entire stock of defined-benefit plan assets would be exhausted by 2043.

It is important to note that this is not a forecast of doom for the defined-benefit plans; it is simply a "what if" exercise. If by magic our rate of return assumptions proved to be precisely accurate, then employers would be forced to increase their pension contributions above the 2.8 percent of aggregate payroll that we have assumed or to curtail the pension benefits they offer workers. While vested benefits of existing workers cannot be cut, certainly the accrual of new benefits can be reduced by changes in the plan design. This tough choice of higher costs or lower pension benefits would occur long before the 2043 date when the model says that the assets of defined-benefit plans would be exhausted. Government regulators and pension actuaries would sound the alarm, hopefully decades before the forecast could come true. The problem may become apparent and the tough choice may have to be faced very early in the next century. One concern we have is that employers may have gotten used to the very low contributions that many of them have had to make to defined-benefit plans in recent years thanks to the extraordinary performance of financial markets. When they face the higher long-run funding costs of their pension plans under more normal return realizations, they may choose to curtail the benefits that they offer. It is also possible that just about the time this is being resolved, we as a society will have to acknowledge that Social Security is not in long-run equilibrium; once again, the choice will be to either raise taxes or lower benefits. In this sense, both Social Security and the funded private defined-benefit pension system will likely face cost pressure to scale back retirement benefits.

Under our assumptions, the outlook for the defined-contribution plans is decidedly more optimistic. Our model shows defined-contribution plan assets growing relative to economy-wide aggregates over the next 30 years or so and then stabilizing at the relatively larger level. Again using total economy-wide private payroll as our scaling factor, defined-contribution assets are now about 37 percent of one year's payroll. We project those assets will climb to 52 percent of private payroll by 2000, to 70 percent by 2010, and to level out at about 85 percent for 2025 and beyond. The defined-contribution system is much less susceptible to "running out of assets," and indeed, we do not project any such occurrence. The private defined-contribution system would be a modest net source of saving in the economy even in the period with the maximum number of baby boom retirees.

5.4   Conclusions

The major result of this paper is that the national saving generated by the private pension system can be expected to decline from current levels, gradually for about a decade, and then far more steeply. With our set of conservative assumptions about the rate of return earned by pension assets, the pension system would cease to be a source of saving roughly in 2024. It is our opinion that this will indeed happen, although there is considerable uncertainty about the timing of the event.

We also find that the defined-benefit portion of the private pension system faces a tough choice. Our model shows that the system would run out of money in 2043 if it were funded according to our assumptions and if rates of return were consistent with those we have projected. The running-out-of-money part of our story will not happen. However, what the model is implicitly predicting is that either corporate pension contributions will have to be substantially raised or pension plans will have to be scaled back. It is highly unlikely that the current low contribution rates, caused by the high realized rates of return on financial assets over the past decade, can be sustained.

We briefly speculated about the impact of the reduced saving of the pension system on asset prices. Even though we do not think the change will be as dramatic as our model predicts (due to adjustments in contributions and plan design), we still feel that the demographic structure is such that a major change in pension saving will occur. The timing and magnitude of the effect on asset prices is impossible to determine. Capital markets are worldwide, interest rates are determined by both supply and demand, and forecasts of financial rates of return some 30 or more years into the future are futile. However, the population bulge that we call the baby boom caused considerable strain on the U.S. education system in the 1950s and 1960s. Absorbing those people into the workforce was a challenge in the 1970s and early 1980s and may have been a factor in slowing the growth in worker productivity. It is probably safe to say that the same numerous cohort will strain the economic system once again during their retirement years, roughly 2010 to 2050.

References

Ballantyne, Harry C. 1983. Long-range projections of Social Security Trust Fund operations in dollars. *Actuarial Notes* (Social Security Administration), no. 117 (October): 2.

Board of Trustees of the Federal OASDI Trust Funds. 1993. *The 1993 annual report.* Washington, D.C.: U.S. Department of Health and Human Services, Social Security Administration.

Ibbotson Associates. 1993. *Stocks, bonds, bills and inflation, 1993 yearbook: Market results for 1926–1992.* Chicago: Ibbotson Associates.

U.S. Bureau of the Census. 1975. *Historical statistics of the United States: Colonial times to 1970.* bicentennial ed. pt. 1. Washington, D.C.: U.S. Government Printing Office.

———. 1991. *Statistical abstract of the United States,* 111th ed. Washington, D.C.: U.S. Government Printing Office.

Wyatt Company. 1987. *The compensation and benefits file,* vol. 3, no. 11. Washington, D.C.: Wyatt Company, November.

———. 1992. *Survey of actuarial assumptions and funding, 1992.* Washington, D.C.: Wyatt Company.

6   The Effects of Aging on National Saving and Asset Accumulation in Japan

Naoto Yamauchi

6.1   Introduction

This paper investigates the effects of population aging on saving behavior and asset accumulation in Japan. There are a lot of empirical studies on the relationship between population aging and household saving behavior, and most economists and policymakers believe that aging has and will lower the household saving rate to some extent. The precise magnitude is still open to question, however.

I shed light on fluctuations in the national saving rate as a whole, as well as in the household and private saving rates. Reasons for emphasizing national saving are as follows. Japan has a huge trade surplus at the moment, and this external balance (or imbalance) is, by the definition of national account, a mirror image of the internal saving-investment balance. It is obvious that national saving has a closer link to the external balance than the savings of individual sectors. Moreover, if households view their saving plans through the corporate and government veils, so that household saving is not independent from corporate and government savings, it makes sense to focus on national saving rather than sectoral saving.

National saving is important not only because it is a source of investment and one of the major determinants of macroeconomic growth but also because it is closely related to the demand for financial and real assets, and it may well affect asset price formation. For instance, how does saving through employer-sponsored private pension funds affect the saving behavior of individual sec-

Naoto Yamauchi is associate professor of economics at Osaka School of International Public Policy, Osaka University.

The author would like to acknowledge numerous comments from participants at the NBER/JCER conference. He especially appreciates the helpful comments of Noriyoshi Oguchi. He is also grateful to Naosumi Atoda for providing a compiled data file of the Family Savings Survey.

tors, the national saving rate, and the demand for various assets? Since private pension funds have become major institutional investors, it is extremely important to know the potential impacts of the future decumulation of pension funds as population aging proceeds.

The paper is organized as follows. Section 6.2 gives an overview of fluctuations of national saving in Japan, and the relationship between aggregate saving rates—either household or national—and demographic variables is examined. Sections 6.3 and 6.4 discuss the effects of population aging on household saving rates and corporate and government saving rates, respectively. I try to decompose the System of National Accounts (SNA) basis for national and sectoral savings consistently into saving by age group or cohort, in order to clarify who (which age cohort) saves and who dissaves. By examining saving rates in this way, I hope to clarify the relationship between population aging and fluctuations of national saving. Section 6.5 focuses on saving through employer-sponsored pension plans, with statistical comparisons between Japan and the United States. Section 6.6 offers a brief conclusion.

6.2 Population Aging and National Saving

6.2.1 Fluctuations of National Saving

National saving consists of household saving, corporate saving, and government saving. Figure 6.1 shows yearly fluctuations in the national saving rate and individual sector saving rates, all defined as ratios to national disposable income. The household saving rate, which is the most familiar to us, increased gradually in the 1960s and increased rapidly during the first half of the 1970s, but since the mid-1970s it has been declining gradually.

The national saving rate, on the other hand, increased until around 1970, but after rather sharp drops in the first half of the 1970s, it did not fluctuate much during the 1970s and the 1980s. The difference between the changing patterns of the household saving rate and the national saving rate is, by definition, explained by fluctuations in corporate and government saving rates. In particular, a sharp increase in the government saving rate more or less offset the decrease in the household saving rate in the 1980s.

6.2.2 Demographic Factors and Saving Rates

Many theoretical and empirical studies have tried to explain fluctuations in the household saving rate, and a number of possible explanations have been identified for the high saving rates up to the mid-1970s and for the recent declining trend.[1] Possible explanations of the high saving rates include the bonus payment system, unavailability of consumer credit, the low level of social secu-

---

1. A comprehensive survey of various explanations for Japan's high household saving rate can be found in Horioka (1990).

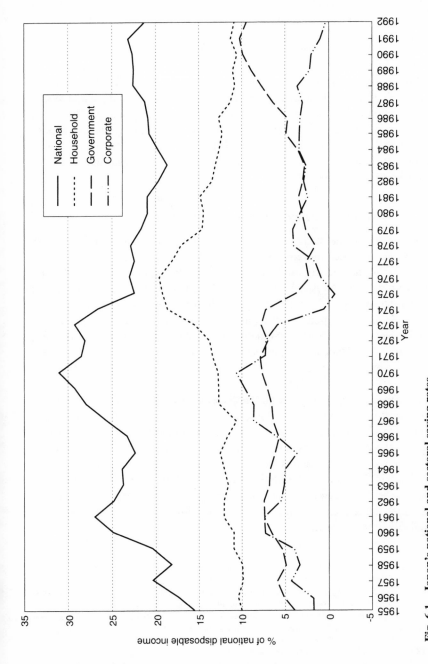

Fig. 6.1 Japan's national and sectoral saving rates
Source: Economic Planning Agency, *Annual Report on National Accounts* (Tokyo: Government Printing Office, various years).

rity benefits, the low level of asset accumulation, the high cost of housing, high economic growth, and the high ratio of working to total population. The recent decline in the saving rate can be explained by reversals of some of these factors.

Some economists emphasize population aging to explain the recent decline of the household saving rate. How do demographic factors affect saving rates? Using conventional time-series regression analysis, Horioka (1991) showed that the coefficient of the demographic variable was larger in the national saving equation than in the private and household saving equations. This result implies that corporate saving and government saving are more sensitive to population aging than household saving is. If this is the case, it may be quite misleading to look at only household saving when investigating the effects of aging on saving behavior.[2]

6.3   Household Saving and Asset Accumulation

According to the standard life-cycle model of saving, people save when young, dissave after retirement, and die without wealth. On the other hand, according to the dynasty model of saving, parents and children are linked by altruistic motives. As Auerbach, Cai, and Kotlikoff (1991) show, the national saving rate is higher for the dynasty (or altruistic family) model than for the life-cycle model. Which model is more applicable to Japan? Several eminent studies have been published. Some of them support the life-cycle model, but many found evidence that fails to support this model.

6.3.1   Data of Cohort Saving

I use the Family Savings Survey (FSS), or Chochiku Doko Chosa, to answer this question. There are several statistics in the survey, including saving data divided by different age groups. The FSS data set is better than other statistics, such as the Family Income and Expenditure Survey (FIES), or Kakei Chosa, in several ways. First, figures for the saving of self-employed households are available in the FSS, but not in the FIES. Second, the FSS saving figures are likely to be more accurate because they are calculated from reported assets and liabilities rather than from income and expenditure.[3] Moreover, FSS data are available for every year.

2. When I regressed national and household saving rate equations on the demographic factor, the ratio of the elderly to the total population in this case, the estimated coefficients on the elderly population ratio were significantly negative when variables that represent asset holding were omitted. However, when the asset variables were included as explanatory variables, the ratio of the elderly population became insignificant. This behavior reflects serious multicollinearity between the demographic and asset variables. Therefore, it is fair to conclude that population aging may lower saving rates, but the results of time-series regression are not robust and the relationship between aging and saving rates may not be straightforward.

3. The FSS asks respondents about outstanding financial wealth at the end of the calendar year and at the end of the year before, and about transactions involving houses and land throughout the year.

It is worth noting that the definition of the FSS saving rate is different from that of the SNA saving rate. There are several technical differences, for instance, the treatment of imputed rent for owner-occupied housing and transfers in kind, such as medical services and public education. I would like to point out two more factors. First, the FSS saving rate is defined as the net increase in the value of assets held divided by annual income. Net increase includes not only the acquisition of financial and real assets, but also capital gains and losses from financial assets (but not real assets) that accrue in a year. The SNA saving rate, however, does not include capital gains and losses. We might interpret the FSS household saving rate as indirectly reflecting the corporate saving rate, if corporate saving in the form of retained profits raises the stock prices of a company and shareholders' asset value.

Second, the SNA saving rate is net of depreciation, whereas the FSS saving rate is a gross saving rate in the sense that it includes capital consumption or depreciation. Therefore, FSS saving is comparable to SNA gross saving, which is the sum of net saving plus depreciation of the household sector.

Figure 6.2 shows that the amount of aggregate household saving based on the FSS gives a good approximation of the amount of SNA gross saving. The differences in movement between the two saving rates reflect the difference in definitions. The FSS saving rate went up in the first half of the 1970s and in the second half of the 1980s. This probably was caused by asset price inflation during these periods.

Fig. 6.2   SNA and FSS gross saving rates
Source: Author's calculation from Economic Planning Agency, *Annual Report on National Accounts* (Tokyo: Government Printing Office, various years) and the FSS.

6.3.2   Saving and Asset Accumulation of the Elderly

According to the FSS, the saving rate of all households ("all" includes self-employed) in 1980–92 period was on average 19.4 percent of annual income. This statistic can be broken down by age of household head. The age distribution of household saving is shown in table 6.1. The saving rate for households with heads aged 65 or older was 16.3 percent, lower than the average, but still positive. The saving rates of households with heads aged 60–64 or 55–59 were slightly higher than the average. In the 1970s the saving rate of households with heads aged 65 or older was even higher than the average.

These facts show that households headed by the elderly do not dissave or decumulate their wealth substantially. This apparently contradicts the life-cycle model of saving. Do elderly households really continue to accumulate wealth? A longitudinal survey is necessary to test this precisely, but such a survey is virtually unavailable in Japan. So instead we used published cross-sectional age-wealth profiles. The National Survey of Family Income and Expenditure (NSFIE), or Zenkoku Shohi Jittai Chosa, and the FSS supply tabulations of this kind. Table 6.2 shows cross-sectional age-wealth profiles in 1992 from the FSS. It shows that households with older heads tended to be wealthier in terms of the current value of financial assets.

However, table 6.2 does not show time-series or cohort age-wealth profiles. I compiled "pseudo"-cohort data on age-wealth profiles by tracking published cross-sectional age-wealth data from annual reports of the FSS. The cohort age-wealth profiles show that the Japanese household continues to accumulate wealth until at least age 65. For example, figure 6.3 shows how personal wealth is accumulated in households where the head was born in 1924. This upward-sloping profile may be exaggerated by the asset price inflation of the second half of the 1980s. However, the age-wealth profiles for households with heads born in years other than 1924 also show clear upward-sloping curves, and these profiles do not include the asset inflation period of the late 1980s. Therefore, the pattern of asset accumulation by Japanese households is quite different from that in the United States.

As Hayashi, Ando, and Ferris (1988) pointed out, there may be some sample

Table 6.1   FSS Saving Rates by Age of Household Head (percent)

Years	Average	–24	25–29	30–34	35–39	40–44	45–49	50–54	55–59	60–64	65+
1970–74	25.7	27.4	19.1	22.8	26.2	27.0	24.8	19.9	30.1	33.3	28.9
1975–79	22.8	5.8	16.9	22.5	23.9	23.0	22.1	21.3	28.9	21.1	24.6
1980–84	17.6	9.7	15.0	16.9	18.4	18.1	16.4	16.9	20.6	18.5	16.2
1985–89	19.8	8.4	14.6	20.7	21.6	21.1	17.6	18.4	22.5	23.3	15.8
1990–92	21.8	1.9	15.0	19.1	19.5	22.5	24.1	22.0	22.0	28.7	17.0
1970–79	24.2	16.6	18.0	22.7	25.1	25.0	23.5	20.6	29.5	27.2	26.8
1980–92	19.4	7.4	14.9	18.9	19.9	20.3	18.6	18.6	21.7	22.7	16.3

Source: FSS data.

Table 6.2 **Composition of Household Financial Wealth by Age of Household Head, 1992**

Financial Asset	−24	24–29	30–34	35–39	40–44	45–49	50–54	55–59	60–64	65+	Total
Total outstanding (1,000 yen)	1,596	4,182	6,739	7,114	10,635	13,841	14,126	19,146	20,825	23,414	14,654
				Composition (percent)							
Demand deposits	19.6	14.8	7.8	8.4	6.9	6.2	6.5	5.8	5.7	6.1	6.4
Time deposits	45.1	39.9	44.7	41.3	47.3	43.7	42.1	43.2	51.3	46.7	45.6
Life Insurance, etc.	26.3	30.7	29.6	34.5	30.3	28.5	30.4	22.9	21.5	16.6	24.4
Corporate equities	0.0	2.2	5.7	5.8	5.4	9.1	8.0	17.8	8.6	14.6	10.9
Bonds	0.0	0.8	1.5	1.5	1.4	1.8	2.1	1.1	2.9	4.0	2.4
Unit and open-end trust	0.0	0.0	1.9	0.6	1.0	1.8	1.7	1.4	1.9	1.8	1.6
Open-end bond trust	7.1	1.1	1.1	0.8	1.1	1.7	0.7	0.9	1.1	1.1	1.1
Loan trust and money in trust	0.0	1.2	1.6	2.7	2.8	3.6	4.8	4.2	5.2	7.3	4.8
Total	100.0	100.0	100.0	100.0	100.0	100.0	100.0	100.0	100.0	100.0	100.0

Source: FSS data.

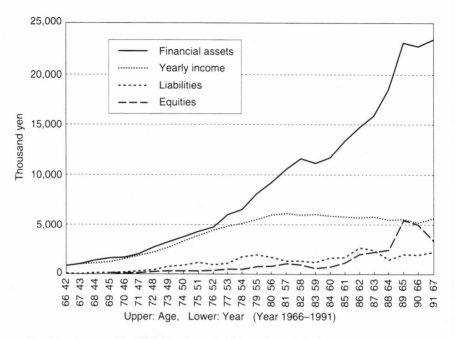

Fig. 6.3   Age-wealth profile for household head born in 1924
Source: Author's calculation from the FSS.

selection biases due to the fact that elderly household heads tend to be wealthier than the elderly living in extended families. They compared the saving rate of the nuclear family with that of the extended family and estimated that the elderly in extended families are likely to continue to save and accumulate wealth until around age 80–84. We expect that similar reasoning is applicable to the FSS, but this has not yet been confirmed. Hayashi et al. also found that U.S. households after retirement dissave on average approximately one-third of their peak wealth by the time of death.

6.3.3   Decomposition of Household Saving by Age Cohorts

The annual saving of the household sector as a whole is the sum of the savings of all age groups. It is not very difficult to decompose household saving by age group. The annual household saving of each age group multiplied by the number of households gives the total saving of each age group. Figure 6.4 shows the results of these calculations. For example, in the period 1990–92, households headed by the elderly, aged 65 or older, saved 8.9 percent of total household savings, whereas households with heads aged 60–64 accounted for 12.8 percent.

The share of saving contributed by older households (with household heads aged 50 or older) increased gradually in the 1970s and 1980s. On the other hand, households with younger household heads (say, up to age 40) have made

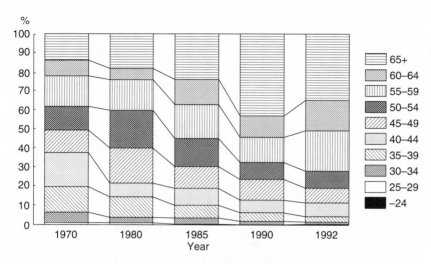

Fig. 6.4   Decomposition of FSS household saving by age of household head

smaller and smaller contributions as time goes on. This more or less reflects population aging in Japan, or in this case the aging of household heads. We can estimate the exact impact of population aging on the aggregate household saving rate from these data.

6.3.4   Role of Intergenerational Transfers

The typical elderly household in Japan continues to accumulate wealth, rather than decumulate it as the standard life-cycle theory implies. Thus a huge amount of wealth is transferred from parents to children by means of bequests. For example, Barthold and Ito (1992) estimated the volume of transferred wealth from published tax statistics and concluded that in Japan at least one-third of household wealth is transferred wealth rather than life-cycle wealth.

The motive for inter vivos transfers may be purely altruistic or a kind of implicit contract between parents and children. If the elderly rarely decumulate their wealth, the macroeconomic impact of aging on the household saving rate may not be large.

6.4   Corporate and Government Savings

6.4.1   Household Saving and National Saving

There have been a number of studies on the relationship between aging and saving rates. Although most previous studies cover only the household saving rate, it is also important to investigate how the aging of the population affects national saving. A reason behind this is that a household may decide its saving rate taking into account the saving rates of firms and the government (see Hayashi 1992, e.g.), or in other words, households may see their saving plans through the corporate and government veils. A review of past studies shows that, while there is a fairly clear negative correlation between household and corporate saving rates, the correlation between household and government saving rates is not so clear.[4]

6.4.2 Who Claims Corporate Wealth?

Who has the final right to use corporate wealth, which is the sum of past corporate saving? This is, in some sense, the same as the question: Who owns the corporate firm? There are several possible answers.

First, employees may own their corporate savings. This is plausible particularly in Japan, where the seniority wage profile and severance payment system still prevail. If firms, rather than their employees, save, because of the sharply rising wage-age profile this corporate saving is just preparation for future wage expenditure. This kind of corporate saving represents an increase in the claim by employees on the firm. In this case, the stock price of the firm will not go up even if the firm accumulates wealth since investors know that the wealth ultimately belongs to the employees.

On the other hand, if corporate saving does not reflect seniority wage profiles, then we can assume that stockholders ultimately own the incorporated enterprises and that they have claims on corporate savings and assets.

It is not easy to determine which of these conjectures is closest to the real world. The real world may in fact be a mixture of these. In this section I assume as a first approximation that corporate savings are ultimately owned by shareholders. Corporate equities held by other firms can be ignored because these claims on corporate savings are canceled out by cross-holding of shares. Thus, it is reasonable to allocate corporate savings to individual shareholders according to the number of equities held.

I decomposed aggregate corporate saving for specific years into savings by various age groups proportional to the share of equities held by households. The age distribution of shareholders is available from the FSS. Figure 6.5 shows the age distribution of equities and unit and open-end trusts for various years. Since the elderly tend to be wealthier in terms of asset holdings and tend to have a larger proportion of corporate equities in their portfolios, the holding of corporate equities is highly concentrated among the elderly. For example, households with heads aged 65 or older have 33.4 percent of the total value of

---

4. I estimated simple household saving rate equations using corporate and government savings and household disposable income as explanatory variables. If households decide their saving behavior taking government and corporate savings into account, the signs of the coefficients on corporate and government savings should be negative. While the coefficients on corporate saving are negative as predicted by the theory, the coefficients on government saving are positive, which contradicts the theory. This implies that households see through the corporate veil (at least partly), but not through the government veil.

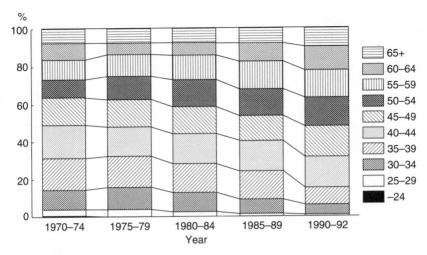

Fig. 6.5   Composition of shareholding by age of household head
Source: Author's calculation from the FSS.

stocks. Households aged 55 and older have about 70 percent of the total. Figure 6.5 also shows that the share of corporate equities held by households with heads aged 65 or older increased drastically from just over 10 percent in 1970 to approximately one-third in 1992.

6.4.3   Aging and Government Saving

Government saving is defined as revenue minus consumption expenditure. Thus, the government surplus is defined as government saving minus capital formation.

In the SNA, general government is divided into three subsectors: the central government, local government, and the social security funds. Thus, the saving of general government is the sum of the savings of the three subsectors.

Figure 6.6 shows the fluctuations in the saving rates of these subsectors, defined as ratios to national disposable income. The saving rate of the central government went negative after 1975, just after the first oil crisis, because of the contraction of tax revenue and the failure to cut government expenditure. But the deficit became smaller and the saving rate of this sector finally became positive in 1987. The saving rate of local government has expanded gradually since 1975 and has accounted for nearly 4 percent of national disposable income in recent years. The saving rate of the social security funds also has increased gradually; it reached more than 3 percent in 1991.

Who contributes to government saving in a specific year? Who dissaves government wealth? An answer is easiest to find for the social security funds.

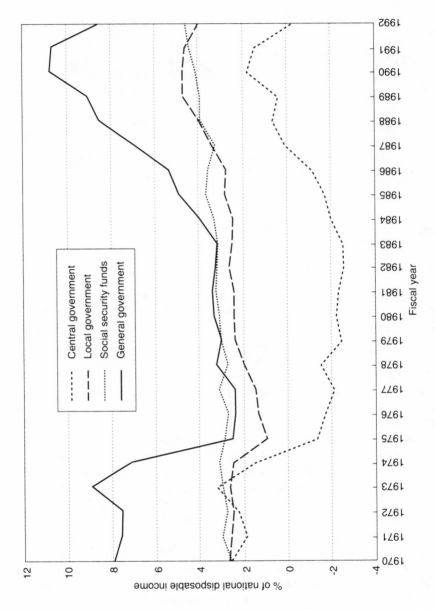

Fig. 6.6 Japan's government saving rates by institutional sector
Source: Economic Planning Agency, *Annual Report on National Accounts* (Tokyo: Government Printing Office, various years).

People of working age make positive contributions, whereas retired people, aged 65 or over, make negative contributions to these savings.

The tax burden for a specific age cohort can be estimated in a similar way. However, it may be difficult to estimate an age-cohort decomposition for government expenditure. Moreover, it is difficult to decompose future government saving by age cohort because we have to predict future government tax and expenditure policies almost perfectly to do so. But we could apply the generational accounting method developed by Kotlikoff and others (see, e.g., Kotlikoff 1992; Auerbach, Gokhale, and Kotlikoff 1991). It would be fruitful for examining the relationship between population aging and government saving, as well as for the evaluation of various policies.

6.4.4 Aging and the Social Security Funds

Two major components of the social security funds are the public pension system and the medical care program. Japan's public pension system consists of several different programs. The balance of the income-expenditure account of the social security funds reflects the balances of all individual programs. Currently, the social security funds have a fairly large surplus (positive savings) and accumulated wealth. However, we can reasonably predict that savings and wealth will decrease and eventually become negative as a result of the rapid aging of the population. Quite a few studies estimate in various ways intergenerational redistribution by means of the public pension system. The internal rates of return of public pensions have been calculated for various age cohorts. Takayama et al. (1990) calculated public pension wealth and the amount of intergenerational transfers using the microdata set from the NSFIE.

We can investigate how much population aging and some possible program reforms (changes of eligible age, rate of contribution, standard of benefit payments, etc.) affect the accounting balance of the social security funds. It is useful to calculate the positive and negative contributions by age group. It is almost certain that population aging will cause a sharp increase in medical care costs. In fact, medical care costs for the elderly are much higher than the average for all age groups. As for the public pension, we can estimate which age cohorts make positive or negative contributions to the medical care balance sheet.

Since the saving of the social security funds will eventually be distributed to the household sector at some time in the future, this saving may have a clearer correlation with household saving than does general government saving.[5]

---

5. To test this, I estimated the household saving rate equations with the saving of the social security funds as one of the explanatory variables. The results show that the estimated coefficient is not significant, just like the coefficient for government saving as a whole. This implies that households do not necessarily take the accumulation of wealth in the social security funds into account in deciding their own saving rate.

6.5   Saving through Private Pension Plans

6.5.1   Development of Employer-Sponsored Pension Plans

In this section, I explore the impact of the development of employer-sponsored or occupational pension funds on national saving and capital markets. Saving through private pension funds has become more and more important in both the United States and Japan.

In the United States, private pension fund assets amounted to $2.3 trillion at the end of 1992. In Japan the one-time severance payment used to be more popular than payment in the form of a pension. Occupational pension plans, however, have recently become an important instrument of saving for retirement. Two major occupational pension schemes are tax-qualified pensions (TQP), or the Tekikaku Nenkin, and semipublic employee pension funds (EPF), or the Kosei Nenkin Kikin.

The TQP scheme was founded in 1962 to replace the traditional severance payment system, whereas the EPF scheme was founded in 1966 to increase the standard of pension payment by combining employer-sponsored private pensions with public employee pensions. In 1992, there were 1,474 EPFs and 86,766 TQPs, covering 31 million employees, or approximately 60 percent of all private sector employees. The amount of accumulated wealth in various private pension funds has increased rapidly. The total amount of wealth accumulated by private pension funds was nearly 50 trillion yen at the end of fiscal 1992. For both EPFs and TQPs, life insurance companies and trust banks are responsible for fund management. Table 6.3 shows this upward trend.

The relative importance of pension fund reserves in household balance sheets is much smaller in Japan than in the United States. Table 6.4 shows this. In the United States, pension fund reserves were 21.4 percent of total household net wealth and 28.3 percent of household financial assets at the end of 1992. In Japan, outstanding employer-sponsored pension wealth was only 2.2 percent of net worth and 4.8 percent of financial assets.

6.5.2   Composition of Pension Wealth

The asset allocation of U.S. private pension funds is quite different from that of Japanese funds. Approximately 50 percent of the financial assets of U.S. pension funds are invested in corporate equities and mutual fund shares (see table 6.5). In Japan, approximately 25 percent of accumulated pension trust wealth is in corporate equities. The share of corporate equities increased gradually beginning in 1971, when the share of equities was only 6 percent. During the same time the share of loans decreased drastically, from 79 percent in 1970 to 14 percent in 1992.

Asset allocation is restricted by various regulations. In the case of Japan's pension trusts, risk-free assets (in the sense that the principal should be maintained) should account for 50 percent or more of total wealth. Moreover, do-

Table 6.3   **Accumulated Private Pension Wealth in Japan (billion yen and percent)**

End of Fiscal Year	Tax-Qualified Plans	Employee Pension Funds	Total Pension Wealth	Percentage of Household Financial Wealth	Net Yearly Increase	Percentage of Household Saving
1965	19	0	19	0.1		
1966	43	2	45	0.1	26	0.7
1967	78	15	93	0.2	48	1.2
1968	130	46	176	0.4	83	1.4
1969	196	100	296	0.5	120	1.8
1970	276	187	463	0.6	167	2.1
1971	375	315	690	0.8	227	2.5
1972	481	486	967	0.8	277	2.5
1973	613	714	1,327	1.0	360	2.4
1974	808	1,032	1,841	1.2	514	2.4
1975	1,040	1,438	2,478	1.4	637	2.6
1976	1,315	1,936	3,251	1.6	773	2.7
1977	1,633	2,536	4,168	1.8	917	3.1
1978	2,008	3,209	5,217	1.9	1,049	3.4
1979	2,478	3,997	6,475	2.1	1,258	4.4
1980	3,052	5,020	8,073	2.4	1,598	5.3
1981	3,707	6,167	9,874	2.6	1,801	5.4
1982	4,456	7,485	11,941	2.9	2,067	6.5
1983	5,277	8,986	14,264	3.1	2,323	7.2
1984	6,199	10,688	16,887	3.3	2.623	7.9
1985	7,188	12,596	19,784	3.5	2,897	8.4
1986	8,257	14,765	23,023	3.6	3,239	8.7
1987	9,432	17,161	26,593	3.7	3,570	10.3
1988	10,459	19,649	30,109	3.7	3,516	9.9
1989	11,859	22,488	34,347	3.6	4,238	11.0
1990	13,027	25,580	38,607	4.1	4,260	10.8
1991	14,095	28,820	42,915	4.3	4,308	9.7
1992	15,027	32,184	47,213	4.8	4,298	9.8

Source: Author's calculation based on SNA and data compiled by the Trust Association.

mestic corporate equities, foreign assets, and real estate should not exceed 30, 30, and 20 percent of total wealth, respectively.

The difference between the positions of U.S. and Japanese pension funds as institutional investors in capital markets reflects the difference between pension fund portfolios or asset mixes between the two countries. In the United States, private pension funds hold 22 percent of their total market value in the form of equities, while in Japan, pension funds hold only 1 percent of their market value in that form (see table 6.6).

The asset composition of employee pension funds is quite different from that of households. In the United States, households invested 22.4 percent of their net worth in equities (including equity in noncorporate business) and 8.4 percent in "credit market instruments" in 1992, while private pension funds

Table 6.4 **Household Sector Balance Sheet in the United States and Japan**

Component	1980[a]	1985[a]	1990[a]	1992[a]
U.S. Households				
Net worth (billion $)	9,644.3	14,072.3	18,839.3	21,414.4
Composition (%)	100.0	100.0	100.0	100.0
Reproducible assets	34.6	31.2	32.3	31.0
Land	14.3	15.9	14.1	13.5
Financial assets	66.3	69.8	74.2	75.6
Checkable deposits and currency	2.7	2.7	2.7	3.1
Small time and saving deposits	11.8	13.0	12.1	10.3
Money market fund shares	0.7	1.5	2.3	2.2
Large time deposits	1.2	0.5	0.6	0.0
Credit market instruments	5.8	7.3	10.0	8.4
Mutual fund shares	0.5	1.5	2.7	4.2
Corporate equities	11.5	11.5	9.8	11.8
Life insurance reserves	2.2	1.8	2.0	2.0
Pension fund reserves	9.5	14.2	17.5	21.4
Equity in noncorporate business	19.3	14.6	13.0	10.6
Security credit	0.2	0.2	0.3	0.4
Miscellaneous assets	0.8	0.9	1.1	1.1
Total assets	115.2	116.9	120.7	120.0
Total liabilities	15.2	16.9	20.7	20.0
Japanese Households				
Net worth (trillion yen)	856	1,237	2,393	2,180
Composition (%)	100.0	100.0	100.0	100.0
Inventory	1.0	0.7	0.4	0.4
Net fixed assets	16.7	13.8	9.5	11.2
Nonreproducible assets	57.7	56.1	64.0	58.4
Land	54.2	53.7	62.5	56.6
Financial assets	39.9	45.2	39.7	45.6
Currencies	1.8	1.6	1.3	1.5
Demand deposits	3.1	2.7	2.2	2.7
Time deposits	21.8	24.0	18.3	23.1
Long-term bonds	3.2	4.1	2.9	2.9
Corporate equities	4.7	5.3	6.8	4.9
Life insurance reserves	4.7	6.5	7.3	9.4
Pension fund reserves[b]	0.9	1.6	1.6	2.2
Miscellaneous assets	0.7	0.9	0.8	0.9
Total assets	115.2	115.8	113.6	115.6
Total liabilities	15.2	15.8	13.6	15.6

Sources: For the United States, Board of Governors of the Federal Reserve System, *Balance Sheet for the U.S. Economy* (Washington, D.C., 1993); for Japan, Economic Planning Agency, *Annual Report on National Accounts* (Tokyo: Government Printing Office, 1994).

[a]End of calendar year.

[b]Pension fund reserves are not included in net worth for Japanese households.

Table 6.5   **Asset Allocation of Private Pension Funds for the United States and Japan (percentage of total)**

Component	1980[a]	1985[a]	1990[a]	1991[a]	1992[a]
	United States				
Checkable deposit and currency	0.9	0.5	0.5	0.7	0.7
Time deposits	5.3	9.5	7.6	4.8	4.9
Money market fund shares	0.6	0.9	1.4	1.0	1.0
Mutual fund shares	1.5	1.8	3.0	3.0	3.2
Corporate equities	47.6	44.5	46.9	44.3	44.8
Credit market instruments	32.2	29.1	28.6	28.6	28.1
U.S. government securities	10.8	15.0	14.5	13.2	13.0
Treasury issues	6.9	8.9	9.8	8.9	9.0
Agency issues	3.9	6.1	4.6	4.2	4.0
Tax-exempt securities	0.0	0.3	0.2	0.2	0.2
Corporate and foreign bonds	16.5	11.1	10.3	9.8	9.7
Mortgages	0.8	0.7	1.7	1.3	1.3
Open-market paper	4.2	1.9	1.9	4.2	4.0
Miscellaneous assets	11.9	13.6	11.9	17.5	17.3
Total	100.0	100.0	100.0	100.0	100.0
	Japan				
Liquidity assets	0.5	2.3	2.1	2.1	2.4
Loans	37.4	20.3	14.1	13.6	14.0
Bonds	51.7	51.2	41.3	42.3	42.2
Corporate equities	9.2	16.0	25.9	25.8	25.0
Foreign bonds	0.6	9.5	16.0	15.6	15.7
Real estate	0.2	0.6	0.6	0.6	0.6
Total	100.0	100.0	100.0	100.0	100.0

Sources: For the United States, Board of Governors of the Federal Reserve System, *Flow of Funds* (Washington, D.C., various years); for Japan, data provided by individual trust banks.
[a]End of calendar year.

invested 44.8 percent of their wealth in corporate equities and 28.1 percent in credit market instruments (cf. table 6.4 with table 6.5). In Japan, households allocated only 4.9 percent of their net worth to equities and 2.9 percent to long-term bonds, whereas pension trusts allocated 25.0 percent of their assets to corporate equities, 42.2 percent to bonds, and 15.7 percent to foreign bonds (again, cf. table 6.4 with table 6.5). In sum, in both the United States and Japan, pension funds tend to allocate a larger part of their wealth to relatively long-term and risky assets than do households.

The difference between the asset portfolios of household investors and institutional investors such as pension funds may be explained by several factors. For instance, since the portfolio of an institutional investor is much larger than that of an individual, the former can allocate more of its wealth to risky assets. Economies of scale in investment may be important as well. Institutional investors may not be just intermediaries or agents of households, that is, "repositories" of household savings invested in capital markets.

Table 6.6   **Holdings of Corporate Equities at Market Value in the United States and Japan**

Investor	1980[a]	1985[a]	1990[a]	1992[a]
United States				
Households	70.7	62.4	52.5	47.1
Foreign	4.1	4.9	6.6	6.5
Commercial banking	0.0	0.0	0.1	0.1
Mutual savings banks	0.3	0.2	0.3	0.2
Insurance	22.0	27.6	33.7	36.4
Life insurance companies	2.9	2.9	2.8	2.7
Other insurance companies	2.1	2.2	2.3	2.6
Private pension funds	14.2	17.9	20.1	21.8
Government retirement funds	2.8	4.6	8.4	9.3
Mutual funds	2.7	4.4	6.7	9.3
Brokers and dealers	0.2	0.5	0.3	0.3
Total	100.0	100.0	100.0	100.0
Japan				
Households	27.9	22.3	20.4	20.7
Foreign	5.8	7.0	4.7	6.3
Commercial and trust banks	19.9	20.9	25.5	25.5
Securities investment trust	1.9	1.7	3.7	3.2
Pension trust	0.4	0.8	1.0	1.2
Insurance	16.1	16.5	15.8	16.2
Life insurance companies	11.5	12.3	12.0	12.4
Other insurance companies	4.6	4.1	3.9	3.8
Other financial institutions	2.3	2.4	1.6	1.2
Nonfinancial business	26.2	28.8	30.1	28.5
Government	0.4	0.3	0.3	0.3
Brokers and dealers	1.5	1.9	1.7	1.2
Total	100.0	100.0	100.0	100.0

Sources: For the United States, Board of Governors of the Federal Reserve System, *Flow of Funds* (Washington, D.C., various years); for Japan, Japan Council on Stock Exchange, *Equity Distribution Survey* (Tokyo, various years).

[a] End of calendar year.

6.5.3   Comparison of Individual Saving and Saving through Firm Pension Funds

Does the development of retirement saving through private pension funds affect individual saving behavior?

Pension plans are classified into two types: defined-contribution plans and defined-benefit plans. In a defined-contribution plan, contributions are determined by a formula agreed to by employers and employees. In a defined-benefit plan, the employee's pension benefit is determined by a formula that takes into account years of service for the employer and wages or salary. While defined-contribution plans are by definition fully funded, in the sense that the value of benefits equals that of the assets, defined-benefit plans can be funded to any degree (for details, see Bodie and Papke 1992). In Japan, so far as EPFs and TQPs are concerned, most corporate pension plans are designed to be defined-benefit plans, and they must be fully funded in the sense that the discounted value of benefits is equal to the discounted sum of contributions.[6]

A simple life-cycle saving model can be used to explain how and to what extent the development of pension plans affects household and national savings. As summarized by Munnell and Yohn (1992), it may seem obvious that aggregate saving will be unchanged by the introduction of pension plans if (1) employees and employers correctly perceive the increase in future income encompassed by pension promises and reduce wages by an equivalent amount, (2) employees reduce their direct personal saving by the increased value of future pension benefits, and (3) the firm transfers to the pension fund or some other firm investment an amount equal to the pension promise.

However, the real world is more complicated than that, and saving through corporate pension funds is not necessarily a perfect substitute for private retirement saving. Important factors in the real world are favorable tax treatment for pension plans and uncertainty about benefits.[7]

In the statistical rules of the SNA, saving through EPFs is included in the saving of social security funds, which is a subsector of general government, while saving through TQPs is included in household saving from the start. Tax-free reserves by corporations to prepare for severance payments are classified as corporate saving.

Hence, if severance payments are replaced by EPFs, corporate saving would be replaced by government saving, whereas if severance payments are replaced by TQPs, corporate saving would be replaced by household saving.

6.5.4 The Impact of Aging on Capital Markets

Aging may affect individual saving behavior and asset markets and prices in two ways: first, through the change in individual portfolio choice—say a shift from bonds to equities as one grows older—and, second, through the behavior of employer-sponsored pension funds. In this section let us examine the latter.

A large fraction of financial assets in the United States is held by employer-sponsored pension funds, as we have already seen. These assets will be sold to finance pension benefits sometime in the future. When the number of retired elderly becomes larger than the number of employees, sales of assets by these funds will be large relative to purchases (saving to fund the future benefits of

---

6. However, a substantial number of EPFs and TQPs have failed to accumulate enough funds to meet future payments in these years because of historically low interest and weak asset market indices. Therefore, it is suggested that some defined-benefit pension plans be reorganized into defined-contribution plans.

7. How strong is the link between pension fund accumulation and household direct saving? To clarify this, I estimated a household saving equation using saving through corporate pension funds (defined as net yearly increase of managed assets) as an explanatory variable. The estimation results show that the coefficients on saving through corporate pension funds are statistically significant, and the values of these coefficients are much higher than unity. This implies that typical households see corporate pension programs as good substitutes for individual retirement saving.

current workers). Thus, the tendency will be for the price of assets to fall. This change in the market for financial assets could have a substantial effect on the accumulated wealth of the elderly.

The effects may differ between Japan and the United States. The negative impact on the capital market may be much smaller in Japan than in the United States. The reasons are as follows: First, in Japan the elderly tend to continue to save, or at least not dissave much, as discussed earlier. Second, it is highly likely that a substantial part of individual retirement saving will be replaced by compulsory or semicompulsory saving through employer-sponsored pension plans, which have a larger demand for corporate equities and long-term bonds. In the transitional period, the selling pressure on equities may be offset by the potential demand for them. Third, in Japan, the regulation of the asset composition of pension funds has been quite restrictive, but the possible deregulation of asset composition would encourage demand for corporate equities. While it is difficult to estimate the possible effect of such deregulation on investment, the present asset mix of U.S. pension funds gives us a good hint. As we have already seen, U.S. pension funds allocate approximately half of their assets to corporate equities. There must be a fair amount of room for Japanese pension funds to increase the share of equities in their portfolios.

6.6 Conclusions

One of the purposes of this paper was to find some statistical evidence about the effects of population aging on national saving, corporate pension funds, and asset accumulation. I have examined these, using the System of National Accounts, Flow of Funds, and Family Savings Survey in Japan and the United States. The main findings of the empirical investigations are as follows.

First, microdata on household saving and wealth by age do not show that the elderly dissave or decumulate their assets drastically in Japan. If this is really the case, aggregate household and national saving rates are not likely to decline sharply in the near future.

Second, indirect saving through employer-sponsored pension plans is gradually replacing a portion of individual direct saving in Japan, just as in the United States. Increasing pension fund wealth tends to lower the household saving rate, but it is not clear whether the growing popularity of corporate pensions lowers the national saving rate.

Third, the demand for corporate equities will increase rather than decrease as long as corporate pension funds cover more and more employees and have a positive attitude toward investment in equities, supported by deregulation of investment. Therefore, in Japan, it is unlikely that the negative impact of aging on the capital market will be serious.

While I have emphasized the interrelationship of saving behavior among individual subsectors, I have not conducted exact statistical tests about this interdependence, apart from some preliminary time-series regression analysis.

Among the subsectors reviewed in this paper, the quantitative impact of aging on the saving behavior of the government sector is not yet clear. We have to develop some sort of simulation model to evaluate effects of aging on the government sector. Every topic listed here is of particular interest to us but is left for future work.

References

Auerbach, A. J., J. Cai, and L. J. Kotlikoff. 1991. U.S. demographics and saving: Predictions of three saving models. *Carnegie-Rochester Conference Series on Public Policy* 34:135–56.

Auerbach, A. J., J. Gokhale, and L. J. Kotlikoff. 1991. Generational accounts: A meaningful alternative to deficit accounting. In *Tax policy and the economy,* vol. 5, ed. D. Bradford, 5–110. Cambridge: MIT Press.

Barthold, T., and T. Ito. 1992. Bequest taxes and accumulation of household wealth: U.S.-Japan comparison. In *The political economy of tax reform,* ed. T. Ito and A. Krueger. Chicago: University of Chicago Press.

Bodie, Z., and L. E. Papke. 1992. Pension fund finance. In *Pension and the economy,* ed. Z. Bodie and A. H. Munnell. Philadelphia: University of Pennsylvania Press.

Hayashi, F. 1992. Explaining Japan's saving: A review of recent literature. *BOJ Monetary and Economic Studies* 10 (2): 63–78.

Hayashi, F., A. Ando, and R. Ferris. 1988. Life cycle and bequest savings: A study of Japanese and U.S. households based on data from the 1984 NSFIE and the 1983 Survey of Consumer Finances. *Journal of the Japanese and International Economies* 2 (4): 450–91.

Horioka, C. Y. 1990. Why is Japan's saving rate so high? A literature survey. *Journal of the Japanese and International Economies* 4:49–92.

———. 1991. The determinants of Japan's saving rate: The impact of the age structure of the population and other factors. *Economic Studies Quarterly* 42 (3): 237–53.

Kotlikoff, L. J. 1992. *Generational accounts.* New York: Free Press.

Munnell, A. H., and F. O. Yohn. 1992. What is the impact of pensions on saving? In *Pensions and the economy,* ed. Z. Bodie and A. H. Munnell. Philadelphia: University of Pennsylvania Press.

Takayama, N., F. Funaoka, F. Ohtake, M. Sekiguchi, T. Shibuya, H. Ueno, and K. Kubo. 1990. Human capital estimation and the redistribution effects of public pension (in Japanese). *Keizai Bunseki,* no. 118.

7   The Impact of Demographics on Housing and Nonhousing Wealth in the United States

Hilary W. Hoynes and Daniel L. McFadden

7.1 Introduction

Equity in housing is a major component of household wealth in the United States. Demographic impacts on housing prices can have potentially large effects on the welfare of households that anticipate using their equity when they are old to finance consumption and insure against risks of major medical costs. Mankiw and Weil (1989) and McFadden (1994a) have argued that population aging in the United States in the coming three decades is likely to induce substantial declines in housing prices, resulting in capital losses for current homeowners. McFadden argues that the welfare impact of these capital losses is small if they are anticipated and savings rates adjust to optimize life-cycle consumption. However, the impact near the end of life of some cohorts could be large if they have failed to adjust savings behavior to compensate for demographically induced losses in housing wealth. This paper examines further the question of whether households anticipate demographic impacts on housing prices and adjust their savings behavior in response.

Section 7.2 summarizes the evidence on the relationship between demographics and behavior of the housing market. Section 7.3 contains an analysis of life-cycle savings behavior using data from the Panel Study of Income Dynamics and examines the question of whether savings rates are correlated with capital gains rates. Zero correlation corresponds to complete behavioral offset, with each increase in savings due to capital gains offset by a reduction in savings from other channels. High correlation corresponds to a failure to anticipate price changes or to adjust savings behavior in response. Section 7.4 concludes.

Hilary W. Hoynes is assistant professor of economics at the University of California, Berkeley, and a faculty research fellow of the National Bureau of Economic Research. Daniel L. McFadden is the Cox Professor of Economics at the University of California, Berkeley, and a research associate of the National Bureau of Economic Research.

7.2 Demographics and the Housing Market

7.2.1 Background

Over the period 1900–1990, McFadden (1994a) finds for the United States a correlation of 0.966 between real constant-quality housing stock and population.[1] This suggests that the force of demographics is a leading determinant of housing demand, even though adjustments in household formation and dissolution, housing consumption in square meters per person, and dwelling quality in response to income and price may be important at the margin.

New construction is a relatively small proportion of the housing stock: real gross investment has averaged 5.3 percent of the real housing stock over 1900–1990. Consequently, the short-run price elasticity of supply of dwellings is relatively low, even though new construction is fairly responsive to price. Then demographic trends that affect housing demand should induce substantial, and largely forecastable, movements in housing prices. The correlation of population and housing prices was 0.883 over 1900–1990.

We shall review the standard theory of the housing market and identify the role of demographic factors in determining stocks and prices. For completeness, we begin by developing the standard consumer model of housing demand and deriving the conventional formula for the user cost of housing. A comparative statics analysis of this model identifies qualitatively the linkage between housing prices and demand. We use the following notation:

π	Cost of living index
d	Dummy variable: one for owner, zero for renter
R	Nominal rental rate per unit of constant-quality housing
P	Nominal purchase price per unit of constant-quality housing
m	Marginal income (and capital gains) tax rate
τ	Property tax rate
δ	Maintenance (or depreciation) rate
θ	Share of purchase mortgaged
r	Mortgage interest rate (nominal)
r'	After-tax interest rate, $r' \equiv (1 - m)r$
μ	Operating cost rate for owned housing, $\mu \equiv (\theta r + \tau)(1 - m) + \delta$
A	Nominal financial assets of the consumer (debt if negative)
W	Nominal wealth
Y	Nominal income

1. The GNP Residential Investment Deflator is assumed to be a valid measure of nominal constant-quality housing price. Residential Investment, deflated by this measure, is then accumulated at a depreciation rate of 2.687 percent to obtain real constant-quality housing stock. The depreciation rate is chosen so that the series is commensurate with the Department of Commerce series on Value of Net Stocks of Residential Structures. The Residential Investment Deflator, divided by the total GNP Implicit Price Deflator, is taken as the measure of the price of constant-quality housing. Details of the construction and sources are given in McFadden (1994a).

g	Real consumption of goods other than housing
h	Real consumption of constant-quality housing units
$\mathring{P}$	Capital gains rate, $\mathring{P} \equiv (P_2 - P_1)/P_1$
α	Consumer's expected capital gains rate
σ^2	Consumer's variance of capital gains rate

Consider for simplicity a consumer who is endowed with initial (after-tax) wealth W_1, lives one period, and then leaves a bequest W_2 in the following period. The consumer must decide on levels of consumption of housing units (h) and goods other than housing (g), and on whether to rent ($d = 0$) or own ($d = 1$). Assume the consumer's utility function has the form

(1) $$\mathcal{U} = U(g, h) + \mathbf{E}\, V(W_2/\pi_2),$$

where U is the utility of current consumption, V is the utility of bequests, and the expectation is taken with respect to future housing prices, which are unknown when consumption decisions must be taken. Although we shall not do so in this paper, it is possible to interpret V as a valuation function, which may depend on age, health, and mortality risk, and to allow U to depend on age and health. Then equation (1) will be the term entering Bellman's equation for the consumer's dynamic stochastic program. We make the following assumptions on U, V, and beliefs about future prices:

1. U is strictly concave and nondecreasing, with $\nabla_g U(0, h) = +\infty$, $\nabla_h U(g, 0) = +\infty$, and $\nabla_h U(g, +\infty) = 0$.
2. Housing and nonhousing consumption are normal goods; that is, $\nabla_g(\nabla_g U/\nabla_h U) \le 0$ and $\nabla_h(\nabla_g U/\nabla_h U) \ge 0$.
3. V is a constant relative risk aversion utility function; that is, $V(w) = -Ce^{-\kappa w}$, where C and κ are positive parameters.
4. All variables except $\mathring{P}$ are in the consumer's initial information set $\mathcal{I}$, and given this information the consumer believes that $\mathring{P}$ has a normal distribution with mean α and variance σ^2.

The consumer's budget constraint in the first period is

(2) $0 = W_1 + (1 - m)Y_1$	Initial after-tax wealth and after-tax income
$\quad - \pi_1 g$	Nonhousing expenditures
$\quad - (1 - d)Rh$	Housing expenditures if renter
$\quad - dh\{(1 - \theta)P_1$	Out-of-pocket housing expenditures
$\quad + P_1 [(\theta r + \tau)(1 - m) + \delta]\}$	if owner
$\quad - A_1$	Financial assets purchased

Line four of equation (2), out-of-pocket housing expenditures, is composed of the down payment $(1 - \theta)P_1 h$, mortgage interest $r\theta P_1 h$, property taxes $\tau P_1 h$, maintenance or depreciation $\delta P_1 h$, and an offset $m(r\theta + \tau)P_1 h$ arising from the deductability of mortgage interest and property taxes from income subject to income taxes. Using the definition of μ, line four can be written compactly as $-dhP_1(1 - \theta + \mu)$. The second period budget constraint is

(3) $0 = [1 + (1 - m)r]A_1$ Financial assets with after-tax interest

      $+ dh[P_2 - \theta P_1 - m(P_2 - P_1)]$ Housing equity net of capital gains tax

      $- W_2$ Bequest

For simplicity, we assume that financial assets are held as savings accounts (resp. consumer loans) that carry the mortgage interest rate r, and that interest income (resp. expense) is taxed (resp. deducted) at the marginal rate m. Then the first line of equation (3) gives financial assets in the second period after taxes. The second line of equation (3) gives the cash received from sale of a house in period 2, less repayment of mortgage principal $(P_2 - \theta P_1)h$ and taxes on nominal capital gains $m(P_2 - P_1)h$, which are assumed to be taxed at the same rate as ordinary income. Using the definitions of r' and $\mathring{P}$, this constraint can be written compactly as

$$0 = (1 + r')A_1 + dhP_1[1 - \theta + (1 - m)\mathring{P}] - W_2.$$

Combining equations (2) and (3) to eliminate A_1 gives an intertemporal budget constraint,

(4) $W_2 = dhP_1[1 - \theta + (1 - m)\mathring{P}] + [1 + r'] \{W_1 + (1 - m)Y_1$
        $- \pi_1 g - (1 - d)Rh - dhP_1(1 - \theta + \mu)\}$
      $= (1 + r')[W_1 + (1 - m)Y_1 - \pi_1 g - (1 - d)Rh]$
        $- dhP_1[(1 + r')\mu + r'(1 - \theta) - (1 - m)\mathring{P}].$

Substituting equation (4) into equation (1) and taking the expectation gives the objective function

(5) $$\mathcal{U} = U(g, h) - C \cdot \exp\left\{ -\frac{\kappa}{\pi_2}\left[\omega - (1 + r')\pi_1 g \right.\right.$$
$$\left.\left. - (1 - d)(1 + r')Rh - dhP_1 c - P_1^2 h^2 d \frac{q}{2} \right]\right\},$$

where

$\omega = (1 + r')[W_1 + (1 - m)Y_1],$
$q = \kappa\sigma^2(1 - m)^2/\pi_2,$
$c = (1 + r')\mu + r'(1 - \theta) - (1 - m)\alpha \approx (1 - m)(r + \tau)$
    $+ \delta - (1 - m)\alpha.$

Then ω is total initial wealth, q is a risk penalty associated with the uncertainty about future house prices, and c is the *expected user cost of housing per dollar purchased*. The last form of c is obtained using the approximation $r'\mu \approx 0$. The first-order conditions for maximization of expression (5) are

(6)
$$\nabla_g U = (1 + r')\kappa\frac{\pi_{1}g}{\pi_2}\mathcal{V},$$

(7)
$$\nabla_h U = \frac{\kappa}{\pi_2}[(1 + r')R(1 - d) + dP_1c + dhP_1^2q]\mathcal{V},$$

where

$$\mathcal{V} \equiv C\cdot\exp\left\{-\frac{\kappa}{\pi_2}\left[\omega - (1 + r')\pi_1 g\right.\right.$$
$$\left.\left. - (1 - d)(1 + r')Rh - dhP_1c - P_1^2h^2d\,\frac{q}{2}\right]\right\}.$$

A consumer whose utility U does not depend on tenure d will choose to own if $P_1c' < R$, where $c' = c + P_1hq/2$, and rent otherwise. If all consumers are identical, then equilibrium in a market in which both purchased and rental housing appear requires that prices and rents adjust so that $R = P_1c'$. On the other hand, if there is a distribution of beliefs, or even a distribution of wealth and income that induces a distribution of c', then the split between owning and renting will be determined by the proportion of consumers with c' satisfying $P_1c' < R$, with R and P_1 adjusting to clear the purchase and rental markets. Of course, if there is a distribution of tastes for tenure entering U, or of degrees of risk aversion κ, this will split the population between owners and renters even if all consumers have common beliefs.

The marginal utility of additional housing is positive. Then when faced with negative c, corresponding to a high rate of positive capital gains, the consumer will choose $d = 1$ and a high level of h, financing the purchase by borrowing financial assets at the after-tax rate $(1 - m)r$. Risk aversion will, however, keep $h \leq -2c/P_1q$. The market will respond to this increase in the demand for purchases by increasing P_1. This arbitrage opportunity implies that very large anticipated capital gains over very short periods will be squeezed out by the market. Similarly, large anticipated capital losses should induce a shift to rental housing, which lowers P_1 and squeezes out some of the capital losses. In practice, consumers are additionally constrained with respect to the proportion of a housing purchase they can mortgage and with respect to financing down payments with borrowed money, and there are substantial transactions costs associated with moves between rental and owner housing or in changing housing consumption levels in owner-occupied housing. These will further limit the scope for arbitrage by consumers and leave the possibility of modest anticipated capital gains and losses that are not arbitraged away. From the last form of the definition of c, the user cost of housing does not depend on equity versus debt financing (θ), a consumer equivalent of the Modigliani-Miller theorem.

A comparative statics analysis of the impact of income and prices on consumer decisions can be carried out given the assumptions below equation (1), plus the following assumptions:

5. The elasticities of g and h with respect to ω are less than one.
6. The elasticity of h with respect to R (for renters) or P_1 (for owners) is less than one in magnitude.
7. The elasticity of substitution between g and h is at most one.
8. The degree of relative risk aversion is less than two.

The directions of change expected under assumptions 1–8 are summarized in table 7.1. The impact of P_1 in this table does not take into account indirect effects arising because P_1 affects consumer beliefs about capital gains. The first row of the table is constructed under the assumption that across consumers there is a continuous distribution of beliefs about capital gains rates and that this distribution divides the population into owners and renters. The expected capital gains rate α is reinterpreted as characterizing the location of this distribution. Details of the construction of the table are given in the appendix.

Define the *ex ante expected savings rate* of the consumer to be $s^e = (W_2^e - W_1)/Y_1$, and the *ex post realized savings rate* to be $s = (W_2 - W_1)/Y_1 \equiv s^e + (1 - m)dhP_1(\mathring{P} - \alpha)/Y_1$. From table 7.1, the ex ante savings rate should fall when P_1 rises and rise when α rises, other things being equal. This effect can be reversed if consumers believe that α is higher when P_1 is higher. Define $\psi = (1 - m)dhP_1/Y_1$, and let $\alpha^r = \mathbf{E}_{\mathring{P}|\mathscr{I}}\mathring{P}$ denote the statistical expectation of $\mathring{P}$, given initial information. Then $s = s^e + \psi(\mathring{P} - \alpha)$, implying that $\mathbf{E}_{\mathring{P}|\mathscr{I}}s = s^e + \psi(\alpha^r - \alpha)$ and $s - \mathbf{E}_{\mathring{P}|\mathscr{I}}s = \psi(\mathring{P} - \alpha^r)$. In the population, the ex post savings rate satisfies

$$(8) \quad \mathrm{Cov}(s, P_1) = \mathbf{E}_{\mathscr{I}}\{s^e + \psi(\alpha^r - \alpha)\}(P_1 - \mathbf{E}_{\mathscr{I}}P_1)$$
$$= \mathbf{E}_{\mathscr{I}}s^e(P_1 - \mathbf{E}_{\mathscr{I}}P_1) + \mathbf{E}_{\mathscr{I}}\psi(\alpha^r - \alpha)(P_1 - \mathbf{E}_{\mathscr{I}}P_1)$$

$$(9) \quad \mathrm{Cov}(s, \mathring{P}) = \mathbf{E}_{\mathscr{I}}\{s^e + \psi(\mathring{P} - \alpha^r) + \psi(\alpha^r - \alpha)\}$$
$$(\mathring{P} - \alpha^r + \alpha^r - \mathbf{E}_{\mathscr{I}}\alpha^r)$$
$$= \mathbf{E}_{\mathscr{I}}s^e(\alpha^r - \mathbf{E}_{\mathscr{I}}\alpha^r) + \mathbf{E}_{\mathscr{I}}\psi\cdot\mathrm{Var}(\mathring{P}|\mathscr{I})$$
$$+ \mathbf{E}_{\mathscr{I}}\psi(\alpha^r - \alpha)(\alpha^r - \mathbf{E}_{\mathscr{I}}\alpha^r).$$

If consumer expectations α do not depend on P_1 and rational expectations α^r are uncorrelated with P_1, then the first term in equation (8) should be negative from table 7.1 and the second term should be zero, so that $\mathrm{Cov}(s, P_1) < 0$. If consumer expectations α are positively correlated with P_1, then the first term in equation (8) can be positive; the second term will reinforce this if rational expectations are more positively correlated with P_1 than beliefs and will offset this otherwise. The first term in equation (9) is nonnegative from table 7.1, provided consumer expectations are nonnegatively correlated with rational expectations. The second term is positive. The third term is zero if expectations are rational and positive if consumer beliefs exhibit "regression to the mean," positively correlated with rational expectations but with smaller deviations from the mean. If the correlation of P_1 and $\mathring{P}$ is low, then the slope coefficients

Table 7.1   **Comparative Statics of Housing Demand**

Quantity	Income Y_1	Rental Rate R	Housing Price P_1	Capital Gains Rate α
Share of owners ($d = 1$)	+	+	−	+
If renter				
Nonhousing consumption (g)	+	?	0	0
Housing consumption (h)	+	−	0	0
Financial assets (A_1)	+	−	0	0
Expected bequest (W_2^e)	+	−	0	0
If owner				
Nonhousing consumption (g)	+	0	?	?
Housing consumption (h)	+	0	−	+
Financial assets (A_1)	+	0	−	−
Expected bequest (W_2^e)	+	0	−	+

in a regression of s on one, P_1, and $\overset{\circ}{P}$ will have the signs of $\text{Cov}(s, P_1)$ and $\text{Cov}(s, \overset{\circ}{P})$, respectively. The magnitude of the coefficient of $\overset{\circ}{P}$ will be relatively small if capital gains are largely anticipated, so that the conditional variance of $\overset{\circ}{P}$ is small and the "bias" $\alpha - \alpha^r$ has a low correlation with α^r. If consumers are naive in forming expectations, believing that $\overset{\circ}{P}$ is more positively correlated with P_1 than is the case, this will make the coefficient of P_1 less positive and have relatively little effect on the coefficient of $\overset{\circ}{P}$.

We have argued that arbitrage by consumers, achieved by varying the level of housing consumption and by moving between rental and owner housing, should limit but not eliminate anticipated capital gains. The behavior of supply will also affect the transmission of demographic trends into housing prices. Poterba (1984), Topel and Rosen (1988), and McFadden (1994a) have found aggregate supply of new housing to be quite price-elastic, with elasticities around 2. Further, real housing investment has averaged 5.3 percent of real constant-quality stocks over the period 1900–1990, and the elasticity of stocks with respect to price is quite low, about 0.11. Then, one would expect short-run changes in housing demand to induce substantial short-run variations in housing prices. However, developers do have some control over the timing of completion and marketing of new houses, giving them some arbitrage opportunities when there are large anticipated capital gains or losses.

We conclude from this analysis that rational consumers should display behavioral response to anticipated capital gains, although arbitrage will limit the magnitude of these gains. If consumers expect no correlation between initial information and future price changes, so that there are no anticipated capital gains, then comparative statics suggests that ex post savings rates are likely to be negatively correlated with initial housing prices and correlated dollar for dollar with ex post realized capital gains. On the other hand, if arbitrage does not eliminate anticipated capital gains, and these are forecastable in part from initial housing prices and other information, then ex post savings can be positively correlated with initial house prices. Further, there may be some behavioral offset to the savings these capital gains are expected to generate.

7.2.2 Demographics and Housing Consumption

An empirical examination of demographics and housing consumption can be made using U.S. census public-use samples of 0.1 percent of the population, which give household size and age composition, status as a renter or owner, and owner-reported dwelling value. McFadden (1994a) analyzes the 1940, 1960, 1970, and 1980 census samples, adapting a model suggested by Mankiw and Weil (1989):

$$(10) \qquad V_{ht} = \sum_{j=0}^{J} \alpha_{jt} K_{jht} + \varepsilon_{ht},$$

where h indexes households, t indexes year, $j = 0, \ldots, J$ indexes five-year age cohorts, V_{ht} is stated dwelling value, K_{jht} is the number of persons in cohort j in household h, α_{jt} is the imputed housing consumption of individuals in cohort j in year t, and ε_{ht} is a disturbance. This model applies to homeowners. To correct for bias due to self-selection between owning and renting, a probit model is first estimated for tenure choice, using observations on both owners and renters:

$$(11) \qquad \text{Pr(Owner)} = \Phi(\gamma_0 + \gamma_1 y_{ht} + \gamma_2 y_{ht}^2 + \sum_{j=0}^{J} \beta_{jt} K_{jht}),$$

where y_{ht} is real household income. Then, an inverse Mills ratio is calculated from this probit equation and added to equation (10) to absorb the nonzero conditional expectation of ε_{ht} induced by selection. Figure 7.1, adapted from McFadden (1994a), plots the coefficients from the selection-adjusted regressions, *relative to the age 40–44 cohort*, for each census year. These profiles are remarkably stable between 1960 and 1980. The profile for 1940 shows less relative housing consumption for the cohorts between ages 25 and 39 than is observed in the later censuses. This is almost certainly attributable to the lack of consumer confidence and shortage of liquidity during the Great Depression, when these cohorts might normally have been rapidly increasing their housing consumption. This figure provides empirical justification for an assumption that the relative housing consumption profile will remain stable in the future. Figure 7.2 gives the 1970 profile, which will be used for further computation, with 95 percent confidence bounds. The profile is quite precisely determined except for the very old, where sample sizes are small.

McFadden (1994a) summarizes U.S. census data on population by sex and five-year age cohort in census years from 1900 through 1990, using *Current Population Reports* and contemporaneous life tables to interpolate in the early part of the century. He then uses the *cohort-component* projection procedure, combined with 1989 U.S. census "midrange" assumptions on fertility, mortal-

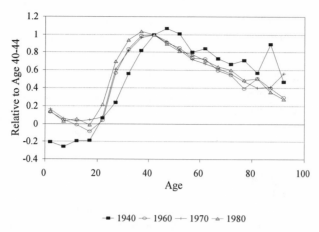

Fig. 7.1   Housing consumption
Source: McFadden (1994a).

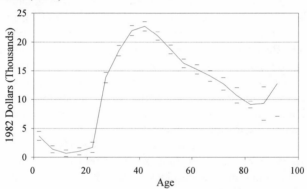

Fig. 7.2   1970 Housing consumption (with 95 percent confidence bounds)
Source: McFadden (1994a).

ity, and immigration, to project population by age cohort in the coming century. Figure 7.3 shows historical and projected population and *housing-consumption-equivalent* population, in which each age cohort is scaled to its equivalent numbers of age 40–44 persons using the coefficients from figure 7.2. Qualitatively, the equivalent population curve shows relatively steady growth from the beginning of the century until about 1975, rises more rapidly from 1975 to 1990 as the post–World War II baby boomers formed households and acquired houses, and is forecast to rise much more slowly after 1990, becoming essentially flat after 2020.

   Equivalent population has a correlation of 0.964 with real constant-quality housing stock over the period 1900–1990 and a correlation of 0.904 with housing prices measured by the GNP implicit price deflator. Further evidence on the correlation of changes in equivalent population and housing prices is obtained by examining 112 metropolitan statistical areas (MSAs) and primary

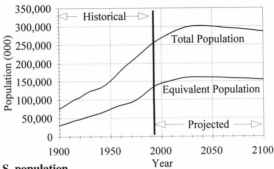

Fig. 7.3   U.S. population
Source: McFadden (1994a).

metropolitan statistical areas (PMSAs) during the decade of the 1980s. We use American Chamber of Commerce Researchers Association (ACCRA) data on prices of "standard 3 bedroom, 2 bath one-family houses suitable for a mid-management level owner" (ACCRA 1992). These data are obtained from quarterly surveys of homebuilders, mortgage bankers, appraisers, and savings and loan officers. Respondents were asked for sales prices of new homes meeting the criteria above and an additional list of detailed specifications. If no new homes meeting the specifications were marketed, then recent resale homes were asked for. A drawback of these prices is that they are not representative of the total housing market and may not be accurate for low-income consumers. Missing quarters are imputed by interpolation. In some cases, missing observations in are imputed by the following method: The National Association of Realtors *Home Sales* and *Home Sales Yearbook* provide data on median sales prices of resale one-family homes by year and MSA (National Association of Realtors 1990). For all MSAs where both the ACCRA and Realtors series are available, we form the ratio of their (unweighted) means in each year. Then we deflate the Realtors series using these ratios and use this deflated series to fill in missing observations in the ACCRA series. The effect of the deflation is to remove quality changes in the Realtors series that are held constant in the ACCRA series. The final extended ACCRA series is then in nominal dollars and is substantially but not completely adjusted to remove quality changes. The housing price data show substantial variation across MSAs. Figure 7.4 shows the distribution of rates of price changes, deflated by the CPI, from 1984 to 1989; the observations on which this distribution is based are weighted by MSA population. Some perspective on the consistency of these prices is provided by comparing them with median house values in the MSAs in census years. There is a mismatch in years (1984–89 for ACCRA, 1980–90 for the census), with some significant macroeconomic changes in the nonoverlapping period. Also, the census values are not quality-adjusted. Figure 7.5 shows a scatter plot of the two price series, along with a fit of census price changes to ACCRA price changes. There is considerable scatter, and a few MSAs, such

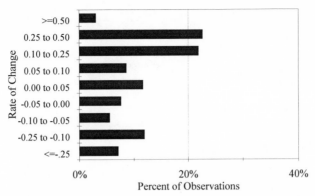

Fig. 7.4   ACCRA housing prices (frequency of 1984–89 rate of change)
Source: Authors' tabulation.

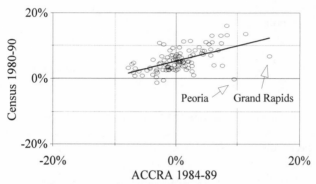

Fig. 7.5   MSA housing prices (annual rates of change)
Source: Authors' tabulation.

as Peoria, Grand Rapids, York, and Lancaster, are outliers. Nevertheless, the correlation of the two variables is 0.56.

Equivalent population for each MSA is approximated by applying the cohort-size-weighted average coefficients from figure 7.2 to the population age segments 0–18, 19–64, and 65+. For 1970, these age distributions were not available by MSA, so the corresponding age distribution in the state containing the MSA was used. Changes in equivalent population are quite forecastable in the short run, even at the MSA level. A regression of the rate of equivalent population change in 1980–90 on the rate of equivalent population change in 1970–80, plus a constant and the rate of change of real median prices in 1970–80, gives a multiple correlation coefficient of 0.407, with the lagged equivalent population change providing most of the explanatory power. The correlation of 1970–80 equivalent population change and 1980–90 equivalent population change is 0.618.

Figure 7.6 gives the scatter plot for the rates of change in real housing prices

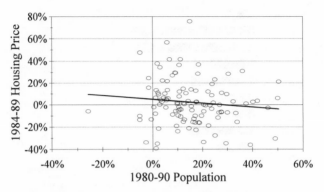

Fig. 7.6   Population and housing prices (rates of change)
Source: Authors' tabulation.

over 1984–89 and population over 1980–90. The figure also shows a regression through these points:

(12)

$$\log(\text{Price}_{89}/\text{Price}_{84}) = 0.050 - 0.175 \cdot \log\left(\text{Equiv. pop.}_{90}/\text{Equiv. pop.}_{80}\right).$$

$$(0.029) \quad (0.146)$$

Our comparative statics analysis suggests that price changes and population changes should be positively correlated in the market, even when the population change is fully anticipated. Unanticipated changes in population should have a stronger positive impact since they will not have increased initial prices via reduced user cost, which increases initial demand. However, the regression does not show the expected positive correlation between housing price change and equivalent population change and suggests instead that population changes are fully anticipated and actively arbitraged away. However, there are also several econometric reasons the regression might fail to exhibit the expected effects, including variations in income growth or economic conditions across MSAs that are omitted from the model, speculative "bubbles" in prices that increase variance and produce outliers, or measurement problems related to the definition of MSA boundaries and the distribution of home sales within each MSA. In addition, there may be self-selection between homeowners and renters that is related to population growth, and there may be endogeneity of population growth, which may respond to price differentials. Examination of the scatter plot suggests that there are outliers. However, a least absolute deviations regression that reduces the influence of outliers does not change the coefficients substantially.

Extending this analysis, we ask whether housing price changes are predictable from initial information on housing price levels (which may be correlates of past population growth) and the rate of change in population growth. The regression

$$(13) \quad \log\left(\frac{Price_{89}}{Price_{84}}\right) = 0.098 + 0.188 \cdot \log\left(\frac{Equiv.\ pop._{.90}}{Equiv.\ pop._{.80}}\right)$$

$$(1.328) \quad (0.202)$$

$$- 0.472 \cdot \log\left(\frac{Equiv.\ pop._{.80}}{Equiv.\ pop._{.70}}\right)$$

$$(0.183)$$

$$-0.112 \cdot \log\left(\frac{Median\ price_{80}}{Median\ price_{70}}\right)$$

$$(0.075)$$

$$+ 0.011 \cdot \log(Price_{84})$$

$$(0.117)$$

has $R^2 = 0.108$, indicating that the initial information embodied in historical housing prices and current population growth has little predictive power but that past population growth does have some predictive power.

A second implication of the housing market model is that as a result of arbitrage the *level* of housing prices should be higher in markets where population growth is higher. To test this, we regress 1984 price on the rates of population change in 1970–80 and 1980–90 and on the 1970–80 rate of housing price change:

$$(14) \quad \log(Price_{84}) = 11.296 + 0.372 \cdot \log\left(\frac{Equiv.\ pop._{.90}}{Equiv.\ pop._{.80}}\right)$$

$$- 0.072 \cdot \log\left(\frac{Equiv.\ pop._{.80}}{Equiv.\ pop._{.70}}\right)$$

$$(0.070) \quad (0.169)$$

$$(0.156)$$

$$+ 0.040 \cdot \log\left(\frac{Median\ price_{80}}{Median\ price_{70}}\right).$$

$$(0.064)$$

This regression indicates that initial price is positively related to future population growth but is not related to past rates of price change or population growth. This suggests that demographic effects are largely translated by arbitrage into initial prices, and consumers are primarily affected through these price changes rather than through capital gains.

Sharper, and somewhat different, results are obtained when the rate of growth of median house values, as reported by the census, is used instead of the ACCRA measure:

$$(15) \quad \log\left(\frac{Median\ price_{90}}{Median\ price_{80}}\right) = 1.042 + 0.893 \cdot \log\left(\frac{Equiv.\ pop._{.90}}{Equiv.\ pop._{.80}}\right)$$

$$(1.076) \quad (0.282)$$

$$+ 0.018 \cdot \log(Price_{80})$$

$$(0.105)$$

$$- 1.116 \cdot \log \left(\frac{\text{Equiv. pop.}_{80}}{\text{Equiv. pop.}_{70}} \right)$$
$$(0.264)$$
$$- 0.531 \cdot \log \left(\frac{\text{Median price}_{80}}{\text{Median price}_{70}} \right).$$
$$(0.111)$$

This regression has $R^2 = 0.35$, suggesting that real housing price changes *are* forecastable. Contemporaneous population growth has predictive power and is positively correlated with price changes. The effect of lagged price change is negative, suggesting that the market overshoots. Measurement error in census data should be modest but if present could also explain the last effect. The negative sign on past population growth rates also suggests a market cycle, with "spurts" of past population growth that are uncorrelated with current population growth possibly leading to "overbuilding," which creates downward pressure on market prices.

Since there is moderately good agreement between the ACCRA and census prices, it is surprising that regressions (13) and (15) are substantially different. In further analysis, we will use the ACCRA prices, which match the dates of the savings data to be analyzed. For the critical question of behavioral response in savings, we will repeat the analysis using the apparently more forecastable census prices.

The pattern of results for MSAs with census median house prices is confirmed by an analysis of changes in population and housing prices across states. We use the median of owner-reported dwelling values by state, not quality-adjusted, from the 1970, 1980, and 1990 U.S. censuses. We use state equivalent population, constructed in the same way as the MSA equivalent populations. The regressions analogous to (14) and (15) are

(16)
$$\log(\text{Price}_{80}) = 10.813 + 1.849 \cdot \log \left(\frac{\text{Equiv. pop.}_{90}}{\text{Equiv. pop.}_{80}} \right)$$
$$(0.103) \quad (0.510)$$
$$- 1.080 \cdot \log \left(\frac{\text{Equiv. pop.}_{80}}{\text{Equiv. pop.}_{70}} \right)$$
$$(0.469)$$
$$+ 1.083 \cdot \log \left(\frac{\text{Median price}_{80}}{\text{Median price}_{70}} \right),$$
$$(0.304)$$

(17) $$\log \left(\frac{\text{Median price}_{90}}{\text{Median price}_{80}} \right) = - 2.391 + 1.580 \cdot \log \left(\frac{\text{Equiv. pop.}_{90}}{\text{Equiv. pop.}_{80}} \right)$$
$$(1.317) \quad (0.481)$$
$$+ 0.258 \cdot \log(\text{Price}_{80})$$
$$(0.122)$$

$$- 1.187 \cdot \log \left(\frac{\text{Equiv. pop.}_{80}}{\text{Equiv. pop.}_{70}} \right)$$
$$(0.413)$$
$$- 0.985 \cdot \log \left(\frac{\text{Median price}_{80}}{\text{Median price}_{70}} \right).$$
$$(0.286)$$

Equation (16) has $R^2 = 0.336$. Initial prices appear to be related to future population growth, indicating that arbitrage occurs. The terms involving equivalent population can be rearranged into the form

$$0.769 \cdot \log \left(\frac{\text{Equiv. pop.}_{90}}{\text{Equiv. pop.}_{80}} \right) + 1.080 \cdot \left\{ \log \left(\frac{\text{Equiv. pop.}_{90}}{\text{Equiv. pop.}_{80}} \right) - \log \left(\frac{\text{Equiv. pop.}_{80}}{\text{Equiv. pop.}_{70}} \right) \right\}.$$

Then initial price is positively related to the rate of change of future population and to the rate of acceleration of equivalent population.

Equation (17) has $R^2 = 0.581$, so housing price changes appear to be forecastable, with current and lagged equivalent population growth and lagged price changes all significant. The directions of the effects are the same as were found in the MSA data. Again, the effects of equivalent population changes can be reinterpreted as positive response to contemporaneous equivalent population growth (with a coefficient of 0.393) and to the rate of acceleration of equivalent population (with a coefficient of 1.187).

The analysis above with ACCRA prices suggests that demographic effects are largely anticipated and arbitraged away in the housing market so that initial prices embody current information about forecastable trends. Because there are essentially no surprises in population growth over a decade, even at the MSA level, there is no significant correlation of ex post population change and ex post price change. However, using census prices, there appears to be evidence for a substantial forecastable component in housing prices. We have indicated several possible sources of differences in the two price series but have not identified any key features that would lead to the differences in fitted regressions using the two different sources. If the market is not perfectly efficient and there is substantial forecastability, then there is at least scope for a behavioral response that would mitigate some of the adverse effects of demographic changes that are expected to weaken the housing market and reduce real capital gains.

Over the 40-year horizon facing a 30-year-old prospective home buyer, birth rates and consequent changes in equivalent population are not so highly forecastable, and one would expect to see a significant positive correlation of ex post population changes and ex post price changes. These conclusions have several implications for life-cycle savings behavior. First, if arbitrage eliminates most forecastable capital gains, then there is little room for demographics to influence savings behavior except via its impact on initial prices. In the long run, the demographic effects may contain innovations that will result in ex post capital gains, but since these are not forecastable, they cannot alter savings behavior. Then most demographic change should have relatively little ex ante impact on behavior, with the consequence that the effects of demographics on market prices should translate directly into changes in welfare, particularly as a result of unanticipated changes late in life.

7.3   Wealth, Expectations, and Savings

7.3.1   Background

In this section we explore the role of ex post measures of capital gains in the housing market on household savings decisions. Equity in housing has traditionally represented a major component of household wealth in the United States. Feinstein and McFadden (1989), Venti and Wise (1990), and McFadden (1994b) have found that housing equity represents more than 50 percent of total wealth in the population over age 65. Housing wealth has increased with age, at least in the past decade, except for the very old, but extraction of equity becomes an important resource after age 75. The trend of rising house prices that has typified the U.S. market for past decades, as noted by McFadden (1994a), has translated into increases in wealth for current cohorts of elderly homeowners. However, Mankiw and Weil (1989) and McFadden (1994a) have argued that population aging in the United States in the coming three decades is likely to result in a reversal of these trends in housing prices. McFadden (1994a) finds that a potential implication of this reversal is capital losses accompanied by nontrivial welfare losses for younger cohorts of current homeowners. However, if households can anticipate changes in housing prices, and if they adjust their *nonhousing* savings accordingly, welfare losses in retirement could be mitigated. The empirical question that we examine in this section is how household savings decisions are affected by capital gains in housing.

Section 7.2 presented a simple two-period model of consumption and savings. An implication of that model is that consumers should show some savings behavior response to the level of housing prices, essentially because housing demand is inelastic, housing consumption cannot be reduced sufficiently to reduce equity, and compensating adjustments in financial savings are not fully offsetting. Another implication is that ex ante savings rates should respond positively to a change in beliefs that increases expected capital gains. Ex post savings rates, which incorporate realized capital gains, will reflect this dependence in addition to the dependence built into the accounting. However, if capital gains cannot be forecast from current information, including demographic trends, then only the accounting dependence will be observed. The results in section 7.2 suggest that this may indeed be the case. This should be seen most clearly by examining the rate of savings for assets other than housing equity.

Of course, if consumers are irrational in their beliefs and fail to use available information, then a behavioral response may be absent even if capital gains are in principle forecastable.

Recent data from the Panel Study of Income Dynamics (PSID) provides an excellent source for the analysis of savings among elderly households. Comprehensive data on housing and nonhousing wealth was collected in 1984 and 1989 for over 7,000 households. We use this wealth data to form measures of real savings rates over the five-year period. Data on average housing prices by MSA are used to form ex post real capital gain rates over the 1984–89 period, which are then matched to each household in the PSID based on their county of residence. If consumers can predict changes in housing prices *and* have full behavioral offset in savings, then we would expect to see very low correlation between changes in area housing prices and savings rates. However, if individuals are naive in forming expectations or do not adjust savings, then we would expect to see a positive correlation between ex post savings rates and ex post capital gains in housing, as suggested by equations (8) and (9) derived from the two-period model.

The MSA-level regression results in section 7.2 present somewhat mixed evidence concerning the degree to which capital gains in housing are forecastable based on current information, including demographics. In view of these results, the household-level savings regressions in this section use both sources of housing price data, those from ACCRA and from the census.

We present estimates of the effect of changes in housing prices on total, housing, and nonhousing savings rates. These regressions contain controls for age of head, health status, demographic characteristics such as marital status, race, education, and sex of head, and income and initial wealth.

7.3.2 Data and Definitions

The data used for our analysis of the determinants of household savings are drawn from the PSID, a longitudinal data set collected by the Institute for Social Research (ISR) at the University of Michigan, which began in 1968 with a sample of about 5,000 households containing 18,000 individuals. All members (and descendants) of these original survey families have been reinterviewed annually such that by the twenty-second year of the panel, more than 38,000 individuals have participated or are currently participating in the survey. All estimates presented here are based on the 1968–89 (or Wave XXII) sample of the PSID.

The PSID contains a detailed accounting of wealth for all survey households in 1984 and 1989. Using these data, we construct measures of net worth in 1984 and 1989 that include home equity (house value less remaining principal), other real estate equity, financial assets (savings accounts, money market accounts, CDs, treasury bills, mutual funds, stocks, and bonds), business equity, and vehicle equity, less household debt. In an assessment of quality of wealth estimates from survey data, Curtin, Juster, and Morgan (1989) found that the PSID provides wealth data that is "of surprisingly high quality, relative to the quality obtainable with much more intensive survey methods and higher costs per case" (477). In addition to the wealth data, the PSID contains data on health status, demographic variables, family composition, household income, and state and county of residence. The demographic data used in this analysis includes age, education, marital status, sex, and race of the head of household.

We limit the sample to include those households that had stable family compositions over the 1984–89 period. Primarily, we seek to exclude those families where there was a divorce, marriage, or remarriage during the five-year period. We choose to limit our analysis to these intact households because a major change in family composition, such as marriage or divorce, could have a large impact on the savings rate over this period that is not necessarily attributable to life-cycle savings behavior. There are a total of 7,114 households in the 1989 sample of the PSID, of which 4,719 satisfy our definition of an intact family. We further limit the sample by excluding families where the head of household was less than 30 years old and dropping observations with missing data on demographic variables, resulting in a sample with 4,360 observations.[2]

The PSID data are augmented with data on changes in housing prices by MSA from two different sources. The first source comes from ACCRA and covers the period 1984–89; the second source is the decennial census and covers the years 1980–90.[3] The ACCRA data are attractive because they measure constant-quality housing price for the same period that the PSID savings rate is measured. The census data represent owner-reported house value. Both sources of data are available at the MSA or PMSA level. Because the PSID identifies county of residence, not MSA, we merge the housing price data with the PSID data using a Census Bureau file that maps counties into MSAs. About 27 percent of the households in our sample live in counties that are not part of one of the 112 PMSAs or MSAs represented in the ACCRA data. In addition, price data were not available for the entire 1984–89 period for all of the MSAs. The resulting number of observations with data on area housing prices from ACCRA is 2,427.[4] Capital gains from housing are measured by the logarithm of the ratio of real housing prices in 1989 to real housing prices in 1984.

The dependent variable in the regressions is real savings rate over the five-

2. Our sample selection is designed to identify those households where there was no change in the head or spouse over the five-year period. The one exception is that we include those households where the head or spouse died between 1984 and 1989 but the surviving spouse did not remarry. Those households with no change in the head or spouse represent almost 98 percent of the observations in our data set. Overall, in the PSID, over 70 percent of the households in the 1989 sample had no change in the head or spouse between 1984 and 1989. We do not limit the sample to homeowners because one of the implications of the model in section 7.2 is that it may be optimal to change ownership status in response to anticipated capital gains or losses.

3. Both sources of housing price data are described in more detail in section 7.2.2.

4. We are able to assign housing price data to 2,694 of the 4,360 observations in the intact sample. The sample is reduced further to 2,427 observations by dropping those households that move out of the county during the five-year period 1984–89.

year period 1984–89. The savings rate is defined as the difference between real wealth in 1989 and real wealth in 1984 divided by the sum of real income over the period 1984–88,[5]

$$s = \frac{W_{89} - W_{84} / p_{84}}{\displaystyle\sum_{t=1984}^{1988} Y_t / p_t}.$$

In order to explore the effect of capital gains in housing on savings, we split total savings into its housing and nonhousing components. Wealth in each of the years can be easily separated into equity in housing and all nonhousing wealth. Housing wealth includes equity in the home and all other real estate equity, while nonhousing wealth includes financial assets (liquid assets, stocks, and bonds), business equity, and vehicle equity, less household debt. Using these wealth measures, the total savings rate over the period is separated into housing savings and nonhousing savings rates.

Summary statistics for the sample of all intact families from the PSID are provided in table 7.2. Table 7.3 provides descriptive statistics for the subsample with housing price data. In order to minimize the impact of outliers in savings rates, we drop observations in the top and bottom 2.5 percent of the total savings rate distribution.[6] The final sample sizes are 4,142 for all intact families and 2,331 for the sample of intact households with area housing price data.[7] Table 7.2 shows that mean wealth (in 1989 dollars) increased from $72,647 in 1984 to $95,707 in 1989. The real savings rate averaged 7.3 percent, about equally split between housing and nonhousing savings. The average age of the head of household in 1989 was 49, and over 1,180 families had a head over the age of 60. The health status variable is self-reported health status of the head in 1984. The values range from 1 (excellent) to 5 (very poor). Over half of the sample reports health to be excellent or very good. Sixty-three percent of the households are married couple households, and about 72 percent are headed by men. The sample of households in MSAs have slightly higher wealth, savings rates, and income. They are older and more likely to be single, black, and headed by a female. Average housing price (in 1989 dollars) increased from

5. The wealth data correspond to the years 1984 and 1989. To create the savings rate, we divide by total (real) income received in the period between the wealth assessments. This corresponds to income received in 1984–88. In the PSID, income received in calendar year t is reported in survey year $t + 1$. Therefore, total income is the real sum of income from calendar years 1984–88, or survey years 1985–89.

6. Trimming the data in this way drops observations with savings rates of less than −118 percent or more than 133 percent. There seem to be a few extreme outliers in the data, such as a savings rate of over 10,000 percent, and the estimates are sensitive to the exclusion of these outliers. Other than dropping these extreme outliers, the results are not sensitive to the amount of trimming of the data.

7. Note that these sample counts are for the ACCRA housing price data. The sample sizes are somewhat smaller for the census housing price because of data availability.

Table 7.2   Descriptive Statistics: Full Sample of Intact Households, 1984–89

Statistic	Mean	Standard Deviation	Median	Minimum	Maximum
Total wealth 1984[a]	72,647	174,684	27,569	−216,200	5,752,500
Housing wealth 1984	39,081	78,008	16,708	−28,046	2,252,400
Nonhousing wealth 1984	33,565	130,267	7,208	−273,960	5,633,100
Total wealth 1989	95,707	235,097	36,675	−107,400	7,460,000
Housing wealth 1989	50,572	94,727	21,500	−100,000	2,270,000
Nonhousing wealth 1989	45,135	182,374	9,500	−126,800	6,675,000
Total savings rate 1984–89	0.073	0.321	0.027	−1.147	1.326
Housing savings rate 1984–89	0.039	0.255	0.000	−2.326	2.228
Nonhousing savings rate 1984–89	0.034	0.244	0.008	−1.873	1.946
Real income 1984–89	174,533	166,017	143,110	2,657	4,251,000
Age[b]	47.8	15.3	46	30	97
Health status 1984	2.528	1.182	2	1	5
Married	0.633				
Male	0.719				
Black	0.357				
Education <8	0.147				
Education 9–11	0.176				
Education 12	0.313				
Education 13–15	0.185				
Education ≥16	0.179				
N	4,142				

Source: Authors' tabulations from the 1989 PSID. See text for definition of sample.

[a]All dollar amounts are in 1989 dollars.

[b]Unless otherwise specified, all demographic characteristics are for the head of household in 1989.

$114,000 in 1984 to $130,952 in 1989, representing a increase of 9.2 percent. Figure 7.4 shows that there is large variation in the housing growth rate over this period. Over 50 percent of the sample had real growth between 10 and 50 percent, while about a third of the sample had capital losses.

7.3.3 Life-Cycle Savings and Wealth

The PSID data show large differences in the level and composition of wealth and savings by age of head of household. Figure 7.7 provides estimates for mean wealth in 1989 by age of head of household, and figure 7.8 plots median

Table 7.3   **Descriptive Statistics: Intact Households with MSA Housing Prices, 1984–89**

Statistic	Mean	Standard Deviation	Median	Minimum	Maximum
Total wealth 1984[a]	74,477	207,399	24,956	−216,200	5,752,500
Housing wealth 1984	41,455	90,802	14,321	−13,128	2,252,400
Nonhousing wealth 1984	33,022	156,676	6,564	−273,960	5,633,100
Total wealth 1989	100,922	283,206	35,000	−72,579	7,460,000
Housing wealth 1989	54,154	105,730	20,000	−71,319	2,270,000
Nonhousing wealth 1989	46,768	227,404	8,153	−126,800	6,675,000
Total savings rate 1984–89	0.080	0.311	0.026	−1.131	1.326
Housing savings rate 1984–89	0.046	0.244	0.000	−1.577	1.736
Nonhousing savings rate 1984–89	0.034	0.218	0.008	−1.873	1.489
Real income 1984–89	183,245	193,901	147,380	2,657	4,251,000
MSA housing price 1984	114,356	26,481	106,371	67,980	212,996
MSA housing price 1989	130,952	53,422	107,680	74,875	344,670
log(HPRY89/ HPRY84)	0.092	0.218	0.063	−0.361	0.758
Age[b]	49.9	14.8	47	30	97
Health status 1984	2.540	1.178	2	1	5
Married	0.586				
Male	0.674				
Black	0.433				
Education <8	0.132				
Education 9–11	0.186				
Education 12	0.317				
Education 13–15	0.195				
Education ≥16	0.170				
N	2,331				

Source: Authors' tabulations from the 1989 PSID. See text for definition of sample.

[a]All dollar amounts are in 1989 dollars.

[b]Unless otherwise specified, all demographic characteristics are for the head of household in 1989.

wealth by age of head of household.[8] Mean wealth rises steeply from ages 30–34 to ages 60–64, an increase from $34,000 to $160,000. Wealth falls to about $100,000 for ages 75 and over. Median wealth also follows this hump-

8. Means by five-year age class are fairly precisely estimated because cell sizes average 200–350. The exception is the oldest age group (85+), which is imprecisely estimated because sample size is 47.

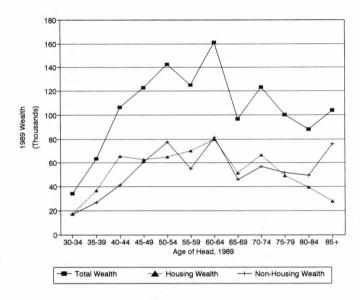

Fig. 7.7   Mean wealth by age of head of household
Source: Authors' tabulation from the 1989 PSID.

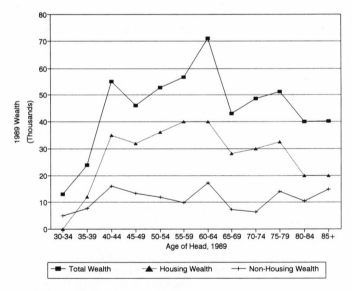

Fig. 7.8   Median wealth by age of head of household
Source: Authors' tabulation from the 1989 PSID.

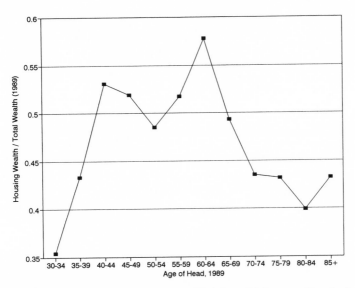

Fig. 7.9   Housing wealth as a percentage of total wealth by age of head of household
Source: Authors' tabulation from the PSID.

shaped pattern, but because of the highly skewed nature of wealth, the levels are consistently lower. Median wealth rises from $13,020 for households with heads aged 30–34 to $70,000 for those aged 60–64, then falls to about $40,000–$50,000 for those aged 70 and over.[9]

Figures 7.7 and 7.8 also plot the housing and nonhousing components of household wealth. The hump-shaped pattern for wealth is particularly apparent for housing wealth, but it is not apparent for nonhousing wealth. Median housing wealth falls from $40,000 among those aged 55–64 to $20,000 for those aged 80 and over. At the same time, median nonhousing wealth remains fairly constant over this age range.

Housing wealth represents the single most important part of total household wealth among families in the United States. Among our sample of intact families in the PSID data, housing wealth represents, on average, over half of total wealth. As shown in figure 7.9, the relative importance of housing wealth varies dramatically over the life cycle. Among younger families homeownership is low; housing wealth peaks as a percentage of total wealth at ages 60–64 and then decreases. Housing wealth as a percentage of total wealth increases from about 35 percent among the youngest cohort to a high of over 55 percent for

9. Because we are only using one year of wealth data, these age effects of wealth could also be generated by cohort effects. That is, those aged 80–84 in the data also belong to the same birth cohort. These data do not allow for the separate identification of age effects and cohort effects. For an analysis of financial wealth holdings by age and birth cohort, see Attanasio (1993).

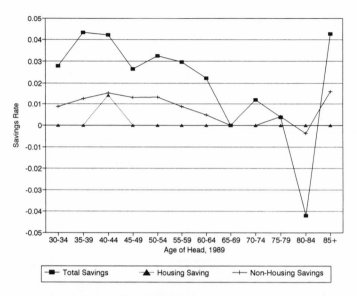

Fig. 7.10   Mean five-year savings rate by age of head of household in 1989
Source: Authors' tabulation from the 1984–89 PSID.

those aged 60–64, then falls to about 40 percent of total wealth for those in the oldest cohorts.

Figure 7.10 summarizes the life-cycle pattern of total, housing, and non-housing savings rates over the period 1984–89. Between the ages of 35 and 60, the total savings rate averages about 9 percent of real income over the five-year period. After age 60, the savings rate decreases to about 5 percent and eventually turns negative only at the highest age levels. Housing savings follows this same pattern, with lower savings rates among the elderly. Nonhousing savings, however, remain more steady over the life cycle.

7.3.4   Savings Rates and Capital Gains in Housing

This section investigates the effect of changes in housing prices on five-year savings rates using a sample of intact families from the PSID. As described above, the savings rate data correspond to the period 1984–89. The housing price data refer to price changes for the MSA that the family resides in. The ACCRA housing price data cover the years 1984–89, while the census data cover the years 1980–90.

Table 7.4A presents parameter estimates for regressions where the dependent variable is the total savings rate.[10] Model (1) relates savings rates to age

10. For each of the models reported in this section, the dependent variable is the savings rate multiplied by 100.

Table 7.4A   **Parameter Estimates for Savings Rate Regressions Where Dependent Variable = Total Savings Rate: Capital Gains in Housing for 1984–89**

Variable	Model							
	(1)	(2)	(3)	(4)	(5)	(6)	(7)	(8)
Constant	-2.117	-5.864	-1.982	-157.838	-151.100	-147.397	-137.785	-134.940
	(6.320)	(6.664)	(8.742)	(36.849)	(41.933)	(42.293)	(42.235)	(42.198)
Age	0.472	0.407	0.347	0.265	0.115	0.034	-0.061	-0.195
	(0.247)	(0.249)	(0.331)	(0.330)	(0.352)	(0.362)	(0.358)	(0.359)
Age^2/100	-0.519	-0.363	-0.339	-0.267	-0.133	-0.060	0.026	0.210
	(0.225)	(0.226)	(0.306)	(0.305)	(0.325)	(0.334)	(0.332)	(0.332)
Married		4.102	4.541	4.410	4.581	4.547	3.628	2.390
		(1.751)	(2.198)	(2.190)	(2.275)	(2.276)	(2.305)	(2.299)
Black		-1.363	-1.182	-1.460	-1.029	-1.045	-0.561	-0.476
		(1.155)	(1.441)	(1.437)	(1.541)	(1.542)	(1.551)	(1.544)
Male		1.420	3.311	3.375	3.730	3.778	3.488	2.982
		(1.879)	(2.306)	(2.297)	(2.386)	(2.387)	(2.385)	(2.365)
Education 9–11		-1.029	-2.984	-2.841	-3.123	-3.156	-3.151	-2.592
		(1.800)	(2.307)	(2.298)	(2.411)	(2.413)	(2.408)	(2.390)
Education 12		1.330	-2.268	-2.135	-2.271	-2.336	-2.585	-2.238
		(1.703)	(2.209)	(2.200)	(2.309)	(2.311)	(2.309)	(2.295)
Education 13–15		3.665	-2.378	-2.672	-2.276	-2.353	-2.892	-2.837
		(1.912)	(2.461)	(2.452)	(2.592)	(2.596)	(2.601)	(2.586)
Education ≥16		8.932	4.713	4.304	3.809	3.807	2.218	1.014
		(2.004)	(2.655)	(2.647)	(2.815)	(2.816)	(2.886)	(2.887)

(continued)

Table 7.4A (continued)

Variable	Model							
	(1)	(2)	(3)	(4)	(5)	(6)	(7)	(8)
Health status		-1.132	-1.473	-1.518	-0.776	-0.763	-0.505	-0.352
		(0.495)	(0.631)	(0.628)	(0.663)	(0.664)	(0.672)	(0.668)
log(HPYR89/HPRY84)[a]			22.800	18.628	20.529		19.910	19.930
			(2.905)	(3.048)	(4.111)		(4.113)	(4.077)
log(HPRY84/100,000)[a]				13.651	13.256	13.108	12.326	11.940
				(3.136)	(3.622)	(3.636)	(3.637)	(3.621)
log(POP80/POP70)[b]					2.357	2.439	1.819	3.764
					(6.135)	(6.141)	(6.131)	(6.086)
log(HPRY80/HPRY70)[c]					-1.180	-1.120	-0.801	-0.364
					(2.626)	(2.630)	(2.628)	(2.606)
log(HPRY89/HPRY84) * Age ≤40						24.556		
						(5.834)		
log(HPRY89/HPRY84) * Age 41–60						18.923		
						(6.417)		

					18.241	1.122	3.789
log(HPRY89/HPRY84) * Age >60					(5.547)	(0.459)	(0.627)
Real income 1984–89[d]						1.122	3.789
						(0.459)	(0.627)
Housing wealth 1984[d]							−1.555
							(0.855)
Nonhousing wealth 1984[d]							−3.161
							(0.554)
Adjusted R^2	0.0027	0.0276	0.0621	0.0693	0.0631	0.0626	0.0654	0.0825
N	4,142	4,142	2,331	2,331	1,996	1,996	1,996	1,996

Note: Based on authors' tabulations from the 1989 PSID. See text for description of sample selection. The dependent variable is the real savings rate over the five-year period 1984–89, which is calculated by dividing the change in real wealth by real income over the five-year period. All specifications include controls for age, sex, race, education, marital status, and health status of the head of household. All dollar amounts are in 1989 dollars. Standard errors are in parentheses.

[a]ACCRA data for constant-quality housing prices.

[b]Population by MSA from decennial census.

[c]Median home value (not quality-adjusted) from decennial census by MSA.

[d]In 100,000 dollars.

Table 7.4B   Parameter Estimates for Savings Rate Regressions Where Dependent Variable = Total Savings Rate: Capital Gains in Housing for 1980–90

		Model	
Variable	(1)	(2)	(3)
Constant	−8.281	−106.709	−106.659
	(9.262)	(22.048)	(23.046)
Age	0.177	0.142	0.093
	(0.349)	(0.348)	(0.351)
Age²/100	−0.194	−0.169	−0.114
	(0.323)	(0.321)	(0.325)
Married	5.355	5.440	4.527
	(2.270)	(2.258)	(2.276)
Black	−1.901	−1.349	−1.583
	(1.506)	(1.501)	(1.522)
Male	3.158	3.212	4.016
	(2.381)	(2.368)	(2.387)
Education 9–11	−2.685	−2.502	−2.672
	(2.412)	(2.398)	(2.415)
Education 12	−1.765	−1.854	−1.881
	(2.296)	(2.283)	(2.307)
Education 13–15	−1.108	−1.918	−2.186
	(2.574)	(2.565)	(2.590)
Education ≥16	5.448	4.572	4.330
	(2.793)	(2.783)	(2.805)
Health status 1984	−0.745	−0.725	−0.777
	(0.662)	(0.659)	(0.661)
log(HPRY90/HPRY80)[a]	13.832	16.154	15.577
	(1.890)	(1.937)	(2.542)
log(HPRY80/100,000)[a]		9.113	9.322
		(1.855)	(2.073)
log(POP80/POP70)[b]			0.076
			(6.152)
log(HPRY80/HPRY70)[a]			−0.511
			(2.866)
Adjusted R^2	0.0582	0.0688	0.0663
N	2,045	2,045	2,024

Note: See table 7.4A note.

[a]Median home value (not quality-adjusted) from decennial census by MSA.

[b]Population by MSA from decennial census.

of head of household, and the results imply a hump-shaped age profile. As shown in figure 7.10, the savings rate decreases with age beginning at about age 45. Model (2) considers a larger set of demographic variables. Savings rates are found to be higher for married couples and those families whose head of household is nonblack or male. However, neither sex nor race of head of household is found to significantly affect savings rates. Higher education levels (education of the head) are associated with higher rates of savings. Self-reported health of the head in 1984 is associated with lower levels of savings. This is consistent with the evidence in Attanasio and Hoynes (1995), where lower levels of household wealth are associated with higher levels of mortality risk. Controlling for these demographic variables shifts out the age profile for savings rates. The parameter estimates in model (2) imply that savings rates are maximized at age 56 and decline after.

The next three models add capital gains in housing prices for the MSA of residence to the savings rate regression.[11] These housing price data correspond to 1984–89 and are from ACCRA. The housing price variable is constructed as the logarithm of the ratio of real housing prices in 1989 to real housing prices in 1984. The estimates in model (3) imply that an increase in the growth rate of real housing prices of 10 percentage points will lead, on average, to an increase in the total savings rate of 2.28 percentage points, or an increase of 37 percent. What does this suggest for the amount of behavioral offset that households are engaging in? At mean levels of income and wealth, an additional real increase of 10 percentage points in home value (with no offsetting change in savings) will lead to an increase in the savings rate of 3.10 percentage points. If individuals are, in fact, forming correct expectations about changes in housing prices, then these estimates suggest that they are making (at the most) very minor changes to their nonhousing savings.

This result can also be seen by considering the effect of capital gains in housing on housing and nonhousing savings rates. Parameter estimates for the housing savings rate regressions are presented in table 7.5A, while the nonhousing savings rate estimates are in table 7.6A.[12] Consider the estimates for model (3) in tables 7.5A and 7.6A. Changes in area housing prices have the same effect on the housing savings rate as was found for the total savings rate. For nonhousing savings, capital gains in housing are associated with both small and statistically insignificant changes in nonhousing savings.

The model presented in section 7.2 suggests that savings rates should be correlated with the initial level of housing prices, as well as with the growth rate. Model (4) adds the logarithm of the 1984 housing price to the regressions. Increases in initial housing prices are associated with increases in the total and

11. Note that the sample size is reduced by half when we include the MSA-level housing price data in the specification. As described in section 7.3.2, this is because of incomplete price data and because about a quarter of the PSID sample does not live in an MSA. Estimates not reported here suggest that there are not large differences in the role of demographic variables among these two samples. Because of the smaller sample, however, the precision of the estimates generally is reduced.

12. The effects of demographic variables on housing and nonhousing savings rates are similar to the results summarized for the total savings rate equation. Notable differences are that health status in 1984 is more important in determining changes in nonhousing as compared to housing wealth. If poor health leads to low savings rates because of an increase in medical costs, reductions in nonhousing wealth would be expected because of the highly illiquid nature of housing wealth. In addition, housing savings is found to peak at an earlier age compared to total savings rates. Model (2) implies that housing savings rates begin to decline at age 49, compared to age 56 for total savings.

Table 7.5A   Parameter Estimates for Savings Rate Regressions Where Dependent Variable = Housing Savings Rate: Capital Gains in Housing for 1984–89

	Model							
Variable	(1)	(2)	(3)	(4)	(5)	(6)	(7)	(8)
Constant	-10.132	-11.288	-6.512	-155.981	-163.530	-161.486	-163.888	-181.460
	(5.004)	(5.313)	(6.859)	(28.855)	(33.692)	(33.982)	(33.985)	(34.071)
Age	0.679	0.618	0.465	0.387	0.393	0.337	0.397	0.521
	(0.196)	(0.198)	(0.259)	(0.258)	(0.282)	(0.291)	(0.288)	(0.290)
Age^2/100	-0.729	-0.629	-0.487	-0.418	-0.430	-0.377	-0.434	-0.499
	(0.178)	(0.181)	(0.240)	(0.239)	(0.261)	(0.268)	(0.267)	(0.268)
Married		3.658	4.827	4.701	4.656	4.639	4.682	4.825
		(1.396)	(1.725)	(1.715)	(1.828)	(1.829)	(1.855)	(1.856)
Black		0.655	0.754	0.488	0.557	0.540	0.545	0.046
		(0.921)	(1.131)	(1.125)	(1.238)	(1.239)	(1.248)	(1.247)
Male		0.371	0.677	0.739	1.234	1.267	1.240	1.250
		(1.498)	(1.809)	(1.799)	(1.917)	(1.918)	(1.919)	(1.909)
Education 9–11		-3.282	-4.386	-4.248	-4.659	-4.674	-4.658	-4.135
		(1.435)	(1.810)	(1.799)	(1.937)	(1.938)	(1.938)	(1.930)
Education 12		-0.949	-3.509	-3.381	-3.960	-3.997	-3.952	-3.237
		(1.357)	(1.733)	(1.723)	(1.855)	(1.857)	(1.858)	(1.853)
Education 13–15		1.517	-2.361	-2.643	-2.677	-2.716	-2.661	-1.895
		(1.524)	(1.931)	(1.920)	(2.082)	(2.086)	(2.093)	(2.088)
Education ≥16		2.667	-1.802	-2.194	-2.014	-2.011	-1.971	-1.200
		(1.598)	(2.083)	(2.073)	(2.262)	(2.263)	(2.322)	(2.331)
Health status 1984		-0.485	-0.780	-0.824	-0.458	-0.447	-0.466	-0.594
		(0.395)	(0.495)	(0.492)	(0.533)	(0.533)	(0.541)	(0.540)
log(HPRY89/ HPRY84)[a]			22.536	18.535	15.609		15.626	16.016
			(2.279)	(2.387)	(3.303)		(3.310)	(3.292)
log(HPRY84/ 100,000)[a]				13.092	13.825	13.762	13.850	14.916
				(2.456)	(2.910)	(2.921)	(2.927)	(2.924)

log(POP80/POP70)[b]				−4.802 (4.929)	−4.778 (4.934)	−4.787 (4.933)	−3.458 (4.914)
log(HPRY80/HPRY70)[c]				−0.590 (2.110)	−0.562 (2.113)	−0.600 (2.115)	−0.150 (2.104)
log(HPRY89/HPRY84) * Age ≤40					18.507 (4.687)		
log(HPRY89/HPRY84) * Age 41–60					13.725 (5.156)		
log(HPRY89/HPRY84) * Age >60					14.426 (4.457)		
Real income 1984–89[d]						−0.030 (0.370)	0.743 (0.506)
Housing wealth 1984[d]							−3.341 (0.690)
Nonhousing wealth 1984[d]							−0.322 (0.448)
Adjusted R^2	0.0082	0.0196	0.0572	0.0683	0.0600	0.0595	0.0597	0.0704
N	4,142	4,142	2,331	2,331	1,996	1,996	1,996	1,996

Note: See table 7.4A note.

[a]ACCRA data for constant-quality housing prices.
[b]Population by MSA from decennial census.
[c]Median home value (not quality-adjusted) from decennial census by MSA.
[d]In 100,000 dollars.

Table 7.5B   **Parameter Estimates for Savings Rate Regressions Where Dependent Variable = Housing Savings Rate: Capital Gains in Housing for 1980–90**

	Model		
Variable	(1)	(2)	(3)
Constant	−14.962	−107.416	−102.791
	(7.414)	(17.608)	(18.425)
Age	0.452	0.419	0.307
	(0.280)	(0.278)	(0.281)
Age^2/100	−0.488	−0.464	−0.353
	(0.259)	(0.257)	(0.260)
Married	5.676	5.756	5.507
	(1.817)	(1.803)	(1.820)
Black	−0.104	0.415	0.423
	(1.205)	(1.199)	(1.217)
Male	0.357	0.408	0.763
	(1.906)	(1.891)	(1.908)
Education 9–11	−4.102	−3.930	−4.179
	(1.930)	(1.915)	(1.931)
Education 12	−3.298	−3.382	−3.688
	(1.837)	(1.823)	(1.845)
Education 13–15	−1.461	−2.223	−2.557
	(2.060)	(2.048)	(2.071)
Education ≥16	−0.931	−1.754	−2.048
	(2.236)	(2.223)	(2.242)
Health status 1984	−0.341	−0.321	−0.382
	(0.530)	(0.526)	(0.529)
log(HPRY90/HPRY80)[a]	12.945	15.126	14.316
	(1.512)	(1.547)	(2.032)
log(HPRY80/100,000)[a]		8.560	8.472
		(1.481)	(1.658)
log(POP80/POP70)[b]			−3.194
			(4.918)
log(HPRY80/HPRY70)[a]			0.472
			(2.292)
Adjusted R^2	0.0515	0.0664	0.0638
N	2,045	2,045	2,024

Note: See table 7.4A note.
[a]Median home value (not quality-adjusted) from decennial census by MSA.
[b]Population by MSA from decennial census.

housing savings rates but have no significant effect on nonhousing savings. A 10 percent increase in initial housing prices increases the (total) savings rate by 1.4 percentage points, an increase of about 17 percent. Finally, model (5) includes past measures of population and price changes for the MSA. Neither of these variables affect household savings.

The savings regressions presented above assume that the behavioral re-

Table 7.6A   Parameter Estimates for Savings Rate Regressions Where Dependent Variable = Nonhousing Savings Rate: Capital Gains in Housing for 1984–89

	Model							
Variable	(1)	(2)	(3)	(4)	(5)	(6)	(7)	(8)
Constant	8.015 (4.821)	5.424 (5.118)	4.529 (6.245)	−1.858 (26.429)	12.429 (29.919)	14.089 (30.181)	26.103 (30.086)	46.520 (29.927)
Age	−0.207 (0.189)	−0.211 (0.191)	−0.118 (0.236)	−0.122 (0.237)	−0.277 (0.251)	−0.303 (0.258)	−0.458 (0.255)	−0.716 (0.255)
Age^2/100	0.210 (0.172)	0.266 (0.174)	0.148 (0.218)	0.151 (0.219)	0.297 (0.232)	0.317 (0.238)	0.461 (0.236)	0.710 (0.235)
Married		0.445 (1.345)	−0.286 (1.570)	−0.291 (1.571)	−0.075 (1.623)	−0.092 (1.624)	−1.054 (1.642)	−2.436 (1.630)
Black		−2.018 (0.887)	−1.937 (1.030)	−1.948 (1.031)	−1.586 (1.099)	−1.584 (1.100)	−1.106 (1.105)	−0.522 (1.095)
Male		1.049 (1.443)	2.634 (1.647)	2.637 (1.647)	2.497 (1.702)	2.511 (1.703)	2.248 (1.699)	1.732 (1.677)
Education 9–11		2.253 (1.382)	1.402 (1.648)	1.407 (1.648)	1.536 (1.720)	1.519 (1.722)	1.507 (1.715)	1.543 (1.695)
Education 12		2.278 (1.308)	1.240 (1.578)	1.246 (1.578)	1.689 (1.647)	1.660 (1.649)	1.367 (1.645)	1.000 (1.628)
Education 13–15		2.148 (1.469)	−0.017 (1.758)	−0.029 (1.759)	0.401 (1.849)	0.362 (1.852)	−0.231 (1.852)	−0.942 (1.834)
Education ≥16		6.264 (1.539)	6.515 (1.897)	6.498 (1.898)	5.823 (2.008)	5.817 (2.010)	4.189 (2.056)	2.214 (2.047)
Health status 1984		−0.647 (0.380)	−0.692 (0.450)	−0.694 (0.451)	−0.318 (0.473)	−0.316 (0.474)	−0.039 (0.479)	0.242 (0.474)
log(HPRY89/HPRY84)[a]			0.264 (2.186)	0.093 (2.933)	4.920	(2.930)	4.285 (2.892)	3.915
log(HPRY84/100,000)[a]		(2.705)		0.559 (2.249)	−0.570 (2.584)	−0.654 (2.595)	−1.524 (2.591)	−2.977 (2.568)

(continued)

Table 7.6A (continued)

Variable	Model							
	(1)	(2)	(3)	(4)	(5)	(6)	(7)	(8)
log(POP80/POP70)[b]					7.159 (4.377)	7.216 (4.382)	6.607 (4.367)	7.222 (4.316)
log(HPRY80/HPRY70)[c]					−0.591 (1.874)	−0.558 (1.877)	−0.201 (1.872)	−0.214 (1.848)
log(HPRY89/HPRY84) * Age ≤40						6.049 (4.163)		
log(HPRY89/HPRY84) * Age 41–60						5.198 (4.579)		
log(HPRY89/HPRY84) * Age > 60						3.815 (3.959)		
Real income 1984–89[d]							1.152 (0.327)	3.046 (0.444)
Housing wealth 1984[d]								1.786 (0.606)
Nonhousing wealth 1984[d]								−2.840 (0.393)
Adjusted R^2	0.0001	0.0118	0.0206	0.0202	0.0152	0.0142	0.0208	0.0471
N	4,142	4,142	2,331	2,331	1,996	1,996	1,996	1,996

Note: See table 7.4A note.

[a] ACCRA data for constant-quality housing prices.

[b] Population by MSA from decennial census.

[c] Median home value (not quality-adjusted) from decennial census by MSA.

[d] In 100,000 dollars.

Table 7.6B   **Parameter Estimates for Savings Rate Regressions Where Dependent Variable = Nonhousing Savings Rate: Capital Gains in Housing for 1980–90**

Variable	Model (1)	(2)	(3)
Constant	6.681	0.706	−3.868
	(6.670)	(15.972)	(16.657)
Age	−0.274	−0.276	−0.214
	(0.252)	(0.252)	(0.254)
Age^2/100	0.294	0.295	0.239
	(0.233)	(0.233)	(0.235)
Married	−0.321	−0.316	−0.980
	(1.635)	(1.635)	(1.645)
Black	−1.797	−1.764	−2.006
	(1.084)	(1.088)	(1.100)
Male	2.801	2.804	3.253
	(1.715)	(1.715)	(1.725)
Education 9–11	1.417	1.428	1.507
	(1.737)	(1.737)	(1.746)
Education 12	1.534	1.528	1.807
	(1.653)	(1.654)	(1.668)
Education 13–15	0.353	0.304	0.371
	(1.854)	(1.858)	(1.872)
Education ≥16	6.379	6.326	6.378
	(2.011)	(2.016)	(2.027)
Health status 1984	−0.404	−0.403	−0.395
	(0.477)	(0.477)	(0.478)
log(HPRY90/HPRY80)[a]	0.887	1.028	1.261
	(1.361)	(1.403)	(1.837)
log(HPRY80/100,000)[a]		0.553	0.850
		(1.344)	(1.498)
log(POP80/POP70)[b]			3.270
			(4.446)
log(HPRY80/HPRY70)[a]			−0.983
			(2.072)
Adjusted R^2	0.0172	0.0168	0.0164
N	2,045	2,045	2,024

Note: See table 7.4A note.
[a]Median home value (not quality-adjusted) from decennial census by MSA.
[b]Population by MSA from decennial census.

sponse to a given change in capital gains is constant across all households. Because older homeowners are closer to retirement and possibly more likely to be considering selling their homes in the near future than younger homeowners, it is possible that the behavioral response would differ with the age of the household head. Model (6) interacts the change in housing prices with dummies for age of the household head. Our results show no significant differences in the responses of households with heads less than age 40, between ages 40 and 60, and over age 60.[13]

Further, we find that adding controls for household wealth and income does not change the conclusions about the role of capital gains in housing. Models (7) and (8) in tables 7.4A, 7.5A, and 7.6A show that higher household income and lower initial wealth are associated with higher savings rates. The results for wealth, however, appear to be spurious: initial housing wealth is significantly negatively correlated with housing savings, while initial nonhousing wealth is significantly negatively correlated with nonhousing savings rates.

These savings regressions imply that households are not engaging in any behavioral offset in response to changes in housing prices. However, if capital gains cannot be forecast from current information, then we would not expect to see the households engaging in any offsetting behavior. The results in section 7.2 suggest that, when the ACCRA data are used, housing prices are not forecastable from current information, including demographics. However, the census data imply that these gains are not arbitraged away and housing prices are forecastable from demographics. Tables 7.4B, 7.5B, and 7.6B present estimates for models that use the census price data to reconsider the issue of behavioral offset.

Model (1) in tables 7.4B, 7.5B, and 7.6B includes the full set of demographic variables and the growth rate in housing prices over 1980–90. The housing price variable is constructed as the logarithm of the ratio of real housing prices in 1990 to real housing prices in 1980. Results using the census data have the same implications about offsetting behavior as we found with the ACCRA housing price data. Increases in capital gains in housing have a large and positive effect on both total and housing savings. The results in table 7.6B, however, show that there is no effect of changes in capital gains in housing prices on nonhousing savings. These results are robust to the addition of 1980 housing price (model [2]) as well as measures of past growth in population and housing prices (model [3]).

If households can perfectly predict capital gains in housing *and* they offset this change by fully adjusting nonhousing savings rates, then we would expect to see zero correlation between changes in housing prices and total savings rates and negative correlation between changes in housing prices and nonhousing savings rates. We find neither. There are several hypotheses, however, that are consistent with our findings: Expectations about capital gains in housing prices may not play any role in savings decisions; that is, even if consumers had perfect foresight about changes in housing prices, they do not change their savings rates to try to achieve some target total savings over the period. Alternatively, expectations play a role but households are "naive" in forming these expectations; that is, they may not be using all available information (e.g., fore-

---

13. We considered several specifications for the interaction between age and price change (e.g., various other dummy variable interactions and an age polynomial), and in each case there were no significant age effects.

castable components of housing price changes such as demographic trends) to form expectations about changes in housing prices.

7.4 Concluding Remarks

Housing equity represents an important part of household wealth in the United States. Steady gains in housing prices over the last several decades have generated large potential gains in household wealth among homeowners. Mankiw and Weil (1989) and McFadden (1994a) have argued that the population aging in the United States is likely to induce substantial declines in housing prices, resulting in capital losses for future elderly generations. However, if households are able to anticipate these housing price changes and they modify their nonhousing savings decisions, then potential losses may be mitigated.

We use data on housing prices and demographic trends for 112 metropolitan statistical areas to investigate whether housing prices are forecastable from current information. We then estimate housing savings rate equations using data on five-year savings rates from the Panel Study of Income Dynamics. We use data from two different sources to examine the effect of demographics on housing prices, and in future research we intend to use alternative data sources to further examine this important issue.

While our results are mixed with respect to the forecastability of housing prices, we found no evidence that households were changing their nonhousing savings in response to expectations about capital gains in housing. This lack of adjustment could result in large welfare losses to current homeowners and large intergenerational equity differences.

Appendix
Comparative Statics for the Housing Demand Model

This appendix analyzes the comparative statics of housing demand and savings in the two-period model. Assumptions will be stated when they are first used, starting with the following basic assumptions:

1. U is strictly concave and nondecreasing with $\nabla_g U(0, h) = +\infty$, $\nabla_h U(g, 0) = +\infty$, and $\nabla_h U(g, +\infty) = 0$.

2. Housing and nonhousing consumption are normal goods; that is, $\nabla_g (\nabla_g U / \nabla_h U) \leq 0$ and $\nabla_h (\nabla_g U / \nabla_h U) \geq 0$.

3. V is a constant relative risk aversion utility function; that is, $V(w) = -Ce^{-\kappa w}$, where C and κ are positive parameters.

4. All variables except $\mathring{P}$ are in the consumer's initial information set $\mathscr{I}I$ and given this information the consumer believes that $\mathring{P}$ has a normal distribution with mean α and variance σ^2.

Using the budget constraint equations (2) and (3) to eliminate A_1, one has

(A1) $W_2 = dhP_1[1 - \theta + (1 - m)\mathring{P}] + [1 + r']\{W_1 + (1 - m)Y_1$
$$- \pi_1 g - (1 - d)Rh - dhP_1 (1 - \theta + \mu)\}.$$

For notational shorthand, define

$$W_2^e = dhP_1 [1 - \theta + (1 - m)\alpha] + [1 + r']\{W_1 + (1 - m)Y_1$$
$$- \pi_1 g - (1 - d)Rh - dhP_1 (1 - \theta + \mu)\},$$
$$\omega = (1 + r')[W_1 + (1 - m)Y_1],$$
$$c = (1 + r')[1 - \theta + \mu] - [1 - \theta + (1 - m)\alpha],$$
$$q = \kappa\sigma^2(1 - m)^2/\pi_2,$$
$$\mathsf{V} = \exp\left\{-\frac{\kappa}{\pi^2}\left[\omega - (1 + r')\pi_1 g\right.\right.$$
$$\left.\left. - (1 - d)(1 + r')Rh - dhP_1 c - P_1^2 h^2 d\frac{q}{2}\right]\right\}.$$

Then W_2^e is the consumer's expected final wealth, ω is total initial wealth, c is the user cost of housing, q is a risk penalty, and V appears in the expression for expected utility of bequests:

(A2) $$\mathbf{E}\, V(W_2/\pi_2) = - C \cdot \mathsf{V}.$$

Substituting this expression into the consumer's objective function gives the problem

(A3) $$\max_{h,\, g} U(g, h) - C \cdot \mathsf{V}.$$

The first-order conditions for this unconstrained problem are

(A4) $$\nabla_g U = b_g C \cdot \mathsf{V},$$
$$\nabla_h U = b_h C \cdot \mathsf{V},$$

where

$$(\nabla_g \mathsf{V})/\mathsf{V} = b_g \equiv (1 + r')\kappa\frac{\pi_1}{\pi_2},$$
$$(\nabla_h \mathsf{V})/\mathsf{V} = b_h \equiv \frac{\kappa}{\pi_2}[(1 + r')R(1 - d) + dP_1 c + dhP_1^2 q].$$

Similarly,

$$(\nabla_\omega \mathsf{V})/\mathsf{V} = b_\omega \equiv -\kappa/\pi_2,$$
$$(\nabla_R \mathsf{V})/\mathsf{V} = b_R \equiv (1 + r')\frac{\kappa}{\pi_2}(1 - d)h,$$
$$(\nabla_{P_1} \mathsf{V})/\mathsf{V} = b_{P_1} \equiv \frac{\kappa}{\pi_2}dh[c + qhP_1],$$
$$(\nabla_\alpha \mathsf{V})/\mathsf{V} = b_\alpha \equiv -1(1 + r')\frac{\kappa}{\pi_2}(1 - m)dhP_1.$$

Define the matrix

$$
\mathbf{M} \equiv \begin{bmatrix} \nabla_{gg}U - b_g^2 C \cdot \mathbf{V} & \nabla_{gh}U - b_g b_h C \cdot \mathbf{V} \\ \nabla_{hg}U - b_h b_g C \cdot \mathbf{V} & \nabla_{hh}U - b_h^2 C \cdot \mathbf{V} - \dfrac{\kappa}{\pi_2} dP_1^2 q C \cdot \mathbf{V} \end{bmatrix} .
$$

Note that $\mathbf{M}$ is the sum of

$$
\begin{bmatrix} \nabla_{gg}U & \nabla_{gh}U \\ \nabla_{hg}U & \nabla_{hh}U \end{bmatrix},
$$

which is negative definite, and

$$
\begin{bmatrix} 0 & 0 \\ 0 & -\dfrac{\kappa}{\pi_2} dP_1^2 q C \cdot \mathbf{V} \end{bmatrix} - \begin{bmatrix} b_g \\ b_h \end{bmatrix} \begin{bmatrix} b_g & b_h \end{bmatrix} C \cdot \mathbf{V},
$$

which is negative semidefinite. Hence, det $\mathbf{M} > 0$, and

$$
\mathbf{M}^{-1} = \frac{1}{\det_\mathbf{M}} \begin{bmatrix} \nabla_{hh}U - b_h^2 C \cdot \mathbf{V} - \dfrac{\kappa}{\pi_2} dP_1^2 q C \cdot \mathbf{V} & -\nabla_{gh}U + b_g b_h C \cdot \mathbf{V} \\ -\nabla_{gh}U + b_g b_h C \cdot \mathbf{V} & \nabla_{gg}U - b_g^2 C \cdot \mathbf{V} \end{bmatrix} .
$$

Define the vectors

$$
\mathbf{A}_\omega = \begin{bmatrix} b_g b_w \\ b_h b_w \end{bmatrix}, \quad \mathbf{A}_{P_1} = \begin{bmatrix} b_g b_{P_1} \\ b_h b_{P_1} + \dfrac{\kappa d}{\pi_2}(c + 2hP_1 q) \end{bmatrix},
$$

$$
\mathbf{A}_R = \begin{bmatrix} b_g b_R \\ b_h b_R + \dfrac{\kappa}{\pi_2}(1 + r')(1 - d) \end{bmatrix}, \quad \mathbf{A}_\alpha = \begin{bmatrix} b_g b_\alpha \\ b_h b_\alpha - \dfrac{\kappa d}{\pi_2} P_1(1 - m) \end{bmatrix} .
$$

The derivatives needed for comparative statics analysis are obtained by differentiating the first-order conditions:

$$
\mathbf{M} \begin{bmatrix} d_g \\ d_h \end{bmatrix} = C \cdot \mathbf{V} \left\{ \mathbf{A}_\omega d\omega + \mathbf{A}_{P_1} dP_1 + \mathbf{A}_R dR + \mathbf{A}_\alpha da \right\}.
$$

First, income/wealth effects satisfy

$$
\begin{bmatrix} \partial g / \partial \omega \\ \partial h / \partial \omega \end{bmatrix} = \frac{b_\omega C \cdot \mathbf{V}}{\det \mathbf{M}} \begin{bmatrix} b_g \nabla_{hh}U - b_h \nabla_{hg}U - b_g \cdot \dfrac{\kappa}{\pi_2} \cdot dP_1^2 q C \cdot \mathbf{V} \\ -b_g \nabla_{gh}U + b_h \nabla_{gg}U \end{bmatrix} .
$$

The terms $b_g \nabla_{hh}U - b_h \nabla_{hg}U \le 0$ and $b_h \nabla_{gg}U - b_g \nabla_{gh}U \le 0$ by normality, along with $b_\omega < 0$, imply that g and h are increasing in ω. Let $\varepsilon(g, x) = \partial \log(g)/$

$\partial \log(x)$ denote the elasticity of a variable g with respect to a variable x. The following assumption appears to be supported empirically:

5. The elasticities of g and h with respect to ω are less than one.

This assumption implies

$$\omega \frac{\partial A_1}{\partial \omega} = \frac{\omega}{1 + r'} - \pi_1 g \varepsilon(g, \omega)$$
$$- [(1 - d)(1 + r')Rh + dhP_1(1 - \theta + \mu)]\varepsilon(h, \omega) \geq A_1,$$

and for α such that expected net equity $1 - \theta + (1 - m)\alpha$ is positive,

$$\omega \frac{\partial W_2^e}{\partial \omega} = \omega - (1 + r')\pi_1 g \varepsilon(g, \omega)$$
$$- dhP_1[1 - \theta + (1 - m)\alpha]\varepsilon(h, \omega) \geq W_2.$$

Second, increasing R has no effect on owners and for renters satisfies

$$\begin{bmatrix} \partial g/\partial R \\ \partial h/\partial R \end{bmatrix} =$$
$$\frac{1}{\det M} \begin{bmatrix} b_R(b_g \nabla_{hh} U - b_h \nabla_{hg} U) - \dfrac{\kappa}{\pi_2}(1 + r')\{b_g b_h C \cdot V - \nabla_{gh} U\} \\ b_R(-b_g \nabla_{gh} U + b_h \nabla_{gg} U) - \dfrac{\kappa}{\pi_2}(1 + r')\{b_g^2 C \cdot V - \nabla_{gg} U\} \end{bmatrix}.$$

Then $\partial h/\partial R < 0$. The cross-price effect $\partial g/\partial R$ is negative if g and h are not very substitutable, and the income effect dominates. The effect of increasing R on financial assets, and hence on savings, is negative if h is inelastic with respect to R and the cross-price effect of R on g is weak.

Third, increasing P_1 has no effect on renters and for owners satisfies

$$\begin{bmatrix} \partial g/\partial P_1 \\ \partial h/\partial P_1 \end{bmatrix} =$$
$$\frac{1}{\det M} \begin{bmatrix} b_{P_1}(b_g \nabla_{hh} U - b_h \nabla_{hg} U) - \dfrac{\kappa}{\pi_2}(c + 2hP_1 q)\{b_g b_h C \cdot V - \nabla_{gh} U\} \\ b_{P_1}(-b_g \nabla_{gh} U + b_h \nabla_{gg} U) - \dfrac{\kappa}{\pi_2}(c + 2hP_1 q)\{b_g^2 C \cdot V - \nabla_{gg} U\} \end{bmatrix}.$$

Then $\partial h/\partial P_1 < 0$. The cross-price effect $\partial g/\partial P_1$ is negative if g and h are not very substitutable, and the income effect dominates. The effects of increasing P_1 on financial assets and final expected wealth satisfy

$$\partial A_1/\partial P_1 = -h[1 + \varepsilon(h, P_1)](1 - \theta + \mu) - \pi_1 \partial g/\partial P_1,$$
$$\partial W_2^e/\partial P_1 = -h[1 + \varepsilon(h, P_1)]c - (1 + r')\pi_1 \partial g/\partial P_1.$$

If h is inelastic with respect to P_1 and the cross-price effect of P_1 on g is weak, then $\partial A_1/\partial P_1$ is negative and $\partial W_2^e/\partial P_1$ is small negative.

Fourth, increasing α has no effect on renters and for owners satisfies

$$\begin{bmatrix} \partial g/\partial \alpha \\ \partial h/\partial \alpha \end{bmatrix} = \frac{1}{\det M} \begin{bmatrix} b_\alpha(b_g\nabla_{hh}U - b_h\nabla_{hg}U) - \dfrac{\kappa}{\pi_2}(1-m)P_1\{b_gb_hC\cdot V - \nabla_{gh}U\} \\ b_\alpha(-b_g\nabla_{gh}U + b_h\nabla_{gg}U) - \dfrac{\kappa}{\pi_2}(1-m)P_1\{b_g^2C\cdot V - \nabla_{gg}U\} \end{bmatrix}.$$

When risk aversion is moderate, the leading terms will dominate, and $\partial g/\partial \alpha$ and $\partial h/\partial \alpha$ will both be positive. The effect of α on W_2^ε satisfies

$$\partial W_2^\varepsilon/\partial \alpha = hP_1(1-m) + (1+r')\partial A_1/\partial \alpha$$
$$+ P_1[1 - \theta + (1-m)\alpha]\partial h/\partial \alpha .$$

This expression is positive when risk aversion is moderate.

The preceding analysis assumed that the P_1 and α varied independently. In practice, the consumer will use the initial information, including P_1, in forming expectations. If the consumer is rational, this dependence will reflect the statistical dependence of $\mathring{P}$ on P_1. If the consumer is irrational, having for example naive expectations that past rates of increase in prices reflected in P_1 will continue, this will also make α positively dependent on P_1. A strong positive dependence of α on P_1 will result in positive total effects of increasing P_1 on A_1 and W_2^ε.

The analysis to this point has dealt with a single consumer, who is either an owner or a renter. Now consider a population of consumers, identical except for heterogeneity in beliefs about expected capital gains; that is, α has a distribution over the population. If supplies of rental and owner housing are fixed, then prices adjust to equilibrate demand and supply, with consumers with high α becoming owners. The comparative statics of demand are then as follows: An increase in R, and under usual circumstances a decrease in P_1 or a shift upward in the α of each consumer, will increase the utility of owning and lead at the margin to moves from renting to owning. If supplies are completely inelastic, this increase in demand for owning will be offset by a combination of increasing R and decreasing P_1.

References

ACCRA (American Chamber of Commerce Researchers Association). 1992. *ACCRA cost of living manual.* Alexandria, Va.: American Chamber of Commerce Researchers Association.

Attanasio, Orazio. 1993. A cohort analysis of life-cycle accumulation of financial assets. *Richerche Economiche* 47:323–54.

Attanasio, Orazio, and Hilary Hoynes. 1995. Differential mortality and wealth accumulation. NBER Working Paper no. 5126. Cambridge, Mass.: National Bureau of Economic Research, May.

Curtin, Richard, F. Thomas Juster, and James Morgan. 1989. Survey estimates of wealth: An assessment of quality. In *Measurement of savings, investment, and wealth,* ed. R. E. Lipsey and H. S. Tice. Chicago: University of Chicago Press.

Feinstein, Jonathan, and Daniel McFadden. 1989. The dynamics of housing demand by the elderly: Wealth, cash flow, and demographic effects. In *The economics of aging,* ed. D. Wise. Chicago: University of Chicago Press.

Mankiw, N. Gregory, and David N. Weil. 1989. The baby boom, the baby bust, and the housing market. *Regional Science and Urban Economics* 19:235–58.

McFadden, Daniel. 1994a. Demographics, the housing market, and the welfare of the elderly. In *Studies in the economics of aging,* ed. D. Wise. Chicago: University of Chicago Press.

———. 1994b. Problems of housing the elderly in the United States and Japan. In *Aging in the United States and Japan,* ed. Y. Noguchi and D. Wise. Chicago: University of Chicago Press.

National Association of Realtors. 1990. *Home sales yearbook 1990.* Washington, D.C.: National Association of Realtors.

Poterba, James. 1984. Tax subsidies to owner-occupied housing: An asset market approach. *Quarterly Journal of Economics* 99:729–52.

Topel, Robert, and Sherwin Rosen. 1988. Housing investment in the United States. *Journal of Political Economy* 96:718–40.

Venti, Steven, and David Wise. 1990. But they don't want to reduce housing equity. In *Issues in the economics of aging,* ed. D. Wise. Chicago: University of Chicago Press.

8 Improvement of After-Retirement Income by Home Equity Conversion Mortgages: Possibility and Problems in Japan

Yukio Noguchi

8.1 Introduction

Population aging is usually regarded as a gloomy phenomenon, exemplified by an increase in taxes to finance increased social security payments. It must be noted, however, that an aged society is typically a society in which a large amount of assets has been accumulated. If these assets are properly utilized, many of the problems associated with the aging of the population can be handled. This is especially true of income support of the elderly. Since a considerable share of assets is held by the elderly, it would be possible to support their after-retirement lives without relying too heavily on public pensions if these assets could be liquidated for consumption purposes.

In many cases, however, the elderly hold their assets in the form of housing, which is difficult to liquidate partially. Thus it is necessary to introduce a system by which residential assets can be liquidated step by step to meet the needs of after-retirement life.

Reverse mortgage programs, or home equity conversion mortgages (HECMs) in general, are schemes designed for this purpose. These are programs by which a person borrows a certain amount of money (usually in the form of an annuity) using his or her residential asset as collateral and repays the loan by selling the house when the contract is terminated.

These schemes are useful because they expand available alternatives for the elderly. Unlike the sale of a house, these schemes have the advantage of allowing the elderly to continue to live in their own homes. Moreover, unlike the case of conventional private pensions, it is possible to reflect future capital gains that can be expected from residential assets.

The potential usefulness of these schemes is greater in Japan than in other

Yukio Noguchi is professor of economics at Hitotsubashi University.

countries because land prices are extremely high. According to the government's *White Paper on Life* (Kokumin Seikatsu Hakusho; Economic Planning Agency 1990), the share of real assets in total household assets is 63.9 percent in Japan (as opposed to 39.2 percent in the United States), and the share of land assets in real assets is 83.4 percent in Japan (36.0 percent in the United States). As a matter of fact, HECMs are already available in Japan in the form of private pension programs offered by trust banks and loan programs offered by local governments. However, these programs are not widely utilized. It is necessary to examine why they are unpopular: Is it because the amount of available loans is not enough to support after-retirement life? Or are there other reasons? This paper examines these issues.

Although there is some Japanese literature on HECMs, there are few studies concerning the problems mentioned above.

This paper is organized as follows. In section 8.2, we review the HECM programs that are presently available in Japan. In spite of their potential usefulness, the programs are not widely utilized mainly because of the objections of heirs. In section 8.3, we review the income and asset holdings of households by age group of household head. We find that the elderly typically live in more spacious houses than younger people. In sections 8.4 and 8.5, we examine the possibilities of HECMs in Japan. We find that the income obtained from HECMs exceeds annual consumption under reasonable assumptions. This is very different from the situation in the United States, and the major reason is the extraordinarily high value of residential assets in Japan in relation to income or consumption. The uncertainty about the future value of housing assets is examined in section 8.5. The conclusion from a simulation analysis is that it is possible to borrow a large fraction of the initial asset value because the expected rate of appreciation is higher than the interest rate. In this regard, too, the situation in Japan is considerably different from that in the United States.

8.2   The Present State of HECMs in Japan

Several HECM programs are already available in Japan. They can be classified into two categories: those provided by trust banks and those provided by local governments.

8.2.1   HECMs Provided by Trust Banks

Several trust banks offer programs by which a person can receive an old-age pension by utilizing his or her residential asset. There are two kinds of schemes: The first type uses the house as collateral, and hence property rights remain with the borrower. The second type is called a "trust scheme," under which the residential asset is entrusted to the bank.

Table 8.1 shows the outlines of the programs that are now available. The common features are as follows: Most programs are directed to relatively old people (aged 60–70) and require that dwellers be single or a couple (i.e., that

Table 8.1   **HECMs Offered by Trust Banks**

	Mitsui	Mitsubishi	Sumitomo	Yasuda
Borrower	Over age 65 Single or couple	Over age 60 Single or couple	Over age 60	Over age 70 Single
Asset	Land or condominium over 100 million yen	Land over 200 million yen	Land over 100 million yen	Real estate
Borrowing limit	Less than 60% assessed land value or 40% of condominium	Less than 50% of land value		Less than 50% of assessed value
Borrowing period	Less than 15 years (land) or 10 years (condominium)	5–15 years		10 years

Source: Pamphlets from each trust bank.

there be no other occupants in the house). The housing asset must be an owner-occupied house built on owned land (only the scheme offered by the Mitsui Trust Bank takes condominium-type houses). This reflects the fact that the land, rather than the structure, is regarded in Japan as the reliable asset.

In many cases, the amount that can be borrowed is less than 50 percent of the assessed value of the house. Payment usually takes the form of a fixed-term annuity rather than a lump sum or lifetime annuity. The borrowing period is less than 15 years (no bank offers lifetime annuities). The interest rate is the long-term prime rate. The contract terminates when the period is over or the borrower dies. Repayment of the loan is supposed to be accomplished by selling the house.

Most banks ask for the consent of the heirs in order to avoid trouble associated with bequests. This reflects the fact that the objection of heirs is the most common and serious obstacle to such schemes.

Unfortunately, no data are available concerning the actual use of these programs. It is said, though, that they are not widely used. The most serious obstacle is said to be difficulty in obtaining the consent of heirs. The unavailability of lifetime annuities and the absence of insurance programs to cope with default risk may also be obstacles to more extensive use of such programs.

8.2.2   HECMs Provided by Local Governments

Some local governments offer HECMs. The most representative program is the one provided by the city of Musashino (a city in the suburbs of Tokyo). This program is so famous that similar programs provided by other local governments are usually called "Musashino schemes."

In Musashino's program a person can receive a certain (lifetime) annuity by using his or her house as collateral. The money is supposed to be used for various welfare programs provided by the city as well as for general living and medical expenses. The welfare programs include a catering service, a care service, and assistance for general housekeeping. The program started in April 1971.

The borrower must be a resident of Musashino (one year of residence is required) and must be a participant in one or more of the city's welfare programs.

The lending rate is 5 percent per annum. The amount of money that can be borrowed is less than 80 percent of the assessed value in the case of land and less than 50 percent in the case of a condominium. When the contract is terminated, the fund must be repaid by the heirs or by selling the house.

As of March 1991, the number of borrowers was 42 households, or 60 persons. This is about 17.8 percent of those who make welfare contracts with the city. The average annual amount of the annuity is about 2.4 million yen per household.

The number of households that have thus far terminated the contract through death or because of other reasons is 21. As of 1990, the average amount of debt per household was 24 million yen (of which 5 million yen was interest). In 20 of the 21 cases, the debt was repaid by the heirs rather than by selling the house.

Why do children tend to "undo" the reverse mortgage by paying off the debt rather than selling the house? One important reason is the tax advantage. If a house is sold, a capital gains tax is imposed. The inheritance tax burden is also significantly different. If the asset is in the form of real estate, it is assessed at a value significantly lower than the market value, whereas if the house is sold, the financial asset is assessed at face value.

Another question is, Why do children not simply pay their parents during their lifetimes rather than let them use a reverse mortgage? One answer to this question is the uncertainty associated with the total amount of payments. If children commit to paying their parents, the total amount could exceed the value of the house if their parents live very long. On the other hand, the amount that the parents can use is limited to less than the house value if they use a reverse mortgage.

8.3 Asset Holdings of the Elderly

There are several surveys and studies concerning the asset holdings of the elderly (e.g., Tokyo Metropolitan Government 1991). Most of them point out the importance of residential assets. In this section, we confirm this point using data from the 1989 National Survey of Family Income and Expenditures (Zenkoku Shohi Jittai Chosa) conducted by the Statistics Bureau.[1]

Table 8.2 shows income, consumption, and assets by age groups of house-

---

1. Sample size is about 59,000 households. The first survey was conducted in 1959 and the subsequent surveys have been conducted every five years. The 1989 survey was the seventh.

Table 8.2   **Income, Consumption, and Assets by Age Group (1,000 yen and percent)**

Age	A Ratio of OOH[a]	B Annual Income	C Consumption	D Financial Assets	E Debt	F Residential Assets	G[b] F/(D+F−E)
Under 30	25.09	5,003	2,944	5,567	6,047	41,670	101.17
30s	56.81	6,124	3,260	6,789	6,163	45,290	98.64
40s	79.35	7,419	4,020	10,094	5,930	50,120	92.33
50s	86.9	8,482	4,343	13,879	4,303	63,040	86.81
60s	90.57	6,335	3,435	18,401	2,295	69,440	81.17
70s and over	88.93	5,514	2,927	20,550	2,632	92,190	83.73
Average	75.43	7,136	3,790	12,500	4,722	58,460	88.26

Age	H Residential Expenditures	H/B	H/C	I Household Members	Three Major Metropolitan Areas[c] OOH	Residential Asset
Under 30	91.66	1.83	3.11	3.55	25.28	60,940
30s	67.03	1.09	2.06	4.48	54.69	70,740
40s	78.04	1.05	1.94	4.37	76.57	76,490
50s	117.47	1.38	2.7	3.62	82.63	106,080
60s	139.4	2.2	4.06	3.17	85.5	130,190
70s and over	128.81	2.34	4.4	2.98	85.76	166,340
Average	98.33	1.38	2.59	3.89	71.82	96,350

Source: 1989 National Survey of Family Income and Expenditure.

Note: Columns B through I are national average figures for households living in owner-occupied houses.

[a]OOH (owner-occupied houses).

[b]The weight of residential assets is the ratio of residential assets to net assets (= financial assets + residential assets − debt). The number for ages under 30 exceeds 100 percent because net financial assets are negative.

[c]The three major metropolitan areas are Keihin, Chukyo, and Keihanshin.

hold head.[2] Column A shows the ratio of households living in owner-occupied houses (national average figure). The ratio becomes higher for higher age groups of household heads except for the oldest. For the 60 and over age groups, the ratio is about 90 percent.

Columns B through I are for households living in houses that they own (national average figures). The numbers in column F are the values of residential assets, which include structures and land. The value of land was assessed using the government's benchmark land price. The average absolute amount of resi-

---

2. Income includes salary income, business income, property income, and social security benefits. Consumption expenditures do not include the following: imputed rents of owner-occupied houses, imputed service of wives, and tax payments.

dential assets for all age groups is about 58 million yen (about $580,000). The amount increases as the age of the household head rises. It as high as 92 million yen for household heads aged 70 and over. This is about 17 times their average annual income, or about 32 times their annual consumption.

Note that the increase in residential asset value as age increases is not necessarily a result of the accumulation of life-cycle savings in the form of residential assets. Rather, it can be interpreted as a reflection of the simple fact that in many cases older generations were able to purchase more spacious residences in more convenient locations because land prices were lower in the past. In other words, the trend observed in the table is mainly due to the cohort effect rather than to the life-cycle effect.

The share of residential assets in net assets (financial assets + residential assets − debt) is very high for all age groups. The average ratio is about 88 percent. The ratio declines as the age of the household head increases up to the 60s age group and rises slightly from the 60s to the 70s and over.

The last two columns in table 8.2 are for the three major metropolitan areas: Keihin (the greater Tokyo area), Chukyo (the greater Nagoya area), and Keihanshin (the greater Osaka area). The ratio of households living in owner-occupied houses in these areas is slightly lower than the national average (except for the age group under 30). But the difference is not significant. On the other hand, the value of residential assets of households living in owner-occupied houses is considerably higher than the national average. On the average, the former is 1.6 times the latter. For the 70 and over age group, the ratio is 1.80. The absolute value of residential assets in these areas exceeds 100 million yen for the 50 and over age groups and becomes as high as 166 million yen for the 70 and over age group.

Column H in the table shows residential expenditures.[3] The ratio to income (H/B) is higher for higher age groups. The ratio to consumption (H/C) also rises with age for those who are 40 and over. For the 60 and over age groups, the annual expense is about 140,000 yen (about $1,400), or over 4 percent of total consumption. If property tax payments (not shown in the table) are added, over 8 percent of total consumption is used for residential purposes.

Column I shows the average number of dwellers per house. This number reaches its peak of 4.37 during the 30s age group and decreases for older age groups. The number becomes less than three for the 70 and over age group. This fact, together with the trend in residential expenditures mentioned above, suggests that on average elderly people live in houses that are too spacious for their needs, at least relative to younger people.

Table 8.3 shows the breakdown by income class. In this table, income classes have been reconstructed from the original data in such a way that about 30

---

3. "Residential expenditures" in the survey include (1) house and land rents and (2) repairs and maintenance (material costs and service charges). In this paper, only expenditure 2 is considered.

Table 8.3   **Income, Consumption, and Assets by Age Group and Income Class (10,000 yen)**

		Income Class		
	Average	Low	Middle	High
50s				
Ratio of households (%)		30.5	41.6	27.9
A. Annual income	848.2	410.2	788.5	1,414.6
B. Annual consumption	434.3	294.4	419.2	609.6
C. Financial assets	1,387.9	813.2	1,169.6	2,314.1
D. Debt	430.3	226.4	367.4	742.2
E. Net assets	957.6	586.8	802.2	1,571.9
F. Residential assets	6,304.0	3,656.7	5,111.6	10,919.9
(weight of F; %)	(86.8)	(86.2)	(86.4)	(87.4)
F/A	7.43	8.91	6.48	7.72
60s				
Ratio of households (%)		35.6	40.2	24.2
A. Annual income	633.5	280.7	576.4	1,246.2
B. Annual consumption	343.5	238.0	346.7	492.9
C. Financial assets	1,840.1	1,109.5	1,745.7	3,026.1
D. Debt	229.5	61.6	170.0	563.3
E. Net assets	1,610.6	1,047.9	1,575.7	2,462.8
F. Residential assets	6,944.0	3,835.0	6,430.5	12,253.9
(weight of F; %)	(81.2)	(78.5)	(80.3)	(83.3)
F/A	11.04	13.70	11.16	9.83
70 and over				
Ratio of households (%)		33.9	37.1	29.0
A. Annual income	551.4	207.8	422.3	1,118.0
B. Annual consumption	292.7	184.5	282.7	432.0
C. Financial assets	2,055.0	871.0	1,809.8	3,692.9
D. Debt	263.2	25.4	166.9	646.1
E. Net assets	1,791.8	845.6	1,642	3,046.8
F. Residential assets	9,219.0	4,839.9	9,130.3	14,412.1
(weight of F; %)	(83.7)	(85.13)	(84.75)	(82.55)
F/A	16.73	23.37	21.63	12.89

Source: 1989 National Survey of Family Income and Expenditure.

Note: Table gives national average figures for households living in owner-occupied houses.

percent of households belong to the "low" class, about 40 percent to the "middle" class, and about 30 percent to the "high" class.

For the low income class, the value of residential assets of the 70 and over age group is about 1.32 times that of the 50s age group. Interestingly, the corresponding figure for the high income class is also 1.32. This may be interpreted to support the conjecture made earlier that the increase in residential assets as age increases is due mainly to rises in land prices rather than life-cycle savings. On the other hand, while the average income of the high income class does not drop significantly as the households get older (the average income of the 70 and over age group is about 79 percent of that of people in their 50s), that of the low income group shows a significant drop (the average income of the 70 and over age group is only about 51 percent of that of people in their 50s).

Consequently, the relative value of residential assets becomes higher for the low income class of higher age groups. For the low income group aged 70 and over, the ratio of housing value to income is as high as 23.4. The average value of houses that the elderly in this group possess is about the same as that for middle-income people in their 50s. On the other hand, the annual income of the former is only about one-fourth that of the latter. This observation reinforces the conjecture mentioned above that the houses of the elderly are too valuable compared with their needs. Thus, the relative increment of income obtained by liquidating residential assets is larger for older people in the lower income group.

8.4   Improvement of After-Retirement Income by HECMs

The observations in the preceding section suggest that HECMs are potentially highly effective in Japan. In this section, we consider a hypothetical program and evaluate the extent to which after-retirement income can be improved by HECMs.

The method is essentially the same as that used by Venti and Wise (1991). We consider the following setting: A borrower receives money in the form of either a lump-sum payment or a lifetime annuity. The contract terminates when the borrower dies, and the loan is repaid. (It may be more natural to assume that the surviving spouse continues the contract and the contract terminates when the surviving partner dies. This assumption, however, is not adopted in the present calculation.)[4] We assume that the borrower is a male household head.

Let L be the maximum amount that can be borrowed at the time the contract is made. L is equal to the expected housing value at the termination of the contract. In this calculation, the discount rate is the mortgage rate (the lending rate of the financial institution), which we denote by m. We calculate the expected value because the termination of the contract is a random phenomenon.[5]

---

4. Most actual contracts are terminated when the borrower moves out of the house. This condition is not considered in the present calculation.

5. Let $d(n)$ be the death rate for age n defined by (number of deaths at age n)/(age n population). In the present calculation, we use the male death rate. Let $l(a, n)$ be the probability that a person who was alive at age a is still alive at age n, and let $c(a, n)$ be the probability that a person who was alive at age a dies at age n. Then,

$$l(a, a) = 1, l(a, n) = l(a, n - 1) \times [1 - d(n)], \quad \text{and } c(a, n) = l(a, n - 1) \times d(n) \text{ for } n > a.$$

The probability $c(a, n)$ is used for calculating the expected present value of the residential asset at the termination of the contract, and $l(a, n)$ is used for calculating the expected present value of the annuity.

In this section, we assume no uncertainty in the future value of the residential asset and assume that the value will appreciate at a constant rate g. Needless to say, this is an unrealistic assumption. To compensate for possible overestimations of the amount that can by borrowed, we assume that the amount the financial institution lends is qL, where q is a fraction not greater than 1. In this section, we assume rather arbitrarily that $q = 0.5$.

In the case where the borrower receives the money in the form of an annuity, the expected present value of the annuity should be equal to qL. In this calculation, the discount rate is the rate of return on private pensions, which we denote by r.

The most crucial parameters are the rate of appreciation of housing values and the interest rate. If the former is greater than the latter, the maximum amount that can be borrowed (L) is greater than the current value of the residential asset.

Table 8.4 shows the amount that can be borrowed on a house with initial value 10,000, in terms of both a lump-sum payment $(L/2)$ and an annuity, for various combinations of g and m where r is 5 percent. If g is greater than m, L is greater the younger the contract age. For example, if $g = 10$ percent and $m = 7$ percent, $L/2$ is 10,418 for age 55 and 6,709 for age 75. This is because the benefit of real appreciation of the residential asset is greater for a longer expected contract period. The relationship is reversed if g is smaller than m.

The annuity amount tends to be greater for an older contract age because the expected period in which the annuity can be received becomes shorter. For example, if m is equal to g, the annuity amount for age 75 is about twice as large as that for age 55. However, if g is enough higher than m, the relationship is reversed. This happens in the table when m is 5 percent and g is higher than 10 percent.

Table 8.4   **Amount That Can Be Borrowed from an HECM**

	Contract Age: 55			Contract Age: 75	
g	$m = 7\%$	$m = 5\%$	g	$m = 7\%$	$m = 5\%$
		Lump Sum Payment			
12	17,452	30,809	12	8,262	10,421
10	10,418	17,894	10	6,709	8,345
7	5,000	8,186	7	5,000	6,090
5	3,167	5,000	5	4,161	5,000
		Annuity			
12	1,246	2,199	12	1,890	1,374
10	743	1,277	10	885	1,101
7	357	584	7	659	803
5	226	357	5	549	659

Note: g is the rate of appreciation of asset value, and m is the lending rate of the financial institution (%). The rate of return of the annuity (r) is assumed to be 5 percent. The initial value of the house is assumed to be 10,000, and q (the fraction that can be borrowed) is assumed to be 0.5.

The annuity amount is very sensitive to the difference between g and m. For example, the amount becomes less than one-half if g is lowered from 10 percent to 7 percent when m is 7 percent and the contract age is 55. The sensitivity becomes smaller for a higher contract age. This is because the expected period in which the contract is exposed to variations in g is shortened.

Thus, a longer contract period is desirable from the point of view of borrowers (assuming g is greater than m), while it is undesirable from the point of view of lenders (assuming that they are risk averse).

In Japan, the value of residential assets consists mostly of land value, rather than the value of the structure. According to the National Survey of Family Income and Expenditures, about 90 percent of residential asset value is accounted for by the land. The ratio is higher for relatively old houses in urban areas where land prices are high. Thus, in this paper, we assume that the rate of increase in residential value is given by that in land prices.

Table 8.5 shows the trend of residential land prices in urban areas as represented by the government's benchmark price.[6] The average annual growth rate in the greater Tokyo area was 11.6 percent for the period 1971–92. As seen in the table, there was a big fluctuation in land prices during the late 1980s due to speculation, and prices still may be falling. If this period is excluded and the average is taken for the period 1971–86, the average growth rate in the greater Tokyo area was 10.0 percent. The national average for the same period was 9.5 percent. This is greater than the average value of the long-term interest rate (the average contracted rate of loans and discounts of all banks) during the same period, which was 7.4 percent.[7]

Considering the above data, we assume in the following calculation that the annual growth rate of land prices (g) is 10 percent, the lending rate of the financial institution (m) is 7 percent, the rate of return of the annuity (r) is 5 percent, and the fraction q is 0.5.[8]

Under the above assumptions, the annuity amount has been calculated for various age groups of household heads using data from the 1989 National Survey of Family Income and Expenditures. The results are shown in table 8.6. The relative annuity amount is evaluated by the following four indices:

H: ratio to current annual income, which is shown in column A in table 8.3

6. It is usually said that the government's benchmark price underestimates the actual fluctuation of land prices. This is especially true when land prices are rising.

7. The difference between the average rate of increase in land prices and the average interest rate does not necessarily imply the absence of arbitrage since the variance of the former is much greater than that of the latter.

8. The average difference between the lending rate (long-term prime rate) and the deposit rate (time deposit rate) of financial institutions over the past 25 years has been about 2 percentage points.

Table 8.5 **Rate of Increase of Land Prices and Interest Rate (%)**

Year	Greater Tokyo	Greater Osaka	Nagoya Nagoya	Three Major Areas	Regional Cities	National Average	Interest Rate
1971	19.9	22.0	18.5	20.3	–	20.3	7.69
1972	15.1	14.9	14.6	15.0	11.0	14.8	7.04
1973	35.9	30.1	30.1	33.7	28.6	33.3	7.18
1974	35.4	31.8	29.0	33.9	43.5	34.7	9.11
1975	−11.5	−9.3	−8.8	−10.4	−7.5	−8.9	9.09
1976	0.6	0.5	0.7	0.6	0.9	0.8	8.25
1977	1.7	1.6	2.6	1.8	2.1	1.9	7.56
1978	3.5	2.8	4.1	3.4	3.2	3.3	6.30
1979	8.8	6.8	8.2	8.1	5.1	6.5	6.36
1980	18.3	13.5	14.2	16.3	9.0	12.3	8.34
1981	14.1	12.6	12.3	13.4	9.8	11.4	7.86
1982	7.4	9.3	7.9	8.0	8.5	8.3	7.31
1983	4.1	5.3	4.5	4.5	5.6	5.1	7.12
1984	2.2	3.6	2.4	2.6	3.5	3.0	6.74
1985	1.7	3.0	1.6	2.0	2.4	2.2	6.60
1986	3.0	2.6	1.4	2.7	1.7	2.2	6.02
1987	21.5	3.4	1.6	13.7	1.2	7.6	5.20
1988	68.6	18.6	7.3	46.6	1.9	25.0	5.03
1989	0.4	32.7	16.4	11.0	4.4	7.9	5.28
1990	6.6	56.1	20.2	22.0	11.4	17.0	6.86
1991	6.6	6.5	18.8	8.0	13.6	10.7	7.53
1992	−9.1	−22.9	−5.2	−12.5	2.3	−5.6	6.15
Average							
1971–92	11.6	11.2	9.2	11.1	7.4	9.7	7.0
1971–86	10.0	9.4	9.0	9.7	8.0	9.5	7.4
Standard deviation							
1971–92	17.1	16.0	9.9	13.7	10.4	10.8	1.1
1971–86	12.3	10.7	10.1	11.6	11.8	11.3	0.9

Sources: For land prices, National Land Agency, *The Government Benchmark Land Price* (Tokyo, various years); for interest rates, Bank of Japan, *Annual Economic Statistics* (Tokyo, various years).

Notes: Land price is the government benchmark price for residential land. The interest rate is the average contracted rate on loans and discounts (before 1978, on loans) of all banks (Zenkoku Ginko), calendar year.

I: ratio to after-retirement income (ARI), which is defined to be the same as the present income of those aged 70 and over in the same income group

J: ratio to current annual consumption, which is shown in column B of table 8.3

K: Ratio to after-retirement consumption (ARC), which is defined to be the same as the present consumption of those aged 70 and over in the same income group

Table 8.6   **Improvement in Income from an HECM**

Improvement Ratios	Income Class			
	Average	Low	Middle	High
50s				
G. Annuity (10,000 yen)	468.9	272.0	380.2	812.3
H. Ratio to income (%)	55.3	66.3	48.2	57.4
I. Ratio to ARI (%)	85.0	130.9	90.0	72.7
J. Ratio to consumption (%)	108.0	92.3	90.7	133.3
K. Ratio to ARC (%)	160.2	147.4	134.5	188.0
60s				
G. Annuity (10,000 yen)	550.5	304.0	509.8	971.4
H. Ratio to income (%)	86.9	108.3	88.4	77.9
I. Ratio to ARI (%)	99.9	146.3	120.7	86.9
J. Ratio to consumption (%)	160.3	127.7	147.0	197.1
K. Ratio to ARC (%)	188.1	167.8	180.3	224.9
70s				
G. Annuity (10,000 yen)	816.0	428.3	808.1	1275.6
H. Ratio to income (%)	148.0	206.1	191.4	114.1
I. Ratio to ARI (%)	–	–	–	–
J. Ratio to consumption (%)	278.8	232.1	285.9	295.3
K. Ratio to ARC (%)	–	–	–	–

Notes: The parameters $g = 10$ percent, $m = 7$ percent, $r =$ percent, and $q = 0.5$ are assumed. Improvement ratios are based on the data in table 8.2.

People in the 50s age group are assumed to make the contract at age 55. Similar assumptions are made for the other age groups.

ARI (after-retirement income) and ARC (after-retirement consumption). Definitions are given in the text.

The calculated annuity exceeds annual consumption for almost all groups. The maximum ratio is 295 percent for the high income group aged 70 and over. This implies that HECMs can provide more than enough after-retirement income in Japan.

In most cases, the ratio of residential asset value to income is higher for lower income groups. Thus the improvement ratio is higher for lower income groups within the same age group. In terms of the ratio to annual consumption, the improvement ratios for higher income groups are high.

Within the same income group, the improvement ratio is higher for higher age groups in terms of both the ratio to income and the ratio to consumption. This is a reflection of the fact that elderly people live in large houses relative to their income or consumption because of the difficulty of liquidating residential assets.

The same trend can be observed when the after-retirement income or after-retirement consumption concepts are used.

According to Venti and Wise (1991), the income of typical married couples in the United States would be affected very little by HECMs. Even for a low-income couple and even under the assumption that $q = 1$, a reverse annuity mortgage would mean only a 4 percent increase in income for the 55–66 age group and about a 10 percent increase for the 65–70 age group. The ratio becomes 35 percent only for the 85 and over age group (the assumptions were $m = 10$ percent, $r = 5$ percent, and $g = 5$ percent). The improvement ratios in Japan are considerably higher because of the relatively high value of residential assets.

The results depend heavily on the assumed values of parameters. Sensitivity analyses can be performed using the data in tables 8.3 and 8.4. Table 8.7 shows the results for people in their 70s with respect to changes in g (the rate of appreciation of asset values). The ratio of annuity to consumption exceeds 100 percent even when g is as low as 5 percent.

There are of course several qualifications to the above results. First of all, we must note that the entire picture of the elderly is not necessarily captured by the National Survey of Family Income and Expenditures because the "elderly" in the survey are only those who are household heads. The elderly who live with their children and are not heads of households do not explicitly appear in the data. Indeed, the number of households whose heads are aged 65 or over is only 1.6 percent of the total number of households in this survey. The ratio is considerably lower than the ratio of people aged 65 or over, which was 12.1 percent in 1990.

For those elderly who are not heads, it would be difficult to put their houses into HECM programs because of the objections of their children. Even for the elderly who are heads, a similar problem may exist because there are, in many

Table 8.7   **Improvements in Income from an HECM for People in Their 70s**

	Income Class			
g (%)	Average	Low	Middle	High
Annuity (10,000 yen)				
12	1742.4	914.7	1725.6	2723.9
10	815.9	428.3	808.0	1275.5
7	607.5	318.9	601.7	949.8
5	506.1	265.7	501.3	791.2
Ratio to income (%)				
12	316.2	440.2	408.6	243.6
10	148.1	206.1	191.3	114.1
7	110.3	153.5	142.5	85.0
5	91.9	127.9	118.7	70.8
Ratio to consumption (%)				
12	595.3	495.8	610.4	630.5
10	278.7	232.2	285.8	295.2
7	207.6	172.9	212.8	219.9
5	172.9	144.0	177.3	183.2

Notes: The parameters $m = 7$ percent, $r = 5$ percent, $q = 0.5$ are assumed. Calculations are performed as in table 8.6

cases, household members other than the elderly couple. (As we have seen, the average number of household members is about three even when the age of the household head is 70 or over.) In fact, as mentioned, the most serious obstacle to HECMs in Japan is said to be the objections of children who expect to inherit their parents' houses.

It must be noted, however, that HECMs can be used even when there are household members other than the elderly couple because, if the heirs repay the loan in cash, they can continue to live in the house. In fact, as mentioned later, this is the typical way of repaying HECM loans in Japan.

The second point is that the above calculations are for average figures. The distribution of assets is fairly unequal. According to Takayama (1992), inequality in asset holding is greater than in income. This is especially true of real estate: there are households that do not own their houses, and the difference in the value of assets is quite large even among households living in owner-occupied houses.

Third, it must be noted that a fixed annuity amount has been assumed in the above demonstration. It may be argued that we should consider a rise in consumer prices because we are assuming a rise in land prices.

There are also some technical problems associated with the specific method used here. For example, in 1989, the year in which the survey was conducted, land prices were fairly high as a result of speculative bubbles. In fact, as shown in table 8.4, recent land prices have been lower by about 5–20 percent. This may have introduced an overestimation bias into the above result.

However, even when the recent fall in land prices is taken into consideration, the potential effectiveness of HECMs in Japan is still very high.

Note also that the above calculations are for national averages. In the major metropolitan areas, where the value of housing assets is greater than the national average, the improvement ratio is higher than in the above calculations. Moreover, the assumed interest rate of 7 percent may be somewhat high considering the recent trend of interest rates shown in table 8.5. If a lower value is assumed for m, the improvement ratio is higher.

8.5   Uncertainty about Future Housing Values

In the preceding section, we assumed that housing values will appreciate at a constant rate. As mentioned before, this is a highly unrealistic assumption. In fact, as shown in table 8.5, the standard deviation of the rate of land price increases is greater than the mean value. In this section, uncertainty in asset appreciation is examined.[9] The model used here is based on Szymanoski (1990).

---

9. In addition to the uncertainty discussed in this section, there may be structural changes in the trend of land prices. In particular, it is argued that the demand for houses will decline in the future as the relative number of elderly people increases. This issue is not explored in this paper.

We assume that the asset value in year t is given by

$$H(t) = H(0)\exp[gt + f(t)],$$

where $H(0)$ is the value when the contract is made ($t = 0$), g is a constant, and $f(t)$ is a random variable that is normally distributed with zero mean and variance s^2t.[10]

On the other hand, we assume that a lump-sum amount qL is borrowed at the time of the contract and that the interest rate is a constant. Therefore, the outstanding debt increases with certainty as time passes. As before, we assume that the contract is terminated when the borrower dies.

To cope with the situation in which the value of the house is less than the outstanding debt at the termination of the contract (let us call this situation "default"), an insurance program is introduced. A fraction (denoted by p_1) of L is collected as the insurance premium when the contract is made, and a fraction (denoted by p_2) of the outstanding amount of debt is collected each year. If the value of the residential asset is greater than the outstanding debt at the termination of the contract, the entire amount of the loan is repaid by the borrower or his heirs (by selling the house), as before. If, on the other hand, the amount of debt is greater than the housing value at the termination, the difference is paid by the insurance program.

The fraction q is computed by an iterative method in the following way: First, we set the fraction q at a certain value. Using this, the time trend of the outstanding debt is calculated. On the other hand, the probability of default and the conditional expected value of the residential asset given that default occurs are calculated for each year.[11] Based on the probability that the contract is terminated because of death, the expected receipt of the insurance premium and expected payment of the insurance program are calculated for each year. In this way, the time trend of the insurance fund is calculated, and the expected outstanding fund in the final year (assumed to be the year when the borrower's age becomes 100) is calculated. If this amount becomes negative (positive), the fraction q is changed to a smaller (greater) value and the same calculation is repeated until the final fund becomes zero. In the present calculation, we assume that the interest rate (the discount rate) is 7 percent. We also assume that $p_1 = 2$ percent and $p_2 = 0.1$ percent, which seem to be modest rates.

Table 8.8 illustrates the time path of a model HECM and insurance program for a specific set of parameter values. The borrower makes the contract at age

10. Whether this is an appropriate formulation is debatable. In particular, the data in table 8.5 seem to suggest that the growth rate is serially correlated. However, this issue is not examined in detail in the present paper.

11. (1) The probability of default is given by the area under the normalized normal distribution curve from minus infinity up to U, where $U = [\ln b(t) - mt]/s\sqrt{t}$, $b(t) = B(t)/H(0)$, and $B(t)$ is the loan balance. (2) The expected value of the residential asset in year t is given by $E[H(t)] = H(0)\exp[mt + s^2t/2]$ (3) The expected value of the residential asset conditional on default is given by $E[H(t)]S/A$ where S is the area under the normalized normal distribution curve from minus infinity up to $U - s\sqrt{t}$ and A is the probability of default calculated in step 1.

Table 8.8   Time Path of Model HECM and Insurance Program

Age	End Balance (1)	Expected Value of House (2)	Default Probability (3)	Conditional Expected Value (4)	Probability of Survival (5)	Expected Premium (6)	Expected Loss (7)
75	104,200	100,000	0.0000	–	1.0000	2,000	0
76	111,844	111,071	0.5475	103,001	0.9494	105	155
77	120,048	123,368	0.4514	108,246	0.8957	107	202
78	128,855	137,026	0.3942	114,497	0.8387	108	238
79	138,307	152,196	0.3525	121,514	0.7787	108	270
80	148,453	169,046	0.3195	129,222	0.7161	107	298
81	159,343	187,761	0.2920	137,633	0.6517	105	321
82	171,031	208,548	0.2685	146,729	0.5865	102	338
83	183,578	231,637	0.2480	156,554	0.5218	98	348
84	197,044	257,281	0.2299	167,152	0.4587	93	351
85	211,499	285,765	0.2137	178,536	0.3979	88	348
86	227,014	317,402	0.1992	190,812	0.3403	81	340
87	243,667	352,542	0.1859	204,035	0.2864	74	326
88	261,541	391,572	0.1739	218,172	0.2368	66	308
89	280,727	434,924	0.1628	233,378	0.1923	58	284
90	301,320	483,074	0.1527	249,808	0.1532	51	255
91	323,424	536,556	0.1433	267,312	0.1196	43	225
92	347,149	595,958	0.1347	286,068	0.0913	36	194
93	372,615	661,937	0.1267	306,255	0.0680	29	163
94	399,949	735,220	0.1192	327,983	0.0495	23	134
95	429,288	816,617	0.1123	351,347	0.0350	18	106
96	460,779	907,025	0.1058	376,142	0.0240	13	83
97	494,580	1,007,442	0.0999	403,317	0.0160	10	61
98	530,861	1,118,977	0.0943	431,477	0.0103	7	45
99	569,803	1,242,860	0.0890	462,356	0.0064	5	32
100	611,602	1,380,457	0.0841	495,405	0.0000	2	53

Note: The $g = 10$ percent, $s = 10$ percent, $m = 7$ percent, $q = 1.042$, $p_1 = 2$ percent, $p_2 = 0.1$ percent, and contract age $= 75$ are assumed. Initial asset value is 100,000.

75, and the initial residential asset value is 100,000. We assume that $g = 10$ percent and $s = 10$ percent. The value of q is chosen as 1.042 (this is the value that makes the final fund zero).

The initial insurance premium of 2,000 (2 percent of 100,000) is subtracted from the lump-sum payment in the first year (hence the borrower receives 102,200). From the second year, an insurance premium of 0.1 percent of the balance and the interest payment are added to the loan balance.

The expected value of the residential asset, which is shown in column (2), grows at the rate $g + s^2/2$. The probability of default is shown in column (3), and the conditional expected value of the housing asset given that default occurs is shown in column (4). Column (5) shows the probability that the borrower is alive and hence that the contract is continued at the corresponding age. The number is calculated from the male death rate (see n. 5). This probability is less than 50 percent after age 84 and less than 10 percent after age 92.

Expected collection of the insurance premium, shown in column (6), is calculated as 0.1 percent of the end balance times the probability that the contract is continued. The expected loss of the insurance program, shown in column (7), is calculated as (end balance − conditional expected value of the housing asset) × (probability of default) × (probability that the contract will be terminated in the year). The probability of termination is given by the decrement in the probability of survival from the preceding year.

In this particular example, the probability of default is high for several years after the contract is made because q is greater than 1. However, the difference between the loan balance and the conditional expectation is not so large during these years. Hence, the expected loss can be covered by the initial insurance premium. Since the rate of appreciation of the asset is assumed to be greater than the interest rate, the expected housing value grows faster than the loan balance. The former becomes greater than the latter, and the probability of default becomes less than 0.5 after age 77. The probability becomes less than 0.1 after age 97. Thus, although the conditional expected value of the asset becomes considerably lower than the loan balance, the expected loss decreases.

The calculated value of q is shown in table 8.9 for several combinations of g and s. For reasonable values of g and s, the value of q becomes fairly high. For example, if $g = 10$ percent and $s = 10$ percent, it is possible to set $q = 1.042$ when the contract age is 75. In many cases shown in the table, the value of q exceeds the 50 percent assumed in the previous section. This means that in Japan, a considerable amount of residential assets can be liquidated by HECMs because the rate of land price increases is high relative to the interest rate.

If the value of g is greater than the interest rate and q is not very large, the value of q is higher for a younger contract age. For example, in the case where $g = 10$ percent and $s = 10$ percent, q is 125.5 percent for age 55 and 104.2 percent for age 75. This is because the period in which real appreciation of residential assets is enjoyed becomes longer for a longer contract period.

However, this trend is reversed when the value of g is lower than the interest rate. For example, in the case where $g = 4$ percent and $s = 10$ percent, q is 35.2 percent for age 55 and 58.6 percent for age 75. This is because the default risk increases as the period of the contract becomes longer.

The value of q for the same value of g and the same age is higher for a higher value of s. For example, when $g = 10$ percent, q is 152.3 percent for $s = 5$ percent, 125.5 percent for $s = 10$ percent, and 98.0 percent for $s = 15$ percent (when the contract age is 55). This is a natural result, since the default risk increases as the uncertainty becomes greater.

In the United States, where the mean value of asset appreciation is relatively low and the interest rate is high, the value of q is low. Szymanoski (1990) shows that the value is somewhere around 0.3–0.4 assuming that $g = 4$ percent, $s = 10$ percent, $m = 10$ percent, $p_1 = 2$ percent, and $p_2 = 0.5$ percent.

We mentioned in the previous section that the degree of improvement of

Table 8.9   **Ratio *q* for Various Values of Mean and Standard Deviation**

		Age of Contract				
s	*g*	55	60	65	70	75
5.0	12.0	186.4	165.7	149.8	137.0	127.6
	10.0	152.3	140.7	131.4	123.7	118.0
	8.0	112.2	109.6	107.5	105.9	104.8
	6.0	70.6	74.2	78.0	82.1	86.2
	4.0	41.6	47.0	53.1	59.8	67.0
	2.0	25.0	30.0	36.0	43.2	51.4
10.0	12.0	163.4	146.5	133.9	123.8	116.5
	10.0	125.5	118.0	112.1	107.5	104.2
	8.0	87.3	87.1	87.2	88.0	89.3
	6.0	55.9	59.6	63.7	68.3	73.2
	4.0	35.2	39.9	45.4	51.6	58.6
	2.0	22.5	26.5	32.3	38.8	46.4
15.0	12.0	133.6	121.2	113.0	106.1	101.4
	10.0	98.0	93.9	91.0	89.0	88.4
	8.0	67.0	68.1	69.7	72.0	74.7
	6.0	44.3	47.8	51.9	56.6	61.8
	4.0	29.4	33.4	38.3	44.0	50.5
	2.0	19.9	23.6	28.3	34.1	41.0
20.0	12.0	105.2	97.7	92.1	88.2	86.0
	10.0	75.3	73.6	72.8	73.0	74.2
	8.0	52.1	53.9	56.2	59.2	62.8
	6.0	35.8	39.0	42.8	47.3	52.5
	4.0	24.9	28.3	32.5	37.6	43.6
	2.0	17.6	20.8	24.9	30.0	36.2

Notes: The numbers in the table are 100 q, where q is the ratio of the amount that can be borrowed to the initial asset value; g is the mean growth rate, and s is the standard deviation (%).

The interest rate (the discount rate) is assumed to be 7 percent, $p_1 = 2$ percent, and $p_2 = 0.1$ percent.

after-retirement income by HECMs is higher in Japan than in the United States. The basic reason for this result is that the value of houses relative to income is higher in Japan. The results obtained in this section reinforce the conclusion because the ratio of the amount that can be borrowed to the initial asset value is also higher in Japan. The basic reason for this result is that both the profitability and the safety of residential assets relative to financial assets are greater in Japan.

8.6   Concluding Remarks

The major findings of this paper can be summarized as follows: First, HECMs are potentially highly important in Japan as a means of providing funds for after-retirement life because the value of residential assets is in general very high compared to income or consumption and is expected to increase at a fairly high rate, at least in urban areas. Second, in spite of this, HECMs are not widely utilized mainly because of the objections of heirs. This also reflects the high value of residential assets in Japan. Therefore, ironically, the factor that makes HECMs a potentially important tool at the same time becomes an obstacle to their implementation.

It can be argued that the present situation is inequitable in the sense that people who could more than afford to support themselves after retirement if they were to utilize HECMs receive the full amount of their public pensions and are able to leave their residential assets to their heirs, for whom the burden of supporting their parents has been reduced by the social security program. This is inequitable because (1) most of the increase in land values is due to external economic effects such as the concentration of population in urban areas, rather than to the owners' efforts, and (2) the public pension program is financed largely on a pay-as-you-go basis, rather than being fully funded.

References

Economic Planning Agency. 1990. *White paper on life* (in Japanese). Tokyo: Government Printing Office.

Szymanoski, E. J., Jr. 1990. *The FHA home equity conversion mortgage insurance demonstration: A model to calculate borrower payments and insurance risk.* Washington, D.C.: U.S. Department of Housing and Urban Development.

Takayama, Noriyuki. 1992. *Stock Economy, Sisan Keisei to Chochiku, Nenkin no Keizaibunseki* (Stock economy, analysis of asset accumulation, saving and social security). Tokyo: Toyo Keizai Shinposha.

Tokyo Metropolitan Government. 1991. *Asset management and life design for after-retirement lives.* Tokyo: Tokyo Metropolitan Government, July.

Venti, Steven F., and David A. Wise. 1991. Aging and the income value of housing wealth. *Journal of Public Economics* 44 (3): 371–97.

III   Aging, Household Saving, and Retirement

9 The Effects of Special Saving Programs on Saving and Wealth

James M. Poterba, Steven F. Venti, and David A. Wise

The last decade has witnessed important changes in the way Americans save for retirement. In particular, individual retirement accounts (IRAs) and 401(k) plans have become popular targeted retirement saving vehicles. The IRA and 401(k) asset accumulation of many households is substantially greater than the combined value of their other financial assets. If current contribution patterns persist, the next generation of retirees will derive a substantial fraction of its support from resources accumulated in these accounts.

This paper provides an overview of the nature of targeted retirement saving programs in the United States and a summary of the effects of these programs on the saving behavior and wealth of U.S. households. The paper is divided into five sections. The first presents descriptive information on the structure of IRAs and 401(k)s and summarizes the changing patterns of participation in these programs during the last decade. Section 9.2 summarizes information on the relative importance of assets in household wealth. Section 9.3 draws on previous studies of both IRA and 401(k) contributors to address the extent to which contributions to these special accounts represent "new saving." Section 9.4 explores the relationship between the enormous increase in personal targeted retirement saving in the 1980s and aggregate measures of personal saving in the United States. There is a brief conclusion.

James M. Poterba is professor of economics at the Massachusetts Institute of Technology and director of the Public Economics Program at the National Bureau of Economic Research. Steven F. Venti is professor of economics at Dartmouth College and a research associate of the National Bureau of Economic Research. David A. Wise is the John F. Stambaugh Professor of Political Economy at the John F. Kennedy School of Government, Harvard University, and director for Health and Retirement Programs at the National Bureau of Economic Research.

The authors are grateful to the Japan Foundation Center for Global Partnership, the U.S. National Institute of Aging, and the National Science Foundation for research support. Sections of this paper draw heavily on earlier papers on this topic by the same authors. They thank Charles Horioka for his thoughtful and detailed comments on the paper.

9.1   The Structure of Special Saving Plans

Employer-provided pension plans have been the dominant retirement saving vehicle for U.S. households throughout much of the postwar period. Employer contributions to these plans can be deducted from corporate income taxes, and income accruing on pension plan assets is also tax-exempt. Employees are not taxed on their pension entitlement until they receive benefits, typically many years after contributions are made.

During the 1980s, however, a number of specialized programs designed to encourage household saving were introduced and, in some cases, subsequently restricted. These programs, principally IRAs and 401(k)s, offer many of the same tax benefits as traditional employer-provided pensions. While a variety of regulatory and tax changes reduced the appeal of traditional pension arrangements during the 1980s, the new retirement saving vehicles flourished. This section describes the increasingly popular specialized saving plans and also presents some information on more traditional pension arrangements.

9.1.1   IRAs and 401(k)s: The Rules

IRAs were created by the Economic Recovery Tax Act of 1981. As originally enacted, taxpayers could make tax-deductible contributions to IRAs subject to a limit of $2,000 per earner and $250 for a nonworking spouse. Withdrawals could be made without penalty any time after the account holder turned 59 and a half, while early withdrawals were subject to a 10 percent tax penalty. Withdrawals are taxed as ordinary income. The power of compound interest makes the IRA an advantageous vehicle for long-term saving.

To reduce the current revenue cost of this program, the Tax Reform Act of 1986 limited access to tax-deductible IRAs by imposing income tests on deductible contributions by taxpayers covered by an employer-sponsored pension plan. Single taxpayers with incomes less than $25,000, and joint filers with taxable incomes less than $40,000, can make fully deductible contributions. Single filers with incomes above $35,000, and joint filers with incomes above $50,000, cannot make tax-deductible contributions. Taxpayers with incomes between the thresholds for tax-deductible and taxable IRAs are eligible for partially deductible IRAs. Taxpayers with employer-sponsored pensions and incomes above the various thresholds can still make after-tax contributions, and the return on the contributions accrues tax-free. As a rough approximation, for those affected by the legislation, about one-half of the advantage of the IRA over conventional saving vehicles was removed.

The 1986 tax changes reduced the attractiveness of saving through IRAs for many households, and we will show below that participation rates in IRAs declined. A second retirement saving program, known as the 401(k) plan after that section of the Internal Revenue Code, was growing in importance throughout the 1980s. The 401(k) plans were established by 1978 legislation, but they expanded rapidly only after the Treasury Department clarified their operation in 1981. These plans are established by employers. They allow employees to contribute before-tax dollars to 401(k) accounts. Like IRAs, assets in 401(k) plans accumulate tax-free, and just as with IRAs, income from these plans is taxed only when the funds are withdrawn. Prior to 1987 the employee contribution limit was $30,000. The Tax Reform Act of 1986 reduced the limit to $7,000 beginning in 1987 and instituted indexation for inflation in subsequent years. The 1993 contribution limit was $8,994.

There are several additional features of 401(k)s that employers may choose to adopt. First, employers can "match" employee contributions. A Hewitt (1991) study of 677 medium-size and large employers found that 84 percent of 401(k) plans provide some employer matching; 31 percent match at 50 cents per dollar, and 11 percent match dollar for dollar. A 1993 survey of 401(k) plans by Papke, Petersen, and Poterba (1996) found that nearly 90 percent of the participants in 401(k) plans face match rates of at least 25 cents per dollar contributed, and one-third face match rates of 100 percent on at least part of their contributions.[1]

A second important feature of many 401(k) plans is "hardship withdrawal," which enables participants to access plan funds, although in some cases with a penalty payment. Such withdrawals have tax consequences since the withdrawal is treated as taxable income in the year when it is received.[2] Employees in many firms may also borrow funds from their 401(k) accounts.

Conventional financial calculations, emphasizing rates of return, demonstrate that the 401(k) investment strictly dominates even a fully deductible IRA whenever the employer match rate is positive. On this criterion, deductible as well as nondeductible IRAs also dominate saving through traditional taxable accounts. For individuals aged 59 and a half or greater there are no penalties associated with withdrawal of IRA or 401(k) funds, so these accounts strictly dominate ordinary investment accounts. For younger investors, the rate of return benefit from investing through a targeted account must be compared with the reduced liquidity of assets in these accounts. Because we believe that most households do not save according to a simple rate-of-return-maximizing strategy, however, we suspect that return considerations affect but are not the most important determinant of saving behavior.[3]

---

1. The response rate to this survey was just over 5 percent, however. Nonetheless, Papke et al. (1996) present some evidence that the attributes of respondent plans are similar to those in other larger surveys of 401(k) plans. Many 401(k) plans provide high employer match rates up to a fixed fraction of salary (often 5 percent) contributed to the plan. After reaching this matching limit, employees may still make contributions, provided they have not reached the IRS limit on contributions, but those contributions will not be matched.

2. Leaving the firm that offers the 401(k) plan can also trigger a withdrawal if an individual has a relatively small 401(k) account balance and the employer chooses to terminate the account. The plan balance is transferred to the participant as a "lump-sum distribution." The recipient can then choose either to reinvest the proceeds in a tax-free account such as an IRA or to treat the lump-sum distribution as current taxable income.

3. For a discussion of this issue, see Venti and Wise (1992) and Poterba, Venti, and Wise (1994, 1995).

Although IRAs and 401(k) plans are the two most important personal retirement saving plans, other programs are available to specific groups. One such program is the 403(b) tax-sheltered annuity plan for employees of educational and other nonprofit institutions. These plans allow taxpayers to make retirement contributions from before-tax dollars, just as with 401(k) plans, and they permit tax-free accumulation subject to some restrictions on withdrawal. The current limit on contributions to a 403(b) plan is $9,500 per year. Another such program, known as a Keogh plan, is a retirement plan for self-employed persons. These plans are effectively substitutes for the employer-provided defined-contribution (and defined-benefit) plans provided for employees and offer the same tax treatment and the same favorable opportunities for investment. There are limits on contributions. In most cases, an individual cannot contribute more than 20 percent of total earnings, or $30,000, whichever is smaller. Because these plans apply to limited segments of the population, our subsequent analysis focuses on IRAs and 401(k)s.

9.1.2   Participation in IRAs and 401(k)s

The number of taxpayers making IRA contributions in each year since the early 1980s is shown in table 9.1. IRAs became popular almost immediately after they were introduced, and at their peak in 1985 more than 16 million taxpayers contributed nearly $40 billion to these accounts. The changes imposed in the Tax Reform Act of 1986 reduced the incentives for some households to contribute by eliminating deductible contributions for some higher-income taxpayers and by reducing marginal tax rates on capital income accruing through traditional channels. There was also a substantial decline in IRA promotion by financial institutions in the post-1986 period. Many taxpayers

Table 9.1   **Number of Tax Returns Claiming IRA Contributions, 1980–90**

Year	Number of IRA Contributor Returns (million tax returns)	Total IRA Contributions (billion $)
1980	2.564	3.431
1981	3.415	4.750
1982	12.010	28.274
1983	13.613	32.061
1984	15.232	35.374
1985	16.205	38.211
1986	15.535	37.758
1987	7.318	14.065
1988	6.361	11.882
1989	5.882	10.960
1990	4.785	9.928

Source: U.S. Department of the Treasury, *Statistics of Income: Individual Tax Returns* (Washington, D.C., various issues).

Table 9.2   **Growth of 401(k) Plans, 1983–89**

Year	Plans (thousands)	Participants (millions)	Contributions (billion $)
1983	1.7	4.4	n.a.
1984	17.3	7.5	16.3
1985	29.9	10.3	24.3
1986	37.4	11.6	29.2
1987	45.1	13.1	33.2
1988	68.1	15.5	39.4
1989	83.3	17.3	46.1

Sources: Data through 1988 from Turner and Beller (1992, table A4); 1989 data from *Private Pension Plan Bulletin* (1993, table E19).

who could have made tax-deductible contributions in the post-1986 period also appear to have been confused about the new IRA rules and therefore erroneously concluded that they were not eligible for the program. The number of contributors fell by half between 1986 and 1987. Indeed, even taxpayers who were unaffected by the new IRA contribution provisions and whose tax rates were unaffected by the legislation reduced their contribution rates by about 40 percent. By 1990, fewer than 6 million taxpayers reported IRA contributions of just under $10 billion.

The number of 401(k) plans, participants, and contributions over the 1980s is reported in table 9.2. The table charts the rapid growth of 401(k) plans during the last decade. Between 1984 and 1989, the number of plans more than quadrupled, and the number of participants more than doubled.[4] Contributions increased even more than the number of participants, even though the Tax Reform Act of 1986 limited the maximum contribution. The number of employees making 401(k) contributions is now substantially larger than the number of IRA contributors. These plans are now available at virtually all large firms and are diffusing through smaller firms as well.

Data on traditional defined-benefit and defined-contribution pension plans are shown in Table 9.3. The number of defined-contribution plans more than doubled between 1975 and 1982 and then rose sharply again after 1985. The value of contributions to these plans, however, peaked in the early 1980s and has remained relatively constant since that time. (The somewhat larger figures in 1982 and 1983 include 401(k) contributions; contributions to defined-contribution plans changed little over the period.) In 1989, contributions to 401(k) plans were substantially greater than contributions to defined-contribution pension plans.[5] The number of defined-benefit plans increased

4. Participation in a plan only indicates that an employee has a 401(k) account, not that the employee made a contribution in a given year.

5. For some purposes, 401(k) plans are considered defined-contribution plans. Our discussion of defined-contribution plans focuses on *non*-401(k) plans.

Table 9.3   Trends in Pension Plans, Participants, and Contributions, 1975–89

Year	Plans (thousands)	Participants (millions)	Contributions (billion $)
Defined-Contribution Plans			
1975	207.7	11.2	12.8
1976	246.0	13.2	14.2
1977	281.0	14.6	15.9
1978	314.6	15.6	18.4
1979	331.4	17.5	20.7
1980	340.8	18.9	23.5
1981	378.3	20.7	28.4
1982	419.5	23.4	31.1[a]
1983	424.9	23.4	36.1[a]
1984	418.1	23.5	27.1
1985	432.1	22.8	28.9
1986	507.6	23.0	29.1
1987	524.9	21.9	29.0
1988	515.9	n.a.	25.5
1989	515.6	19.1	27.1
Defined-Benefit Plans			
1975	103.3	27.2	24.2
1976	114.0	27.5	28.5
1977	121.7	28.1	31.2
1978	128.4	29.0	27.6
1979	139.5	29.4	40.6
1980	148.1	30.1	42.6
1981	167.3	30.1	47.0
1982	175.0	29.8	48.4
1983	175.1	30.0	46.3
1984	168.0	30.2	47.2
1985	170.2	29.0	42.0
1986	172.6	28.7	33.2
1987	163.1	28.4	29.8
1988	146.0	n.a.	26.3
1989	132.5	27.3	24.9

Sources: Data through 1988 from Beller and Lawrence (1992, table 4.9). Data for number of plans and flow of contributions from Turner and Beller (1992, tables A1, A4, A5, resp.). Data for 1989 from *Private Pension Plan Bulletin* (1993, tables A3, E1, E10).

Note: Entries for defined-contribution plans *exclude* 401(k) plans. This may cause some underestimate for the number of defined-contribution plan participants since the entries in the first panel are computed by subtracting the number of plans, participants, and value of contributions for 401(k)s from the total for defined-contribution plans. Participants refer to active participants.

[a]Includes 401(k) contributions, without which defined-contribution plan contributions were essentially flat over the 1981–84 period.

during the 1975–82 period, but the increase was slower than that for defined-contribution plans. Between 1986 and 1989, however, the number of defined-benefit plans declined by 23 percent. The number of active participants in defined-benefit plans peaked in 1984 and declined 9.6 percent by 1989. Contributions to defined-benefit plans reached a peak in 1982 and declined by 48.6

Table 9.4   **Eligibility and Participation for Selected Years: 401(k) and IRA Compared**

	Percentage 401(k) Eligibility (1)	Percentage 401(k) Participation Given Eligibility (2)	Percentage 401(k) Participation (3)	Percentage with IRA Account (4)
1984	13.3	58.1	7.7	25.4
1987	20.0	62.6	12.5	28.8
1991	34.7	70.8	24.6	27.1

Source: Authors' tabulations from the SIPP, as described in the text.

percent by 1989. These trends in the flow of pension contributions are important factors in aggregate personal saving, an issue we consider in more detail below.

A key difference between IRAs and 401(k)s is that, while all taxpayers are eligible for IRAs, with varying degrees of tax-deductibility, 401(k) eligibility is conditional on the individual's employer's offering a plan. To estimate the participation rate in 401(k) plans *conditional on eligibility* therefore requires data on either individuals or firms. Table 9.4 presents information on both 401(k) eligibility and participation given eligibility, based on tabulations from the Survey of Income and Program Participation (SIPP). The analysis is limited to households with heads between the ages of 25 and 65 and excludes households with self-employment income. Conditional on eligibility, the participation rate in 401(k) plans increased from 58.1 percent in 1984 to 70.8 percent in 1991. Column (3) in table 9.4 gives the overall 401(k) participation rate, which is the product of the eligibility rate in column (1) and the conditional participation rate in column (2). By 1991 almost one-quarter of all families participated in a 401(k).[6]

For comparison, column (4) in table 9.4 shows the participation rate in IRAs. The percentage of families with an IRA has never exceeded 30 percent. These figures are the percentage of families that have a positive balance in an IRA each year. Since many families may have an IRA but no longer make contributions, the figures overestimate the IRA participation rate.

Eligibility and participation rates by age and income are shown for 1991 in table 9.5. Eligibility for a 401(k) increases with income but is not strongly related to age. Given eligibility, participation is unrelated to age but increases somewhat with income; conditional participation is above 60 percent for all income groups, however. The relationship between income and 401(k) partici-

6. One important feature of 401(k) plan participation, underscored by Papke et al.'s (1996) cross-tabulations of plan characteristics in several different years, is a strong persistence in participation. Because participation rates in most 401(k)s are high, and consistently high, there is strong evidence that individuals who begin saving through 401(k) arrangements will continue to do so.

Table 9.5   Eligibility and Participation Rates by Age and Income in 1991: 401(k) and IRA Compared

Age	<10	10–20	20–30	30–40	40–50	50–75	>75	All
				Income (thousand $)				
			A. Percentage 401(k) Eligibility					
25–35	5.1	14.8	30.2	40.1	38.9	51.3	51.2	31.4
35–45	11.2	20.2	34.6	42.8	46.0	53.9	47.1	39.2
45–55	2.1	16.5	27.6	32.8	48.7	56.4	52.5	35.9
55–65	7.9	14.4	20.9	36.5	37.7	51.9	37.0	28.9
All	6.4	16.6	29.7	39.0	43.7	53.8	48.1	34.7
			B. Percentage 401(k) Participation Given Eligibility					
25–35	79.8	63.2	70.3	74.1	73.8	76.1	86.2	73.5
35–45	58.4	67.7	59.8	63.7	68.7	67.2	83.8	67.7
45–55	72.5	51.5	57.6	58.5	81.6	75.1	88.1	72.3
55–65	85.2	68.3	49.0	72.5	67.8	84.0	85.7	72.3
All	70.8	63.0	61.7	67.3	72.9	73.3	85.8	70.8
			C. Percentage 401(k) Participation					
25–35	4.1	9.4	21.2	29.7	28.7	39.1	44.2	23.0
35–45	6.6	13.6	20.7	27.3	31.6	36.3	39.5	26.5
45–55	1.5	8.5	15.9	19.2	39.8	42.3	46.3	25.9
55–65	6.7	9.8	10.2	26.5	25.6	43.6	31.7	20.9
All	4.5	10.5	18.4	26.2	31.8	39.4	41.3	24.6
			D. Percentage with IRA Account					
25–35	3.8	4.8	9.3	14.8	17.9	23.6	43.2	13.2
35–45	10.1	6.8	15.4	20.0	33.0	38.7	59.9	26.3
45–55	6.0	12.9	24.9	31.3	47.3	50.2	66.3	35.3
55–65	14.8	24.1	37.6	45.7	59.5	63.4	75.5	43.8
All	7.9	9.7	18.6	24.7	35.6	41.1	61.6	27.1

Source: Authors' tabulations from the SIPP.

pation shown in panel C of the table is due largely to the relationship of eligibility to income. In contrast, participation in an IRA, for which all wage earners were eligible until 1986, is strongly related to both age and income. Thus, comparing panels B and D of the table, conditional 401(k) participation is much more equally distributed than IRA participation, across age and income groups.

The data in table 9.5 suggest that the diffusion of 401(k) plans may have the greatest effect on retirees who reach retirement age in two or three decades. Indeed, the eligibility rate for 401(k)s is highest among workers between the ages of 35 and 45.

The high 401(k) participation rates suggest that the special features of 401(k) plans—payroll deduction of contributions, other employees also contributing, and often-generous employer match rates—are important aspects of the plan. The high 401(k) participation rates also suggest that as these plans

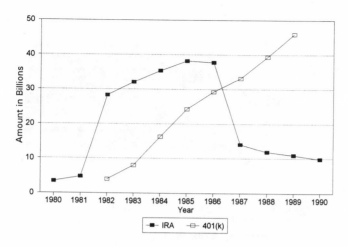

Fig. 9.1   401(k) and IRA contributions, 1980–90 (billions of dollars)

diffuse across firms, and more workers become eligible, there will be increased use of 401(k)s for retirement saving.

9.1.3   Contributions to IRAs and 401(k)s

Figure 9.1 shows the trend in total contributions to 401(k) and IRA accounts. IRA contributions increased from less than $5 billion to almost $30 billion as soon as IRAs became available to all wage earners in 1982. Thereafter, annual contributions increased to almost $40 billion in 1986. But the Tax Reform Act of 1986 led to a dramatic reduction in IRA contributions, which were less than $10 billion by 1990. Annual contributions to 401(k) plans began at a low level in 1982 and then increased continuously, reaching almost $46 billion in 1989. Contributions were probably close to $60 billion by the early 1990s. The graph shows little relationship between IRA and 401(k) saving. In particular, the data show no increase in the rate of growth in 401(k) contributions after the Tax Reform Act of 1986 and the subsequent fall in IRA contributions.

A useful measure of the importance of IRA and 401(k) contributions is their level relative to other contributions that are targeted to providing retirement income. There is an obvious difficulty in measuring such retirement saving since it is not possible to "track" all dollars of saving as targeted for particular uses. Nevertheless, it is plausible to define total new private retirement saving contributions as the sum of employer contributions to defined-benefit and defined-contribution pension plans and individual contributions to IRAs, Keogh plans, and 401(k) plans.

The relative importance of the different components of retirement saving during the 1980s is plotted in figure 9.2. By 1989, IRAs, 401(k)s, and Keogh plans together accounted for almost 53 percent of total retirement saving, up from 7.6 percent in 1980. It seems evident that if IRA contributions had not

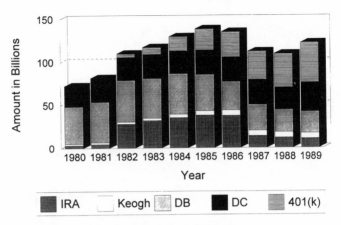

Fig. 9.2   Retirement saving by saving plan, 1980–88
Note: 401(k) data for 1982 and 1983 are estimates.

been reduced by the Tax Reform Act of 1986, this proportion would be substantially higher. Thus these new saving vehicles have rapidly become an extremely important component of the future financial support of the elderly. Counting defined-contribution pension plans, 76 percent of 1988 retirement saving was in "individual" accounts, with a value that the individual can track and assets that the individual can manage to some degree. By comparison, only 43 percent of retirement saving flowed into such accounts in 1980.

Figure 9.2 shows that total retirement saving increased sharply until 1985 and fell substantially thereafter, following the Tax Reform Act of 1986. Essentially, the pattern of total retirement saving follows the pattern of IRA contributions. Indeed, if it had not been for 401(k) contributions, the data suggest that total retirement saving would have fallen much more than it did. In spite of the increase in the number of defined-contribution pension plans, total contributions to these plans remained almost constant over the entire period. There was a large drop in contributions to defined-benefit pension plans.[7] Bernheim and Shoven (1988) discussed a number of explanations for this development, principally increases in the value of pension funds invested in the stock market and thus lower required additional contributions to meet projected benefit entitlements. Schieber and Shoven (chap. 5 in this volume) discuss in addition the effect of legislation in the 1980s that limited contributions to defined-benefit plans.

7. The rapid expansion of 401(k) plans at a time when more traditional retirement saving arrangements were either stable or declining raises a question about whether 401(k)s were substitutes for other pension programs. The evidence in Papke et al. (1996) suggests most 401(k) participants are in plans that supplement other pension plans. There is some evidence that small firms may now choose 401(k)s rather than other types of retirement saving programs.

Table 9.6A   Median IRA Balances versus Other Financial Asset Balances, 1984, 1987, and 1991

Family and Asset Category	Excluding Stocks and Bonds			Including Stocks and Bonds		
	1984	1987	1991	1984	1987	1991
Families with IRA						
Total financial assets	13,000[a]	16,000	22,000[a]	16,170[a]	19,300	26,000[a]
	(562)		(788)	(807)		(562)
Other than IRA	**6,550**	**6,100**	**7,867**[a]	**9,400**	**9,483**	**10,900**
	(432)		(605)	(586)		(821)
IRA	4,500[a]	7,400	10,500[a]	4,500[a]	7,400	10,500[a]
	(224)		(316)	(224)		(316)
Debt	500	500	500	500	500	500
	(100)		(110)	(100)		(110)
Families without IRA						
Total financial assets	650	754	1,200[a]	800[a]	960	1,500[a]
	(57)		(71)	(53)		(66)
Non-401(k)	650	600	800[a]	800	800	1,000[a]
	(30)		(37)	(17)		(21)

Source: Authors' tabulations from the SIPP.
[a]Significantly different from 1987 estimate, at 0.95 confidence level.

9.2   Account Balances in Targeted Saving Plans

The U.S. wealth distribution is highly skewed, and mean holdings of virtually all assets are much greater than median holdings. To provide information on the saving patterns of representative households, we therefore focus on *median* balances in IRAs and 401(k) accounts, as well as median holdings of other financial assets.

Table 9.6A shows the median holdings of all financial assets and median balances in targeted saving plans, by individuals with and without IRAs, in 1984, 1987, and 1991. In 1984, the median IRA balance of households with IRAs was $4,500. The median of non-IRA financial assets, excluding (including) stocks and bonds, was $6,550 ($9,400).[8] By 1991, the median IRA balance in households with an IRA was $10,500, and the median non-IRA balance was $7,867 ($10,900 including stocks and bonds). While the characteristics of the median IRA household may have changed between 1984 and 1991, the striking feature of these statistics is the small increase in non-IRA asset holdings, measured with or without stocks and bonds. Moreover, these statistics demonstrate that balances in IRA accounts represent a substantial fraction of the financial asset holdings of households with these accounts.

8. Because table 9.6B reports medians, and medians are not additive, there is no requirement for the median of the sum of two exhaustive asset categories, e.g., IRA balances and non-IRA balances, to add to the median of total financial assets.

Table 9.6B   **Median 401(k) Balances versus Other Financial Asset Balances, 1984, 1987, and 1991**

Family and Asset Category	Excluding Stocks and Bonds			Including Stocks and Bonds		
	1984	1987	1991	1984	1987	1991
Families with 401(k)						
Total financial assets	–	6,061	8,858[a]	–	7,299	10,449[a]
			(765)		(585)	
Other than 401(k) or IRA	**1,800**	**1,500**	**1,500**	**3,000[a]**	**2,149**	**2,209**
	(243)		(150)	(229)		(370)
401(k)	–	2,800	4,560[a]	–	2,800	4,560[a]
			(349)			(349)
Debt	1,000	1,200	1,500	1,000	1,200	1,500
	(220)		(189)	(220)		(189)
Families without 401(k)						
Total financial assets	1,500	1,500	1,500	1,949	2,000	2,000
	(64)		(86)	(87)		(116)
Non-IRA	1,000	1,050	1,150	1,400	1,430	1,500
	(58)		(78)	(87)		(116)

Source: Authors' tabulations from the SIPP.
[a]Significantly different from 1987 estimate, at 0.95 confidence level.

The lower panel of table 9.6A presents summary information on households without IRAs. The median financial assets for this group was only $1,500 in 1991, including holdings of stocks and bonds, and had been only $800 seven years earlier. The low level of median asset holdings indicates that a majority of households save very little. The finding that median non-IRA financial assets change very slowly for both groups of households is important evidence on the net effect of IRAs on personal saving, a subject we consider in more detail below.

Table 9.6B presents statistics similar to those in table 9.6A, except it divides households based on whether they have a 401(k) plan, rather than an IRA. The broad pattern of results is similar to that for IRAs. Households without 401(k)s have very low levels of total financial assets. The median non-401(k), non-IRA assets of households with 401(k)s declines slightly between 1984 and 1987 and changes relatively little in the next four years. The difference between 1984 and 1987 may not reflect actual asset decumulation by 401(k) households, but rather changes in the composition of the set of households with 401(k) plans over the time period.

Two caveats are important in interpreting table 9.6. First, because most households have at least some net worth in owner-occupied real estate in addition to the financial assets described in the table, 401(k) and IRA accounts are a smaller fraction of net worth, even for the median household, than table 9.6 suggests. Second, because both IRAs and 401(k)s are relatively recent financial innovations and because there are contribution limits preventing very wealthy households from developing large balances in these accounts, the total assets in these accounts still represent a small share of total household net worth. In 1989, for example, the total balance in IRAs and Keogh plans was $501.7 billion, and that in 401(k) plans was approximately $357 billion.[9] This corresponds to roughly 5.3 percent of total household sector net worth.

9.3   Retirement Saving Contributions and Saving Behavior

The data presented in figure 9.2 above show that from their widespread introduction in 1982 until the Tax Reform Act of 1986, contributions to IRAs were a substantial share of the flow of personal saving in the United States and that 401(k) contributions are an increasingly important share. This observation alone does not imply that such retirement saving plans have increased personal saving. Resolving this issue requires information on how the *other* components of private saving respond to changes in saving through targeted retirement programs. Because much of the variation in IRA and 401(k) availability and contribution levels is over time, there is a temptation to examine the overall level of private saving before and after these programs became available. Many factors besides the availability of these programs affect the level of private saving, however, so such time-series comparisons can be unreliable.

Studying the net saving effects of these programs using household-level data is also subject to a number of difficulties. It is tempting to compare the levels and growth rates of financial assets for households that do and do not participate in retirement saving programs. A key problem in interpreting such cross-sectional comparisons is the heterogeneity in saving behavior among individuals. Some people save and others do not, and the savers tend to save more in all forms. For example, families with IRA accounts have larger financial asset balances than families without IRAs. But this does not necessarily mean that IRAs explain the difference.

An accumulating body of evidence, however, suggests that contributions to IRAs and 401(k) plans represent new saving. For example, Venti and Wise (1990, 1991), based on the U.S. Consumer Expenditure Surveys and the SIPP, find no evidence that saving rates in non-IRA channels are lower for households that were accumulating IRA balances in the early 1980s than for non-IRA households who were demographically similar and had comparable prior saving behavior. These estimates imply that increases in the IRA limits would lead to substantial increases in IRA saving and very little reduction in other saving. If the IRA limit were raised, the estimates imply that one-half to two-thirds of the increase in IRA saving would be funded by a decrease in current consumption and about one-third by reduced taxes. Only a small share of the

---

9. The value of IRAs and Keogh accounts is drawn from the Employee Benefit Research Institute, Issue Brief no. 119 (1991). The value of 401(k) plan assets is from the *Private Pension Plan Bulletin* (1993, table E19).

IRA contributions, at most 20 percent, would come from reductions in other saving.[10]

With the availability of better data covering a longer time span, later-generation studies have used nonparametric methods to control for heterogeneity in individual saving behavior. The methods exploit "quasi-experimental" differences in household "exposure" to IRA or 401(k) saving opportunities to investigate the effect of these programs on household saving behavior. Venti and Wise (1992) consider the accumulation of IRA assets of successive random samples of IRA contributors who were exposed to the IRA option for increasing periods of time, but who were alike in other demographic respects. Their accumulation of IRA assets is compared to the change in non-IRA financial assets. While there was a large increase in IRA assets, there was essentially no change in the level of other assets. Poterba et al. (1993, 1994) report results from two such quasi-experimental identification strategies. The first, like the Venti and Wise (1992) analysis, compares the assets accumulated by individuals of similar age and income but in different birth cohorts, and who have therefore been able to save through IRAs and 401(k) plans for different lengths of time. This analysis represent the first study of the saving effect of 401(k) plans. Data from the SIPP—for 1984, 1987, and 1991—provide the basis for these comparisons. Evidence from the 1993 analysis is shown in table 9.6.

Since age, income, and other characteristics of the three cross sections are similar, one would expect saving balances also to be similar. The different cohorts do face different historical patterns of asset returns, but for households with relatively little wealth, this should not have much effect on observed holdings. The critical differences between these cohorts, from the standpoint of retirement saving accounts, are that the 1984 sample had only about two years (1982–84) to accumulate 401(k) and IRA balances, while the 1987 sample had about five years, and the 1991 sample about nine years. The central question is whether longer exposure to IRAs, or 401(k)s, results in higher levels of saving.

The summary statistics in table 9.6 provide important evidence on this issue. Non-IRA, non-401(k) assets do not appear to decline as either IRA or 401(k) assets increase. There were large increases between 1984 and 1991 in the total financial assets of families with both IRA and 401(k) accounts, but little change in their non-IRA, non-401(k) financial assets. There were also substantial increases in the total financial assets of families that had IRAs only or 401(k)s only, but no decline in their non-IRA, non-401(k) financial assets. It is difficult to argue that these differences are due to some form of unobserved heterogeneity across households in different cohorts.

---

10. Results using different data sets and different methodologies are presented in Venti and Wise (1986, 1987). These studies also find very little substitution of IRA for other personal financial asset saving. Gale and Scholz (1990) find essentially no net saving from IRAs. Feenberg and Skinner (1989), like Venti and Wise, find that IRA contributions represent new saving for the most part. Joines and Manegold (1991) conclude that about half of IRA contributions represent new saving.

Table 9.7   **Median Asset Balances by 401(k) Eligibility and Income**

Asset Category and Eligibility Status	Income (thousand $)						
	<10	10–20	20–30	30–40	40–50	50–75	>75
Results for 1991							
Total financial assets							
Eligible for a 401(k)	1,499[a]	2,800[a]	4,608[a]	8,649[a]	15,005[a]	26,000[a]	52,500[a]
Not eligible for a 401(k)	30	350	1,124	2,260	5,600	10,675	31,000
Non-401(k), non-IRA assets							
Eligible for a 401(k)	300	500	1,099	2,550[a]	5,000[a]	8,839[a]	18,100
Not eligible for a 401(k)	20	310	1,000	1,750	4,000	5,800	18,000
Results for 1987							
Total financial assets							
Eligible for a 401(k)	1,090[a]	1,190[a]	4,000[a]	9,205[a]	12,650[a]	25,343[a]	58,119[a]
Not eligible for a 401(k)	22	400	1,366	4,000	6,630	14,650	30,900
Non-401(k), non-IRA assets							
Eligible for a 401(k)	361	305	1,250[a]	3,250[a]	5,800[a]	11,200[a]	25,500[a]
Not eligible for a 401(k)	20	350	1,052	2,800	4,245	8,737	21,200

Source: Authors' tabulations from the SIPP.

[a]Difference between eligibles and noneligibles is statistically significant at the 95 percent confidence level.

The growing importance of 401(k) plans provides a second quasi-experimental way to assess the net effect of retirement saving programs. Assuming that 401(k) eligibility is largely exogenous, the result of decisions by employers, then comparisons between non-401(k) asset accumulation of those who are and who are not eligible for such plans provides another way to assess their saving effects. This approach views 401(k) *eligibility* as the "treatment" in a "natural experiment" to evaluate the saving effect of a plan with 401(k) tax incentives, employer payroll deductions, and other provisions. In this case the key question is whether families who were eligible for 401(k)s in a given year had larger total financial asset balances than families who were not eligible, or equivalently, did non-401(k) financial assets decline enough to offset the 401(k) contributions of eligible families?

Table 9.7 presents the results of this comparison using data from the 1987 and 1991 SIPP. The values in the table are reported by income interval to control for income-related differences in 401(k) eligibility. It presents the median level of 401(k) assets, as well as the median for total financial assets.

If families reduced saving in other forms when they became eligible for a 401(k) plan, the typical family eligible for a 401(k) plan in 1991 should have accumulated less wealth in other (non-401(k)) financial assets than the typical family who was not eligible for a 401(k). This is not the case. The median level of total financial assets of families with incomes above $75,000, for example, who are eligible for a 401(k) is $52,500, whereas the median for families who are not eligible is only $31,000. There is little difference between the other

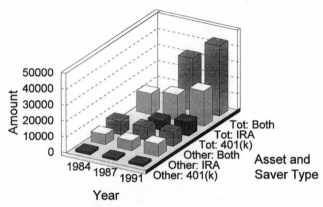

Fig. 9.3   Total and other assets by saver type

Note: Families with both 401(k)s and IRAs had large increases in total financial assets but little change in other assets. Families with IRAs only or with 401(k)s only also had substantial increases in total financial assets but no decline in other financial assets.

financial assets of families who are and are not eligible for a 401(k). Indeed, the eligible families have somewhat higher levels of other financial assets. The data show no substitution of 401(k) contributions for other financial asset saving.

Figure 9.3 presents the information in tables 9.6A and 9.6B, as well as separate data for the changing wealth holdings of households with *both* IRAs and 401(k)s. The figure shows that households with either or both personal retirement saving accounts experienced large increases in total financial assets but in no case was there substantial decumulation of other financial assets, and thus no evidence of substitution of 401(k) and IRA saving for saving in other financial asset forms.

Poterba et al. (1993, 1994) also explore the interaction between IRA and 401(k) saving. Somewhat paradoxically, there is little apparent substitution between saving in these two tax-deferred vehicles. The data on individual saving patterns suggest a number of "economic" anomalies. For example, many households make IRA contributions even though they have not made the maximum allowable contribution to their 401(k) plans. Because of employer matching, 401(k) plans are typically more generous than IRAs. These results call into question standard assumptions about the determinants of saving and the degree to which different forms of saving are treated as close substitutes.

9.4   Personal Saving Trends and Contributions to IRAs and 401(k)s

The decline of the aggregate personal saving rate in the United States during the last decade is poorly understood. While a number of studies, including Summers and Carroll (1987) and Bosworth, Burtless, and Sabelhaus (1991), have tried to link this decline to demographic change, revisions in the structure of social insurance programs, increased household wealth, and other changes in the financial environment, they have failed to identify any single factor, or set of factors, that can explain the decline. The decline in personal saving is particularly surprising in light of the evidence presented above on the growth in IRAs and 401(k)s during the 1980s.

9.4.1 The Measurement of Aggregate Personal Saving

There are two widely cited measures of personal saving: the National Income and Product Accounts (NIPA) and the Federal Reserve Board Flow of Funds (FOF) measure. These two measures differ both in conceptual intent and in the data on which they are based. The NIPA personal saving measure is intended to reflect the difference between personal disposable income and personal spending. The FOF saving measure, in contrast, is intended to reflect the change in net financial assets and liabilities between two points in time, plus net household investment in tangible assets. The two most important categories of tangible assets are consumer durables, primarily automobiles, and owner-occupied housing. Because each of these measures of personal saving is computed from large and sometimes offsetting gross flows, measurement errors in income, spending, or asset flows are reflected in the reported saving flows.

The levels of the NIPA and FOF saving measures sometimes differ by several hundred billion dollars. As shares of personal disposable income, the FOF measure was more than twice the NIPA measure in the late 1980s. To illustrate conceptual differences in what the measures attempt to capture, as well as the differences in the data that underlie the measures, it is helpful to consider a saving concept that is intermediate between the FOF and NIPA: the NIPA saving concept computed using FOF data. This saving flow, which is also published by the Federal Reserve Board, equals the FOF saving flow *less* three components: net household investment in consumer durables, the change in the insurance and pension reserves of federal and state and local governments, and the net saving of corporate farms. The first two adjustments are much larger than the third. In 1990, for example, net investment in consumer durables equaled $85.1 billion, and the change in government insurance liabilities was $88 billion. The government insurance and pension reserve adjustment consists of the change in the financial reserves of three federal retirement programs—veterans, railroad employees, and other federal workers—plus the change in the reserves of state and local government retirement funds.[11]

After making these three adjustments to the FOF personal saving flow, the resulting series (which we call the FOF NIPA basis) and the NIPA series are conceptually the same and in principle are measuring the same thing. Differ-

---

11. The NIPA attributes the assets and liabilities of *private* pension plans to the household sector, but they do not perform a similar adjustment with government pension plans. This is the reason this adjustment is required.

ences remain, however, in the way the same saving concept is measured in the two series. The FOF estimate of personal saving begins with financial securities transactions, such as net purchases of saving bonds and corporate stock, and net deposits to various financial intermediaries. These are added to the increase in private pension reserves and the net acquisition of tangible assets. The latter is computed as gross purchases of various assets less an estimate of depreciation of existing holdings.

In contrast to the FOF estimate, the NIPA estimate of the saving rate is the difference between personal disposable income and personal outlays. Several features of the NIPA measure are important. First, outlays include expenditures on all durable goods *except* owner-occupied housing. While a newly purchased car is counted as consumption in the national income accounts, a new house is capitalized: personal income rises by an estimate of the imputed income the new homeowner receives from the house, and outlays rise by an estimate of the rental cost of the house. Second, the NIPA personal income estimate includes a number of imputations for income that households never receive as cash. These include the interest and dividends received by private employer-provided pension funds, the estimated market value of in-kind transfers such as Medicare, and the differential between the interest earned and paid by financial intermediaries (labeled "imputed interest income"). These imputations lead to potentially large differences between actual personal saving on a cash basis, the type of saving that IRAs and 401(k)s may have encouraged, and NIPA-reported personal saving.[12]

Both the NIPA and FOF measures include directly *employer* contributions to 401(k) plans. In the NIPA, these show up as other labor income, one of the components of personal disposable income. In the FOF, these are additions to the reserves of private insured and noninsured pension funds. The FOF accounts also include *individual* contributions to these plans, but the NIPA does not include such contributions directly; they are part of the residual between income and outlays. A similar situation applies to IRA contributions: they do not directly enter the NIPA calculation, although they directly enter the FOF calculation when individuals add to IRAs.

9.4.2 Trends in Aggregate Personal Saving

Table 9.8 reports the time series for both the NIPA and FOF personal saving rates for the 1956–92 period. The two measures display substantially different levels, with the FOF measure between 5 and 8 percent higher than the NIPA measure during the 1980s. The two measures of personal saving also follow very different trends during the 1980s, as shown in figure 9.4. The NIPA measure fell almost 50 percent over the 1980s, declining more or less continuously

---

12. Bosworth et al. (1991, 228) present a calculation of cash basis saving in an appendix to their paper. While the saving rate computed on a cash basis is the same as that on a NIPA basis for 1989, there is no reason to expect such strong agreement in general. There are numerous required adjustments to the NIPA saving flow.

Table 9.8   **Personal Saving Rate, 1956–92 (percentage of disposable income)**

Year	NIPA	FOF Unadjusted	FOF NIPA Basis
1956	7.1	13.0	9.2
1957	7.2	12.2	9.0
1958	7.4	11.3	9.3
1959	6.3	10.4	7.4
1960	5.7	10.6	7.7
1961	6.6	10.1	8.0
1962	6.5	11.2	8.1
1963	5.9	11.7	8.0
1964	6.9	13.4	9.1
1965	7.0	13.9	8.8
1966	6.8	15.5	10.1
1967	8.1	14.8	10.1
1968	7.1	13.3	8.0
1969	6.5	12.3	7.3
1970	8.0	12.6	8.7
1971	8.3	13.2	8.7
1972	7.0	14.3	8.8
1973	9.0	16.4	10.9
1974	8.9	11.7	7.7
1975	8.7	13.5	9.7
1976	7.4	13.3	8.6
1977	6.3	13.9	8.5
1978	6.9	13.0	7.6
1979	7.0	12.2	7.9
1980	7.9	11.0	7.8
1981	8.8	11.0	7.9
1982	8.6	11.3	8.4
1983	6.8	12.5	8.3
1984	8.0	13.9	8.6
1985	6.4	12.3	6.5
1986	6.0	14.0	7.9
1987	4.3	10.3	4.9
1988	4.4	10.7	5.1
1989	4.0	12.1	6.7
1990	4.3	10.3	6.0
1991	4.7	8.7	5.8
1992	4.8	9.6	6.3

Sources: NIPA and FOF accounts.

from around 8 percent in 1980 to 4 percent in 1990, with the most precipitous decline after 1984. In contrast, the FOF measure rose from 11 percent in 1980 to 14 percent in 1986—the period over which IRAs expanded—and then declined to around 10 percent, ending the decade about 10 percent below its starting value (as opposed to the 50 percent decline in the NIPA measure). The FOF NIPA basis measure remained relatively constant at around 8 percent until 1986 and then fell to 5 percent, ending the decade at 6 percent. An apparent

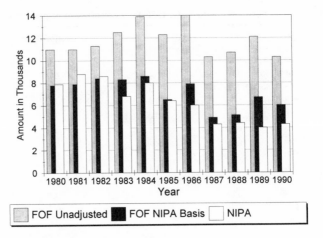

Fig. 9.4   National saving rates

agreement over all the measures is a sharp decline in the saving rate following the Tax Reform Act of 1986, when IRA contributions plummeted.

Although the measures differ in important respects, when compared as a group to the growth in total contributions to IRAs and 401(k) plans reported in figure 9.1, it may be surprising that national personal saving was not higher at the end than at the beginning of the decade.

To place the national personal saving flows in perspective with respect to targeted saving contributions, table 9.9 reports the annual flow of national personal saving for each year beginning in 1956. We emphasize the data for the 1980s. The flow of national personal saving based on the NIPA and the two FOF measures is shown in figure 9.5 together with the total of contributions to retirement saving plans, reported in figure 9.2. It is evident that retirement saving contributions represent a large fraction of national personal saving. In addition, it is evident that the FOF measures show an *increase* in other personal saving at the same time that contributions to personal retirement plans were increasing rapidly. The national series also show a sharp drop after the Tax Reform Act of 1986 and the subsequent fall in IRA contributions. Possibly most striking is that, while total retirement contributions *declined* as a proportion of FOF national saving over the 1980s, retirement contributions *increased* as a percentage of NIPA saving. Indeed, by 1989 retirement contributions represented 80 percent of NIPA saving. We question whether this number is believable and suggest that it brings into question the validity of the most widely cited measure of national saving.

The individual components of retirement saving relative to national saving are also striking. Recall that in their peak year (1985) IRA contributions totaled $39 billion. Personal saving measured on a FOF basis was $361.1 billion, and on a NIPA basis, $189 billion. The NIPA saving rate was 6.4 percent of dispos-

Table 9.9   **Personal Saving Flows, 1956–92 (billion current dollars)**

Year	NIPA	FOF Unadjusted	FOF NIPA Basis
1956	21.3	38.8	27.6
1957	22.7	38.4	28.4
1958	24.1	36.8	30.4
1959	22.0	36.1	25.5
1960	20.7	38.1	27.7
1961	25.0	38.0	30.2
1962	25.9	44.5	32.4
1963	24.6	49.0	33.4
1964	31.6	61.1	41.6
1965	34.5	68.1	43.1
1966	36.3	82.5	53.7
1967	45.8	84.2	57.4
1968	43.9	82.4	49.3
1969	43.4	81.9	48.6
1970	57.5	91.1	62.7
1971	65.4	103.3	68.4
1972	59.8	121.2	75.1
1973	86.1	157.4	104.5
1974	93.4	122.5	80.6
1975	100.3	155.0	111.9
1976	93.0	168.3	108.8
1977	88.0	193.0	118.7
1978	107.8	204.2	118.5
1979	123.3	214.0	138.3
1980	153.9	213.9	151.9
1981	191.8	239.0	171.7
1982	199.5	262.8	196.0
1983	168.6	312.5	207.8
1984	222.0	384.4	238.0
1985	189.3	361.1	192.1
1986	187.5	438.2	247.5
1987	142.0	339.4	161.7
1988	155.7	381.0	182.2
1989	152.1	456.5	252.1
1990	175.6	417.5	242.3
1991	199.6	368.3	242.8
1992	212.7	425.2	277.1

Sources: NIPA and FOF accounts.

able income, so the flow of IRA contributions equaled 1.3 percent of disposable income. In more recent years, the flow of 401(k) contributions has been a larger share of the reported saving flow. In 1990, for example, we estimate that 401(k) contributions were approximately $60 billion. These contributions were roughly one-third as large as the total personal saving flow estimate from the NIPA ($175.6 billion), and slightly under one-sixth of the FOF personal saving estimate ($417 billion). If the amount that individuals and their firms contrib-

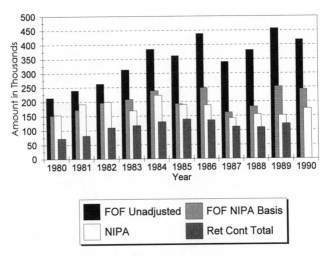

Fig. 9.5   National saving levels and total retirement contributions

uted to 401(k) accounts in 1990 had been channeled to consumption rather than saving, the NIPA personal saving rate would have been less than 3 percent of disposable income.

An apparently important factor in the decline of the personal saving rate during the last 10 years is the decline in contributions to employer-provided pension plans. Although contributions to defined-contribution plans remained constant over the period, defined-benefit plan contributions fell substantially. Contributions to these plans together fell from 3.5 percent of disposable income in 1981 to 1.4 percent in 1989.

This example demonstrates clearly that the personal saving rate as usually reported includes some components beyond household control and suggests that future research on the source of declining saving should focus on the imputations and other factors that make personal saving in the NIPA and FOF different from cash saving. Another approach to measuring saving trends is to construct a time series of saving rates from household surveys. There is some evidence from household surveys, presented in Bosworth et al. (1991), that personal cash saving has declined since the mid-1960s. This work does not bear on the timing, magnitude, or source of the personal saving decline in the late 1980s, however.

9.5   Conclusions

Individual saving through targeted retirement saving accounts—IRAs and 401(k)s, in particular—grew rapidly during the 1980s. While aggregate measures of personal saving show a sharp decline in the late 1980s, following the Tax Reform Act of 1986 and the fall in IRA saving, the 401(k) component of saving was rising, forestalling what could have been an even sharper decline in personal saving. Contributions to targeted saving accounts currently account for approximately one-third of the flow of personal saving measured in the NIPA. Studies of asset accumulation patterns for those who do, and do not, contribute to these plans suggests very little substitution between saving in these plans and other forms of personal saving. This suggests that most of the contributions to these plans represent saving that would not otherwise have occurred.

In a stable economic and tax environment, contributions to IRAs and 401(k)s appear strongly persistent from year to year. If current contribution patterns persist, the accumulation of assets in these accounts will represent a very important component of wealth at retirement for those who reach retirement in the early twenty-first century. Unlike other traditional forms of retirement income provision, such as Social Security or defined-benefit pension plans, individuals make portfolio decisions about their investments in targeted accounts. This may introduce more heterogeneity into the distribution of wealth at retirement, as there may be greater variation in the returns that individuals earn on their retirement investments. On the other hand, contributions to personal retirement plans are likely to be much more equally distributed than other forms of personal financial asset saving.

References

Beller, Daniel J., and Helen H. Lawrence. 1992. Trends in private pension plan coverage. In *Trends in pensions 1992*, ed. John A. Turner and Daniel J. Beller. Washington, D.C.: U.S. Government Printing Office.

Bernheim, B. Douglas, and John B. Shoven. 1988. Pension funding and saving. In *Pensions in the U.S. economy*, ed. Z. Bodie, J. Shoven, and D. Wise. Chicago: University of Chicago Press.

Bosworth, Barry, Gary Burtless, and John Sabelhaus. 1991. The decline in saving: Evidence from household surveys. *Brookings Papers on Economic Activity*, no. 1: 183–241.

Feenberg, Daniel, and Jonathan Skinner. 1989. Sources of IRA saving. *Tax Policy and the Economy* 3:25–46.

Gale, William G., and John Karl Scholz. 1990. IRAs and household saving. University of Wisconsin. Mimeograph.

Hewitt Associates. 1991. 401(k) plan design and administration. Lincolnshire, Ill.: Hewitt Associates.

Joines, Douglas H., and James G. Manegold. 1991. IRAs and saving: Evidence from a panel of taxpayers. University of Southern California. Mimeograph.

Papke, Leslie, Mitchell Petersen, and James M. Poterba. 1996. Did 401(k) plans replace other employer-provided pensions? In *Advances in the economics of aging*, ed. D. Wise. Chicago: University of Chicago Press.

Poterba, James M., Steven F. Venti, and David Wise. 1994. 401(k) plans and tax-deferred saving. In *Studies in the economics of aging*, ed. D. Wise, 105–138. Chicago: University of Chicago Press.

————. 1993. Do 401(k) contributions crowd out other private saving? NBER Working Paper no. 4391. Cambridge, Mass.: National Bureau of Economic Research.

Summers, Lawrence, and Chris Carroll. 1987. Why is U.S. national saving so low? *Brookings Papers on Economic Activity,* no. 2: 607–35.

Turner, John A., and Daniel J. Beller, eds. 1992. *Trends in pensions 1992.* Washington, D.C.: U.S. Government Printing Office.

Venti, Steven F., and David A. Wise. 1986. Tax-deferred accounts, constrained choice and estimation of individual saving. *Review of Economic Studies* 53:579–601.

————. 1987. IRAs and saving. In *The effects of taxation on capital accumulation,* ed. M. Feldstein. Chicago: University of Chicago Press.

————. 1990. Have IRAs increased U.S. saving? Evidence from the Consumer Expenditure Surveys. *Quarterly Journal of Economics* 105:661–98.

————. 1991. The saving effect of tax-deferred retirement accounts: Evidence from SIPP. In *National saving and economic performance,* ed. B. Douglas Bernheim and John Shoven, 103–31. Chicago: University of Chicago Press.

————. 1992. Government policy and personal retirement saving. In *Tax policy and the economy,* ed. J. Poterba, vol. 6, 1–41. Cambridge: MIT Press.

10 The Economic Status of the Elderly in Japan: Microdata Findings

Noriyuki Takayama

10.1 Introduction

A rapid aging of the population has taken place in Japan. In 1994, 14.1 percent of the population was aged 65 or over. This proportion will increase by 0.5 percent every year for the next 25 years and will be more than 30 percent by around 2040. Previously, the peak proportion of the elderly was projected to be 25 percent and to occur around 2020, just after the first baby boom generation (born between 1947 and 1949, called the Dankai-No-Sedai) reaches age 65. That projection has been adjusted to account for a recent sharp decline in the fertility rate, and the peak is now expected to come around 2045 and be more than 30 percent.

The social cost of supporting the growing elderly population will increase by 0.5 percent of GDP every year. If the Japanese economy grows at more than 0.5 percent per year in real terms, the Japanese will be able to provide for their elderly without any real sacrifices. If they enjoy 1 percent real growth per year, active generations will probably be richer than their parents' generations. Economic growth will mitigate the financial problems associated with an aging population in the future.

This paper gives an overview of the current economic status of the elderly. By estimating personal savings rates, it also tries to predict the future economic status of the elderly.

Section 10.2 makes clear the economic status and savings behavior of the Japanese elderly in 1989. Section 10.3 analyzes the possible adverse effects of

Noriyuki Takayama is professor of economics at the Institute of Economic Research, Hitotsubashi University.

The author is grateful to Michael Hurd, Hilary Hoynes, and Charles Horioka for their valuable comments.

public pensions on personal savings and estimates the age effect on consumption expenditures. Section 10.4 presents concluding remarks.

The range of problems we examine in this paper is by no means comprehensive. A detailed study is required to predict more accurately the future economic status of the elderly in Japan.

10.2   Economic Status of the Elderly in 1989

It is well known that in Japan most of the elderly are now living with their children. About 57 percent of persons aged 65 or over were living with their children in 1992. That percentage, however, has decreased rapidly, and in the near future a minority of elderly persons will be living with their children. Note that 42 percent of the elderly living with their children were living as heads of households or spouses of heads[1] and that 67 percent of the total elderly population were living as heads or spouses of heads. The "head of household" is defined as the person who earns the principal income in the household.

This section examines the economic status of elderly couples and singles. The data came from the microdata of the 1989 National Survey of Family Income and Expenditure (NSFIE).

10.2.1   Public Pension Benefits and Annual Income: Elderly Couples

Today the proportion of the Japanese elderly blessed with high income and considerable assets is steadily growing. The elderly may even feel better off than the young in terms of living conditions (see fig. 10.1).

By elderly couples, we mean two-person households consisting of a husband and a wife, with the husband at least 60 years old and receiving public pension benefits. The 1989 NSFIE contains 4,743 observations of elderly couple households.

Table 10.1 summarizes main economic indicators for the elderly population. The mean annual public pension benefits received by elderly couples in 1989 were about 2.4 million yen (200,000 yen per month).[2] The median benefits were the same. Sixteen percent of the couples received annual benefits of less than 1.2 million yen, while 25 percent enjoyed annual benefits of 3 million yen or more. These findings imply that more than 80 percent of elderly couples were salaried workers or retired employees.

The mean annual income of elderly couples was about 4.3 million yen, and the median was nearly 3.4 million yen. One-sixth had an annual income of 6 million yen or more, while 20 percent (one-fifth) had an income of less than 2.4 million yen.

The 1989 NSFIE breaks household income into 10 categories and includes

---

1. See Takayama (1994, sec. 4.6, 104–107) for more details.
2. As of 23 September 1994, 10,000 yen = U.S.$102.4 = £65.6 = DM 158.1.

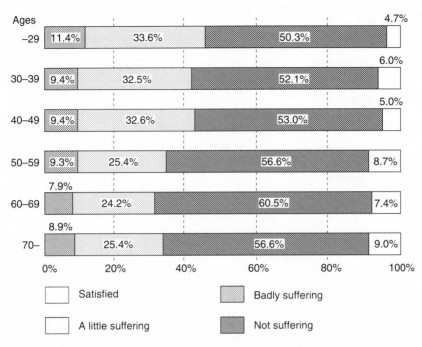

Fig. 10.1 Feelings of household heads about living conditions
Source: Ministry of Health and Welfare, *Basic Survey on Japanese Living Conditions* (Tokyo, 1991).

**Table 10.1   Main Economic Indicators for Elderly Couples and Singles, 1989
            (10,000 yen)**

Indicator	Elderly Couples		Elderly Singles	
	Mean	Median	Mean	Median
Annual public pension benefits	239	241	127	119
Annual income	430	338	189	160
Annual consumption expenditures	275	234	162	131
Monetary asset holdings in gross terms	1,956	1,135	898	542
Housing assets including residential land	6,488	2,728	4,201	2,384
Net worth	7,797	3,891	5,077	1,852

Source: 1989 NSFIE

income earned by individual household members. Income is classified as wages and salaries; income from agriculture, forestry, or fishing; business income; income from homework; social security pension benefits; remittances from relatives; income from rent; income from interest and dividends; other cash income; and income in kind. By investigating the NSFIE microdata, we

Table 10.2　　Distribution of Annual Income of Elderly Couples

Income Category and Receiver[a]		Annual Amount of Public Pension Benefits (10,000 yen)								
		−59	60–	120–	180–	240–	300–	360–	420+	Total
		Receiving Ratio (%)								
Wages and salaries	H	37.5	28.7	25.9	19.7	19.2	22.5	27.1	16.3	22.7
	W	21.8	13.8	13.8	10.9	8.1	4.5	3.3	4.1	9.6
Income from agriculture	H	20.5	22.2	14.8	6.9	4.6	5.2	1.6	2.6	8.8
	W	5.5	1.4	0.4	0.5	0.3	0.9	0.0	0.1	0.8
Business income	H	23.4	20.0	10.5	5.9	2.8	4.0	3.4	4.8	7.5
	W	4.7	3.5	2.0	0.4	0.9	1.2	0.0	0.8	1.4
Income from homework	H	2.8	4.3	3.6	2.6	2.7	4.3	3.4	1.7	3.2
	W	10.6	10.1	8.3	7.2	7.1	8.8	1.8	2.4	7.5
Public pensions	H	100.0	100.0	100.0	100.0	100.0	100.0	100.0	100.0	100.0
	W	15.9	54.7	50.1	42.4	39.2	54.5	65.4	85.1	47.7
Remittances	H	6.6	8.0	4.8	3.2	1.9	2.3	1.3	1.0	3.4
	W	1.0	1.4	0.5	0.9	0.4	0.4	1.8	0.7	0.7
Income from rent	H	14.2	14.4	13.6	9.4	9.2	11.4	13.6	9.1	11.1
	W	3.7	1.6	1.7	2.1	1.4	1.1	1.5	3.1	1.8
Interest and dividends	H	23.4	26.8	25.0	29.7	41.0	48.5	54.0	47.0	36.5
	W	1.6	3.7	5.1	6.5	7.8	11.7	19.7	27.1	8.7
Other cash income	H	10.5	13.1	12.3	10.0	9.8	11.3	16.9	8.7	11.1
	W	3.0	3.8	3.0	2.7	2.7	3.1	4.8	2.9	3.0
Income in kind	H	19.5	31.5	22.6	21.0	18.7	22.0	12.9	20.5	21.3
		Average Income (receivers only, 10,000 yen)								
Wages and salaries	H	345	401	309	292	313	342	292	405	330
	W	133	177	138	199	198	176	152	160	175
Income from agriculture	H	109	126	79	62	67	41	55	55	88
	W	29	64	28	28	31	17	–	100	35
Business income	H	343	358	471	229	201	292	131	239	323
	W	138	125	92	74	131	89	–	175	117
Income from homework	H	66	49	61	47	43	64	10	54	50
	W	40	45	41	46	47	33	53	42	43
Public pensions	H	35	65	125	190	248	284	316	369	206
	W	23	38	50	49	48	71	104	199	69
Remittances	H	68	44	30	52	31	59	46	158	47
	W	96	51	14	40	40	38	98	57	52
Income from rent	H	184	133	168	154	190	155	142	81	159
	W	102	37	326	190	152	96	19	80	153
Interest and dividends	H	34	50	46	46	44	92	49	53	55
	W	34	27	32	30	28	34	33	33	31
Other cash income	H	51	81	92	94	78	71	117	57	83
	W	237	50	50	49	119	54	31	25	73
Income in kind	H	13	16	17	23	24	16	14	17	19
		Average Distribution (% in column)								
Wages and salaries	H	34.7	29.3	21.2	15.8	14.6	15.1	14.3	9.7	17.4
	W	7.8	6.2	5.1	5.9	3.9	1.6	0.9	1.0	3.9
Income from agriculture	H	6.0	7.1	3.1	1.2	0.8	0.4	0.2	0.2	1.8
	W	0.4	0.2	0.0	0.0	0.0	0.0	–	0.0	0.1

(continued)

Table 10.2 (continued)

Income Category and Receiver[a]		Annual Amount of Public Pension Benefits (10,000 yen)								
		−59	60−	120−	180−	240−	300−	360−	420+	Total
Business income	H	21.6	18.2	13.1	3.7	1.4	2.3	0.8	1.7	5.7
	W	1.8	1.1	0.5	0.1	0.3	0.2	−	0.2	0.4
Income from homework	H	0.5	0.5	0.6	0.3	0.3	0.5	0.1	0.1	0.4
	W	1.1	1.2	0.9	0.9	0.8	0.6	0.2	0.2	0.8
Public pensions	H	9.4	16.6	33.2	52.2	60.0	55.7	57.0	54.1	48.0
	W	1.0	5.3	6.7	5.7	4.5	7.6	12.2	24.9	7.6
Remittances	H	1.2	0.9	0.4	0.5	0.1	0.3	0.1	0.2	0.4
	W	0.3	0.2	0.0	0.1	0.0	0.0	0.3	0.1	0.1
Income from rent	H	7.0	4.9	6.0	4.0	4.2	3.5	3.5	1.1	4.1
	W	1.0	0.2	1.4	1.1	0.5	0.2	0.5	0.4	0.6
Interests and dividends	H	2.1	3.4	3.1	3.7	4.4	8.7	4.8	3.6	4.6
	W	0.1	0.3	0.4	0.5	0.5	0.8	1.2	1.3	0.6
Other cash income	H	1.4	2.7	3.0	2.6	1.9	1.6	3.6	0.7	2.1
	W	1.9	0.5	0.4	0.4	0.8	0.3	0.3	0.1	0.5
Income in kind	H	0.7	1.3	1.0	1.3	1.1	0.7	0.3	0.5	1.0
		Average Annual Income (10,000 yen)								
Total		372	394	377	363	413	510	555	682	430

Source: 1989 NSFIE.
[a]Receiver: H (husband) and W (wife).

can find out, for example, which member of each household had labor income and how much it was.

Table 10.2 and figure 10.2 present the distribution of the annual income of elderly couples. They show that public pension benefits were the major source of income for the elderly, accounting for more than 50 percent of total income. Furthermore, as pension benefits increased, they made up a greater proportion of income. For example, when the amount of benefits was 4.2 million yen or more, benefits accounted for 79 percent of income; when benefits were between 0.6 and 1.2 million yen, they accounted for only 22 percent of income.

For 23 percent of elderly couples, public pension benefits were their only source of income. For 71 percent of couples, public pension benefits accounted for 50 percent or more of their total income.[3]

The proportion of public pension benefits as related to total income varied with the employment status of the household head and with age. Overall, couples whose public pension benefits accounted for a large part of their total income received a large amount of pension benefits (for more details, see Takayama and Kitamura 1994).

3. For nearly three-quarters of nonworking elderly couples public pension benefits accounted for more than 80 percent of their income, and about 40 percent of them had no income other than public pension benefits.

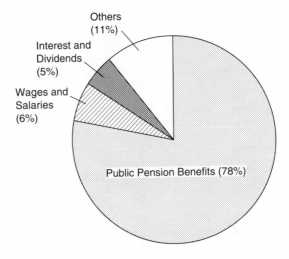

Fig. 10.2   Distribution of income for elderly couples with annual income between 3.0 and 3.6 million yen
Source: 1989 NSFIE.

In 1989, about 23 percent of husbands earned wages and salaries. The annual mean was 3.3 million yen in 1989, as shown in table 10.2. Elderly couples with public pension benefits of less than 1.2 million yen were likely to have income from either business or agriculture. One out of nine husbands had income from rent, and the annual mean was 1.6 million yen.[4] Only 3 percent of husbands received remittances from relatives, with annual mean remittances of 470,000 yen.

10.2.2   Consumption Expenditures and Savings: Elderly Couples

The mean annual consumption expenditure (in cash) of elderly couples was 2.75 million yen (see table 10.1).[5] The modal value was between 1.8 and 2.4 million yen, and the median was about 2.34 million yen. The consumption expenditure of 10 percent of elderly couples was less than 1.2 million yen, while that of 20 percent of the couples was 3.6 million yen or more.

From the 1989 NSFIE, we know that the mean annual consumption expenditure of younger four-person households (defined as a couple with two children, with household head aged 30–49) was 3.56 million yen, and the median was

4. Almost all elderly couples held financial assets, but more than 60 percent of them did not report interest and dividends. The interest and dividends given in table 10.2 and figure 10.2 therefore reflect underreporting.
5. The sample of elderly couples included actively working households (41 percent in 1989). There needs to be a control for retirement; the life-cycle hypothesis allows continuing asset accumulation during one's work life.

3.24 million yen. Forty percent of these households spent less than 3 million yen on consumption. Adjusted for household size and composition, the consumption expenditure of the elderly was about the same as that of the younger generation. This implies that elderly couples were as well-off as their children in terms of consumption expenditure.

Table 10.3 presents annual consumption expenditure of elderly couples classified by annual income. It indicates that the majority of elderly couples (especially those with an annual income of 1.8 million yen or more) lived within their incomes; only a small proportion (21 percent) dissaved. Those with less annual income were proportionately more likely to dissave. Elderly couples in present-day Japan generally persist in earning some part of their incomes, and they are careful consumers. Consequently, a majority of them continue to save.

The elderly probably dissave considerably if they receive terminal care services, although these dissavings have not been statistically verified. Only monetary assets would likely be dissaved; housing assets would probably not be disposed of until after death.

In 1989, the cost of housing for elderly couples in Japan was quite high. Although their housing costs in cash were rather small (162,000 yen annually on average) since their homeownership rate was very high (90 percent), their mean annual imputed rent was estimated to be about 1.50 million yen, a little more than 50 percent of their total consumption expenditure in cash.[6]

Japan has a generous system of social security health care. The elderly in Japan enjoy health care services with very low user charges (copayments). In 1989, the annual mean of in-kind social security health care services per person was 330,000 yen (ages 65–69) and 530,000 yen (ages 70 and up). If we add imputed rent and in-kind social security health care services to annual consumption expenditure in cash, the consumption level of the elderly looks very different from the level in cash only.

10.2.3   Monetary and Housing Asset Holdings: Elderly Couples

The mean gross monetary asset holdings of elderly couples in 1989 was nearly 20 million yen (see table 10.1). This figure corresponded roughly to the 70th percentile. The median was a little over 11 million yen, while the mode was in the range of 3.0–4.0 million yen. Clearly, monetary asset holdings differed widely among the elderly.

As for the distribution of gross monetary assets by different categories, elderly couples' portfolios varied with differing amounts of monetary asset holdings. It may be interesting to point out that the elderly hold a considerable amount of demand deposits, amounting to two or three months' worth of consumption expenditure even in the lower asset classes. According to the 1989

---

6. The median annual imputed rent of elderly couples was estimated to be nearly 1.2 million yen in 1989. Compare this amount with the median annual income of active working generations, 5.5 million yen.

Table 10.3   Annual Consumption Expenditures of Elderly Couples by Annual Income

	Annual Income (million yen)										
	−1.19	1.2–	1.8–	2.4–	3.0–	3.6–	4.8–	6.0–	9.0–	12.0+	Total
Household distribution (% in row)	2.8	5.6	11.7	19.3	15.2	18.8	10.6	9.9	3.0	3.0	100.0
Average age	72.0	71.0	70.1	67.9	67.5	67.0	66.6	66.7	66.1	68.3	67.9
Average annual income (million yen)	0.9	1.5	2.1	2.7	3.3	4.1	5.3	7.1	10.3	18.9	4.3
Average annual pension benefits (10,000 yen)	70	120	175	226	255	261	302	301	273	274	239
Average annual pension benefits, husband (10,000 yen)	48	96	150	205	226	226	248	247	254	240	206
Average monetary assets (million yen)	5.3	6.2	6.8	11.2	16.1	19.8	24.1	29.0	35.6	112.1	19.6
Average equity in own home (million yen)	26	33	28	36	43	47	88	116	101	217	58.9
Average annual consumption expenditure (10,000 yen)	163	156	174	218	251	281	350	367	437	486	275
Dissaving households (%)	73.9	40.8	29.0	25.8	19.6	14.3	14.6	6.2	1.6	0.0	21.2

Source: 1989 NSFIE.

NSFIE, only 8.1 percent of elderly couples had annuity-type monetary assets (other than social security).

The homeownership rate of elderly couples was about 90 percent. The mode of housing asset holdings (including residential land) was between 10 and 15 million yen. The median and mean were about 27 and 65 million yen, respectively (see table 10.1). The mean corresponded roughly to the 75th percentile. The amount of landholdings increased sharply between 1985 and 1989, especially in the three major metropolitan areas. In 1989, mean housing assets for elderly persons living in Tokyo were 240 million yen, and median assets were 160 million yen. A young person will never be able to buy a home in the suburbs of Tokyo if he or she is solely dependent on his or her own earnings.

Income and wealth distributions do not necessarily overlap. There are wide gaps in asset holdings even among households belonging to the same income group (see Takayama 1992a, 79, table 3.3). Flow and stock do not necessarily run parallel. Income and wealth are different, and an argument based on only one of the two would be incomplete.

Table 10.4 presents the distribution of net worth for elderly couples. By net worth, we mean net monetary assets plus home equity plus golf club membership certificates. Mean net worth was 78 million yen in 1989. The median was 39 million yen, and the mode was 21.0–21.9 million yen. Note that the mean corresponded to the 74th percentile.

From table 10.4, we can verify that the homeownership rate of households with a net worth of 10 million yen or more was around 90 percent. For the group with less than 10 million yen in assets, the homeownership rate was only 40 percent. Apparently, home equity was the most important component of household assets; in 1989 it amounted to 76 percent of net worth on average.[7] We can see that the larger the net worth, the higher the proportion of home equity in net worth.

Twenty-three percent of elderly couples still had liabilities. All elderly couples whose net worth was negative had liabilities. Some of them received housing rents, implying that they had rental housing assets with big liabilities. These liabilities might be strategically held to lessen payments of inheritance tax by their children.

10.2.4   Income, Consumption, and Asset Holdings: Elderly Singles

Table 10.1 also presents main economic indicators for elderly singles in 1989. By elderly singles, we mean one-person households in which the person is aged 60 or over and receives public pension benefits. The 1989 NSFIE contains 1,107 observations of elderly single households. Eighty-six percent of them were female. Their homeownership rate was 66 percent, much lower than the figure for elderly couples.

---

7. It is interesting that couples in their early sixties had a mean gross social security (pension) wealth of around 57 million yen in 1989.

Table 10.4   Distribution of Net Worth of Elderly Couples

| | Net Worth (million yen) | | | | | | | | |
	-0	0-	10-	20-	30-	50-	100-	200+	Total
Household distribution (% in row)	0.2	9.2	13.0	13.5	18.7	22.9	13.4	9.0	100.0
Ownership rate of own home (%)	30.7	40.2	85.2	95.1	98.1	98.8	99.0	99.6	89.4
Percentage receiving rents	24.6	2.0	4.4	6.0	8.3	13.1	23.6	43.9	12.2
Average annual income (10,000 yen)	867	299	357	388	413	483	598	930	481
Average public pension benefits (10,000 yen)	168	158	198	220	238	260	263	257	233
Average monthly consumption expenditure (10,000 yen)	21.6	14.8	17.6	20.1	2.2	24.6	27.2	33.8	22.4
Average net worth (million yen)	-29	5	15	25	39	71	138	433	78.0
Holding Ratio (%)									
Monetary assets (gross)	100.0	100.0	100.0	100.0	100.0	100.0	100.0	100.0	100.0
Liabilities	100.0	21.7	25.3	27.3	19.4	21.3	23.3	23.8	23.0
Golf club membership certificates	–	1.1	3.1	4.8	5.1	9.2	16.3	30.5	8.4
Home equity	30.7	43.0	87.6	96.8	99.3	99.4	99.9	100.0	90.8
Average Amounts (holders only, million of yen)									
Monetary assets (gross)	8.8	3.6	6.8	10.0	14.4	22.9	31.3	71.3	19.6
Liabilities	74.9	1.7	2.3	2.1	2.7	2.4	7.6	31.4	5.8
Monetary assets (net)	-67.9	3.2	6.2	9.4	13.9	22.4	29.5	63.9	18.2
Golf club membership certificates	–	0.4	1.6	0.8	2.0	3.3	11.4	23.4	10.2
Home equity	122	5	10	16	25	48	107	362	64.9
Average Distribution (% in column)									
Monetary assets (gross)	-30.9	68.3	45.3	39.9	36.8	32.4	22.6	16.5	25.4
Liabilities	262.5	-7.0	-3.9	-2.3	-1.3	-0.7	-1.3	-1.7	-1.7
Monetary assets (net)	231.5	61.4	41.4	37.6	35.4	31.7	21.4	14.7	23.4
Golf club membership certificates	0.0	0.1	0.3	0.2	0.3	0.4	1.3	1.7	1.1
Home equity	-131.5	38.5	58.3	62.3	64.3	67.9	77.3	83.6	75.5

Source: 1989 NSFIE.

Table 10.5   **Annual Consumption Expenditure of Elderly Singles by Annual Income**

	Annual Income (10,000 yen)							
	−59	60–	120–	180–	240–	300–	360+	Total
Household distribution (% in row)	6.7	20.0	29.9	18.9	10.9	7.0	6.6	100.0
Average age	74.5	69.9	69.6	69.7	68.0	67.7	68.5	69.6
Average annual income (10,000 yen)	41	95	146	201	268	320	521	189
Average annual pension benefits (10,000 yen)	34	77	118	143	171	227	183	127
Average monetary assets (10,000 yen)	363	440	735	984	1045	1423	2516	898
Average equity in own home (million yen)	14.7	15.4	52.6	32.4	53.8	32.2	119.9	42.0
Average annual consumption expenditure (10,000 yen)	79	106	149	178	176	203	275	162
Dissaving households (%)	87.1	48.8	39.1	11.4	14.8	6.3	10.5	40.4

Source: 1989 NSFIE.

The mean annual public pension benefit for elderly singles was 1.27 million yen, and the median and the mode were more or less the same. Nineteen percent of singles received annual benefits of less than 600,000 yen, while 20 percent enjoyed annual benefits of 1.8 million yen or more.

The mean annual income for elderly singles was about 1.9 million yen. While 29 percent had an annual income of 2.4 million yen or more, 27 percent had an income of less than 1.2 million yen. The only source of income for 36 percent of elderly singles was public pension benefits.

Table 10.5 shows annual consumption expenditure of elderly singles classified by annual income. The mean was 1.62 million yen per year, the median 1.31 million yen, and the mode 1.20–1.31 million yen. The majority of singles (60 percent) lived within their incomes, but many in the lower income classes were likely to dissave.

The mean monetary asset holdings of elderly singles was about 9.0 million yen, but the median was much lower, about 5.4 million yen. One-third had assets worth less than 3 million yen, while 29 percent had assets worth 10 million yen or more (10 percent had assets of 20 million yen or more). The mean home equity of elderly singles amounted to 42 million yen, with a median of 24 million yen.

Overall, the economic conditions of elderly couples and singles per person were about the same. Home equity, on a household basis, was also not so different.

10.3   Some Evidence on Personal Savings

Using a simulation model, Horioka (1991, 1992) showed that the savings rate in Japan will decline sharply and become negative as the rapid aging of the population proceeds in the next 50 years. Asoh and Tamura (1993) predicted more or less the same result. Their simulations have given a new dimension to discussions about personal savings in Japan.

As Yashiro and Oishi (chap. 3 in this volume) convincingly argue, labor-augmenting technological progress will occur during the population aging process, preventing the declining savings rate from turning negative. Horioka (1991) and Asoh and Tamura (1993) ignored such progress.

Horioka (1991) assumed that the elderly will dissave, but this has not been verified by statistics available in Japan. Rather, as tables 10.3 and 10.5 indicate, elderly people seem to continue saving long after their retirement.

Social security wealth has an effect on savings. The age structure of consumption should also be studied before estimating the savings rate in the population aging process. We examine these two problems in this section.

10.3.1   Impact of Public Pensions on Consumption and Savings

The question of whether the public pension system discourages personal savings is important to Japanese policymakers who are concerned about possible adverse effects on capital formation and, therefore, on future economic growth.

A simple life-cycle model is assumed. Consumption expenditure (C) is assumed to depend on asset holdings. More specifically, the consumption function estimated here is as follows:

$$\frac{C}{YD} = \frac{a_0}{YD} + a_1 * \frac{HW}{YD} + a_2 * \frac{FA}{YD} + a_3 * \frac{RA}{YD}$$
$$+ a_4 * \frac{GSSW}{YD} + a_5 * \frac{RET}{YD} + a'Z + \mu,$$

where HW is the present value of current and future salaries, FA is the value of financial assets, RA is the value of real (nonfinancial, tangible) assets, GSSW is the present value of public pension wealth, and RET is the present value of lump-sum retirement benefits. Z is a vector that includes other variables such as age dummies and the number of household members. YD is current disposable income, and μ is an unobserved error term. We shall examine effects of the gross value of social security wealth (GSSW) using the 1979 and 1984 NSFIE.

Table 10.6 presents the estimated consumption function for workers' households. In 1984, the parameter estimates of $GSSW_i$ were all in the range of 1.2–1.8 percent for those under age 55. Overall, the presence of social security wealth is estimated to increase the 1984 consumption expenditure of workers'

Table 10.6   **Estimates of the Consumption Function for Workers' Households**

Variable	1984		1979	
1/YD	84.0	(37.3)	71.6	(35.3)
HW1/YD	−0.0002	(−0.12)	−0.0020	(−1.50)
HW2/YD	0.0012	(1.36)	0.0022	(3.91)
HW3/YD	0.0029	(4.27)	0.0016	(2.84)
HW4/YD	0.0012	(1.74)	0.0036	(6.57)
HW5/YD	0.0011	(1.45)	0.0023	(4.01)
HW6/YD	0.0008	(0.97)	0.0018	(3.12)
HW7/YD	0.0041	(4.80)	0.0018	(3.23)
HW8/YD	0.0099	(12.3)	0.0082	(11.1)
GSSW1/YD	0.0149	(3.07)	0.0077	(2.64)
GSSW2/YD	0.0134	(6.00)	0.0100	(8.20)
GSSW3/YD	0.0182	(11.2)	0.0104	(10.4)
GSSW4/YD	0.0158	(10.6)	0.0089	(9.25)
GSSW5/YD	0.0147	(9.38)	0.0091	(9.11)
GSSW6/YD	0.0122	(7.66)	0.0071	(6.82)
GSSW7/YD	0.0061	(3.75)	0.0085	(7.08)
GSSW8/YD	0.0263	(19.8)	0.0310	(30.6)
RET1/YD	−0.0108	(−1.81)	0.0076	(1.33)
RET2/YD	−0.0010	(−0.37)	−0.0081	(−3.47)
RET3/YD	−0.0044	(−2.28)	−0.0024	(−1.25)
RET4/YD	0.0039	(2.00)	0.0008	(0.39)
RET5/YD	0.0050	(2.21)	0.0054	(2.30)
RET6/YD	0.0101	(3.68)	0.0102	(3.77)
RET7/YD	0.0289	(8.90)	0.0196	(5.75)
RET8/YD	0.0606	(17.1)	–	
FA/YD	0.0134	(10.3)	0.0022	(1.40)
RA1/YD	0.0086	(22.2)	0.0140	(25.0)
N	0.0292	(24.5)	0.0298	(22.2)
D-AGE1	0.3137	(5.46)	0.4008	(7.29)
D-AGE2	0.2650	(9.02)	0.2264	(9.32)
D-AGE3	0.1646	(8.43)	0.2312	(11.5)
D-AGE4	0.2332	(13.5)	0.2058	(10.9)
D-AGE5	0.2688	(15.9)	0.2586	(14.0)
D-AGE6	0.3393	(22.4)	0.3373	(19.8)
D-AGE7	0.3187	(21.7)	0.3137	(20.0)
Observations	29,078		30,501	
R^2	0.9238		0.9109	

Consumption Function: $\dfrac{C}{YD} = \dfrac{\alpha_0}{YD} + \Sigma\beta * \dfrac{W_i}{YD} + \gamma * N + \Sigma\delta_j * D\text{-}AGE_j + \mu.$

Variables:

C/YD	Dependent variable
HW	Present value of future lifetime wages minus present value of future lifetime contributions for public pensions
C	Annual consumption expenditure
YD	Disposable income
GSSW	Present value of public pension benefits

(continued)

Table 10.6   (continued)

NSSW	GSSW − PPT − FPT
PPT	Present value of past contributions for public pensions
FPT	Present value of future contributions for public pensions
RET	Present value of lump-sum retirement benefits
FA	Net financial assets
RA1	Net real assets (homeowners only)
N	Number of household members
D-AGE1	Age dummy (less than 25)
D-AGE2	Age dummy (25–29)
D-AGE3	Age dummy (30–34)
D-AGE4	Age dummy (35–39)
D-AGE5	Age dummy (40–44)
D-AGE6	Age dummy (45–49)
D-AGE7	Age dummy (50–54)
	Standard = age 55–59

Numbers following the human capital variables indicate the dummy variable for age class with which variable is interacted.

households by about 1.5 percent of GSSW. This increase in consumption expenditure is equivalent to 12 percent of disposable income in 1984, or 13.9 percent in 1979. The evidence confirms the hypothesis that social security wealth discourages personal savings in Japan.

Remember, however, that the current public pension system will probably be reformed in the future. Benefits and contributions will be more closely balanced. The social security wealth of each individual will also be reduced by raising the normal retirement age or decreasing real levels of monthly benefits.[8] These reforms should *encourage* personal savings.[9]

8. It is a growing concern of the Japanese people to change the benefits level to relate to the net, rather than gross, income of economically active generations. With this method, take-home pay will be expected to grow, keeping the same pace across different generations. See Takayama (1992b, 1995).

9. Effects of occupational pensions or lump-sum retirement benefits in Japan should also be analyzed. The average lump-sum retirement benefit paid to mandated career male retirees was 20–24 million yen in large firms and 10–13 million yen in smaller firms in 1989. Employers have occupational pension plans, not to pay annuities, but mainly to accumulate funds under favorable tax treatment. In fact, almost all retiring employees choose to take their retirement benefits in a lump sum, even though their employers have a formal pension plan whose basic form is an annuity. Currently, the coverage of occupational retirement benefits is about 90 percent in Japan, although the coverage of occupational pension plans is about 50 percent. The appendix contains a sketch of major schemes that employers can use to prepare for paying retirement benefits.

In April 1991, a special type of individual retirement pension account, called the Kokumin-Nenkin-Kikin, became available for nonemployees and their spouses (ages 20–59). Contributions of up to 68,000 yen per month per person are now tax-exempt, which is very generous compared with 50,000 yen per year (for all) for individual "pension" insurance policy premiums.

10.3.2   Impact of Age on Consumption and Savings

Are there any differences in consumption expenditure depending on differences in the ages of household heads? Using data from the 1984 NSFIE, we can estimate an age effect on consumption, controlling for main factors other than age.[10]

A Keynesian consumption model is used. Consumption expenditure (C) is assumed to basically depend on disposable income (YD). The marginal propensity to consume is assumed not to be constant. More specifically,

$$C = \alpha + \Sigma_i \beta_i * \text{YD-Class}_i + \Sigma_i \gamma_i * \text{YD} * \text{YD-Class}_i + \Sigma_i \Sigma_j \delta_{ij} * Z_j^i + \mu,$$

where Z is a vector of household attributes (including age of household head) and μ is an unobserved error term. After carefully examining statistically significant variables, we came up with the consumption model in table 10.7.

The model indicates that consumption expenditure increases with the age of the household head, reaching a peak at ages 45–54. People in their twenties consume at a relatively high level, whereas people in their sixties or older consume at a low level.[11] The elderly, especially those aged 60–69, are still careful in consuming. They may be preparing for their futures, which will probably be much longer than they expected in their active days.

Population aging in Japan will continue as members of the Dankai-No-Sedai now in their mid-forties get older. Other things being constant, the household savings rate in Japan might decline for the next 10 years, but it will return to a higher level after the Dankai-No-Sedai reach age 55. The task of simulating the age effect, considering other changes, such as a fall in the disposable income of the Dankai-No-Sedai after retirement, remains.

10.4   Concluding Remarks

The future economic status of the elderly in Japan will not be as gloomy as previously thought. Many factors will offset the decreasing savings rate: labor-augmenting technological progress, reforms in social security pensions, and the careful consumption behavior of the elderly. In addition, growing anxieties about who will provide health care services for the elderly will no doubt encourage pensioners to save more even after retirement.

Conversely, slower growth of the Japanese economy will probably lower the savings rate. The consumption habit persistence hypothesis states that consumption lagged behind the rapid increase in income, but the savings rate will rarely become negative.

10. Consumption expenditure and disposable income in section 10.3.2 are given on an SNA basis.

11. Takayama et al. (1990) examined cohort effects, if any, on consumption by comparing the 1979 and 1984 NSFIEs; they concluded that few cohort effects were verified between the two periods. Takayama and Arita (1992a, 1992b) studied the economic status of the elderly in Japan, using the microdata from the 1984 NSFIE.

Table 10.7   **Estimates of the Consumption Function**

Parameter	Variable	Estimate	(t-value)
α	Constant (10,000 yen)	-102.4	(-2.7)
	Disposable Income Dummies[a]		
β	(YD-CLASS1: 1.0–2.0)	-227.2	(-7.5)
	(YD-CLASS2: 2.0–3.0)	-243.6	(-8.2)
	(YD-CLASS3: 3.0–4.0)	-237.5	(-8.0)
	(YD-CLASS4: 4.0–5.0)	-229.6	(-7.7)
	(YD-CLASS5: 5.0–6.0)	-181.6	(-5.9)
	(YD-CLASS6: 6.0–8.0)	-158.7	(-5.2)
	(YD-CLASS7: 8.0–10.0)	-115.1	(-3.3)
	(YD-CLASS8: 10.0+)	Standard	
	Disposable Income		
γ	YD (YD-CLASS1)	0.6000	(16.4)
	YD (YD-CLASS2)	0.6240	(29.3)
	YD (YD-CLASS3)	0.5752	(36.3)
	YD (YD-CLASS4)	0.5358	(34.6)
	YD (YD-CLASS5)	0.4577	(27.5)
	YD (YD-CLASS6)	0.4315	(33.7)
	YD (YD-CLASS7)	0.3883	(20.0)
	YD (YD-CLASS8)	0.2692	(11.7)
	Age Dummies		
δ_1	D-AGE1 (Less than 25)	63.9	(6.8)
	D-AGE2 (25–29)	55.0	(8.0)
	D-AGE3 (30–34)	38.3	(5.8)
	D-AGE4 (35–39)	36.8	(5.7)
	D-AGE5 (40–44)	47.4	(7.3)
	D-AGE6 (45–49)	69.3	(10.7)
	D-AGE7 (50–54)	70.0	(10.9)
	D-AGE8 (55–59)	47.8	(7.5)
	D-AGE9 (60–64)	23.6	(3.7)
	D-AGE9 (65–69)	5.7	(0.9)
	D-AGE11 (70–74)	2.10	(3.0)
	D-AGE12 (75+)	Standard	
	Occupation Dummies[b]		
δ_2	D-OC1 (Nonoffice workers)	-32.8	(-9.3)
	D-OC2 (Temporary and day workers)	-45.4	(-4.1)
	D-OC31 (Office workers 1 in private sector)	19.4	(-4.5)
	D-OC32 (Office workers 2)	-10.4	(-2.7)
	D-OC33 (Office workers 3)	-4.7	(-0.8)
	D-OC34 (Office workers 4)	10.0	(2.5)
	D-OC35 (Office workers 5)	10.9	(0.8)
	D-OC4 (Civil servants)	1.1	(0.3)
	D-OC5 (Merchants/craftsmen)	-24.8	(-7.2)
	D-OC6 (Business operators)	-4.8	(-0.9)
	D-OC7 (Corporate managers)	67.6	(12.7)
	D-OC8 (Independent workers)	13.3	(2.5)
	D-OC9 (Other professionals)	-41.5	(-6.0)
	D-OC10 (Jobless)	Standard	

(continued)

Table 10.7   (continued)

Parameter	Variable	Estimate	(*t*-value)
	Family Composition Dummies		
δ_3	D-FAM1 (Couples only)	18.1	(4.4)
	D-FAM2 (Couples + 1 child)	23.1	(6.5)
	D-FAM3 (Couples + 2 children)	28.8	(8.8)
	D-FAM4 (Couples + 3 or more children)	29.5	(7.8)
	D-FAM5 (One parent + children)	11.2	(2.1)
	D-FAM6 (Couples + parents)	17.4	(3.2)
	D-FAM7 (Couples + parents + children)	19.0	(5.2)
	D-FAM8 (Others)	Standard	
	Dummies for Home Acquisition Planning[c]		
δ_4	D-HPLAN1 (HO:WB in less than 3 years)	−22.1	(−5.3)
	D-HPLAN2 (HO:WB in 3–5 years)	−28.7	(−6.0)
	D-HPLAN3 (HO:WB in more than 5 years)	−14.0	(−4.3)
	D-HPLAN4 (HR:Without any plans)	−25.6	(−13.1)
	D-HPLAN5 (HR:WL in 3–5 years)	−51.1	(−2.0)
	D-HPLAN6 (HR:WB in 3–5 years)	−10.9	(−1.6)
	D-HPLAN7 (HR:WLB in 3–5 years)	−33.1	(−5.6)
	D-HPLAN8 (HR:WL in 3–5 years)	−44.6	(−1.8)
	D-HPLAN9 (HR:WB in 3–5 years)	−16.3	(−2.0)
	D-HPLAN10 (HR:WLB in 3–5 years)	−34.0	(−5.1)
	D-HPLAN11 (HR:WL in more than 5 years)	−19.1	(−1.1)
	D-HPLAN12 (HR:WB in more than 5 years)	−24.2	(−4.4)
	D-HPLAN13 (HR:WLB in more than 5 years)	−22.4	(−5.1)
	D-HPLAN14 (HR:Without any plans)	Standard	
δ_5	Real assets (homeowners)	0.01029	(33.2)
δ_6	Bonus (annual amount)	−0.1335	(−24.2)
δ_7	Number of household members	15.1	(14.0)
δ_8	Cost of living index by district	418.7	(17.3)
	Observations	42,009	
	R^2	0.5352	

Notes: The figures are for 1984 and for multimember households (excluding those households whose disposable income is less than 1.0 million yen and agricultural households).

$$C = \alpha + \Sigma_i \beta_i * \text{YD-Class}_i + \Sigma_i \gamma_i * \text{YD} * \text{YD-Class}_i + \Sigma_i \Sigma_j \delta_{ij} * Z_j^i + \mu.$$

[a]Amounts given in million yen.

[b]Office workers: 1 (less than 30 employees), 2 (30–499 empoyees), 3 (500–999 employees), 4 (1,000 employees or more), or 5 (not identified).

[c]HO (homeowner households) and HR (home-renter households). WB (with a plan to acquire a home building), WL (with a plan to acquire residential land), or WLB (with a plan to acquire residential land with a home building).

Appendix
Major Schemes for Financing Occupational Retirement Benefits in Japan

There are three major schemes that employers can use to prepare for paying retirement benefits. One is a pay-as-you-go plan with book reserve accounting (started in 1952, similar to the practice in West Germany). Book reserves are tax-deductible within certain limits: namely, 40 percent of the benefit liability can be deducted from income tax calculations as a corporate expense. Originally, a deduction was permitted on 100 percent of the liability.

Another scheme is a tax-qualified plan (started in 1962). The plan must be funded outside, through a group annuity contract or a trust agreement. The employer's contributions to a tax-qualified plan are 100 percent tax-deductible as business expenses. A special 1.173 percent corporate tax is levied annually on fund assets. The plan must contain a provision for annuity payments, although a lump-sum option is permitted.

The third scheme is a contracted-out plan (started in 1966) through the Kosei-Nenkin-Kikin (KNK; Employee's Pension Fund). The benefits of the KNK have two components: the equivalent benefit of the earnings-related portion of social security (excluding the benefit resulting from indexing) and the supplementary benefit. The latter is financed primarily by the employer. It can be received in a lump sum at the discretion of the employee, although in principle it should be in the form of an annuity. The plan must be funded through a trust fund or an insurance contract. The tax treatment of a contracted-out plan is substantially the same as that of a tax-qualified plan, except that the KNK does not pay taxes on accrued benefit liabilities equal to 2.7 times the equivalent benefit.

Book reserves are not funded outside but are actually retained as profits inside, contributing to further investment in the firm. The funded reserve of tax-qualified plans and contracted-out plans has been growing rapidly. It has contributed to an increase in national savings in Japan.

References

Asoh, Y., and H. Tamura. 1993. Estimating the future saving rate in Japan (in Japanese). Discussion Paper no. 1993–18. Tokyo: Institute for Posts and Telecommunications Policy.

Horioka, C. Y. 1991. The determinants of Japan's saving rate: The impact of the age structure of the population and other factors. *Economic Studies Quarterly* 42 (3): 237–53.

———. 1992. Future trends in Japan's saving rate and the implications thereof for Japan's external imbalance. *Japan and the World Economy* 3 (4): 307–30.

Takayama, N. 1992a. *The greying of Japan: An economic perspective on public pensions.* Tokyo: Kinokuniya; New York: Oxford University Press.

————. 1992b. *Nenkin Kaikaku No Koso* (Reforming public pensions in Japan). Tokyo: Nihon-Keizai-Shimbun-Sha.

————. 1994. Household asset- and wealthholdings in Japan. In *Aging in the United States and Japan,* ed. Y. Noguchi and D. Wise, 85–108. Chicago: University of Chicago Press.

————. 1995. The 1994 reform bill for public pensions in Japan: Its main contents and related discussion. *International Social Security Review* 48 (1): 45–65.

Takayama, N., and F. Arita. 1992a. Income, consumption and wealth of elderly couples in Japan (in Japanese). *Keizai Kenkyu* 43 (2): 158–78.

————. 1992b. Income, consumption and wealth of elderly singles in Japan (in Japanese). *Hitotsubashi Review* 107 (6): 780–98.

Takayama, N., F. Funaoka, F. Ohtake, M. Sekiguchi, T. Shibuya, H. Ueno, and K. Kubo. 1990. Household assetholdings including social security wealth in Japan. *Keizai Bunseki,* no. 118: 1–73.

Takayama, N., and Kitamura, Y. 1994. Household saving behavior in Japan. In *International comparisons of household saving,* ed. J. M. Poterba, 125–67. Chicago: University of Chicago Press.

11 Retirement Incentives: The Interaction between Employer-Provided Pensions, Social Security, and Retiree Health Benefits

Robin L. Lumsdaine, James H. Stock, and David A. Wise

The retirement effects of U.S. Social Security provisions have been the subject of study for some time. The scheduled phased increase in the Social Security normal retirement age motivates continued interest in the effects of the provisions. In considering changes in Social Security provisions and in contemplating the effects of the changes, attention has been directed primarily to the Social Security provisions themselves. The potential interaction between the effects of Social Security and the effects of employer-provided pension plan provisions has been largely ignored. Yet about half of American workers are covered by employer pension plans, and about two-thirds of these are covered by defined-benefit plans. These plans typically have very substantial retirement incentives and in a large proportion of cases are likely to dominate the effect of Social Security provisions. This paper considers the interaction between the effects of Social Security and employer-provided pension plans. We also give attention to the retirement effects of health benefits and to other provisions that may affect retirement.

The analysis rests on and continues our ongoing study of the retirement effects of employer-provided pension plans. The illustrations in this paper are based on data from "Firm III." We analyzed the Firm III data in an earlier paper (Lumsdaine, Stock, and Wise 1994), and this paper uses the results from that paper as a starting point for the analysis presented here. Our work to date has

Robin L. Lumsdaine is assistant professor of economics at Princeton University and a faculty research fellow of the National Bureau of Economic Research. James H. Stock is professor of political economy at the John F. Kennedy School of Government, Harvard University, and a research associate of the National Bureau of Economic Research. David A. Wise is the John F. Stambaugh Professor of Political Economy at the John F. Kennedy School of Government, Harvard University, and director for Health and Retirement Programs at the National Bureau of Economic Research.

This work was sponsored by the Japan Foundation Center for Global Partnership. Additional support was provided by the U.S. National Institute on Aging and the Hoover Institution (Wise).

emphasized the dramatic effect of employer-provided pension plan provisions on age of retirement and the enormous effects of changing the provisions. The work has also highlighted the important limitations of using Social Security provisions to predict retirement behavior, without accounting for the effect of employer pension plan provisions, which, for employees who have such plans, is typically much more powerful than the effect of Social Security provisions.

In two initial papers, Stock and Wise (1990a, 1990b) developed an "option value" model of retirement. The central feature of this model is that in deciding whether to retire, employees are assumed to compare the "value" of retiring now to the *maximum of the expected values* of retiring at all future retirement ages. If the maximum of the future values is greater than the value of retirement now, the employee continues to work. We tested the predictive validity of this model in two ways: First, we considered the "within-sample fit" of the model by comparing the actual pattern of retirement by age to the pattern predicted by the model, based on the data used for estimation. Second, in papers by Lumsdaine, Stock, and Wise (1990, 1991) we emphasized an external "out-of-sample" check of predictive validity by considering how well the model predicted the effect on retirement of an unanticipated and temporary change in the pension plan provisions occasioned by an early retirement window plan. In a subsequent paper, Lumsdaine, Stock, and Wise (1992) compared the predictive validity of the option value model and two versions of stochastic dynamic programming models. The stochastic dynamic programming model is close in spirit to the option value model, but the prediction of retirement is based on the comparison of the value of retirement now to the *expected value of the maximum* of the values of future retirement ages. The evidence was that the option value model predicted just as well as the stochastic dynamic programming models but had the advantage of being much less complex numerically. This finding was repeated in Lumsdaine et al. (1994) using Firm III data. Ausink (1991) pursued a similar comparison based on retirement from the military and found that the option value version was noticeably better than the stochastic dynamic programming versions. The simulations in this paper are thus based on the option value model.

The use of firm data was motivated by the absence of information on pension plan provisions in standard data sources, such as the Retirement History Survey, and by the realization that the incentives inherent in such plans could be very substantial and varied widely among firms (see, e.g., Bulow 1981; Lazear 1983; Kotlikoff and Wise 1985, 1987, 1988). Our work to date shows quite similar results for three firms. Thus, although the results in this paper are based on a single illustrative employer pension plan, we believe that the findings are representative of typical firms with defined-benefit plans.

The results are presented in the form of simulated effects of changes in the employer pension plan and Social Security provisions. The predicted retirement rates based on option value model estimates serve as the base with which simulated retirement rates under new provisions are compared. We begin in section 11.1 with a description of the firm plan, emphasizing its key provisions. The model used in the analysis and the empirical results are then explained. This material is largely abstracted from Lumsdaine et al. (1994). The effects of changes in provisions are discussed in section 11.2. A summary of findings is presented in section 11.3.

11.1   The Firm III Pension Plan and the Retirement Model

11.1.1   The Employer-Provided Pension Plan

Employees are covered by a defined-benefit pension plan with normal retirement at age 65 and early retirement at age 55. Cliff vesting occurs at 10 years of service, with the exception that employees are vested at age 65 even if they have fewer than 10 years of service. The normal retirement benefit at age 65 depends on earnings, age, and years of service at retirement (i.e., at the time of departure from the firm). A person can retire and elect to start receiving benefits before age 65, but the normal benefit will be reduced by 5 percent for each year that receipt of benefits precedes age 65, as shown in figure 11.1. A person who retired at age 55, for example, would receive 50 percent of the normal retirement benefit of a person who left the firm at age 65. (The normal benefit also depends on years of service at the time of retirement.)

However, if a person has 30 years of service at retirement and is aged 60 or older, the person is eligible for 100 percent of the normal benefit. Benefits are

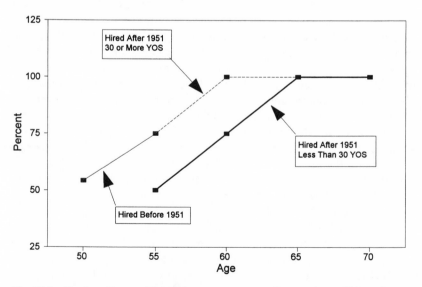

Fig. 11.1   Early retirement benefit as a percentage of normal age 65 benefit
Note: YOS = years of service.

reduced 5 percent for each year that retirement precedes age 60, if the person has 30 years of service. For example, a person who retired at age 55 with 30 years of service would receive 75 percent of the normal benefit.

Even a person who retires before age 55 and is vested can elect to receive benefits from the pension plan as early as age 55, but as for the post-55 retiree, benefits are reduced 5 percent for each year that receipt of the benefits precedes age 65. Of course, this person's benefits would be based on earnings, age, and years of service at the time of retirement, unadjusted for earnings inflation, and would thus be lower than the benefits of a person who retired later.

Employees who joined the firm before 1951 can retire as early as age 50 and begin to receive benefits immediately, but at a reduced rate. An employee hired before 1951 had at least 31 years of service in 1982. The reduction for this group is indicated by the extended line that indicates benefits at age 50 of 54.3 percent of the age 60 benefits for an employee who has 30 or more years of service at retirement.

To demonstrate the effect of the pension plan provisions, figure 11.2A shows the expected future compensation of a person from our sample who is 51 years old and has been employed by the firm for 23 years. To compute the data graphed in figures 11.2A–11.2E, a 5 percent real discount rate and a 6 percent inflation rate are assumed. The discount rate is estimated in the empirical analysis, and the inflation rate is assumed to be 6 percent. Total compensation from the firm can be viewed as the sum of wage earnings, the accrual of pension benefits, and the accrual of Social Security benefits. (This omits medical and other unobserved benefits that should be included as compensation, but for which we have no firm data.) As compensation for working another year the employee receives salary earnings. Compensation is also received in the form of future pension benefits. The annual compensation in this form is the change in the present value of the future pension benefit entitlement due to working an additional year. This accrual is comparable to wage earnings. The accrual of Social Security benefits may be calculated in a similar manner and is also comparable to wage earnings. Figure 11.2A shows the present value at age 51 of expected future compensation in all three forms. Wage earnings represents cumulated earnings, by age of retirement from the firm (more precisely, by age of departure from the firm, since some workers might continue to work in another job). For example, the cumulated earnings of this employee between age 51 and age 60 were he to retire at age 60 would be about $482,000, discounted to age 51 dollars. The slope of the earnings line represents annual earnings discounted to age 51 dollars.

The pension line shows the accrual of firm pension benefits, again discounted to age 51 dollars. It is graphed separately with Social Security accrual in figure 11.2E. The shape of this profile is determined by the pension plan provisions. The present value of accrued pension benefit entitlement at age 51 is about $54,000. The present value of retirement benefits increases between ages 51 and 57 because years of service and nominal earnings increase. An employee could leave the firm at age 53, for example. If he were to do that and were vested in the firm's pension plan, he would be entitled to normal retirement pension benefits at age 65, based on his years of service and nominal dollar earnings at age 53. He could choose to start receiving benefits as early as age 55, the pension early retirement age, but the benefit amount would be reduced 5 percent for each year that the receipt of benefits preceded age 65. Because 5 percent is less than the actuarially fair discount rate, the present value of benefits of a person who leaves the firm before age 55 are always greatest if receipt of benefits begins at age 55.

Recall that a person who has accumulated 30 years of service and is age 55 or older is entitled to increased retirement benefits that would reach 100 percent of normal retirement benefits at age 60. No early retirement reduction is applied to benefits if they are taken then. So a person at age 60 with 30 years of service who continues to work will no longer gain 5 percent a year from fewer years of early retirement reduction, as occurs before age 60. There is a jump in the benefits of a person younger than age 60 who attains 30 years of service. That accounts for the jump in the benefits of the person depicted in figure 11.2A, when he attains 30 years of service at age 58.

The Social Security accrual profile is determined by the Social Security benefit provisions. The present value of accrued Social Security benefit entitlement at age 51 is about $33,000. Social Security benefits cannot begin until age 62. If real earnings do not change much between ages 51 and 62, then real Social Security benefits at age 62 will not change much either. After age 62, the actuarial adjustment is such that the present value of benefits, evaluated at the age of retirement, does not depend on the retirement age. But the present value of the benefits discounted to the same age (51 in this case) declines. There is a further drop after age 65 because the actuarial adjustment is reduced from 7 percent to 3 percent.

The top line in fig. 11.2 shows total compensation. For example, the wage earnings of an employee who left the firm at age 60 would increase $482,000 between ages 51 and 60, shown by the wage earnings line. Thereafter, the employee would receive firm pension plan and Social Security retirement benefits with a present value—at age 51—of about $170,000. The sum of the two is about $652,000, shown by the top line. Compared to total compensation of $575,000 between ages 51 and 60, an average of $63,000 per year, total compensation between ages 60 and 65 would be only $100,000, or $23,000 per year. Thus the monetary reward for continued work declines dramatically with age.

Figures 11.2B through 11.2D show comparable compensation profiles for employees who are aged 57, 60, and 64, respectively, in 1982; they have 29, 38, and 45 years of service, respectively. The person depicted in figure 11.2B attains 30 years of service at age 58, thus the jump in pension benefits at that age. The present value of pension plus Social Security compensation reaches a maximum at age 59 and declines thereafter. Were this employee to continue

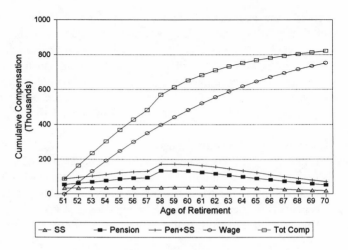

Fig. 11.2A   Future compensation for person aged 51 with 23 years of service in 1982

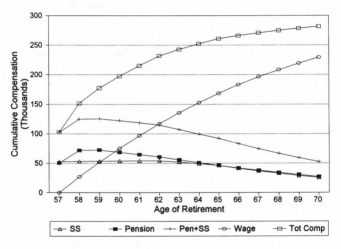

Fig. 11.2B   Future compensation for person aged 57 with 29 years of service in 1982

to work after age 59, until age 65, the present value of total retirement benefits would fall by $33,000, offsetting about 28 percent of the present value of wage earnings over this period ($117,000). A similar prospect faces the employee depicted in figure 11.2C, but this employee is already entitled to 100 percent of normal retirement benefits and loses benefits for each year that he continues to work.

The employee who faces the figure 11.2D compensation profile is 64 years old and loses both pension and Social Security benefits for each year that re-

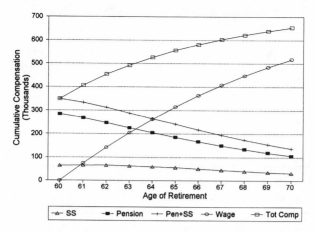

Fig. 11.2C   Future compensation for person aged 60 with 38 years of service in 1982

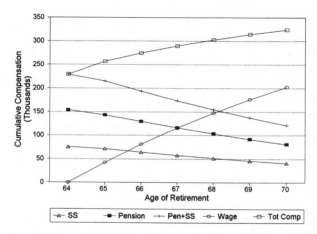

Fig. 11.2D   Future compensation for person aged 64 with 45 years of service in 1982

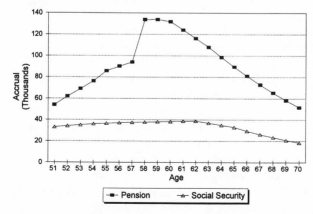

Fig. 11.2E   Future Social Security and pension compensation only, for person aged 51 with 23 years of service in 1982

tirement is postponed. At age 65, for example, about 54 percent of expected wage earnings would be offset by a reduction in retirement benefits, if retirement were postponed.

11.1.2   The 1983 Window

To evaluate the predictive validity of the estimated model, we use estimates based on data for an earlier year to predict retirement under the subsequent 1983 window plan. Under the window plan, which was in effect from January 1 to February 28, all employees were eligible for a separation bonus, but the most generous payments were available to persons aged 55 and older who had at least 21 years of service. Retirement benefits for this group were increased depending on age and years of service. For example, a person aged 59 with 28 years of service could receive 100 percent of normal retirement benefits, instead of 70 percent under the regular plan. That is, this person's retirement benefit would be increased by 43 percent. A person aged 55 with 21 years of service could receive 55 percent of normal benefits, instead of 50 percent. Persons aged 60 or older with 30 years of service were eligible for 100 percent of normal benefits under the regular plan.

In addition, all employees were eligible for a separation bonus equal to one week's pay for every year of service, with a minimum of 2 and a maximum of 26 weeks of pay. Thus even persons who were under 55 years old and those who were eligible for 100 percent of normal retirement benefits faced an added inducement to retire.

11.1.3   Estimation

The Data

The data used in the analysis are drawn from the personnel records of all persons employed by the firm at any time between 1979 and 1988. A year-end file is available for each year. Earnings records back to 1979 (or to the date of hire if after 1979) are available for each employee. In addition, the data contain some demographic information such as date of birth, gender, marital status, and occupational group. The retirement date of employees who retire is also known. (More generally, the date of any departure is known, and the reason for the departure is recorded.) Thus we are able to determine whether a person who was employed at age a was also employed at age $a + 1$, and if not, the exact age at which the employee left the firm.

The estimation of the retirement model in this paper is based on 1982 data, whether or not an employee left the firm in 1982. (To simplify the determination of age of retirement, only employees born in January and February who had not retired before 1 March 1982 are used in this analysis.) The primary test of the predictive validity of the model is based on how well the model, estimated on 1982 data, predicts retirement under the 1983 window plan that substantially increased standard retirement benefits.

The Option Value Model

The model is described in detail in Stock and Wise (1990b) and is explained only briefly here. At any given age, based on information available at that age, it is assumed that an employee compares the expected present value of retiring at that age with the value of retiring at each age in the future through age 70. The maximum of the expected present values of retiring at each future age minus the expected present value of immediate retirement is called the option value of postponing retirement. A person who does not retire this year maintains the option of retiring at a more advantageous age later on. If the option value is positive, the person continues to work; otherwise she retires. With reference to figure 11.1, for example, at age 51 the employee would compare the value of the retirement benefits that she would receive were she to retire then—approximately $87,000—with the value of wage earnings and retirement benefits in each future year. The expected present value of retiring at age 60 (discounted to age 51), for example, is about $652,000. Future earnings forecasts are based on the individual's past earnings, as well as the earnings of other persons in the firm. The precise model specification follows.

A person at age t who continues to work will earn Y_s at subsequent ages s. If the person retires at age r, subsequent retirement benefits will be $B_s(r)$. These benefits will depend on the person's age and years of service at retirement and on his earnings history; thus they are a function of the retirement age. We suppose that in deciding whether to retire the person weighs the indirect utility that will be received from future income. Discounted to age t at the rate β, the value of this future stream of income if retirement is at age r is given by

$$(1) \qquad V_t(r) = \sum_{s=t}^{r-1} \beta^{s-t} U_w(Y_s) + \sum_{s=r}^{S} \beta^{s-t} U_r(B_s(r)),$$

where $U_w(Y_s)$ is the indirect utility of future wage income and $U_r(B_s(r))$ is the indirect utility of future retirement benefits. It is assumed that the employee will not live past age S. The expected gain, evaluated at age t, from postponing retirement until age r is given by

$$(2) \qquad G_t(r) = E_t V_t(r) - E_t V_t(t).$$

Letting r^* be the age that gives the maximum expected gain, the person will postpone retirement if the option value, $G_t(r^*)$, is positive,

$$(3) \qquad G_t(r^*) = E_t V_t(r^*) - E_t V_t(t) > 0.$$

The utilities of future wage and retirement income are parameterized as

$$(4a) \qquad U_w(Y_s) = Y_s^\gamma + \omega_s,$$

$$(4b) \qquad U_r(B_s) = [kB_s(r)]^\gamma + \xi_s,$$

where ω_s and ξ_s are individual-specific random effects, assumed to follow a Markovian (first-order autoregressive) process

(5a) $\omega_s = \rho\omega_{s-1} + \varepsilon_{\omega s}, \qquad E_{s-1}(\varepsilon_{\omega s}) = 0,$

(5b) $\xi_s = \rho\xi_{s-1} + \varepsilon_{\xi s}, \qquad E_{s-1}(\varepsilon_{\xi s}) = 0.$

The parameter k is incorporated to recognize that in considering whether to retire, the utility *associated* with a dollar of income while retired may be different from the utility associated with a dollar of income accompanied by work. Abstracting from the random terms, at any given age s, the ratio of the utility of retirement to the utility of employment is $[k(B_s/Y_s)]^\gamma$.

Parameter Estimates

The parameter estimates for men and women are shown in table 11.1. The estimates for γ suggest some risk aversion. We have typically found estimates closer to 1, suggesting that with respect to retirement income, employees are essentially risk neutral. The estimated value of k is 2.580 for men and 1.329 for women. The estimate for men, for example, suggests that a dollar of retirement benefit income—unaccompanied by work—is valued more than 2.5 times as much as a dollar of income that is accompanied by work. The estimated values of β suggest discount rates between 3 and 25 percent.

The model fits the data quite well, and this is shown graphically in figures 11.3A through 11.3C for men. The principal discrepancy between actual and predicted rates occurs at age 65, with the actual rate substantially greater than the predicted rate. The predicted and actual cumulative departure rates are very close. The primary test of the predictive validity of the model is how well it predicts retirement rates under the 1983 window plan. The model predictions capture the general pattern of retirement under the window, but underpredict retirement rates of persons aged 55 or older, as shown in figure 11.3C.

Table 11.1   Parameter Estimates by Gender

Parameter	Men	Women	Men and Women
γ	0.546	0.738	0.574
	(0.063)	(0.173)	(0.069)
k	2.580	1.329	2.434
	(0.175)	(0.241)	(0.320)
β	0.987	0.720	0.979
	(0.024)	(0.235)	(0.022)
σ	0.110	0.071	0.112
	(0.010)	(0.023)	(0.028)
Log-likelihood			
At maximum	381.56	100.98	486.51
Age averages	362.55	91.26	461.30
Chi square			
Fitted data	27.67	15.14	30.47
Window	99.77	54.66	125.80

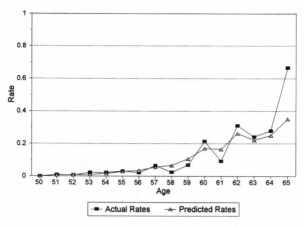

Fig. 11.3A Predicted versus actual annual departure rates—option value
for men

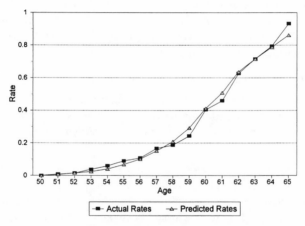

Fig. 11.3B Predicted versus actual cumulative departure rates—option value
for men

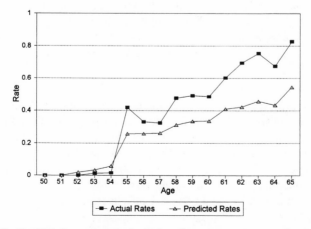

Fig. 11.3C Predicted versus actual window departure rates—option value
for men

Simulated retirement rates under the plan changes discussed below are typically compared to the predicted rates in figures 11.3A and 11.3B.

11.2 Simulations

We consider first the effect on retirement of several provisions of the firm pension plan. The effect of specific changes in Social Security provisions are then considered. These are the actual changes that are scheduled to be phased in over the next 30 years. Then changes in both firm pension and Social Security provisions are considered. We explore in a very provisional manner the effect of retiree health insurance on retirement. To understand how the elimination of mandatory retirement may have affected departure rates, we consider departure rates if 65 were the mandatory retirement age. The effects of a defined contribution instead of the firm defined-benefit plan are also investigated. Finally, we simulate, again in a very provisional manner, the effect of postretirement employment at a reduced salary, compared to the currently typical move from full-time work to retirement.

11.2.1 Changes in the Firm Plan Provisions

We consider each of several firm plan provisions: the early retirement reduction factor, increased benefits for persons with 30 years of service (which we refer to as the "30-year provision"), and the early retirement age.

Actuarially fair early retirement reduction. An important feature of the firm plan is that the 5 percent per year reduction in benefits if they are taken before normal retirement—the early retirement reduction—is less than actuarially fair. An actuarially fair reduction would be about 7 percent, instead of 5 percent. The effect of changing to an actuarially fair reduction is shown in figure 11.4. The effect is concentrated among employees 56–59 years old. With the fair reduction, only 22 percent of persons employed at age 50 would have retired by age 59, compared to 29 percent under the 5 percent reduction factor. The effect at older ages would apparently be greater were it not for the 30-year provision, which has an important effect on retirement as employees approach age 60.

The 30-year provision. As described with reference to figure 11.1, the firm plan also provides for increased benefits when 30 years of service are attained. At age 60, for example, a person with 30 years of service is eligible for 100 percent of normal retirement benefits. The effect of eliminating this provision is shown in figure 11.5. The effects are substantial, reducing from 41 percent to 29 percent the proportion retired by age 60 and from 64 percent to 46 percent the proportion retired by age 62. The age 60 departure rate is reduced by more than 50 percent.

Figure 11.4A   **Simulation—Firm Actuarially Fair Early Retirement Reduction: Data**

	Retirement Rates			Cumulative Rates		
Age	Base	Simulation	Difference	Base	Simulation	Difference
50	0	0	0	0	0	0
51	0.007	0.006	−0.001	0.007	0.006	−0.001
52	0.009	0.008	−0.001	0.016	0.015	−0.001
53	0.01	0.012	0.002	0.025	0.026	0.001
54	0.016	0.018	0.002	0.041	0.044	0.003
55	0.029	0.026	−0.003	0.068	0.069	0.001
56	0.036	0.03	−0.006	0.102	0.097	−0.005
57	0.056	0.044	−0.012	0.152	0.136	−0.016
58	0.067	0.051	−0.016	0.208	0.18	−0.028
59	0.106	0.051	−0.055	0.292	0.223	−0.069
60	0.169	0.161	−0.008	0.412	0.348	−0.064
61	0.165	0.158	−0.007	0.509	0.451	−0.058
62	0.262	0.25	−0.012	0.637	0.588	−0.049
63	0.22	0.222	0.002	0.717	0.68	−0.037
64	0.249	0.235	−0.014	0.788	0.755	−0.033
65	0.35	0.35	0	0.862	0.841	−0.021

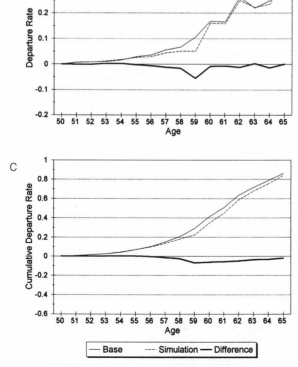

Figs. 11.4B and 11.4C   Simulation—Firm Actuarially Fair Early Retirement Reduction

Note: (*B*) Retirement rates. (*C*) Cumulative rates.

Figure 11.5A   Simulation—Eliminate Firm 30-Year Provision: Data

Age	Retirement Rates			Cumulative Rates		
	Base	Simulation	Difference	Base	Simulation	Difference
50	0	0	0	0	0	0
51	0.007	0.008	0.001	0.007	0.008	0.001
52	0.009	0.011	0.002	0.016	0.018	0.002
53	0.01	0.013	0.003	0.025	0.031	0.006
54	0.016	0.016	0	0.041	0.046	0.005
55	0.029	0.022	−0.007	0.068	0.068	0
56	0.036	0.029	−0.007	0.102	0.095	−0.007
57	0.056	0.047	−0.009	0.152	0.138	−0.014
58	0.067	0.056	−0.011	0.208	0.186	−0.022
59	0.106	0.057	−0.049	0.292	0.232	−0.06
60	0.169	0.081	−0.088	0.412	0.294	−0.118
61	0.165	0.083	−0.082	0.509	0.353	−0.156
62	0.262	0.164	−0.098	0.637	0.46	−0.177
63	0.22	0.182	−0.038	0.717	0.558	−0.159
64	0.249	0.215	−0.034	0.788	0.653	−0.135
65	0.35	0.35	0	0.862	0.774	−0.088

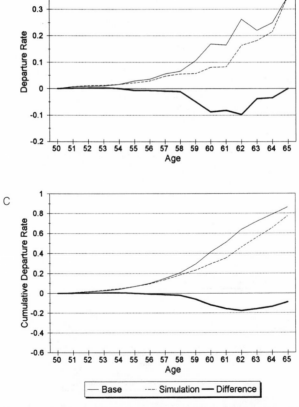

Figs. 11.5B and 11.5C   Simulation—Eliminate Firm 30-Year Provision
Note: (*B*) Retirement rates. (*C*) Cumulative rates.

Early retirement at age 60 instead of age 55. Under the current firm plan, employees can begin to receive pension benefits at age 55. Suppose that the early retirement age were 60 instead of 55. There would be a very substantial reduction in departure rates before age 60, as shown in figure 11.6. Indeed, in this firm, almost no employee would retire before age 60. Under the current plan, 41 percent of persons employed at age 55 would have retired before age 60, according to our predictions. But if early retirement were at age 60, only 4 percent would retire before age 60.

Early retirement at age 62 instead of age 55. In this case, we suppose that early retirement is at age 62—the same as the Social Security early retirement age— and that the 30-year provision provides 100 percent benefits at age 62, instead of age 60. The results are much like those discussed just above, except that in this case retirement tends to be delayed until age 62, as shown in figure 11.7. The percentage retired before age 62 is reduced from 51 percent to 8 percent. The simulations make it clear that employees are unlikely to retire before pension retirement benefits can be received. This is consistent with the evidence that most American families have very limited personal financial assets on the eve of retirement and would be unable to support themselves in retirement without employer-provided pension or Social Security benefits.

In general, the firm pension plan provisions have an important effect on retirement. The simulations below show that for persons with a firm plan like the one presented here, changes in Social Security provisions are much less important.

11.2.2   Changes in Social Security Provisions

We consider three changes in Social Security provisions: actuarially fair increases in benefits after age 65, an increase in the normal retirement age to 67, and both changes together.

Actuarially fair post-65 benefit increases. Under current Social Security provisions, benefits are increased only 3 percent per year if receipt of benefits begins after age 65. An actuarially fair increase would be close to 7 percent. The effect of this change is shown in figure 11.8. The aggregate effects are small, although the age 65 departure is reduced from 35 percent to 29 percent. The proportion retired by age 65 is reduced only from 86 percent to 85 percent. This is because a large fraction of firm employees have already retired by age 65, and thus an increase in the retirement rate of the small proportion that is still working at that age has only a small effect on cumulative retirement.

An increase in the Social Security normal retirement age from 65 to 67. Over the next three decades the Social Security normal retirement age is scheduled to increase from 65 to 67. The Social Security early retirement age will remain at 62, but benefits will be reduced actuarially from full benefits at age 67,

Figure 11.6A   Simulation—Firm Early Retirement at Age 60, Not Age 55: Data

Age	Retirement Rates			Cumulative Rates		
	Base	Simulation	Difference	Base	Simulation	Difference
50	0	0	0	0	0	0
51	0.007	0.007	0	0.007	0.007	0
52	0.009	0.005	−0.004	0.016	0.012	−0.004
53	0.01	0.005	−0.005	0.025	0.018	−0.007
54	0.016	0.004	−0.012	0.041	0.021	−0.02
55	0.029	0.004	−0.025	0.068	0.025	−0.043
56	0.036	0.004	−0.032	0.102	0.029	−0.073
57	0.056	0.004	−0.052	0.152	0.033	−0.119
58	0.067	0.005	−0.062	0.208	0.038	−0.17
59	0.106	0.007	−0.099	0.292	0.044	−0.248
60	0.169	0.169	0	0.412	0.206	−0.206
61	0.165	0.165	0	0.509	0.337	−0.172
62	0.262	0.262	0	0.637	0.511	−0.126
63	0.22	0.22	0	0.717	0.618	−0.099
64	0.249	0.249	0	0.788	0.713	−0.075
65	0.35	0.35	0	0.862	0.813	−0.049

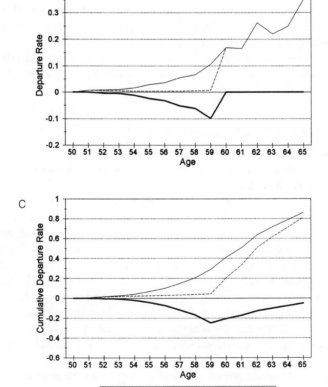

Figs. 11.6B and 11.6C   Simulation—Firm Early Retirement at Age 60, Not Age 55
Note: (*B*) Retirement rates. (*C*) Cumulative rates.

Figure 11.7A   **Simulation—Firm Early Retirement at Age 62, Not Age 55: Data**

	Retirement Rates			Cumulative Rates		
Age	Base	Simulation	Difference	Base	Simulation	Difference
50	0	0	0	0	0	0
51	0.007	0.01	0.003	0.007	0.01	0.003
52	0.009	0.008	−0.001	0.016	0.017	0.001
53	0.01	0.008	−0.002	0.025	0.025	0
54	0.016	0.006	−0.01	0.041	0.031	−0.01
55	0.029	0.006	−0.023	0.068	0.037	−0.031
56	0.036	0.006	−0.03	0.102	0.043	−0.059
57	0.056	0.006	−0.05	0.152	0.049	−0.103
58	0.067	0.007	−0.06	0.208	0.056	−0.152
59	0.106	0.009	−0.097	0.292	0.064	−0.228
60	0.169	0.008	−0.161	0.412	0.071	−0.341
61	0.165	0.011	−0.154	0.509	0.081	−0.428
62	0.262	0.262	0	0.637	0.321	−0.316
63	0.22	0.22	0	0.717	0.471	−0.246
64	0.249	0.249	0	0.788	0.602	−0.186
65	0.35	0.35	0	0.862	0.741	−0.121

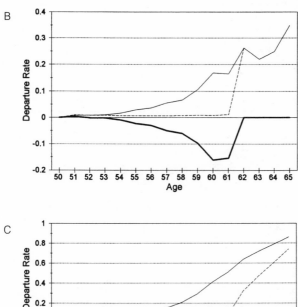

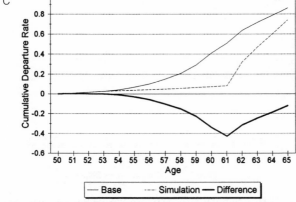

Figs. 11.7B and 11.7C   Simulation—Firm Early Retirement at Age 62, Not Age 55
Note: (*B*) Retirement rates. (*C*) Cumulative rates.

Figure 11.8A   Simulation—Actuarially Fair Post-65 Social Security Benefit: Data

	Retirement Rates			Cumulative Rates		
Age	Base	Simulation	Difference	Base	Simulation	Difference
50	0	0	0	0	0	0
51	0.007	0.007	0	0.007	0.007	0
52	0.009	0.009	0	0.016	0.016	0
53	0.01	0.01	0	0.025	0.025	0
54	0.016	0.016	0	0.041	0.041	0
55	0.029	0.029	0	0.068	0.068	0
56	0.036	0.036	0	0.102	0.102	0
57	0.056	0.056	0	0.152	0.152	0
58	0.067	0.067	0	0.208	0.208	0
59	0.106	0.061	0	0.292	0.292	0
60	0.169	0.169	0	0.412	0.412	0
61	0.165	0.165	0	0.509	0.509	0
62	0.262	0.262	0	0.637	0.637	0
63	0.22	0.22	0	0.717	0.717	0
64	0.249	0.249	0	0.788	0.787	−0.001
65	0.35	0.292	−0.058	0.862	0.849	−0.013

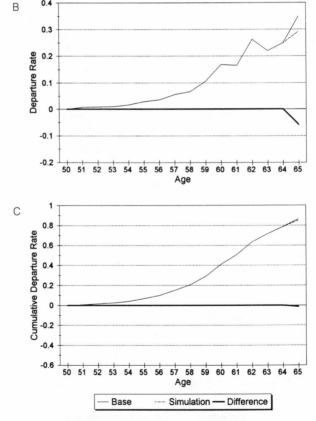

Figs. 11.8B and 11.8C   Simulation—Actuarially Fair Post-65 Social Security Benefit

Note: (*B*) Retirement rates. (*C*) Cumulative rates.

instead of age 65. The simulated effects of this change are shown in figure 11.9. Again, although the retirement rates of persons over age 60 are reduced, the aggregate effect is small. The retirement rate of persons aged 62, for example, is reduced from 26 percent to 23 percent and the rate of persons aged 65 from 35 percent to 26 percent. But the percentage of 50-year-olds retired by age 65 is reduced only from 86 percent to 83 percent.

An increase in the Social Security normal retirement age from 65 to 67 and actuarially fair post-67 benefit increases. Combining the two changes above yields results much like the latter change alone, as shown in figure 11.10. There is a noticeable effect on retirement rates of persons aged 62 or older, but the cumulative effect is small, reducing the percentage retired by age 65 only by 3 percentage points, from 86 percent to 83 percent. Thus, compared to changes in the firm plan provisions, the effect of the scheduled changes in Social Security provisions is very small.

No Social Security early retirement or no Social Security. Although the effect of the proposed Social Security changes is small, and even eliminating Social Security early retirement would have a small effect, no Social Security at all would have a substantial effect. As shown in figure 11.11, eliminating Social Security early retirement would have only a modest effect on cumulative departure rates from this firm, reducing departures by age 65 from 86 percent to 80 percent, although departure rates for ages 62–64 are reduced substantially. But no Social Security benefits at all would reduce departure rates by age 65 from 86 percent to 67 percent, as shown in figure 11.12. Thus it would be inaccurate to say, with respect to its effect on retirement, that Social Security by itself does not matter.

11.2.3   Social Security and Firm Provisions "Coordinated"

If the scheduled Social Security changes are imposed and the firm provisions were changed to "correspond" to the Social Security provisions, the effects would be much like the corresponding effects if only the firm plan provisions were changed. We consider two versions: (1) the firm early retirement age is increased to 62 and the firm 30-year provision applies at age 62 instead of age 60 (as in fig. 11.7 above) and (2) the firm early retirement age is increased to 62 and the 30-year provision applies at age 62 instead of age 60 and the firm normal retirement age is increased from 65 to 67.

Social Security scheduled changes and firm early retirement at age 62. The effect of this change can be compared to the firm change without any change in Social Security provisions, described in figure 11.7. The effect of the joint change—shown in figure 11.13—is very large, but the comparison with figure 11.7 makes clear that most of the effect is due to the change in the firm plan. Retirement before age 62 is reduced from 51 percent to 8 percent, the same as

Figure 11.9A   **Simulation—Social Security Retirement at Age 67, Not Age 65: Data**

Age	Retirement Rates			Cumulative Rates		
	Base	Simulation	Difference	Base	Simulation	Difference
50	0	0	0	0	0	0
51	0.007	0.007	0	0.007	0.007	0
52	0.009	0.01	0.001	0.016	0.017	0.001
53	0.01	0.01	0	0.025	0.026	0.001
54	0.016	0.016	0	0.041	0.042	0.001
55	0.029	0.03	0.001	0.068	0.071	0.003
56	0.036	0.037	0.001	0.102	0.105	0.003
57	0.056	0.053	−0.003	0.152	0.153	0.001
58	0.067	0.063	−0.004	0.208	0.206	−0.002
59	0.106	0.099	−0.007	0.292	0.285	−0.007
60	0.169	0.162	−0.007	0.412	0.401	−0.011
61	0.165	0.154	−0.011	0.509	0.493	−0.016
62	0.262	0.233	−0.029	0.637	0.611	−0.026
63	0.22	0.208	−0.012	0.717	0.692	−0.025
64	0.249	0.233	−0.016	0.788	0.764	−0.024
65	0.35	0.262	−0.088	0.862	0.826	−0.036

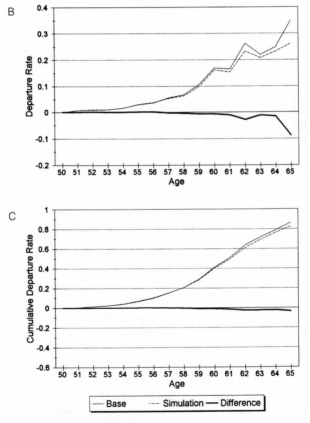

Figs. 11.9B and 11.9C   Simulation—Social Security Retirement at Age 67, Not Age 65

Note: (*B*) Retirement rates. (*C*) Cumulative rates.

Figure 11.10A

Figure 11.10A   **Simulation—Social Security Retirement at Age 67 and Actuarially Fair Post-67 Benefit: Data**

	Retirement Rates			Cumulative Rates		
Age	Base	Simulation	Difference	Base	Simulation	Difference
50	0	0	0	0	0	0
51	0.007	0.007	0	0.007	0.007	0
52	0.009	0.01	0.001	0.016	0.017	0.001
53	0.01	0.01	0	0.025	0.026	0.001
54	0.016	0.016	0	0.041	0.042	0.001
55	0.029	0.03	0.001	0.068	0.071	0.003
56	0.036	0.037	0.001	0.102	0.105	0.003
57	0.056	0.053	−0.003	0.152	0.153	0.001
58	0.067	0.063	−0.004	0.208	0.206	−0.002
59	0.106	0.099	−0.007	0.292	0.285	−0.007
60	0.169	0.162	−0.007	0.412	0.401	−0.011
61	0.165	0.154	−0.011	0.509	0.493	−0.016
62	0.262	0.233	−0.029	0.637	0.611	−0.026
63	0.22	0.208	−0.012	0.717	0.692	−0.025
64	0.249	0.233	−0.016	0.788	0.764	−0.024
65	0.35	0.262	−0.088	0.862	0.826	−0.036

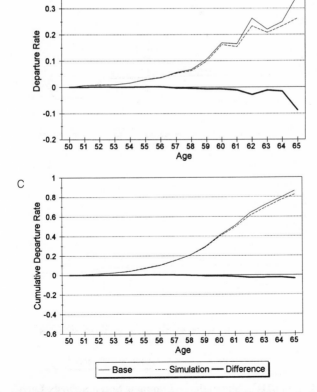

Figs. 11.10B and 11.10C   **Simulation—Social Security Retirement at Age 67 and Actuarially Fair Post-67 Benefit**

Note: (*B*) Retirement rates. (*C*) Cumulative rates.

Figure 11.11A   **Simulation—Eliminate Social Security Early Retirement: Data**

Age	Retirement Rates			Cumulative Rates		
	Base	Simulation	Difference	Base	Simulation	Difference
50	0	0	0	0	0	0
51	0.007	0.006	−0.001	0.007	0.006	−0.001
52	0.009	0.009	0	0.016	0.015	−0.001
53	0.01	0.009	−0.001	0.025	0.024	−0.001
54	0.016	0.015	−0.001	0.041	0.038	−0.003
55	0.029	0.026	−0.003	0.068	0.064	−0.004
56	0.036	0.033	−0.003	0.102	0.095	−0.007
57	0.056	0.05	−0.006	0.152	0.14	−0.012
58	0.067	0.06	−0.007	0.208	0.192	−0.016
59	0.106	0.098	−0.008	0.292	0.271	−0.021
60	0.169	0.161	−0.008	0.412	0.389	−0.023
61	0.165	0.154	−0.011	0.509	0.483	−0.026
62	0.262	0.177	−0.085	0.637	0.574	−0.063
63	0.22	0.138	−0.082	0.717	0.633	−0.084
64	0.249	0.161	−0.088	0.788	0.692	−0.096
65	0.35	0.35	0	0.862	0.8	−0.062

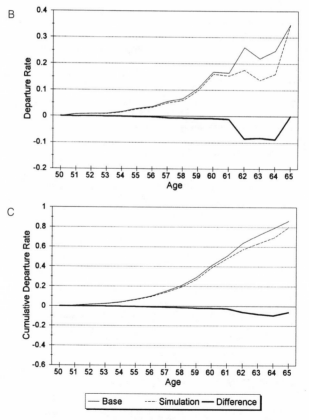

Figs. 11.11B and 11.11C   Simulation—Eliminate Social Security Early Retirement

Note: (*B*) Retirement rates. (*C*) Cumulative rates.

Figure 11.12A   Simulation—Eliminate Social Security: Data

	Retirement Rates			Cumulative Rates		
Age	Base	Simulation	Difference	Base	Simulation	Difference
50	0	0	0	0	0	0
51	0.007	0.005	−0.002	0.007	0.005	−0.002
52	0.009	0.008	−0.001	0.016	0.013	−0.003
53	0.01	0.007	−0.003	0.025	0.02	−0.005
54	0.016	0.012	−0.004	0.041	0.032	−0.009
55	0.029	0.021	−0.008	0.068	0.052	−0.016
56	0.036	0.024	−0.012	0.102	0.075	−0.027
57	0.056	0.034	−0.022	0.152	0.106	−0.046
58	0.067	0.04	−0.027	0.208	0.142	−0.066
59	0.106	0.075	−0.031	0.292	0.206	−0.086
60	0.169	0.133	−0.036	0.412	0.312	−0.1
61	0.165	0.124	−0.041	0.509	0.397	−0.112
62	0.262	0.149	−0.113	0.637	0.487	−0.15
63	0.22	0.111	−0.109	0.717	0.544	−0.173
64	0.249	0.135	−0.114	0.788	0.605	−0.183
65	0.35	0.16	−0.19	0.862	0.668	−0.194

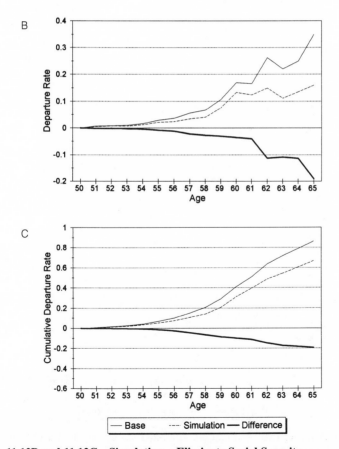

Figs. 11.12B and 11.12C   Simulation—Eliminate Social Security
Note: (*B*) Retirement rates. (*C*) Cumulative rates.

Age	Retirement Rates			Cumulative Rates		
	Base	Simulation	Difference	Base	Simulation	Difference
50	0	0	0	0	0	0
51	0.007	0.01	0.003	0.007	0.01	0.003
52	0.009	0.008	−0.001	0.016	0.017	0.001
53	0.01	0.008	−0.002	0.025	0.025	0
54	0.016	0.006	−0.01	0.041	0.031	−0.01
55	0.029	0.006	−0.023	0.068	0.037	−0.031
56	0.036	0.006	−0.03	0.102	0.043	−0.059
57	0.056	0.006	−0.05	0.152	0.049	−0.103
58	0.067	0.007	−0.06	0.208	0.056	−0.152
59	0.106	0.009	−0.097	0.292	0.064	−0.228
60	0.169	0.008	−0.161	0.412	0.071	−0.341
61	0.165	0.011	−0.154	0.509	0.081	−0.428
62	0.262	0.262	0	0.637	0.321	−0.316
63	0.22	0.22	0	0.717	0.47	−0.247
64	0.249	0.249	0	0.788	0.602	−0.186
65	0.35	0.292	−0.058	0.862	0.718	−0.144

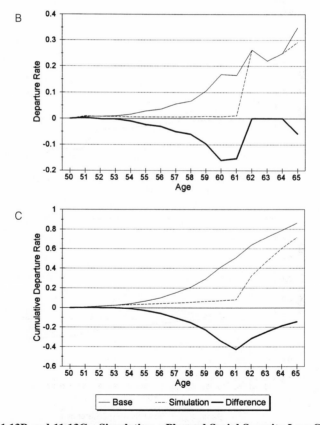

**Figs. 11.13B and 11.13C   Simulation—Planned Social Security Law Changes
and Firm Early Retirement at Age 62, Not Age 60**
Note: (*B*) Retirement rates. (*C*) Cumulative rates.

in figure 11.7. Retirement by age 65 is reduced from 86 percent to 72 percent; the reduction in figure 11.7 is from 86 percent to 74 percent.

Social Security scheduled changes, firm early retirement at age 62, and firm normal retirement at age 67. If in addition to increasing the firm early retirement age to 62 the firm normal retirement age were increased to 67, the effect on retirement—shown in figure 11.14—would be much like the effect shown above. But increasing the firm normal retirement age has a substantial effect on the departure rates of older employees. Cumulative departure by age 65 would be 64 percent as compared to 72 percent in the case just above and 86 percent in the base case. Cumulative departure by age 62 would be 27 percent as compared with 32 percent above and 64 percent in the base case.

11.2.4   Firm Retiree Health Insurance

Health insurance coverage under Medicare does not begin until age 65. Whether an employee is eligible for retiree health insurance before age 65 may affect the retirement decision. This issue has been analyzed in some detail by Gruber and Madrian (1996). Employees in Firm III are covered by employer health insurance while they are working and are covered by retiree health insurance after retirement. An employee who retires at age 55, for example, would be covered by retiree health insurance. The retiree plan is essentially the same as the current employee plan. After age 65, however, the plan pays only for care that is not covered by Medicare but is covered by the employer plan; the employer is the payer of last resort. It is unclear how persons value health insurance. In particular, the dollar cost of purchasing the insurance may not be an adequate measure of the value of the insurance. Nonetheless, to gain some insight as to how retiree insurance coverage might affect retirement, suppose there were no retiree insurance so that employees who retired before age 65 would have to purchase insurance privately. We assume that the cost would be $1,000 per year until age 65, when the person would be covered by Medicare. Therefore, before age 65, we assume that the dollar amount of retirement benefits would be $1,000 lower, the cost of the health insurance that the retiree would have to purchase. The effect on retirement is shown in figure 11.15. Retirement rates before age 65 are importantly lower, but compared to the effect of pension plan provisions, the effect is small. For example, the cumulative percentage retired by age 61 is reduced from 51 percent to 45 percent. In contrast, increasing the firm plan early retirement age from 55 to 62 would reduce cumulative retirement by age 61 from 51 percent to 8 percent, as shown in figure 11.7.

11.2.5   Mandatory Retirement

Before 1978 mandatory retirement at age 65 was common in the United States. It is still common in Japan. We consider here how mandatory retirement in Firm III would change retirement rates. The results are described in figure 11.16. Only departure rates at ages 64 and 65 are affected by the change; the

Figure 11.14A   **Simulation—Planned Social Security Law Changes and Firm Early Retirement at Age 62, Normal Retirement at Age 67: Data**

Age	Retirement Rates			Cumulative Rates		
	Base	Simulation	Difference	Base	Simulation	Difference
50	0	0	0	0	0	0
51	0.007	0.003	−0.004	0.007	0.003	−0.004
52	0.009	0.009	0	0.016	0.012	−0.004
53	0.01	0.009	−0.001	0.025	0.021	−0.004
54	0.016	0.008	−0.008	0.041	0.029	−0.012
55	0.029	0.007	−0.022	0.068	0.035	−0.033
56	0.036	0.007	−0.029	0.102	0.042	−0.06
57	0.056	0.007	−0.049	0.152	0.048	−0.104
58	0.067	0.007	−0.06	0.208	0.055	−0.153
59	0.106	0.007	−0.099	0.292	0.062	−0.23
60	0.169	0.006	−0.163	0.412	0.068	−0.344
61	0.165	0.008	−0.157	0.509	0.075	−0.434
62	0.262	0.213	−0.049	0.637	0.272	−0.365
63	0.22	0.191	−0.029	0.717	0.411	−0.306
64	0.249	0.209	−0.04	0.788	0.534	−0.254
65	0.35	0.232	−0.118	0.862	0.642	−0.22

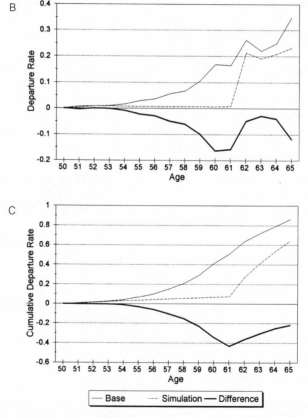

Figs. 11.14B and 11.14C   Simulation—Planned Social Security Law Changes and Firm Early Retirement at Age 62, Normal Retirement at Age 67
Note: (*B*) Retirement rates. (*C*) Cumulative rates.

Age	Retirement Rates			Cumulative Rates		
	Base	Simulation	Difference	Base	Simulation	Difference
50	0	0	0	0	0	0
51	0.007	0.006	−0.001	0.007	0.006	−0.001
52	0.009	0.008	−0.001	0.016	0.013	−0.003
53	0.01	0.008	−0.002	0.025	0.021	−0.004
54	0.016	0.012	−0.004	0.041	0.032	−0.009
55	0.029	0.02	−0.009	0.068	0.052	−0.016
56	0.036	0.026	−0.01	0.102	0.077	−0.025
57	0.056	0.044	−0.012	0.152	0.117	−0.035
58	0.067	0.053	−0.014	0.208	0.164	−0.044
59	0.106	0.089	−0.017	0.292	0.238	−0.054
60	0.169	0.149	−0.02	0.412	0.352	−0.06
61	0.165	0.144	−0.021	0.509	0.445	−0.064
62	0.262	0.24	−0.022	0.637	0.578	−0.059
63	0.22	0.201	−0.019	0.717	0.663	−0.054
64	0.249	0.23	−0.019	0.788	0.741	−0.047
65	0.35	0.35	0	0.862	0.831	−0.031

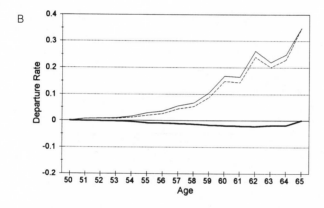

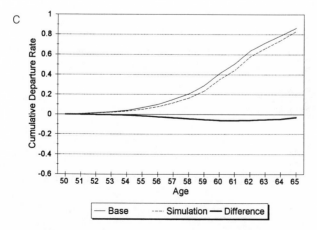

Figs. 11.15B and 11.15C   Simulation—Eliminate Firm Retiree Health Insurance
Note: (*B*) Retirement rates. (*C*) Cumulative rates.

Figure 11.16A   Simulation—Firm Mandatory Retirement at Age 65: Data

Age	Retirement Rates			Cumulative Rates		
	Base	Simulation	Difference	Base	Simulation	Difference
50	0	0	0	0	0	0
51	0.007	0.007	0	0.007	0.007	0
52	0.009	0.009	0	0.016	0.016	0
53	0.01	0.01	0	0.025	0.025	0
54	0.016	0.016	0	0.041	0.041	0
55	0.029	0.029	0	0.068	0.068	0
56	0.036	0.036	0	0.102	0.102	0
57	0.056	0.056	0	0.152	0.152	0
58	0.067	0.067	0	0.208	0.208	0
59	0.106	0.106	0	0.292	0.292	0
60	0.169	0.17	0.001	0.412	0.412	0
61	0.165	0.165	0	0.509	0.509	0
62	0.262	0.262	0	0.637	0.638	0.001
63	0.22	0.22	0	0.717	0.718	0.001
64	0.249	0.357	0.108	0.788	0.818	0.03
65	0.35	0.5	0.15	0.862	0.909	0.047

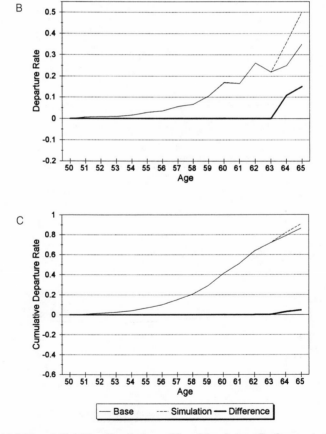

Figs. 11.16B and 11.16C   Simulation—Firm Mandatory Retirement at Age 65
Note: (*B*) Retirement rates. (*C*) Cumulative rates.

cumulative effect is small. The age 64 retirement rate, for example, is increased from 25 percent to 36 percent. Departure by age 65 is increased from 86 percent to 91 percent.

11.2.6   Defined-Contribution versus Defined-Benefit Plan

Unlike the firm defined-benefit plan under which benefits are determined by a formula that can incorporate substantial incentives, benefits under a defined-contribution plan are typically determined only by the cumulated assets that the employee has in the plan at retirement. Other than the level of assets, there are no plan incentive effects that encourage or discourage retirement at specific ages. To provide some idea of how retirement might change under such a plan, we assume that individual pension assets accumulate with years of employment through pension plan contributions equal to 7.5 percent of wage earnings. The benefit at retirement is the annuity value of the accumulated assets. Retirement rates under this plan are described in figure 11.17. Cumulative retirement at age 55 is *increased* from 7 percent to 14 percent; cumulative retirement at age 62 is reduced from 64 percent to 60 percent. At age 65, the cumulative rate is reduced from 86 percent to 80 percent. In particular, there are no noticeable jumps in retirement rates between ages 55 and 61, as there are under the current defined-benefit plan. The increased departure rates at younger ages occur because under the defined-contribution plan there is no incentive to wait for the jump in benefits that would occur at age 55 or at 30 years of service, when the 30-year provision would apply.

11.2.7   Postretirement Work

The typical American employee goes from full-time work to retirement, although a small proportion of workers are employed for a short period of time after retirement, typically fewer than three years. It may be that gradual withdrawal from the labor force would be preferred to the current practice. Our model estimation does not adequately recognize such possibilities. Nonetheless, to explore how a large change in retirement policy might affect departure rates, we consider an option to the present plan that *requires* persons who retire to work half-time (and, correspondingly, receive one-half current salary, with no salary increases) until age 70. In this case, we assume that the parameter k is 1 until age 70 and is the estimated value after age 70. The results suggest that such a plan would lead to much earlier retirement (see fig. 11.18). For example, cumulative retirement by age 55 is increased from 7 percent to 44 percent; the departure rate at age 55 is increased from 3 percent to 12 percent. The implication is that under this arrangement the discounted value of retirement plus pension benefits outweighs the value of continuing to work for many employees at a relatively young age. The implementation of the simulation, however, does not recognize the value of the leisure associated with half-time work. Were the value of leisure accounted for, the departure rates at younger ages would presumably be higher than the simulation implies.

Figure 11.17A   Simulation—Defined-Contribution Plan of 7.5 Percent: Data

	Retirement Rates			Cumulative Rates		
Age	Base	Simulation	Difference	Base	Simulation	Difference
50	0	0	0	0	0	0
51	0.007	0.011	0.004	0.007	0.011	0.004
52	0.009	0.017	0.008	0.016	0.028	0.012
53	0.01	0.022	0.012	0.025	0.05	0.025
54	0.016	0.036	0.02	0.041	0.084	0.043
55	0.029	0.056	0.027	0.068	0.135	0.067
56	0.036	0.06	0.024	0.102	0.187	0.085
57	0.056	0.084	0.028	0.152	0.255	0.103
58	0.067	0.091	0.024	0.208	0.323	0.115
59	0.106	0.086	−0.02	0.292	0.381	0.089
60	0.169	0.106	−0.063	0.412	0.447	0.035
61	0.165	0.105	−0.06	0.509	0.505	−0.004
62	0.262	0.19	−0.072	0.637	0.599	−0.038
63	0.22	0.189	−0.031	0.717	0.674	−0.043
64	0.249	0.182	−0.067	0.788	0.734	−0.054
65	0.35	0.259	−0.091	0.862	0.803	−0.059

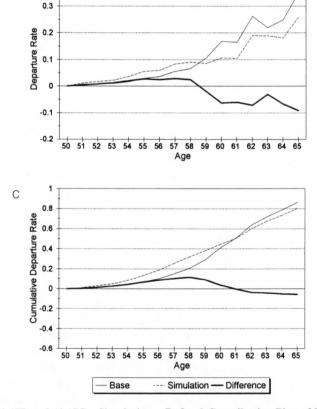

Figs. 11.17B and 11.17C   Simulation—Defined-Contribution Plan of 7.5 Percent
Note: (*B*) Retirement rates. (*C*) Cumulative rates.

Figure 11.18A   Simulation—Require Postretirement Work: Data

| Age | Retirement Rates | | | Cumulative Rates | | |
	Base	Simulation	Difference	Base	Simulation	Difference
50	0	0	0	0	0	0
51	0.007	0.107	0.1	0.007	0.107	0.1
52	0.009	0.104	0.095	0.016	0.199	0.183
53	0.01	0.108	0.098	0.025	0.286	0.261
54	0.016	0.105	0.089	0.041	0.361	0.32
55	0.029	0.123	0.094	0.068	0.439	0.371
56	0.036	0.127	0.091	0.102	0.511	0.409
57	0.056	0.148	0.092	0.152	0.583	0.431
58	0.067	0.159	0.092	0.208	0.65	0.442
59	0.106	0.186	0.08	0.292	0.715	0.423
60	0.169	0.225	0.056	0.412	0.779	0.367
61	0.165	0.22	0.055	0.509	0.828	0.319
62	0.262	0.246	−0.016	0.637	0.87	0.233
63	0.22	0.214	−0.006	0.717	0.898	0.181
64	0.249	0.219	−0.03	0.788	0.92	0.132
65	0.35	0.3	−0.05	0.862	0.944	0.082

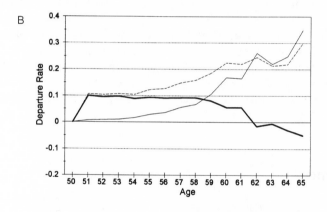

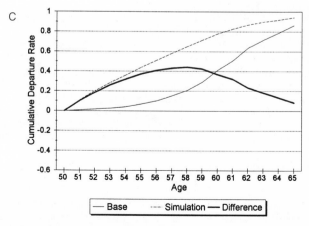

Figs. 11.18B and 11.18C   Simulation—Require Postretirement Work
Note: (*B*) Retirement rates. (*C*) Cumulative rates.

11.3 Summary

The results of the analysis support several conclusions. First, changes in key firm pension plan provisions would have very substantial effects on retirement. For example, increasing the firm early retirement age from 55 to 60 would reduce cumulative departure by age 59 from 29 percent to 4 percent. Second, the scheduled changes in Social Security provisions would have only a modest effect on firm retirement. The firm pension plan provisions dominate the Social Security provisions. Third, if changes in firm pension plan and Social Security provisions were coordinated—for example, if in both early retirement were at age 62 and normal retirement at age 67—the effect on retirement would be very substantial. For example, cumulative departure by age 61 would be reduced from 51 percent to 8 percent. Cumulative departure at age 65 would be 64 percent as compared with 86 percent in the base case. Although the individual simulations cannot be treated as exact, we have confidence in the general order of magnitude. In addition, the simulations suggest that the availability of retiree health insurance is associated with some increase in retirement between ages 55 and 65, although the effect is modest compared to the effect of pension plan provisions on retirement. We also considered the effect of very large changes in retirement policy—half-time work from retirement to age 70. Although these simulations must be considered as exploratory, the results suggest that such changes could change current retirement practices very substantially.

References

Ausink, John A. 1991. The effect of changes in compensation on a pilot's decision to leave the air force. Ph.D. diss., Harvard University.
Bulow, J. 1981. Early retirement pension benefits. NBER Working Paper no. 654. Cambridge, Mass.: National Bureau of Economic Research.
Commerce Clearing House. Business Law Editors. 1992. *Social Security explained.* Chicago: Commerce Clearing House, Inc.
Gruber, Jonathan, and Brigitte C. Madrian. 1996. Health insurance and early retirement: Evidence from the availability of continuation coverage. In *Advances in the economics of aging,* ed. D. Wise, 115–46. Chicago: University of Chicago Press.
Kotlikoff, Laurence J., and David A. Wise. 1985. Labor compensation and the structure of private pension plans: Evidence for contractual versus spot labor markets. In *Pensions, labor, and individual choice,* ed. D. Wise. Chicago: University of Chicago Press.
———. 1987. The incentive effects of private pension plans. In *Issues in pension economics,* ed. Z. Bodie, J. Shoven, and D. Wise, 283–339. Chicago: University of Chicago Press.
———. 1988. Pension backloading, wage taxes, and work disincentives. In *Tax policy and the economy,* ed. L. Summers, vol. 2. Cambridge: MIT Press.

Lazear, Edward P. 1983. Pensions as severance pay. *In Financial aspects of the United States pension system,* ed. Z. Bodie and J. Shoven. Chicago: University of Chicago Press.

Lumsdaine, Robin L., James H. Stock, and David A. Wise. 1990. Efficient windows and labor force reduction. *Journal of Public Economics* 43:131–59.

————. 1991. Windows and retirement. *Annales d'Économie et de Statistique* 20/21:219–42.

————. 1992. Three models of retirement: Computational complexity versus predictive validity. In *Topics in the economics of aging,* ed. D. Wise, 19–57. Chicago: University of Chicago Press.

————. 1994. Pension plan provisions and retirement: Men and women, Medicare, and models. In *Studies in the economics of aging,* ed. D. Wise, pp. 183–212. Chicago: University of Chicago Press.

Stock, James H., and David A. Wise. 1990a. The pension inducement to retire: An option value analysis. In *Issues in the economics of aging,* ed. D. Wise, 205–24. Chicago: University of Chicago Press.

————. 1990b. Pensions, the option value of work, and retirement. *Econometrica* 58, no. 5 (September): 1151–80.

12 Labor Market Implications of Social Security: Company Pension Plans, Public Pensions, and Retirement Behavior of the Elderly in Japan

Atsushi Seike

12.1 Introduction

As the proportion of older people in the Japanese population increases, the need for employment of the elderly also increases, for two reasons. First, an adequate ratio must be maintained between the number of pensioners and the number of pension taxpayers within the public pension system in order to keep the system financially healthy. Second, the size of the younger workforce will decline after the mid-1990s. To cope with the possible consequent labor shortage, we will need more labor supply from the older segment of the population.

The reality, however, is that more and more older workers have been retiring early in the past three decades. Figure 12.1 shows that the labor force participation rate among Japanese males aged 60–64 has been declining since the beginning of the 1960s. In 1962 it was around 83 percent, but toward the end of the 1980s it had declined to 71 percent, although there has been a small recovery in the past few years.

In fact, neither the employment system nor the pension system is consistent with the policy of promoting the employment of older workers in Japan. Among firms with 30 or more employees, 90 percent have mandatory retirement systems, and within these firms only 5.4 percent have a mandatory retirement age above the age of 60.[1] In addition, employers generally try to reduce the number of older employees even before they reach age 60 through several practices, such as early retirement options.[2]

Atsushi Seike is professor of business and commerce at Keio University.

1. According to the Employment Management Survey conducted by the Ministry of Labor, about 71 percent of firms with mandatory retirement have a mandatory retirement age of 60, about 12 percent have one of 56–59, and about 12 percent have one of 55.

2. According to the Severance Payment, Pensions and Mandatory Retirement Survey conducted by the Secretariat of Central Labor Arbitration Board, about two-thirds (66 percent) of large firms with 1,000 or more employees have some kind of early retirement option.

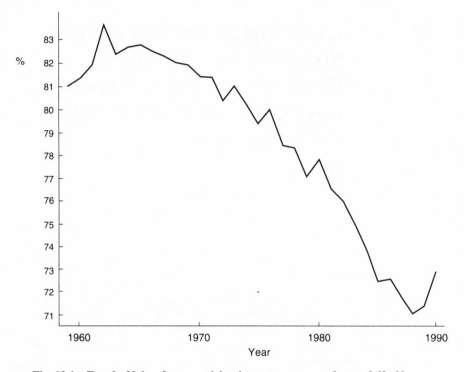

Fig. 12.1   Trend of labor force participation rate among males aged 60–64
Source: Management and Coordination Agency, *Annual Report on the Labor Force Survey* (Tokyo, 1960–90).

Furthermore, public pension policy may discourage older persons from continuing to work. Since the public pension plan has a rather strict earnings test, workers who are eligible for pension benefits cannot receive those benefits if their earnings exceed 250,000 yen per month. The typical male worker with a high school education who has contributed to the public pension plan for 32 years would have to forfeit a lifetime pension benefit equal to 10 percent of his annual salary each year if he worked full-time making more than 250,000 yen per month (Seike 1991).

The aim of this paper is to examine to what extent the ongoing institutional structures in Japan are inconsistent with the recent attempt to promote the employment of the elderly. For this purpose, we focus on one aspect of employment practice concerning older workers below the mandatory retirement age and on one aspect of the public pension scheme for older workers after mandatory retirement from their first job. These two aspects are the company severance payments of large Japanese corporations and the earnings test for the public pension plan.

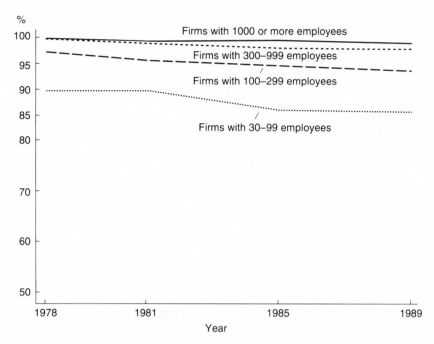

Fig. 12.2   Trend of proportion of firms with firm severance payments
Source: Ministry of Labor, *Retirement Allowance Survey* (Tokyo, 1978, 1981, 1985, 1989).

12.2   Company Severance Payments

A company severance payment is a payment from a company to an employee at separation. It is a very widespread practice among Japanese firms. Separations happen for one of two reasons—by the employee's quitting or through company discharge—and severance payments are made in both cases. The payment is usually more generous in the case of discharge.

Figure 12.2 shows the proportion of firms with severance payment options among firms with 30 or more employees. As shown in figure 12.2, almost 100 percent of large (1,000 or more employees) and large-medium (300–999 employees) firms offer severance payments. Even among medium-small (100–299 employees) and small (30–99 employees) firms, almost 90 percent offer severance payments.

The separation payment at the age of mandatory retirement, which is regarded as discharge or termination of the employment contract due to the employee's age, is the most generous such severance payment and is called the "retirement allowance." Figure 12.3 shows the average retirement allowance of workers retiring at the mandatory retirement age, broken down by educational level and length of service. Workers with a college degree and more than 35 years of service receive 24 million yen. This amount is equivalent to 44

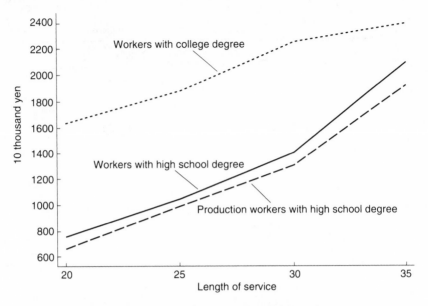

Fig. 12.3   Amount of retirement allowance by length of service
Source: Ministry of Labor, *Retirement Allowance Survey* (Tokyo, 1989).

months' salary at age 60. The amount of the payment clearly depends on the length of service, and payments increase disproportionately as the length of service increases. As the most extreme case in figure 12.3, a production worker with a high school degree who has more than 35 years of service will receive almost three times more than one who has 20–24 years of service.

These company severance payments, particularly the retirement allowance, are believed to be an important way for employers to encourage employees to stay with the same firm (e.g., see Odaka 1984). Lumsdaine and Wise (1994), however, described a conspicuous tendency among American employers to design company pension plans that encourage employees to leave the firm at the normal retirement age, which is designated by the employer. Japanese employers, who are legally allowed to institute a mandatory retirement practice, do not seem to have built this incentive into their companies' pension schemes.

Figure 12.4 shows company severance payments by age for regular workers with a college degree who have quit their companies. "Regular worker" is defined here to be a worker who joined the firm right after graduation from school (in this case from college) and who has been working for the same firm since. Thus, regular workers of the same age will have the same length of service. For example, regular workers who have a college degree and are 27 years old will always have 5 years of service, and those 55 years old will have 33 years of service. Here we observe company severance payments only in the case of employees who have quit because we are interested in the effect of the incen-

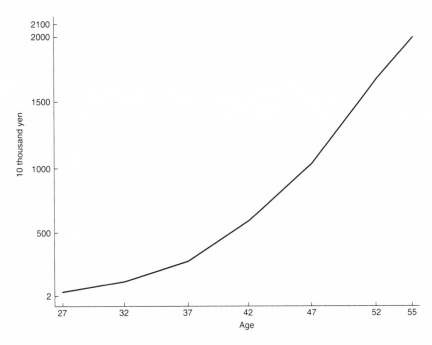

Fig. 12.4   Firm severance payment by age (regular workers with college degree)
Source: Secretariat of Central Labor Arbitration Board, *Severance Payment, Pensions and Mandatory Retirement* (Tokyo, 1992).

tive scheme of severance payments on the company attachment behavior of employees. No cases of separation by discharge are shown.

As seen in figure 12.4, the amount of the company severance payment increases as the employee ages within the firm. Thus the employee is rewarded for staying with the firm longer. Company severance payments certainly seem to be designed to promote employee attachment to the company.

Theoretically, however, firms that have age/tenure-related wage profiles may have an incentive to let employees leave when their wages exceed their marginal productivity (see Lazear 1982). In fact, in the current recession, many interesting casual observations suggest that Japanese employers are willing to let their middle-aged and older managers leave before the mandatory retirement age.

Figure 12.5 shows the ratio of company severance payments by age for regular workers who have quit compared to those who have been discharged. This ratio should always be smaller than 1, and the gap between severance payments for workers who have quit and those for workers who have been discharged can be regarded as the penalty for quitting. The company severance payment in discharge cases is the severance payment paid when the employer wishes to let the employee leave. If the ratio between severance payments for workers

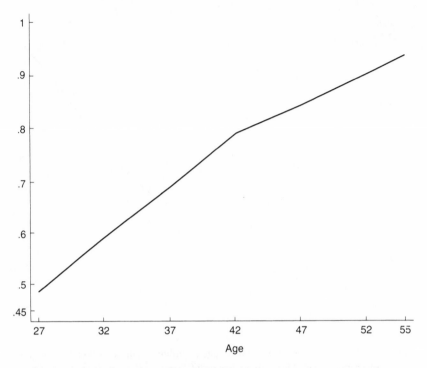

Fig. 12.5   Severance payments in quitting cases as a proportion of those in discharge cases
Source: Secretariat of Central Labor Arbitration Board, *Severance Payment, Pensions and Mandatory Retirement* (Tokyo, 1987).

who quit versus those for workers who are discharged equals 1, there is no motivation for employers to keep their employees or to penalize those who quit. In other words, the penalty for quitting should be zero when the ratio between firm severance payments for workers who have quit and those for workers who have been discharged is 1. As the employers' motivation to keep employees increases, the penalty becomes larger and the ratio becomes smaller. Figure 12.5 clearly shows that the proportion increases as the age of regular workers—that is, their length of service to the company—increases. The proportion goes up to 0.95 for regular workers aged 55.

This observation suggests that employers' motivation to encourage their employees to stay longer weakens as the employees get older. When regular workers reach age 55, employers have almost the same degree of motivation to let them leave the firm voluntarily as to discharge them. It seems that company severance payments in Japan encourage employees to stay longer while they are young but to leave when they get old. This hypothesis is examined in the next section.

2.3   Net Severance Payment Wealth

Kotlikoff and Wise (1985) calculated vested pension benefit wealth for U.S. company pensions. The same kind of calculation is not available in Japan because of data limitations and because most Japanese firms do not pay retirement allowances for employees who quit before the mandatory retirement age. Instead, as noted in the previous section, Japanese firms usually make severance payments to employees who quit. We can calculate "net severance payment wealth" by using the figures for these payments. There is a net gain in the amount of company severance payments if workers postpone quitting for one year.

Net severance payment wealth for regular workers is defined as

$$(1) \qquad \text{NSPW}(a) = \text{SP}(a + 1) - \text{SP}(a) \times (1 + r),$$

where $\text{NSPW}(a)$ is the net severance payment at age a, $\text{SP}(a)$ is the severance payment at age a, and r is the market interest rate.[3] If the principal and interest of the severance payment at age a is smaller than the severance payment at age $a + 1$, namely, if $\text{SW}(a + 1) > \text{SW}(a) \times (1 + r)$, the employee gains positive net severance payment wealth by postponing quitting for a year.

The data we used for calculating net severance payment wealth is from the Severance Payment, Pensions and Mandatory Retirement Survey conducted in 1985 and 1987 by the Secretariat of Central Labor Arbitration Board. These are the most detailed data currently available on company severance payments in Japan. One noteworthy limitation of this data set is that it comes from a survey only of large firms with 1,000 or more employees.

The observed company severance payment here, called the "model severance payment," shows severance payments for workers who have quit. These are regular workers who joined the firm right after graduation from school and stayed with the firm until each observed age and length of service category. The age and length of service categories are observed as a pair. For example, they are observed as age 25 and 3 years of service, age 27 and 5 years of service, . . . , age 55 and 33 years of service, and so forth, for regular workers with a college degree. Therefore, both age and length of service are the same time variable, and here we just use age as the time variable.

Although age is categorized at two- or five-year intervals in this data set, we need severance payments by each age to calculate equation (1). To obtain that age through the age figures of firm severance payments, we must interpolate it from the age severance payments. Because the shape of severance payments is nonlinear, as seen in figure 12.4, we estimate the following quadratic equation as the firm severance payment function:

$$(2) \qquad \text{SP}(a) = \alpha_0 + \alpha_1 a + \alpha_2 a^2 + u,$$

3. We used the government bond yield as the market interest rate.

Table 12.1   Estimated Results of Firm Severance Payment Functions

Industry and Type of Worker	Year	Constant	Age (t-value)	Age^2 (t-value)	Adjusted R^2
Manufacturing					
Workers with college degree	1985	18,443.6	−1,346.53	24.9618	0.9959
		(4.54)	(−6.57)	(10.09)	
	1987	19,769.7	−1,425.32	26.1744	0.9985
		(7.73)	(−11.05)	(16.81)	
Workers with high school degree	1985	6,327.53	−599.823	14.3442	0.9983
		(4.43)	(−7.86)	(14.93)	
	1987	7,079.49	−651.216	15.2529	0.9991
		(6.70)	(−11.53)	(21.45)	
Banking					
Workers with college degree	1985	24,789.6	−1,723.15	30.3828	0.9631
		(1.83)	(−2.52)	(3.68)	
	1987	29,808.6	−2,028.04	35.1522	0.9901
		(3.82)	(−5.16)	(7.41)	
Railway and bus					
Workers with college degree	1985	23,847.7	−1,912.13	37.9930	0.9959
		(3.45)	(−5.88)	(9.05)	
	1987	21,700.5	−1,777.71	36.0295	0.9953
		(3.01)	(−4.89)	(8.20)	
Department store and supermarket					
Workers with college degree	1985	22,864.6	−1,607.15	28.7393	0.9900
		(3.36)	(−4.67)	(6.94)	
	1987	21,290.5	−1,514.01	27.4003	0.9916
		(3.49)	(−4.92)	(7.38)	

where $SP(a)$ is the firm severance payment at age a, $\alpha_0 \sim \alpha_2$ are parameters, and u is a normally distributed random term. Estimated results of severance payment equation (2) are shown in table 12.1. We estimated the equation by industry and by educational category for the manufacturing industry.

By using these equations, we can interpolate firm severance payments by age. Although equation (1) is the net severance payment wealth for one year, the interval of the survey data is two years. Therefore, we have to calculate net severance payment wealth as follows:

(3) $NSPW(a) = SP(a + 2) - SP(a) \times (1 + r)^2.$

Thus $NSPW(a)$ actually calculated here is the net severance payment wealth gained by postponing quitting for two years.

Figure 12.6 shows the calculated net severance payment wealth of regular workers with a college degree in the manufacturing industry by age. As seen in figure 12.6, employees receive 100,000–1,550,000 yen of net severance payment wealth by postponing quitting for two years. The rate of increase of net severance payment wealth by age rises when employees are relatively young

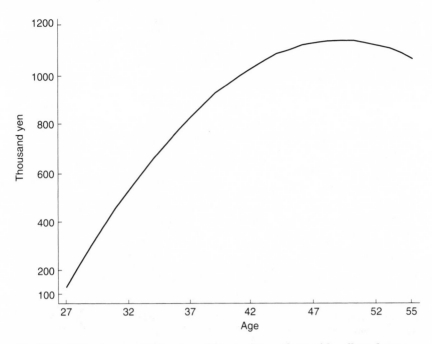

Fig. 12.6   Net severance payment wealth: regular workers with college degree in the manufacturing industry

and peaks in the mid-forties. After reaching this peak, the net severance payment wealth profile begins to decline.

Figure 12.7 shows the same calculated result of net severance payment wealth for regular workers with a high school degree in the manufacturing industry. Again the net severance payment wealth increases with age up to the mid-forties and begins to decline thereafter. Net severance payment wealth is distributed between 20,000–65,000 yen, a narrower range of distribution than for workers with a college degree, as shown in figure 12.6.

Figures 12.8, 12.9, and 12.10 show net severance payment wealth by industry for regular workers with a college degree. Figure 12.8 represents the banking industry, and unlike the manufacturing industry, net severance payment wealth increases steadily. Figure 12.9 shows the railway and bus industry, and figure 12.10 shows the department store and supermarket industry. For both these industries, net severance payment wealth peaks in the latter half of the thirties and the early forties and declines thereafter. Furthermore, net severance payment wealth turns out to be negative after age 50, and employees who postpone quitting for two years at age 55 have to sustain a 600,000-yen net loss.

The fact that net severance payment wealth is positive and increases in the earlier part of an employee's career within a firm suggests that employers have a growing motivation to keep employees in their twenties to mid-forties, when

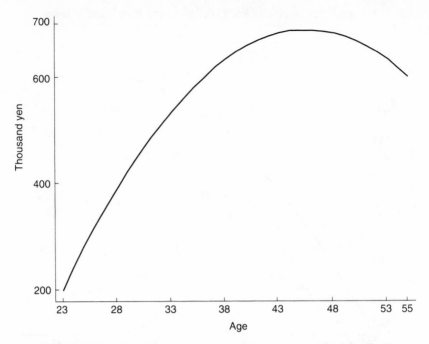

Fig. 12.7 Net severance payment wealth: regular workers with high school degree in manufacturing industry

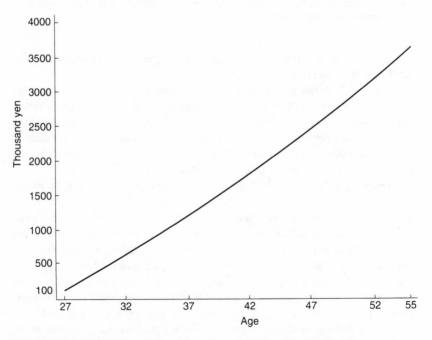

Fig. 12.8 Net severance payment wealth: regular workers with college degree in banking industry

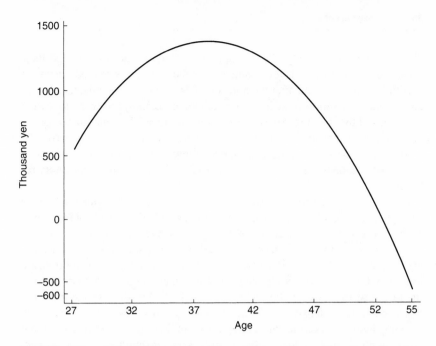

Fig. 12.9 Net severance payment wealth: regular workers with college degree in railway and bus industry

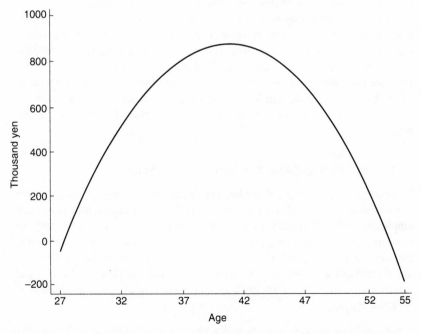

Fig. 12.10 Net severance payment wealth: regular workers with college degree in department store and supermarket industry

the marginal productivity of these employees is more likely to exceed their wages in the long-term labor contract. The fact that net severance payment wealth begins to decline after the mid-forties is consistent with the theory that employers' motivation to keep their middle-aged employees decreases when the wages of these employees are more likely to exceed their marginal productivity. In some industries, net severance payment wealth is even negative for workers aged 50 and over. This fact suggests that employers in some industries have a motivation to let their older workers leave the firm before mandatory retirement.

One curious case shown above is the banking industry, in which net severance payment wealth increases steadily up to age 55. Does the banking industry have a strong need to keep its older employees? On the contrary, it is a well-known phenomenon that in large banking firms, only several selected managers can survive after age 50. Most of the other workers aged 50 and over are transferred to other firms with which the banks have enough influence to force the hiring of these ex-employees. One possible explanation for the inconsistency is that the extensive use of this transfer practice gives employers in the banking industry room to cut an expensive middle-aged workforce without encouraging voluntary leave. And if only selected employees can be kept within a bank as higher-level managers, it is even wise for the employers to maintain a severance payment scheme that fosters strong loyalty and attachment to the bank in the remaining employees until their retirement.

The above results may have two implications. First, they reconfirm the theory that the firm severance payment is designed to encourage employees to stay longer, at least during the earlier part of their career within a firm. Second, it confirms that this characteristic of the firm severance payment—its use to promote firm attachment among employees—begins to weaken after workers are in their forties. Indeed, in some industries, firm severance payment schemes are designed to encourage employees to leave early, when they reach their fifties.

12.4   The Effect of Public Pensions on Labor Supply

Although in some cases described above firm severance payments give employees an incentive to leave the firm before the age of mandatory retirement, employees' jobs are usually guaranteed up until the mandatory retirement age. Now more than 80 percent of firms with mandatory retirement set the mandatory retirement age at 60. However, employment conditions for workers who are searching for second job opportunities beyond age 60 are relatively bad. For example, an average monthly wage may be as low as half of the employee's previous wage.[4]

4. Average monthly wages for a male worker with 1–2 years of service aged 60–64 are about 210,000 yen, whereas those for workers with 30 years of service aged 55–59 are about 420,000 yen.

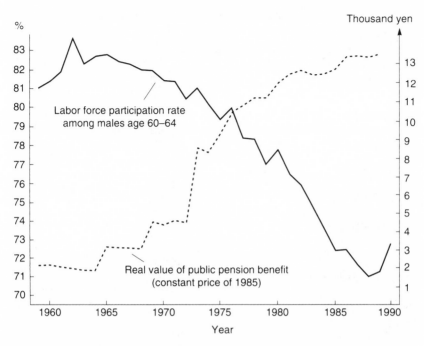

Fig. 12.11   Contrast between trend of labor force participation rate and public pension benefit

Sources: Social Security Agency, *Annual Report* (Tokyo, 1959–90); Management and Coordination Agency, *Annual Report on the Labor Force Survey* (Tokyo, 1959–90).

These undesirable employment conditions undoubtedly discourage older workers who are 60 years old or over from continuing to work. On the other hand, conditions that enable older workers to retire at age 60 and over have been established in the past two decades. Figure 12.11 shows the sharp contrast between the declining labor force participation rate among older males aged 60–64 and the improvement of public pension benefits in Japan in the past several decades. Particularly remarkable is the increase in the real benefit of public pensions after 1973, when the Japanese Ministry of Welfare substantially revised the pension system. This revision introduced an indexation of past wages, which is the principal determinant of public pension benefits, and introduced an indexation of the determined benefit level to allow the real value of future benefits to keep up with inflation.

The "model public pension benefit" for regular workers who have paid tax to the public pension system for 35 years is now about 220,000 yen per month. This is about 65 percent of the average monthly wage, not including bonus payments. Although this amount does not seem to be enough to live a comfortable life, pensioners are at least able to refuse undesirable jobs with low wages and are able to retire on their public pension benefits.

Table 12.2   Empirical Results of the Labor Supply of the Elderly

Variable	Participation Function	Market Wage Function
Constant	4.142	1.263
	(11.348)	(4.321)
Age	−0.017	−0.028
	(−8.378)	(−5.803)
Health dummy	−0.331	−0.282
	(26.861)	(−4.935)
High school dummy	0.037	0.391
	(2.745)	(15.438)
College dummy	0.087	0.670
	(2.616)	(12.333)
Social Security eligiblity dummy	−0.153	
	(−11.429)	
Other nonearned income	−0.0002	
	(−4.386)	
Mandatory retirement dummy	−0.177	−0.361
	(−13.103)	(−8.298)
Tokyo metropolitan residence dummy	0.056	0.211
	(3.688)	(7.338)
Lambda		0.544
		(5.143)
Sample size	7,014	4,559
Log-likelihood	−3859.3	
Adjusted R^2		0.1273
		($F = 96.073$)

Source: Seike (1989).

The impact of the public pension on labor supply behavior has already been confirmed by a cross-sectional study. Table 12.2 shows estimated results using Heckman's labor supply model for older male workers in Japan. Table 12.2 has two parts: (1) the estimated result of the probit function of the labor supply, which includes a public pension eligibility variable, which is free from the simultaneous bias that the pension benefit variable has, and (2) the estimated result of the market wage function, which is free from sample selection bias by including the lambda variable, which eliminates the bias (Heckman 1979).

As seen in table 12.2, all parameters were estimated in a statistically significant fashion, and eligibility to receive pension benefits reduces the possibility of labor force participation by 15 percent. It is clear that the public pension has a significant negative impact on the labor supply.

The effect of the public pension on the labor supply includes not only the income effect of benefits but also the effect of the earnings test, which may discourage labor supply more than the income effect alone would. The public pension system has an earnings test, which is not an implicit tax scheme like the U.S. Social Security System, but a lump-sum tax at several pensioner earn-

Table 12.3   **Earnings Test of Public Pension System in 1983**

Earnings (thousand yen)	Rate of Reduction (%) = Lump-Sum Tax Rate on Benefits
0	0
–95	20
95–130	50
130–155	80
155+	100

Source: Health and Welfare Statistics Association, *Trends of Insurance and Pension* (Tokyo, 1985).

ings levels. For example, in the scheme that was used until 1985, public pension benefits had to be reduced by 20–100 percent depending on the earnings level of the pensioner (table 12.3). This lump-sum tax makes the budget line of pensioners kinked as in figure 12.12. In figure 12.12, suppose the original budget line of a person is OE (market wage rate is w). The person becomes eligible to receive public pension benefits, and the full pension benefits for the person, shown as OA, may shift his or her budget line from OE to AE'. However, the earnings test described in table 12.3 makes this person's budget line like AA'BB'CC'DD'E.

The kinked budget constraint shown in figure 12.12 may allow pensioners to reach an equilibrium at a kinked point of the budget line, for example, point B. This means that the beneficiary chooses to reduce labor supply to avoid the lump-sum tax at the earnings level of 95,000 yen per month. We confirmed the equilibrium of public-pension-eligible workers at the kinked points in a previous study.

Figure 12.13 shows the earnings distribution of public-pension-eligible and noneligible workers in 1983.[5] The earnings distribution of public-pension-eligible workers has a clear mode at the earnings level of 90,000–100,000 yen per month, which corresponds to the kinked point of the budget constraint, beyond which pension-eligible workers had to pay 50 percent of a lump-sum tax on their pension benefits. Because the earnings distribution of noneligible workers does not have this shape, the characteristics of the earnings distribution of pension-eligible workers could be regarded as singular. This shows that there was a clear effect of the earnings test on the labor supply behavior of public-pension-eligible workers under the earnings test scheme of 1983.

12.5   The Revision of the Earnings Test

The effect of the earnings test on the labor supply may not be consistent with the current policy that attempts to promote the employment of older people in

---

5. We controlled the data to include only workers in good health and with mandatory retirement experience from their previous job.

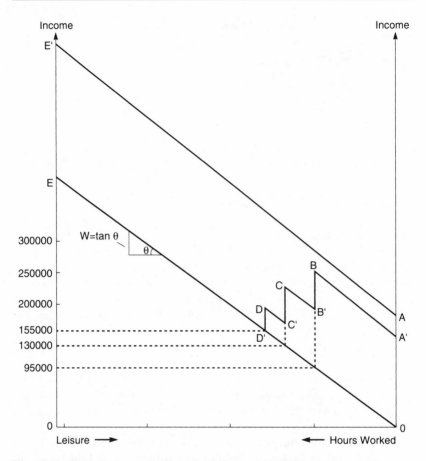

Fig. 12.12   Budget constraint line of public-pension-eligible workers under earnings test scheme in 1983

Japan. Although the improvement in public pension benefits that enables older workers to retire is an important achievement of our society, it is not necessary to discourage the working incentive of older people excessively by the lump-sum tax of the earnings test. We need to have a more neutral earnings test scheme so as not to unduly influence labor supply behavior.

Of course the earnings test does not always cause an equilibrium of public-pension-eligible workers at the kinked point that corresponds to earnings of 95,000 yen, as described in figure 12.13. The equilibrium point depends particularly on the full level of pension benefits for pensioners. For example, if the full level of pension benefits is small enough, as shown in figure 12.14, the point C or D could be chosen as the equilibrium point. However, it is not adequate for us to reduce the level of original full pension benefits in order to

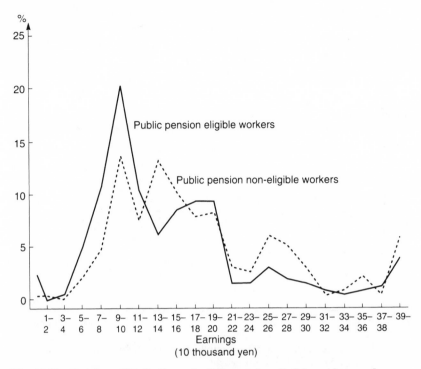

Fig. 12.13   **Earnings distributions of public-pension-eligible workers and noneligible workers in 1983**

minimize the likelihood that an individual equilibrium will fall at one of kinked points of the budget line corresponding to lower earnings levels.

The other way to minimize the influence of the earnings test is to subdivide the its steps. In fact, the Ministry of Welfare revised the earnings test scheme in this way in 1985. The revised scheme is shown in table 12.4. The graduations in the earnings test were increased from three steps under the previous scheme to seven steps under the revised scheme.

According to this revised earnings test the budget line of the public-pension-eligible person is as shown in figure 12.15. Unlike the three steps in the budget line in figure 12.12, which is based on the previous earnings test scheme, the budget line of an eligible person under the revised earnings test scheme becomes more precise, as described by AA′BB′CC′DD′EE′FF′GG′HH′J in figure 12.15. As figure 12.15 shows, it is not only the kinked point B that represents lower earnings but also the kinked points C to H, which, corresponding to higher earnings, could be chosen as equilibrium points of public-pension-eligible workers, although the reward for working past point B is still very small.

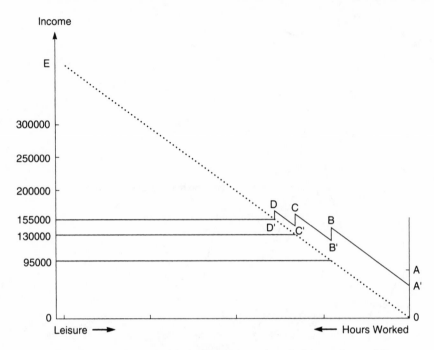

Fig. 12.14   Budget constraint line of public-pension-eligible workers with relatively low level of full pension benefit

Table 12.4   Earnings Test of Public Pension System in 1988

Earnings (thousand yen)	Rate of Reduction (%) = Lump-Sum Tax Rate on Benefits
0	0
–95	20
95–114	30
114–138	40
138–165	50
165–185	60
185–210	70
210–250	80
250+	100

Source: Health and Welfare Statistics Association, *Trends of Insurance and Pension* (Tokyo, 1985).

If the distribution of equilibrium points of public-pension-eligible workers becomes more widely spread under the revised scheme than under the previous scheme, the distribution of earnings should also be more widely spread than it was under the previous scheme, as shown in figure 12.13.

Figure 12.16 is the earnings distribution of working pensioners in 1988. The

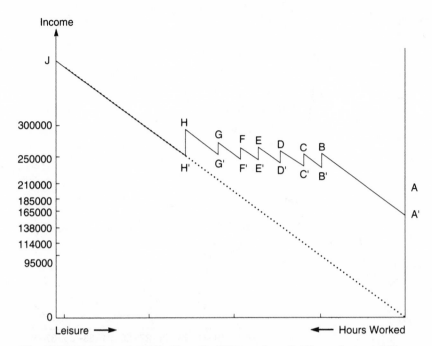

Fig. 12.15   Budget constraint line of public-pension-eligible workers under revised earnings test scheme

data we used to make the distribution here are from the Survey on the Working Situation of the Elderly (1988) conducted by the Ministry of Labor. Unfortunately, unlike those from the previous survey in 1983, which we used to describe the distribution of public-pension-eligible workers shown in figure 12.13, the data from 1988 do not identify public-pension-eligible workers but only workers who are actually receiving pension benefits. The distribution of earnings of working pensioners under the revised earnings test scheme has a clear mode at the earnings level 90,000–100,000 yen, which is quite similar to that of pension-eligible workers in 1983. This suggests that the revision introduced by the Ministry of Welfare to reduce the likelihood of equilibria at the kinked points corresponding to lower earnings had little effect on the labor supply behavior of public-pension-eligible workers. This difficulty may be that the revision provided a very limited increase in reward for working beyond the first kinked point of the budget line (point B of figure 12.15).

12.6   Conclusions

It is important for us to promote more employment of older people in order to cope with the growing number of elderly in the years to come. But employ-

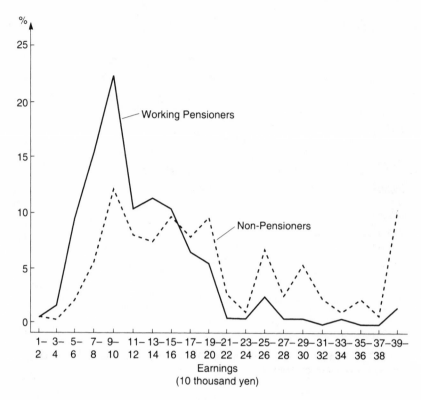

Fig. 12.16   Earnings distribution of working pensioners and nonpensioners in 1988

ment practice in Japanese firms—designed as an efficient instrument for focusing on younger workers within a pyramid-shaped population—has not utilized older workers and has not offered them attractive employment conditions so far. Also, public systems, including the public pension system, were designed when we did not need to promote the employment of older people.

In this paper we examined to what extent systems that were established under the old circumstances of the Japanese economy are disturbing the policy target under new circumstances. Of these systems we focused on firm severance payments and public pension policies.

Our analysis of firm severance payment policy suggests that employers are motivated to keep younger workers whose wages are relatively cheap and to let older workers whose wages have become expensive relative to their productivity leave the firm.

The Japanese public pension system has given older people the freedom to choose retirement in the past two decades. However, its earnings test scheme, particularly its lump-sum tax on pension benefits according to the pensioner's earnings level, excessively discourages pension-eligible workers from supplying more labor. The 1985 revision that tried to minimize this negative effect seems not to have succeeded in its original purpose so far.

References

Heckman, J. J. 1979. Sample selection bias as a specification error. *Econometrica* 47:153–62.

Kotlikoff, L. J., and D. A. Wise. 1985. Labor compensation and the structure of private pension plans: Evidence for contractual versus spot labor markets. In *Pensions, labor and individual choice,* ed. D. A. Wise. Chicago: University of Chicago Press.

Lumsdaine, R. L., and D. A. Wise. 1994. Aging and labor force participation: A review of trends and explanations. In *Aging in the United States and Japan: Economic trends,* ed. Y. Noguchi and D. A. Wise. Chicago: University of Chicago Press.

Lazear, E. P. 1982. Severance pay, pensions, and efficient mobility. NBER Working Paper no. 854. Cambridge, Mass.: National Bureau of Economic Research.

Odaka, Konosuke. 1984. *Labor market analysis* (in Japanese). Tokyo: Iwanami Shoten.

Seike, Atsushi. 1989. The effect of the employee pension on the labor supply of the Japanese elderly. Rand Note no. 2862. Santa Monica, Calif.: RAND Corporation.

———. 1991. Pension wealth and labor supply (in Japanese). *Economic Review* 42:12–20.

IV Public Pension Reform

13   Changing Social Security Survivorship Benefits and the Poverty of Widows

Michael D. Hurd and David A. Wise

13.1 Introduction

Survivorship benefit is a feature of most public pension systems. In the United States a widow can receive Social Security benefits following the death of her husband even though she may not have made contributions to the Social Security system during her lifetime. Such a benefit is based on her deceased husband's record of contributions to the Social Security system. The survivor's Social Security benefit is determined by a complex set of rules. A 33 percent reduction in the prior couple's benefit is typical. There is no reason, however, to believe that this reduction is optimal. It is not based on a theoretical principle or on empirical findings. We consider in this paper how changes in U.S. Social Security survivorship benefits might be expected to change the income and poverty rate of surviving spouses and of prior couples. We focus on widows because they constitute more than three-fourths of elderly unmarried persons in the United States.

In principle, a widower can receive benefits based on his deceased wife's earnings record, but in practice this is quite rare because usually his benefit based on his own earnings record will be higher than his widower's benefit and he is entitled to the higher benefit. For this reason, we shall often refer to the survivor's benefit under the U.S. Social Security system as a widow's benefit.

Although the Social Security benefit can fall by as much as 50 percent at

Michael D. Hurd is professor of economics at the State University of New York, Stony Brook, and a research associate of the National Bureau of Economic Research. David A. Wise is the John F. Stambaugh Professor of Political Economy at the John F. Kennedy School of Government, Harvard University, and director for Health and Retirement Programs at the National Bureau of Economic Research.

Financial support from the Japan Foundation Center for Global Partnership and from the Commonwealth Fund (grant 11180) is gratefully acknowledged. The authors thank Kathleen McGarry for excellent research assistance.

the death of the husband, a decline of about one-third is typical. Using the Retirement History Survey (RHS), Hurd and Wise (1989) calculate the average Social Security wealth (the expected present value of Social Security benefits) of couples and surviving spouses among families in which the husband died between 1975 and 1977. The average wealth of the couples was $63,700 in 1975. The average Social Security wealth of the surviving spouses was $40,400 in 1977. This implies a reduction in Social Security income of about one-third.

Social Security is the most important component of the income of most elderly families in the United States.[1] In 1988, Social Security benefits were 45.9 percent of the income of elderly unmarried women (Grad 1990).[2] One-third of unmarried women relied on Social Security for at least 90 percent of their income; 20 percent had income only from Social Security. It is not surprising, therefore, that the drop in Social Security benefits at the death of her husband could have large effects on the economic status of the surviving widow, particularly a widow at the lower end of the income distribution, and that the incidence of poverty would be high among elderly widows.

In the United States a single elderly person is said to be "in poverty" if his or her income is below the poverty line, $5,674 in 1988 ($6,729 in 1992). In 1988, 21 percent of unmarried elderly women lived in poverty, and 34 percent had incomes less than 125 percent of the poverty line. The poverty rate depends on living arrangements and age. Among women aged 85 or older who were not living with family members, the poverty rate was 28 percent. In contrast, the poverty rate among couples aged 85 or over was just 6 percent.

Panel data show clearly that the transition to widowhood increases poverty substantially. Table 13.1, taken from Hurd and Wise (1989), shows the poverty rates of couples in which the husband survived between 1975 and 1977 and of couples in which the husband died between 1975 and 1977. In 1975 the poverty rates were about the same, but in 1977 the poverty rate of surviving widows was 42 percent. Even among couples with incomes above the poverty line in 1975, the poverty rate of the surviving widow was 37 percent in 1977 (last column of table 13.1). These results, which are representative of the transitions over other two-year periods, show that the high poverty rates of widows are not just due to widows' being the long-lived survivors of the household; the transition to widowhood is, itself, associated with an increase in poverty rates. The issue is also discussed by Holden, Burkhauser, and Feaster (1988).

The difference between the poverty rates of elderly widows and elderly couples and the importance of Social Security benefits to widows suggest that a restructuring of benefits could have an important effect on poverty. An increase in the widow's benefit financed by a reduction in the couple's benefit—so that expected costs are unchanged—could reduce the poverty rate of widows in a

---

1. In this paper by "elderly" we mean those aged 65 or over.
2. The great majority of unmarried elderly women are widows.

Table 13.1   **Poverty Rates (percent) According to Marital Transition 1975–77**

| | Entire Sample | | Not Poor in 1975 | |
Year	Couple to Couple[a]	Couple to Widow[b]	Couple to Couple[a]	Couple to Widow[b]
1969	5	8	3	5
1971	7	11	4	7
1973	8	8	4	4
1975	8	9	0	0
1977	7	42	4	37
1979	11	40	11	35

Source: Hurd and Wise (1989).
[a]Husband survived between 1975 and 1977.
[b]Husband died between 1975 and 1977.

material way, possibly without increasing substantially the poverty rate of couples.[3] Indeed, such a restructuring could increase aggregate economic welfare.

13.2   Methods and Data

All of our illustrations are designed to be cost-neutral: an increase in the survivor's benefit must be offset by a reduction in the benefit of couples. For example, consider a 70-year-old husband and his 67-year-old wife. If their couple's benefit is $100, typically the surviving spouse would have a benefit of about $67. Suppose that benefit were increased by 20 percent to about $80. What would the reduction in the couple's benefit have to be to keep the expected present value of the Social Security benefits of the couple and surviving spouse (widow or widower) constant? The solution requires iterations using life tables and interest rate assumptions.[4] It depends on the ages of both husband and wife, so it varies from couple to couple. The average required reduction in our data is about 11 percent.

The primary data source for our calculations is the Retirement History Survey (RHS).[5] The RHS is a 10-year panel of about 11,000 households whose heads were aged 58–63 in 1969. The households were interviewed every two

3. Couples cannot by themselves accomplish such a restructuring by saving part of their Social Security benefit so as to increase the resources of the widow because they cannot buy indexed annuities with their savings; therefore, they lose the inflation protection and mortality premium of Social Security. Furthermore, the saving decision by the couple may not be in the best interest of the widow. For example, prior to the Retirement Equity Act of 1984, most private pensions, which were typically in the husband's name, had no survivorship rights (Myers, Burkhauser, and Holden 1987). This suggests that the husband, who typically controls any pension, does not adequately value the utility of the widow.
4. We use a real interest rate of 3 percent in these calculations.
5. See Hurd and Shoven (1985) for a description of the RHS and the data.

Table 13.2   **Average Social Security Benefits (1979 dollars)**

Year	Couples			Widows			Singles
	$k=1.0$	$k=1.1$	$k=1.2$	$k=1.0$	$k=1.1$	$k=1.2$	$k=1.0$
1969	402	384	366	683	752	820	283
1971	854	814	773	987	1,085	1,184	572
1973	2,144	2,036	1,929	1,643	1,807	1,972	1,315
1975	3,325	3,152	2,978	2,149	2,351	2,553	2,157
1977	4,528	4,279	4,031	2,661	2,913	3,164	2,698
1979	4,690	4,419	4,148	2,667	2,921	3,176	2,722

Source: Authors' calculations from the RHS.

years. In addition to extensive data on income and assets, the RHS reports the Social Security earnings records of both husbands and wives through 1974. By combining these data with observed earnings after 1974 we can calculate with considerable accuracy the Social Security benefits of husbands and of wives.

We investigate several alternative increases in the Social Security benefits of survivors. We represent the increase by k. For example, $k = 1.1$ means that the widow's benefit would be increased by 10 percent; $k = 1.2$ means that the widow's benefit would be increased by 20 percent. Given an assumed value of k, we calculate for each couple in the sample the reduction in the Social Security benefit of the couple that would make the assumed increase in the widow's benefit actuarially neutral. By making the calculations for each couple we preserve the distribution of Social Security income and total income so that we can calculate poverty rates.

Our measure of poverty is based on money income: no income is imputed to owner-occupied housing or to noncash transfers such as Medicare. Imputations for owner-occupied housing and Medicare reduce poverty rates very substantially (see, e.g., Hurd and Wise 1989; Hurd 1990).

Social Security benefits in 1979 dollars are reported in table 13.2. Actual Social Security benefits averaged over all households (not just those receiving benefits) are shown in the columns headed "$k = 1.0$." The heads of the households were aged 58–63 in 1969 and 68–73 in 1979. The averages include Supplemental Security Income (SSI) payments, which are additional payments to low-income households. We have not changed SSI by the value of k because SSI is not really an old-age pension; rather it is old-age assistance. As a consequence, the entries for widows for $k = 1.1$ and 1.2 are not exactly 10 percent and 20 percent higher than the entries for $k = 1.0$. We show the mean Social Security benefits of singles for reference. Their benefits are not increased under this system because there is no corresponding couple to pay for the increase through a benefit reduction. The means increase with age primarily because more households receive benefits as household members retire.

Consider the data for 1979. Under the actual Social Security provisions ($k = 1.0$), the mean benefit to married couples was \$4,690 in 1979 and the mean

Table 13.3   **Effects of Changes in Social Security Benefits on Average Poverty Rates: Marital Transition 1971–73**

Poverty Status and Year	Couple to Couple[a]			Couple to Widow[b]		
	$k=1.0$	$k=1.1$	$k=1.2$	$k=1.0$	$k=1.1$	$k=1.2$
Total sample						
1969	0.06	0.06	0.06	0.10	0.10	0.10
1971	0.08	0.08	0.08	0.11	0.11	0.12
1973	0.09	0.09	0.10	0.38	0.38	0.36
1975	0.10	0.10	0.11	0.25	0.23	0.20
1977	0.11	0.11	0.12	0.24	0.21	0.20
1979	0.13	0.13	0.14	0.27	0.22	0.17
Not poor in 1971						
1969	0.03	0.03	0.03	0.03	0.03	0.02
1971	0.00	0.00	0.00	0.00	0.00	0.00
1973	0.05	0.05	0.06	0.34	0.33	0.31
1975	0.07	0.07	0.08	0.21	0.19	0.16
1977	0.08	0.08	0.08	0.20	0.17	0.14
1979	0.10	0.10	0.10	0.22	0.17	0.11
Poor in 1971						
1969	0.47	0.47	0.46	0.61	0.61	0.63
1971	1.00	1.00	1.00	1.00	1.00	1.00
1973	0.55	0.55	0.58	0.71	0.71	0.70
1975	0.50	0.51	0.52	0.61	0.57	0.44
1977	0.51	0.52	0.54	0.57	0.57	0.60
1979	0.55	0.54	0.53	0.67	0.67	0.60

Source: Authors' calculations from the RHS.
[a]Husband survived at least to 1973.
[b]Husband died between 1971 and 1973.

benefit paid to widows was $2,667. With k set to 1.1, the mean benefit paid to widows would have been increased to $2,921 and the mean benefit paid to couples would have been reduced to $4,419 to offset in an actuarially fair way the increase for widows. That is, an increase in the widow's benefit of 10 percent would require a decrease in the couple's benefit of about 6 percent. With k equal to 1.2, the mean benefit for widows would have been $3,176 and the mean for married couples would have been $4,148. As mentioned above, these figures include SSI benefits, which are not adjusted; but SSI is very small on average, so excluding SSI would not change the results in any material way.

Examples of the effects of the Social Security changes on poverty rates are shown in table 13.3. This table shows poverty rates by marital transition between two RHS survey years, 1971 and 1973. To understand the table, consider the heading "Couple to Couple," which pertains to households that continued as couples between 1971 and 1973. Of all couples in this group, 8 percent were poor in 1971 (with $k = 1.0$), and 9 percent were poor in 1973. With $k = 1.1$, 9 percent would also have been poor in 1973, and with $k = 1.2$, 10 percent would

Table 13.4   Average Poverty Rates at Transition to Widowhood

Year	N	k=1.0	k=1.1	k=1.2
Prewidowhood year	926	0.10	0.10	0.12
Postwidowhood year	926	0.38	0.36	0.34
Last year of survey (1979)	530	0.30	0.25	0.22

Source: Authors' calculations from the RHS.

Note: Average poverty rates are calculated over households that changed from couple to widow status between 1971 and 1973, 1973 and 1975, 1975 and 1977, and 1977 and 1979.

have been poor. The increase in the poverty rate of couples comes from the actuarial reduction in their Social Security benefits to finance the increased benefits of the surviving spouse.

The next three columns of the table pertain to households that changed from couple to widow status between 1971 and 1973: that is, the husband was alive in 1971 and had died by 1973. Only 11 percent of the couples in this group were poor in 1971 (with $k = 1.0$). Of the spouses surviving in 1973, 38 percent were poor. Had the widow's benefit been 20 percent higher ($k = 1.2$), 36 percent of the surviving widows would have been poor in 1973. By 1979, 27 percent of the widows were poor under the existing Social Security system; 17 percent would have been poor had Social Security benefits been 20 percent higher.

Comparable data are shown for households that were not poor in 1971 and for households that were poor in 1971. The table records considerable movement into and out of poverty. This apparent movement is partly caused by observation error on income, which causes misclassification of poverty status, and partly by true changes in income. Two features of these data stand out. The first is the high rate of poverty among widows who, when their husbands were alive in 1971, were not in poverty. By definition, none were in poverty in 1971; yet 34 percent were in poverty in 1973 following the husband's death. There is some underreporting of income in the year following the husband's death, as emphasized by Burkhauser, Holden, and Myers (1986), but the table makes clear that poverty persists in large part; by 1979, 22 percent of the widows were still poor. The Social Security adjustments have rather large effects on this group: if the survivor's benefit were increased by 20 percent, the poverty rate of widows in 1979 would be reduced from 22 percent to 11 percent.

The second feature that stands out is the small effect of benefit changes on the financial status of surviving widows of households that were poor in 1971. A Social Security increase of 20 percent would reduce poverty in 1979 by only a small amount, from 67 percent to 60 percent. Apparently, most surviving spouses of couple households already in poverty have incomes—including Social Security benefits—too far below the poverty line to be raised above the line by the simulated increases.

The effects of widowhood on poverty are summarized in table 13.4. The

Table 13.5   **Poverty Rates by Age**

	Couples			Surviving Widows			Original Widows		
Age	N	$k=1.0$	$k=1.1$	$k=1.2$	N	$k=1.0$	$k=1.1$	$k=1.2$	N	$k=1.0$	$k=1.1$	$k=1.2$
58–59	1,602	0.05	0.05	0.05	218	0.42	0.42	0.41	356	0.35	0.35	0.34
60–61	3,526	0.07	0.07	0.07	316	0.36	0.35	0.34	902	0.35	0.35	0.34
62–64	7,827	0.09	0.09	0.09	661	0.35	0.32	0.29	2,227	0.39	0.37	0.34
65–69	11,103	0.09	0.10	0.10	1,319	0.36	0.30	0.25	3,375	0.39	0.34	0.30
70+	4,369	0.09	0.11	0.12	655	0.31	0.25	0.22	1,627	0.43	0.36	0.30

Source: Authors' calculations from the RHS.

first row shows the average poverty rate of couples in the last survey year in which the husband was alive. The averages are over the years 1971, 1973, 1975, and 1977. The second row shows the average poverty rate of widows in the survey year following widowhood. The last row shows the average poverty rate of widows in the last year of the survey, 1979. In the actual data ($k = 1.0$), the poverty rate increased from 0.10 to 0.38 following widowhood. Increasing Social Security benefits by 20 percent would increase the poverty rate of the couples from 0.10 to 0.12. But it would have a rather large effect on the final poverty rate of widows: the rate would fall from 0.30 to 0.22. We conclude that a rather sizable reduction in the poverty rate of widows could be achieved at the cost of a small increase in the poverty rate of couples.

Poverty rates by age of household head are shown in table 13.5. For example, the row labeled 65–69 shows poverty rates for couples in which the household head is aged 65–69 and for widows aged 65–69. Surviving widows are those whose husbands died during the course of the RHS; original widows were already widowed when the RHS began in 1969. Under the existing Social Security provisions ($k = 1.0$), 36 percent of surviving widows aged 65–69 were poor. With $k = 1.1$, only 30 percent would have been poor, and with $k = 1.2$, only 25 percent would have been poor. The effects for original widows are similar. Restructuring the benefit stream has a substantial effect on the poverty rate of older widows (aged 70+) as desired, with little effect on the poverty rate of couples.

In summary, these calculations show that the changes that we consider would have a noticeable effect on the Social Security benefits of widows and would have a significant effect on their poverty rates. Nonetheless, the poverty rate among widows would remain high relative to the poverty rate of couples. For example, a 10 percent increase in the widow's Social Security benefit would reduce the poverty rate of surviving widows aged 65–69 from 36 percent to 30 percent; a 20 percent increase in the widow's benefit would reduce the poverty rate among widows aged 65–69 to 25 percent. Although the poverty rate of couples would increase slightly, from 9 percent to 10 percent, with a 10 or 20 percent increase in the widow's benefit, it would still be substantially below the poverty rate of widows.

13.3   Future Poverty Rates

As the RHS respondents aged beyond the last survey year, 1979, household changes could not be observed. It is clear, however, that some 1979 widows died, while new widows were added after 1979, when their husbands died. The results presented in this section estimate the poverty rates of these additional widows as the 1979 RHS households aged. As in the previous section, the goal is to show the effect on poverty rates of changing the Social Security survivor's benefit levels, but in this case the focus is on future poverty rather than poverty during the period of the RHS, 1969–79.

The procedure involves several steps. First, future poverty rates of couples and widows under the current Social Security provisions are established. These baseline rates are found by forecasting to 2001 the future income of each couple and widow household in the 1979 RHS data. The forecasts are based on a behavioral model of wealth decumulation by singles and an observed rate of wealth decumulation by couples. The forecasting method and model estimation are described in Hurd (1989a, 1989b). During each year, individuals in the sample are assumed to die in accordance with mortality probabilities taken from life tables. Widows in 1979 leave the sample based on their mortality rates, and new widows are added as husbands die, also according to the life tables. Income and wealth in each future period are estimated from a model of consumption that depends on 1979 wealth and on future Social Security and other annuity income. Based on the resulting income estimate, poverty rates are calculated in each future year (at two-year intervals). In the baseline simulations, the surviving widow is assumed to receive 67 percent of the couple's Social Security benefit. These baseline simulations show what the poverty rates of the 1979 RHS sample will be as it ages to 2001, when the median age of the sample will be about 91. (An alternative interpretation is that the simulations show the poverty rates of an entire elderly population in which each successive cohort has the same resources as the 1979 RHS population.) The average poverty rate over all future years is the weighted (by the number of survivors) average of the poverty rates by age.

In the second step, the forecasts are repeated, but the Social Security survivor's benefit is increased according the factor k, taken to be 1.1 or 1.2, and the couple's benefit is reduced in an actuarially fair way that depends on the ages at which the husband and wife began to draw benefits. Thus the reduction will vary from couple to couple. (On average, the couple's benefit is reduced by about 5 percent when $k = 1.1$.) Based on the new Social Security benefits, income and wealth in each future year are determined according to the model, and these results are used to determine future poverty rates. The differences between the baseline poverty rates and those with $k = 1.1$ and $k = 1.2$ indicate the change in the future poverty rates of couples and of widows that could be expected from changing survivorship benefits. The results are shown in table 13.6. In 1979, when the median age of the RHS widows was about 71, the

Table 13.6   **Probability of Poverty: 1979 Income Levels**

	Widows					Couples				
Year	N	Median Age	k=1.0	k=1.1	k=1.2	N	Husband's Age	Wife's Age	k=1.0	k=1.1	k=1.2
1979	5,766	71	0.43	0.39	0.35	7,254	71	69	0.09	0.10	0.11
1981	6,172	72	0.41	0.37	0.33	6,275	73	71	0.09	0.10	0.11
1983	6,514	74	0.39	0.35	0.31	5,296	75	73	0.09	0.10	0.11
1985	6,695	76	0.38	0.33	0.30	4,291	77	74	0.09	0.10	0.12
1987	6,706	78	0.37	0.33	0.29	3,372	79	76	0.09	0.11	0.12
1989	6,537	80	0.37	0.33	0.29	2,568	81	78	0.10	0.11	0.12
1991	6,227	81	0.37	0.32	0.29	1,830	83	80	0.10	0.11	0.13
1993	5,723	83	0.38	0.33	0.28	1,266	84	82	0.10	0.12	0.13
1995	5,059	85	0.38	0.33	0.28	804	86	84	0.10	0.11	0.13
1997	4,262	87	0.38	0.32	0.28	484	88	86	0.10	0.10	0.12
1999	3,355	89	0.38	0.32	0.27	254	90	88	0.10	0.11	0.13
2001	2,573	91	0.39	0.32	0.27	110	92	90	0.11	0.13	0.15
Total	65,589		0.39	0.34	0.30	33,804			0.09	0.10	0.11

Source: Authors' calculations from the RHS.

poverty rate of widows was 43 percent; the rate for couples was 9 percent. If the survivor's benefit were increased by 20 percent ($k = 1.2$) the poverty rate of widows would be reduced to 35 percent and the rate for couples increased to 11 percent. By 2001, when the median age of widows will be about 91, the poverty rate of widows is forecast to be 39 percent. Increasing the survivor's benefit level by 20 percent would reduce this poverty rate to 27 percent, a substantial reduction for the very old. The increase has a larger effect on the poverty rate of couples than previous examples. The poverty rate of couples who survive to 2001 would be increased from 0.11 to 0.15, an increase of 36 percent. However, only 1.5 percent of couples are expected to survive to that year. Overall (averaging over all ages), increasing the survivor's benefit by 20 percent would reduce widows' poverty from 39 percent to 30 percent. This change would increase couples' poverty by about 2 percentage points, from about 9 to about 11 percent.

In summary, the projections show future poverty rates of widows that are somewhat lower than the 1979 rates even without an increase in the Social Security survivor's benefit. The reduced poverty rate of widows results from the greater wealth of the prior couples. There is a positive relationship between life expectancy and wealth. Thus households in which the husband dies later have greater wealth than households in which the husband died at a younger age. And, therefore, the surviving widows also have greater wealth. The effect of increasing survivorship benefits is somewhat larger (in percentage terms) in the future than in 1979. Consistent with the estimates for the RHS survey period that ended in 1979, the poverty rate of future elderly widows is reduced substantially at the cost of a modest increase in the poverty rate of couples.

13.4   Updating Wealth and Income Using the SIPP

The poverty rates reported in sections 13.2 and 13.3 are based on the economic resources of the 1979 RHS respondents. Since 1979, however, the economic resources of the elderly have grown and elderly poverty has declined. For example, in 1979 the elderly poverty rate was 15.1 percent; in 1984 it was 12.4 percent. We consider in this section how such changes affect projected future poverty rates, based on alternative Social Security survivor's benefit provisions. To do this, we adjust the income and wealth reported by the RHS respondents so that on average they are the same as the income and wealth of like households in 1984. We base the adjustments on the 1984 Survey of Income and Program Participation (SIPP). The SIPP is a series of two-and-one-half year panels. The first panel began in 1984 (the last quarter of 1983) and covered 15,000 households, of which about 4,000 had heads who were age 65 or older. Every four months the respondents were asked detailed questions about income, assets, and other household characteristics. Thus, as with the RHS, it is possible to construct a financial picture of a representative sample of the elderly in 1984 and in 1985.

We use Wave 4 of the 1984 SIPP panel to find average levels of income and asset variables in the latter part of 1984. For each variable, we calculate the average over respondents who report a positive value for that income source or asset. We use these values to adjust the levels of the RHS respondents who report a positive value for that income source or asset. That is, the value reported by each RHS respondent for each category is adjusted by the ratio of the SIPP average to the RHS average for that category. Thus, for each household type, the average RHS adjusted level among holders of each income or asset category is the same as the SIPP average.

Based on these adjusted income and wealth values the projections described in section 13.3 are repeated. The new poverty rates indicate how the projected rates are affected by the overall increase in elderly income and wealth. Again, the results are reported for alternative changes in Social Security survivor's benefit provisions.

We compared economic resources in the SIPP and the RHS for the following categories:

Wealth
- Bequeathable wealth excluding housing
- Housing

Income
- Nominal annuities (mostly private pensions)
- Real annuities (military, government, etc.)
- Earnings
- Social Security benefits

Table 13.7   **Comparison of Average Income and Assets: RHS and SIPP**

Household Type and Survey	Bequeathable Wealth Excluding Housing	Housing Wealth	Social Security Income
Widows			
RHS (1979$)	21,444	35,348	2,856
SIPP (1984$)	30,090	46,892	5,035
SIPP (1979$)	21,025	32,766	3,518
Couples			
RHS (1979$)	50,772	48,003	5,419
SIPP (1984$)	82,912	58,404	9,177
SIPP (1979$)	57,935	40,810	6,389

Source: Authors' calculations from the RHS and the 1984 SIPP, Wave 4.

For each resource category we calculated the average level in the 1984 SIPP among holders of the resource, by household type and by age. The household types were couples, widows, widowers, single males, and single females. Calculations were made for each age from 65 to 74. For each category of economic resource this defined a total of 50 cells. Because the SIPP is a self-weighting sample, the number of observations was rather small in some of the cells. This resulted in considerable variation in wealth with age, variation that is undoubtedly due to the small sample size. For example, bequeathable wealth excluding housing was about $30,000 among 68-year-old widows, $42,000 among 69-year-old widows, and $32,000 among 70-year-old widows. These averages are based on about 50 observations in each age group. Were we to use these averages to construct adjustment factors to apply to the RHS variables, considerable random variation would be introduced into the adjusted RHS wealth levels.

Our solution was to calculate age-weighted averages by household type for each of the resource categories in the SIPP, where the weights are the number of households in each age cell in the RHS. This procedure led to the average levels of bequeathable wealth, housing wealth, and Social Security in the RHS and in the SIPP shown in table 13.7. The results for all the variables are presented in appendix table 13A.1.

The most important difference between the SIPP and the RHS variables is the growth in Social Security, the most important source of income for poorer widows. This growth is the result of increases in the Social Security benefit schedule and increases in wages over time. Hurd (1990) reports that new Social Security benefit awards increased by 51 percent in real terms between 1968, when the RHS cohort would have been retiring, and 1977, when the SIPP cohort would have been retiring. This implies that the SIPP cohorts would have retired with substantially higher Social Security benefits than the RHS cohorts, consistent with the values reported in table 13.7.

Table 13.8 shows poverty rates calculated from the new projected incomes of widows and couples. Comparison of tables 13.6 and 13.8 shows that among

Table 13.8   Probability of Poverty: 1984 Income Levels

		Widows					Couples			
Year	N	Median Age	k=1.0	k=1.1	k=1.2	N	Husband's Age	Wife's Age	k=1.0	k=1.1	k=1.2
1979	5,766	71	0.29	0.26	0.23	7,254	71	69	0.06	0.06	0.07
1981	6,172	72	0.28	0.25	0.22	6,275	73	71	0.06	0.07	0.08
1983	6,514	74	0.27	0.24	0.21	5,296	75	73	0.05	0.06	0.08
1985	6,695	76	0.26	0.23	0.20	4,291	77	74	0.05	0.06	0.07
1987	6,706	78	0.25	0.23	0.20	3,372	79	76	0.05	0.07	0.08
1989	6,537	80	0.25	0.22	0.19	2,568	81	78	0.06	0.07	0.08
1991	6,227	81	0.25	0.22	0.18	1,830	83	80	0.06	0.08	0.09
1993	5,723	83	0.25	0.22	0.18	1,266	84	82	0.06	0.08	0.09
1995	5,059	85	0.26	0.22	0.18	804	86	84	0.07	0.08	0.09
1997	4,262	87	0.25	0.21	0.18	484	88	86	0.08	0.09	0.09
1999	3,355	89	0.25	0.21	0.17	254	90	88	0.09	0.09	0.10
2001	2,573	91	0.25	0.21	0.17	110	92	90	0.10	0.11	0.11
Total	65,589		0.26	0.23	0.20	33,804			0.06	0.07	0.08

Source: Authors' calculations from the RHS and the 1984 SIPP, Wave 4.

widows the increases in economic resources between 1979 and 1984 (between the SIPP and the RHS) caused a large fall in the poverty rate. For example, with no change in Social Security provisions ($k = 1.0$) the overall poverty rate through 2001 would be 39 percent with the economic resources of the 1979 RHS respondents. With the larger resources of the same age groups in 1984 (the SIPP respondents), the poverty rate is projected to be only 26 percent. The overall rate for couples is reduced from about 9 to about 6 percent. Undoubtedly, the major cause of the reduction in poverty was the increase in Social Security benefit levels.

As above, the effect on poverty of changing the Social Security survivor's benefit, given the economic resource levels in the SIPP, can be found by comparing the poverty rates in the columns for $k = 1.1$ and $k = 1.2$ with the rates in the $k = 1.0$ column. Among all widows, increasing the survivor's benefit by 20 percent ($k = 1.2$) would decrease projected poverty rates overall from 0.26 to 0.20, a percentage decrease of 23 percent. This is the same percentage decrease obtained using the RHS levels of the variables (table 13.6).[6] As before, the increase in the poverty rate of couples is small in absolute terms but comparable to the fall for widows in percentage terms (about 33 percent).

13.5 Conclusion

The illustrative simulations presented in this paper show that the poverty rates of widows could be materially reduced by an increase in survivorship

6. This leads us to believe that a similar percentage fall in the poverty rate would be found if current levels of the economic resources were used in the forecast.

benefits funded by a reduction in the benefits of couples. The increase in Social Security benefits in the 1970s—between the RHS and the SIPP surveys—can be expected in itself to reduce the future poverty rates of the elderly. If this increase in Social Security benefits were accompanied by a 20 percent increase in the survivor's benefit, the poverty rate of widows would be reduced from about 39 percent (table 13.6, $k = 1.0$) to 20 percent (table 13.8, $k = 1.2$).

Appendix

Table 13A.1   **Means and Medians over Households with Positive Values and Number of Observations with Positive Values: RHS and SIPP**

Household Type	Bequeathable Wealth Excluding Housing	Housing Wealth	Real Annuities	Nominal Annuities	Earnings	Social Security Income
RHS data						
Widow						
Mean	21,444	35,348	2,410	1,767	3,478	2,856
Median	6,200	29,999	1,316	1,270	2,400	2,808
N	1,677	1,195	577	314	369	1,656
Widower						
Mean	26,247	38,965	3,759	2,498	5,255	3,294
Median	8,637	30,000	2,262	1,962	2,400	3,361
N	350	247	112	144	87	360
Single male						
Mean	22,700	32,715	3,791	2,502	5,140	2,968
Median	4,899	25,000	1,687	1,800	2,500	2,856
N	291	132	88	105	76	292
Single female						
Mean	17,072	34,440	3,177	2,316	3,228	2,877
Median	6,675	25,999	2,040	1,765	1,741	2,852
N	457	211	233	105	118	448
Couple						
Mean	50,772	48,003	5,697	3,118	6,835	5,419
Median	18,984	39,000	4,063	2,400	3,429	5,536
N	2,359	2,075	638	931	88	2,328
SIPP data						
Widow						
Mean	30,090	46,892	5,991	2,649	7,557	5,035
Median	14,074	40,000	5,520	1,902	3,252	5,088
N	482	360	89	108	84	491
Widower						
Mean	46,317	51,477	9,382	3,528	8,441	5,754
Median	18,763	30,000	7,416	2,122	7,620	5,760
N	84	57	15	30	13	85

(continued)

Table 13A.1   (continued)

Household Type	Bequeathable Wealth Excluding Housing	Housing Wealth	Real Annuities	Nominal Annuities	Earnings	Social Security Income
Single male						
Mean	39,244	44,120	11,375	3,638	8,744	5,559
Median	12,375	38,500	9,876	3,558	6,000	5,622
N	100	53	22	36	25	96
Single female						
Mean	27,153	45,468	4,971	2,299	4,502	4,743
Median	5,752	40,000	4,818	1,884	5,025	4,758
N	147	81	26	42	28	146
Couple						
Mean	82,912	58,404	10,243	4,093	14,305	9,177
Median	34,864	50,000	8,433	3,600	8,400	9,114
N	987	855	260	399	286	934

Source: Authors' calculations from the RHS and the 1984 SIPP, Wave 4.

References

Burkhauser, Richard V., Karen C. Holden, and Daniel A. Myers. 1986. Marital disruption and poverty: The role of survey procedures in artificially creating poverty. *Demography* 23 (4): 621–31.

Grad, Susan. 1990. Income of the population 55 or older, 1988. Washington, D.C.: U.S. Department of Health and Human Services, Social Security Administration.

Holden, Karen, Richard Burkhauser, and Daniel J. Feaster. 1988. The timing of falls into poverty after retirement and widowhood. *Demography* 25 (3): 405–14.

Hurd, Michael D. 1989a. Mortality risk and bequests. *Econometrica* 57 (4): 779–813.

———. 1989b. The poverty of widows: Future prospects. In *The economics of aging*, ed. David Wise, 201–22. Chicago: University of Chicago Press.

———. 1990. Research on the elderly: Economic status, retirement, and consumption and saving. *Journal of Economic Literature* 28 (June): 565–637.

Hurd, Michael D., and John B. Shoven. 1985. Inflation vulnerability, income, and wealth of the elderly, 1969–1979. In *Horizontal equity, uncertainty, and economic well-being*, ed. Martin David and Timothy Smeeding, 125–72. Chicago: University of Chicago Press.

Hurd, Michael D., and David A. Wise. 1989. The wealth and poverty of widows: Assets before and after the husband's death. In *The economics of aging*, ed. D. Wise, 177–99. Chicago: University of Chicago Press.

Myers, Daniel A., Richard V. Burkhauser, and Karen C. Holden. 1987. The transition from wife to widow: The importance of survivor benefits to the well-being of widows. *Journal of Risk and Insurance* 54 (4): 752–59.

14   The Net Pension Debt of the Japanese Government

Tatsuo Hatta and Noriyoshi Oguchi

14.1 Introduction

A public pension system can be viewed as an arrangement by which the government issues IOUs to the currently working population, promising that a specified amount of benefits will be paid out in the future, in return for pension contributions. Under this system, the government accumulates a "pension debt" to the private sector. However, the balance of the existing pension fund represents the government's loans to the private sector. Thus, the difference between the pension debt and the balance of the pension fund represents the net government debt to the private sector stemming from the pension system, hereafter called the "net pension debt."

The imaginary pension fund that would exist if a pension system had been started as a fully funded system is called the "full fund" of the pension system. The balance of the full fund is always equal to the pension debt of the government. Hence, we have

(1)   Net pension debt = Full fund − Actual pension fund.

‖

(Pension debt)

If a pension system were fully funded, the balance of the pension fund and the pension debt would be equal, and the net pension debt would be zero. In

Tatsuo Hatta is professor of economics at the Institute of Social and Economic Research, Osaka University. Noriyoshi Oguchi is professor of economics at the Faculty of Commerce, Senshu University.

The authors would like to thank Robin Lumsdaine, Noriyuki Takayama, Atsushi Seike, and other conference participants for their valuable comments. They are also grateful to Naozumi Atoda, Kiyoshi Murakami, and Hiroshi Miyajima for useful comments on various occasions. This research was partly supported by Grant-in-Aid for Scientific Research 06301075 from the Japanese Ministry of Education.

1990, however, the net pension debt of the Japanese government exceeded the gross national product (GNP). In other words, the pension debt was much larger than the balance of the pension fund. This difference was distributed to the following two groups: current and past retirees, whose benefits exceeded their contributions, and those current workers who had been promised benefits greater than their past contributions. In other words, the net pension debt has been caused by the government's overcommitment in the past.[1]

If the net pension debt continues to expand, the pension fund will eventually be bankrupt. However, even if the balance of the pension fund becomes negative temporarily, the public pension system will be financially healthy as long as a permanent expansion of the net pension debt is prevented.

In this paper, we estimate the net pension debt of the Japanese government that existed in 1990 and predict its future fluctuations under the contribution and benefit schedules set by the government's 1994 Pension Reform Plan.[2] This analysis will reveal the following:

1. The net pension debt in 1990 was 578 trillion yen, 137 percent of the GDP for that year.[3]

2. The net pension debt will grow until the year 2045 then start to decline and become zero in the year 2090 (see fig. 14.4 below).

3. The "excess fiscal burden" for the pension system—that is, the fiscal burden that exceeds the actuarially fair contributions—will be spread unevenly over years, peaking at 3.0 percent of GDP in the year 2020 and dropping to less than 1 percent after the year 2080 (see fig. 14.5 below).

These findings show that the most serious problem of the Japanese pension system is not its financial health, but the uneven distribution of the excess fiscal burden across generations.

The paper also considers the effects of the Pension Reform Plan, which maintains the excess fiscal burden at 1 percent of GDP throughout the forecasted period. We show that this reform not only will make the intergenerational distribution of the excess burden uniform but also will give a sufficient fiscal infusion to make the system fully funded in the year 2155.

Section 14.2 explains the various concepts used in the estimation of the net

---

1. Under a pure pay-as-you-go system, there is no accumulation of the pension fund, and hence the pension debt itself is equal to the net pension debt. The debt is mainly caused by the fact that the first generation of the pension system received benefits without paying any contributions.

2. The estimates given in the present paper differ from those given in Hatta and Oguchi (1993). First, we include the Public Sector Employee Pension in our estimation. Second, our estimates here are based on the benefit and contribution schedule of the government's 1994 Pension Reform Plan, while the estimates in the 1993 paper were based on the schedule of the 1986 Fiscal Reappraisal. Third, the estimates in the present paper are based on 1991 population projections by the Ministry of Welfare, while the estimates in the 1993 paper were based on 1986 population projections. A detailed explanation of the differences between the two estimates is available on request.

3. This value is fairly close to Oshima's (1981) back-of-the-envelope estimate of 460 trillion yen. Note, however, that Oshima's estimate was for 1981 and that the pension system was restructured in 1986.

pension debt. Section 14.3 presents the estimated values of the net pension debts for each of the Japanese public pension systems. Section 14.4 discusses how the net pension debt will grow in the future. Section 14.5 focuses on the excess fiscal burden as a determinant of the growth of the net pension debt. Section 14.6 discusses the economic impacts of the Pension Reform Plan, which maintains the excess fiscal burden at 1 percent of GDP. Section 14.7 runs a few sensitivity analyses, and section 14.8 contains some concluding remarks. The appendix discusses the meaning of the net pension debt.

14.2 Estimation Method of the Net Pension Debt

To calculate the net pension debt at a given point in time, the full fund must be known. The full fund is the sum of the pension debts to all living generations. We first discuss the procedure for estimating the pension debt to the working generations. In section 14.2.4 we discuss the debt to retired generations.

14.2.1 Lifetime Pension Contribution

The sum of the present values of the contributions a person made in the past is called the "past contribution." The sum of the present values of his or her expected contributions is called the "future contribution." The sum of the past contribution and the future contribution is called the "lifetime contribution." Thus,

(2)   Lifetime contribution = Past contribution + Future contribution.

A person's lifetime contribution is the present value of the pension contributions to be paid throughout his or her lifetime. The person's past and future contribution profiles can be estimated based on his or her wage profile.

14.2.2 Pension Wealth

We define an individual's "lifetime benefit" as the present value of his or her expected benefits under the present pension system from the beginning of retirement to the end of his or her life. This is shown by the fine dashed line in figure 14.1. If a pension system is fully funded, the lifetime benefit should be the same as the lifetime contribution as calculated above. Under a pension system that is not fully funded, these two values are not the same.

We define the "pension wealth" of an individual as the present value of his or her expected benefits from a given moment in time to the end of his or her life. This is shown by the heavy dotted line in figure 14.1. For a person who is still working, pension wealth is equal to lifetime benefit, as figure 14.1 shows.

14.2.3 Promised Benefit and To-Be-Earned Benefit

We divide pension wealth into two parts: the portion corresponding to the past contribution and the portion corresponding to the future contribution. The

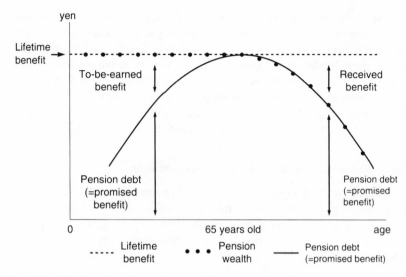

Fig. 14.1   Lifetime benefit, pension wealth, and pension debt

former is called the "promised benefit," and the latter the "to-be-earned bene-fit." Thus,

(3)   Pension wealth = Promised benefit + To-be-earned benefit.

$$\parallel$$

(Pension debt)

The solid line in figure 14.1 depicts the promised benefit. The to-be-earned benefit is shown as the vertical distance between pension wealth and promised benefit. It is positive only for people under age 65.

In practice, there are various ways of calculating the promised benefit and the to-be-earned benefit. In this paper, we simply divide pension wealth in proportion to the two terms in equation (2) to obtain the estimates of the two terms in equation (3).[4]

If a pension system is fully funded, the promised benefit in equation (3) must be equal to the past contribution in equation (2). Everybody must have accumulated contributions exactly equal to the promised benefit.

If a system is not fully funded, these two terms are not necessarily the same. For example, the promised benefit exceeds the past contribution for a person older than age 50 in the Japanese Private Sector Employee Pension. This person receives a net transfer of income from the government based on his or her past contribution. For a person under 30 years of age, the promised benefit is

4. This implies that the following holds:

Lifetime contribution : Pension wealth = Past contribution : Promised benefit.

Table 14.1   **Division of Pension Wealth of Working Generations**

Pension Wealth (present value of benefits to be received)			
Promised Benefit = Pension Debt (present value of benefit attributable to the past contribution)		To-Be-Earned Benefit (present value of benefit attributable to the future contribution)	
Past Contribution	1. Transfer on the Past Contribution	Future Contribution	2. Transfer on the Future Contribution

less than the past contribution (see, e.g., Takayama 1981; Oguchi, Kimura, and Hatta 1993).

The second line of table 14.1 shows the decomposition of pension wealth by equation (3), and the bottom line shows the decomposition by equation (2). The difference between the first terms on the right-hand sides of equations (2) and (3) is the transfer income one receives from the government based on one's past contribution. This is represented by item 1. The difference between the second terms of those equations is the transfer income based on one's future contribution. This is represented by item 2. If the future contribution is larger than the to-be-earned benefit, item 2 becomes negative; its absolute value is called the "excess contribution."

14.2.4   Pension Wealth of Retired Generations

Pension wealth represents the present value of expected future benefits. For retired generations, the annual benefit is already determined. Therefore, pension wealth is simply the properly discounted product of the annual benefit and the expected number of years retirees will receive this benefit.

Regardless of a person's age, the following equation holds true:

(4)   Lifetime benefit = Received benefit + Pension wealth.

The received benefit is the present value of the benefit received in the past. For working generations, the received benefit is nil and pension wealth is the lifetime benefit. For retired generations, pension wealth is less than the lifetime benefit. This relationship is shown in figure 14.1.[5]

For the retired generations, the to-be-earned benefit in equation (3) is nil, and hence pension wealth is equal to the promised benefit.

5. For working generations, the following inequality holds: Lifetime benefit > Pension debt. The lifetime benefit is necessarily equal to pension wealth, and as table 14.1 shows, pension wealth is greater than the pension debt of the government to these generations.

The inequality holds for retired generations as well. For them, the lifetime benefit is greater than pension wealth, and pension wealth is equal to pension debt.

In sum, only for those who have just retired and are about to receive benefits is the lifetime benefit equal to pension debt. That is, for an individual, the pension debt by the government reaches the maximum on his or her retirement, and the maximum value is equal to the lifetime benefit. The relationship among these concepts is shown in fig. 14.1.

14.2.5   Net Pension Debt

The promised benefit is that part of pension wealth attributable to the past contribution. Hence, it may be considered to have been "promised" by the government. In other words, for the government the promised benefit is the payable pension debt. Therefore, the above discussion holds, with the term "promised benefit" replaced by the term "pension debt." For retired people, the pension debt of the government is equal to pension wealth. This is shown by the solid line and the heavy dotted line in figure 14.1.

The sum of the pension debt over all participants is the full fund.[6] The difference between the full fund and the actual fund is the net pension debt.

14.3   Estimation of the Net Pension Debt as of 1990

In this section, we estimate the net pension debt as of 1990 as described in the previous section.

14.3.1   Assumptions for Estimation

In estimation, we followed the government's 1994 Pension Reform Plan (hereafter called the "Reform Plan") for assumptions regarding economic parameters, benefit and contribution schedules, and population projections. Specifically, the economic parameters were set as follows: nominal interest rate 5.5 percent, rate of nominal wage increase 4.0 percent, rate of increase in nominal basic consumption expenditure 4.0 percent, and inflation rate 2.0 percent. The population projection is the one published in 1991 by the Research Institute of Population Problems of the Ministry of Welfare, which was based on the 1990 census.

We made our own estimation of the following parameters: the number of participants and recipients of benefits of the pension system by age group, and the lifetime wage profile of workers. These parameters were not given explicitly in the reappraisal.

The number of participants by age group in each pension system was estimated based on the data on participation rate by age group for 1985. The number of beneficiaries by age group was estimated based on the data for 1988 published in the Reform Plan.

The lifetime wage profile was estimated from the data in the Wage Census, which includes cross-sectional wage data by age group. We created a lifetime profile by taking the wages for the same cohort from the series of censuses.

The pension contribution and the benefits in the future are given in the Reform Plan. Following the plan, we assumed that the wage-proportional part of the private and public sector employee pensions will continue to be paid from

6. The full fund may be viewed as the "pension debt to the participants." The net pension debt is, of course, the difference between this pension debt and the actual fund.

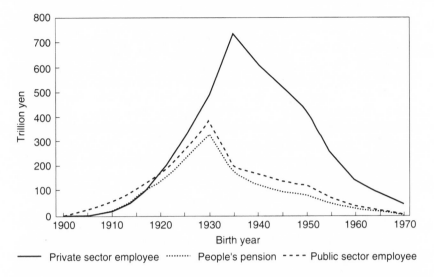

Fig. 14.2   Pension debt as of 1990: case 1

age 60, but the starting age of the fixed portion of the benefit (the basic benefit) will be gradually raised to age 65. Also, the reference wage of the replacement ratio will be shifted from monthly average gross wage to monthly average take-home wage after taxes, pension contribution, and so on.

14.3.2   Estimation Results

Pension debt by age group as of 1990. Figure 14.2 depicts the estimated pension debts owed to different age groups in 1990. The fine dotted line shows the People's Pension, the solid line shows the Private Sector Employee Pension, and the dashed line shows the Public Sector Employee Pension.

For the Private Sector Employee Pension, the largest pension debt is owed to the age group born in 1935 because the people in this age group are just starting to receive benefits. For this group, the lifetime benefit is the pension debt. The pension debt is smaller for each of the older groups because their life expectancies are shorter. For the People's Pension, the pension debt is largest for those born in 1930 because a smaller portion of the younger generations receiving this pension is engaged in agriculture.

For an age group born after 1935, the pension debt was estimated to be the product of its lifetime benefit and the ratio of its past contribution to its lifetime contribution, as explained in section 14.2. Figure 14.3 shows pension wealth (lifetime benefit), past contribution, and lifetime contribution for these age groups.

There are two reasons for the smaller pension debt owed to the younger age groups. First, the younger the age group, the smaller the ratio of past contribu-

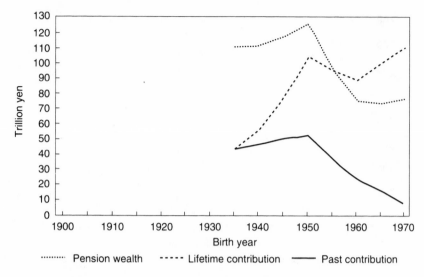

Fig. 14.3   Pension wealth and contributions, 1990: case 1

Table 14.2   Full Fund and Net Pension Debt as of 1990 (trillion yen)

Pension	Full Fund	Actual Fund	Net Pension Debt
Private Sector Employee Pension	387	77	310
People's Pension	133	4	129
Public Sector Employee Pension	171	32	139
Total	691	113	578

Source: Authors' calculations.

tion to lifetime contribution, because the contribution period is shorter. Second, as figure 14.3 shows, the lifetime benefit is smaller the younger the age group. This is due to the schedule, in which the replacement ratio is lower for younger generations. The full benefit of the Private Sector Employee Pension is about 69 percent of the lifetime average of standard monthly pay after taxes and social security contributions, of which 30 percent is the wage-proportional portion and 39 percent is the basic pension benefit (fixed) portion. The wage-proportional portion will decline in percentage as the deductions from wages increase when the pension contribution rate is raised.

Net pension debt as of 1990. The first column of table 14.2 shows the pension debt (full fund) for the Private Sector Employee Pension, the People's Pension, and the Public Sector Employee Pension at the end of 1990. The actual fund and net pension debt also are shown.

As the table shows, the balance of the full fund for all pensions was 691 trillion yen, of which 387 trillion yen was for the Private Sector Employee

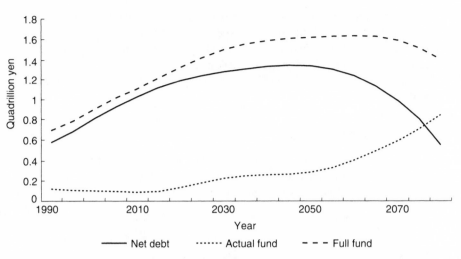

Fig. 14.4   Net debt, actual fund, and full fund: case 1

Pension, 133 trillion yen for the People's Pension, and 171 trillion yen for the Public Sector Employee Pension. The overall balance of the actual fund was 113 trillion yen—77 trillion yen for the Private Sector Employee Pension, 4 trillion yen for the People's Pension, and 32 trillion yen for the Public Sector Employee Pension, resulting in an overall net pension debt of 578 trillion yen.

14.4   Growth of the Net Pension Debt

We now analyze the time path of the net pension debt after 1990. According to equation (1), the net pension debt is the difference between the full fund and the actual pension fund. Here we examine the time paths of the full fund, the actual pension fund, and the net pension debt.

Forecast of the full fund. The dashed line in figure 14.4 shows the future time path of the full fund. First, it expands as the number of retired people increases. It reaches its peak in 2060 then starts to decline.

Forecast of the actual fund. The dotted line in figure 14.4 represents the balance of the actual fund. It starts with 113 trillion yen in the year 1990 and declines slightly until the year 2005. Then it starts to grow slowly and picks up speed after 2060. Thus the actual fund will not be depleted even during the period of rapid aging, as long as the assumptions of the 1994 Reform Plan are realized.[7]

---

7. The fund can be depleted if the assumptions are not realized. Raising the pension contribution rate and the income tax rate in early years will help reduce this possibility. See, e.g., Noguchi (1986), Ueda, Iwai, and Hashimoto (1987), and Ogura and Yamamoto (1993).

Forecast of the net pension debt. In view of equation (1), the net pension debt is equal to the vertical difference between the dotted line and the dashed line in figure 14.4. This difference is depicted by the solid line in the figure. It grows until the year 2045. After its peak in 2045, it declines steadily and becomes zero in 2090. Thus the public pension system can become fully funded in the year 2090.

14.5 Excess Fiscal Burden

In this section, we examine the determinants of the growth of the net pension debt. We first define the concept of the excess fiscal burden, then use this concept in explaining the growth of the net pension debt.

14.5.1 Definition

The revenue of a general pension fund consists of the following three elements:

- Interest income from the balance of the fund
- Pension contribution (equivalent to the Social Security tax in the United States)
- Subsidy from the general account

The sum of the last two may be called the "revenue from outside the fund." If this exceeds the actuarially fair level of the pension contribution, the difference is the fiscal burden for the pension beyond the actuarially fair contribution. We will call this difference the "excess fiscal burden":

(5)   Excess fiscal burden = Actual contribution
                             − Actuarially fair contribution
                             + Subsidy from the general account.

In other words, the excess fiscal burden represents a net transfer that the working generation in a given year makes to other generations.

14.5.2 Interest on the Net Pension Debt

The revenues of the pension fund under a fully funded system consist of the following:

- Interest income from the full fund
- Actuarially fair pension contribution

These revenues will be used to maintain the actual fund at the level of the pension debt, and hence to keep the net pension debt at zero.

Consider a reform of the current Japanese pension system that equates the pension contribution to the actuarially fair level and abolishes the subsidy. Under this reform, the net pension debt will continue to grow. The reason is that the interest income from the actual fund is much less than the interest income from the full fund. We call this difference the "interest on the net pension debt":

(6) Interest on the net pension debt = Interest on the full fund
$$- \text{Interest on the actual pension fund.}$$

The interest on the net pension debt represents the increase in the debt under this hypothetical reform. To keep the net pension debt from growing after this reform, revenues equal to the amount of the interest on the net pension debt must be infused into the pension fund.

14.5.3 Determinants of the Net Pension Debt

We can express the increase in the net pension debt as[8]

(7) Δ Net pension debt = Interest on the net pension debt
$$- \text{Excess fiscal burden,}$$

where the interest on the net pension debt is as defined in equation (6). This equation shows that the change in the net pension debt is determined solely by the difference between the interest on the net pension debt and the excess fiscal burden.

The solid line in figure 14.5 represents the interest on the net pension debt in the ratio to GDP. (Throughout this paper we assume that GDP grows 3.5 percent per year, which is equal to the real interest rate.) Before the year 2020, when excess fiscal burden peaks, this interest far exceeds the excess fiscal burden shown by the dashed line. After this peak, the ratio of the excess fiscal burden to GDP declines gradually and falls below 1 percent after the year 2080. Thus this figure indicates the unequal burdens borne by different generations.

Figure 14.6 directly shows the unequal burden and benefit of the public pen-

---

8. Since the net pension debt is the difference between the full fund and the actual fund, we have

(*) Δ Net pension debt $\equiv \Delta$ Full fund $- \Delta$ Actual fund.

The two terms on the right-hand side can be rewritten as follows:

Δ Full fund = Interest incurred on balance of full fund
        + Actuarially fair pension contribution $-$ Benefit payment,
Δ Actual fund = Interest incurred on balance of actual fund
        + Subsidy from general account + Actual pension contribution $-$ Benefit payment.

Substitution of these two relations into eq. (*) gives:

Δ Net pension debt = (Interest on full fund $-$ Interest on actual fund)
        $-$ (Actual contribution $-$ Actuarially fair contribution
                + Subsidy from general account)

This immediately yields eq. (7).

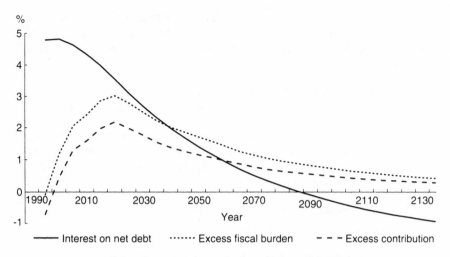

Fig. 14.5   Ratio of debt interest, excess fiscal burden, and excess contribution to GDP

sion system by generation. The lifetime contribution rate, represented by the solid line, rises from below 10 percent for the generation born in 1935 to above 20 percent for the generation born in 1970. In contrast, the lifetime benefit rate, shown by the dashed line, declines from nearly 20 percent to below 15 percent. These two lines cross for the generation born in 1950; for those born after 1950, the pension contribution exceeds the benefits, and the difference becomes larger for younger generations.

14.5.4   Policy Instruments

We now break down the excess fiscal burden into two terms:

(8)   Excess fiscal burden = Excess contribution
                                                + Subsidy from the general account,

where

Excess contribution = Actual contribution − Actuarially fair contribution.

The "excess contribution" is the portion of the actual contribution in excess of the actuarially fair amount.

Let us now examine the future movement of the two terms on the right-hand side of equation (8). First, the time path of the excess contribution in its ratio to GDP is shown by the dashed line in figure 14.5. The excess contribution was −1.7 trillion yen in 1990. It will increase over time and become positive around 2000. This upward trend of the excess contribution reflects the scheduled increase in the pension contribution rate by 2.5 percent every five years

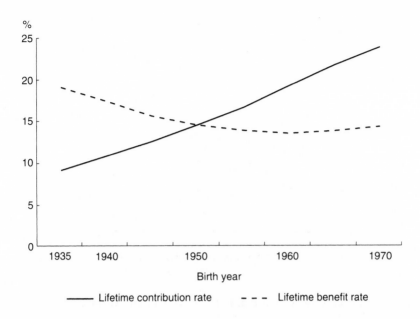

Fig. 14.6   Lifetime contribution rate and benefit rate

from 1995 to 2025, when it will be 29.6 percent.[9] The fact that the excess contribution is negative now implies that working generations are making pension contributions below the actuarially fair contribution.

Second, the subsidy from the general budget account is found by the vertical difference between the dotted line and the dashed line in figure 14.5 because the excess fiscal burden, depicted by the dotted line, is the sum of the excess contribution and the subsidy from the general budget account. In the present system, one-third of the basic pension benefit is subsidized from the general budget account. This is the only subsidy from the general budget account.

Figure 14.5 reveals that the main cause of fluctuation in the excess fiscal burden is fluctuation in the excess contribution, rather than fluctuation in the subsidy from the general account. In particular, the negative excess contribution at present is mainly responsible for the negative excess fiscal burden.[10]

9. The actuarially fair contribution is estimated to be about 14 percent after 2020 from an individual's wage profile and scheduled pension benefits. This is for private sector employees, assuming that they contribute for 40 years and receive benefits for 20 years. For public sector employees, the actuarially fair rate is about 3 percent higher.

10. Suppose that the actual contribution rate is raised to the actuarially fair level. Then the excess contribution will be zero, and hence eqs. (7) and (8) yield

Δ Net pension debt = Interest on the net pension debt − Subsidy from the general account.

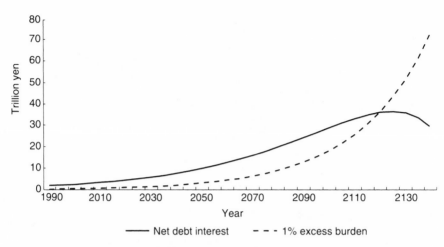

Fig. 14.7   Excess fiscal burden of 1 percent of GDP and interest on net debt

14.6   Pension Reform: Flattening the Excess Fiscal Burden

Let us now consider a pension reform that maintains the excess fiscal burden at 1 percent of GDP throughout the period considered. According to figure 14.5, the ratio of the excess fiscal burden to GDP will be approximately 1 percent in the year 2000. This reform assumes that the scheduled ratio for that year will be maintained throughout the period. Figures 14.7 and 14.8 depict the results of this reform,[11] which will make the intergenerational distribution of the excess burden uniform once and for all. It will also eventually make the Japanese pension system fully funded.

The solid line in figure 14.7, representing the interest on the net pension debt, reflects the shape of the net pension debt itself. This curve will intersect with that representing the excess fiscal burden when the burden reaches its peak in 2120. After that year, the excess fiscal burden will exceed the interest on the net pension debt. That is why the net pension debt will start to decline after this year. The solid line in figure 14.7 shows that it will reach zero in 2155. As a result of this reform, therefore, the Japanese public pension system will become fully funded in 2155.

The solid line in figure 14.8 shows that the ratio of the net pension debt to GDP steadily declines until it reaches zero in the year 2155. Since the growth

---

This implies that the net pension debt will continue to increase as long as the interest on the net pension debt is larger than the subsidy from the general account.

Thus, even if the actual contribution rate had been actuarially fair since 1990, the net pension debt would have continued to grow, for fig. 14.5 indicates that the subsidy to the pension fund from the general account was much smaller than the interest on the net pension debt. See n. 13.

11. The dotted line in fig. 14.8 shows that the ratio of the excess fiscal burden to GDP is 1 percent.

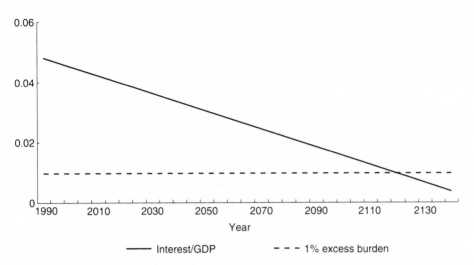

Fig. 14.8   Ratio of excess fiscal burden of 1 percent and interest on net debt to GDP

rate of GDP is the same as the interest rate on the net pension debt, as long as there is an infusion of excess fiscal burden to the pension account, the ratio of the net pension debt to GDP declines. The steady decline in figure 14.8 shows this relationship.

Thus, if the percentage of the excess fiscal burden is maintained at 1 percent of GDP, not only can the intergenerational distribution of the excess fiscal burden be equalized, but also the growth of the net pension debt can be controlled.

14.7   Sensitivity Analyses

We conducted a few sensitivity analyses under the contribution and benefit schedules of the 1994 Reform Plan by changing the assumed economic conditions. First, we changed the assumed nominal interest rate from 5.5 percent to 4 percent and called this case 2. In this case, the net pension debt was about 870 trillion yen as of 1990. This is larger than in the base case because the nominal interest rate is lower. The actual fund will also become negative for certain periods of time as a result of the lower interest rate; but it will start to grow again and eventually turn positive. Finally, the net pension debt will keep growing until 2115, after which time will decline and eventually reach zero in the second half of the twenty-first century.

We also ran another simulation, assuming the same interest rate of 5.5 percent as in the base case but assuming that the growth of the wage rate and basic consumption will also be 5.5 percent. The qualitative nature of the solution in this case was identical to that in case 2.

14.8 Conclusion

The net pension debt has been accumulated as a result of the pure income transfer to the first generation participating in the pension system. Hence, it may be repaid as the war debt was, being financed from the general account by many generations rather than from the pension account.

The revenues of the pension fund from outside sources can be divided into two parts: the actuarially fair part and the excess fiscal burden. The magnitude of the latter determines whether the net pension debt will grow or decline.

We found that the ratio of the net pension debt to GDP will decline under the 1994 Reform Plan and will reach zero in the year 2090. Moreover, we found that the excess fiscal burden will be unevenly distributed across generations and that of current working generations is negative. These generations are not even paying the actuarially fair level of pension contribution.

We considered a pension reform plan that will maintain the percentage of excess fiscal burden at 1 percent of GDP throughout the entire period. We found that this reform will not only equalize the burden across generations but also eventually make the Japanese pension system fully funded. This plan will reduce the fiscal burden of working generations during the early twenty-first century.

Appendix
The Net Pension Debt and Pension Reforms

To illustrate the meaning of the net pension debt, we examine how various hypothetical reforms of a pension system would affect this debt.

The first reform is one that adjusts current and future contribution rates so that they will become actuarially fair to that part of the benefits that corresponds to these contributions.[12] The pension system after this reform will be called an "actuarially fair" system.

If the current Japanese pension system is reformed to be an actuarially fair one, the contributions that flow into the pension fund account will be the same as under a fully funded system. An important revenue of a pension fund is the interest income that the fund itself yields. The actual pension fund, however, yields only a portion of the interest income that a full fund would yield since the balance of the former is lower than that of the latter. This means that even

12. Note that even when contribution rates are reformed this way, the present values of the lifetime contributions and the lifetime benefits are not equalized. In other words, this reform keeps the transfer payments corresponding to the past contributions as the vested interest of each generation. See Hatta (1993), Hatta and Oguchi (1992), and Oguchi et al. (1993) on the actuarially fair pension system.

if our pension system is transformed to an actuarially fair one, the net pension debt may continue to rise and the actual pension fund may become delinquent sometime in the future.[13]

If a sufficient subsidy comes from the general budget every year, the expansion of the pension debt can be contained. We call the interest that has to be paid on the net pension debt the "interest on the net pension debt." If the subsidies from the general budget account equal the interest on the net pension debt every year, the balance of the net pension debt will be kept constant, and the balances of the full fund and the actual fund will fluctuate in parallel. An actuarially fair system accompanied by such subsidies from the general budget is called an "actuarially fair system in the narrow sense." Under this system, the balance of the pension fund will not decline endlessly. (In the text, the term "actuarially fair system" is used to mean that current and future pension contributions are related to the benefits attributable to those contributions in an actuarially fair manner, whether or not subsidies from the general budget account are taking place.)

If the subsidy from the general budget to the pension fund is greater than the interest on the net pension debt, the balance of the net pension debt will decline. If the balance of the net pension debt eventually disappears, it will be possible to switch to a fully funded system. Thus, it is useful to know the amount of interest on the net pension debt in designing pension reforms. To estimate the amount of interest, we need to estimate the amount of the net pension debt itself.

The second reform we consider switches the current system to a fully funded system accompanied by an increase in the general tax to immediately establish a full fund. This reform consists of two components: switching to an actuarially fair system and raising tax revenues so as to equalize the actual pension fund and the full fund. In other words, current workers' actuarially fair contributions will be accumulated to finance their own future benefits. This, however, will deplete the source of benefits for retirees who are currently receiving benefits.[14] This plan necessitates the immediate accumulation of the full fund by means of an increase in revenues so that the benefit payments of both current and future retirees are guaranteed.

To carry out this reform, current workers will have to pay this incremental tax in addition to the actuarially fair contributions for their own future benefits.

13. Note that this means that the contribution rate will be raised now and reduced in the future. In the actual Japanese system, the general budget subsidizes a part of the benefits to the People's Pension. The fact that this is sufficiently small is assumed. See n. 10.

14. This eliminates the revenue source not only for the benefits of current retirees but also for the benefits corresponding to the contributions that current workers have already made. This is because the contributions they have made have already been used for the benefits of current retirees. In the text, the phrase "the benefits of the first generation of the pension system" is used to mean "the sum of (a) the benefits of current retirees and (b) the benefits corresponding to the contributions already made by current workers," or equivalently "the pension benefits of the currently living people corresponding to their contributions."

In other words, this generation will have to bear the burden for two generations.

After this reform, the net pension debt will become zero. The required amount of the incremental tax will be equal to the net pension debt immediately prior to the reform. As we saw in section 14.3, this amount was equal to 578 trillion yen in 1990. It is often said that once a pay-as-you-go system is established, it is difficult to return to a fully funded system. The estimate of the required tax for this reform shows that it is practically impossible to return to the fully funded system immediately by means of an increased tax.

The third reform switches the current system to a fully funded one through the issuing of a public bond rather than raising taxes. The reform is a combination of a shift to an actuarially fair system and the issuing of a government bond in the amount equal to the net pension debt. We call the required government bond "the liquidation bond."[15]

Immediately after the reform, the net pension debt will not be affected by the reform and will be equal to the amount of the liquidation bond issued. Let us assume that this bond is redeemed by subsidies from the general budget financed by increased taxes over time. During the redemption period, the balance of the liquidation bond will always equal the balance of the net pension debt.

Under this reform, the government will simultaneously issue a public bond and increase the size of the pension fund. The former is the government debt to the private sector, while the latter is its loan to the private sector. This reform will not change the net pension debt position of the government in relation to the private sector.

The first and third reforms are equivalent from the point of view of the government's indebtedness to the private sector, even though they are different reforms from an accounting point of view. In particular, if, after the third reform, the subsidy from the general budget to the pension fund were set exactly equal to the amount of the interest on the net pension debt, the balance of the liquidation bond would be kept constant over time. The pension system after this reform would be equivalent to the actuarially fair system in the narrow sense from the point of view of the government's indebtedness to the private sector.[16]

15. See Hatta (1988) and Hatta and Oguchi (1992) for the liquidation bond.

16. We can interpret the current Japanese pension system as having already issued a government bond equivalent to the liquidation bond.

Under the pay-as-you-go system, the contributions made by working generations are not accumulated in the pension fund but are used to finance the benefits of current retirees in return for a government promise to current workers that the benefits will be paid to them in the future. This implies that the government has issued IOUs to current working generations in return for the pension contributions they make. When these IOUs are repaid in the future, new IOUs will be issued to younger generations to finance the repayment. The pay-as-you-go system can thus be viewed as a system that successively issues IOUs. The fact that the government issues IOUs in return for pension contributions implies that the government has been issuing implicit public bonds. The pay-as-you-go system continuously issues implicit public bonds, but with widely fluc-

For the purpose of attaining long-run fiscal solvency of the pension system and of equalizing the fiscal burdens across different generations, it is not important whether the system is reformed to a fully funded one or merely to an actuarially fair one. Regardless of the accounting appearance of the system, what really counts is the amount of additional tax revenues needed beyond the actuarially fair pension contributions. The strategic variables that need to be examined in any pension reform are the net pension debt and the interest that has to be paid on this debt.

References

Hatta, T. 1988. *Reform of direct taxation* (in Japanese). Tokyo: Nihon Keizai Shinbunsha.
———. 1993. Is pension contribution tax or saving? (in Japanese). *Bulletin of the Japan Center for Economic Research,* no. 674: 26–38.
Hatta, T., and N. Oguchi. 1992. Changing the Japanese social security system from pay as you go to actuarially fair. In *Topics in the economics of aging,* ed. David Wise. Chicago: University of Chicago Press.
———. 1993. The public pension debt of the Japanese government (in Japanese). *Nihon Keizai Kenkyu,* no. 25: 101–21.
Noguchi, Y. 1986. The future of the public pension system (in Japanese). In *Softnomics follow-up report,* vol. 4, no. 4. Tokyo: Ministry of Finance.
Oguchi, H., Y. Kimura, and T. Hatta. 1993. Redistribution effects of the Japanese public pension system (in Japanese). In *Distribution of income and wealth in Japan,* ed. Tsuneo Ishikawa. Tokyo: Tokyo University Press.
Ogura, S., and K. Yamamoto. 1993. Projection of Japanese public pension costs in the first half of the twenty-first century and the effects of three possible reforms. *Nihon Keizai Kenkyu,* no. 25: 7–33.
Oshima, O. 1981. *The collapse of the public pension system* (in Japanese). Tokyo: Nihon Seisansei Honbu.
Takayama, N. 1981. Intergenerational redistribution in private sector employee pensions (in Japanese). *Kikan Gendai Keizai,* no. 43: 114–25.
Ueda, K., M. Iwai, and M. Hashimoto. 1987. Public pension and intergenerational income transfer (in Japanese). *Financial Review,* no. 6: 44–57.

---

tuating rates of return for each generation caused by the demographic composition of different generations.

Thus, switching to a fully funded system while issuing a liquidation bond is equivalent to stopping the issuance of new implicit bonds and making explicit the implicit bonds that have already been issued. Only by making these implicit public bonds visible can the government establish a redemption plan that equalizes the burdens on different generations.

Contributors

Tatsuo Hatta
Institute of Social and Economic
  Research
Osaka University
6–1, Mihogaoka, Ibaraki
Osaka 567
Japan

Hilary W. Hoynes
National Bureau of Economic
  Research
1050 Massachusetts Avenue
Cambridge, MA 02138

Michael D. Hurd
RAND Corporation
1700 Main Street
Santa Monica, CA 90407

Robin L. Lumsdaine
Department of Economics
Princeton University
Princeton, NJ 08544

Daniel L. McFadden
Department of Economics
549 Evans Hall 3880
University of California
Berkeley, CA 94707

Yukio Noguchi
Research Center for Advanced Science
  and Technology
The University of Tokyo
Komaba, Tokyo
Japan

Noriyoshi Oguchi
Faculty of Commerce
Senshu University
2-1-1, Higashimita, Tamaku, Kawasaki
Kanagawa 214
Japan

Seiritsu Ogura
Faculty of Commerce
Hosei University
4342, Aiharacho, Machida
Tokyo 194–02
Japan

Akiko Sato Oishi
Japan Center for Economic Research
2-6-1, Nihombashi Kayabacho, Chuo-ku
Tokyo 103
Japan

James M. Poterba
Department of Economics
Massachusetts Institute of Technology
E52–350
Cambridge, MA 02139

Sylvester Schieber
Vice President
The Wyatt Company
601 13th Street NW, Suite 1000
Washington, DC 20005–3808

Atsushi Seike
Faculty of Business and Commerce
Keio University
2–15–45, Mita, Minato-ku
Tokyo 108
Japan

John B. Shoven
Dean's Office of Humanities and
   Sciences
Building One
Stanford University
Stanford, CA 94305

James H. Stock
Kennedy School of Government
Harvard University
79 JFK Street
Cambridge, MA 02138

Noriyuki Takayama
Institute of Economic Research
Hitotsubashi University
2–1, Naka, Kunitachi
Tokyo 186
Japan

Steven F. Venti
Department of Economics
Dartmouth College
6106 Rockefeller Center
Hanover, NH 03755

David A. Wise
National Bureau of Economic Research
1050 Massachusetts Avenue
Cambridge, MA 02138

Naoto Yamauchi
Osaka School of International Public
   Policy
Osaka University
1–1, Machiganeyamacho, Toyonaka
Osaka 560
Japan

Naohiro Yashiro
Institute of International Relations
Sophia University
7–1 Kioicho, Chiyoda-ku
Tokyo 102
Japan

Author Index

Subject Index